Malcolm X's
Michigan
Worldview

Malcolm X's Michigan Worldview

An Exemplar for Contemporary Black Studies

Edited by Rita Kiki Edozie and Curtis Stokes

Michigan State University Press | East Lansing

Michigan State University Press
East Lansing, Michigan 48823-5245

Library of Congress Control Number: 2014954451
ISBN: 978-1-61186-162-4 (cloth)
ISBN: 978-1-60917-450-7 (ebook: PDF)
ISBN: 978-1-62895-172-1 (ebook: ePub)
ISBN: 978-1-61186-504-2 (paperback)

Book design by Charlie Sharp, Sharp Designs, Lansing, MI
Cover design by Shaun Allshouse, www.shaunallshouse.com

Visit Michigan State University Press at *www.msupress.org*

Contents

Foreword

Herb Boyd

Malcolm Little was born on May 19, 1925 in Omaha, Nebraska. Forty years later, renamed El-Hajj Malik El-Shabazz through the course of his short but impactful life, the leader that we came to know as Malcolm X was assassinated on February 21, 1965 in Washington Heights, New York. Between those two dates and names, Malcolm X acquired an acclaim as a human rights activist, freedom fighter, and revolutionary that has enshrined him forever in the hearts of those who seek justice and equality.

Malcolm may have gained his greatest recognition on the streets of Harlem, but it was in the several cities of Michigan—Lansing, Mason, and Detroit—that his familial roots were planted and where the trajectory of his life and his moral compass first signaled a course toward liberation. Most Americans familiar with Malcolm's odyssey know that what formal education he attained occurred in Lansing and Mason, Michigan. It was during these formative years that he encountered his first taste of racism and white supremacy that would mark his journey as a civil rights activist. "When Malcolm went to Mason, you could see the change in him," recalled his oldest brother, Wilfred.

> Some for the better, some for the worse. . . . After a while he started feeling somewhat at home. Sometimes he would complain about some of the things the

teachers would try to do—they would try to discourage him from taking courses that Black people weren't supposed to take; in other words keep him in his place. (Strickland 1994, 34)

But as the world has come to know, Malcolm would not stay "in his place," unless that place was beyond the limitations imposed by his teachers, one of whom told him that dreaming of becoming a lawyer "was no realistic goal for a nigger." (Malcolm X, 1965a, 43). This astonishing statement from his English teacher put an end to Malcolm's schoolroom experiences in the eighth grade, but it did not stop his self-educational quest, which would be a fruitful and never-ending one.

In his journey toward self-discovery, the names that Malcolm acquired practically mirrored his locations as he ventured from Roxbury to Harlem, to prison and back to Michigan. Getting back to Michigan—and especially Detroit after nearly seven years in prison—would reunite him with family members and pave the way to spiritual and political enlightenment. It was at Temple Number One in Detroit that Malcolm shored up his understanding of Islam, concentrated his loyalty to the Honorable Elijah Muhammad, and began to gather a wider reputation as a leader and speaker, particularly upon being appointed the national spokesperson of the Nation of Islam (NOI).

Malcolm soared into the country's collective mind and the mainstream media after the televised airing of "The Hate That Hate Produced," giving him and the NOI the notoriety and popularity that would put him on a path to immortality. Even so, whenever he returned to Detroit, no matter the location, hundreds would turn out to welcome him.

I can still vividly recall Malcolm's appearances at the temple on Linwood Avenue in Detroit. I fondly recall his mesmerizing lectures and the aura of charisma that seemed so pervasive and invigorating. Only those moments almost in the bell of John Coltrane's tenor saxophone at the Minor Key compare to my being totally absorbed and completely overwhelmed by Malcolm's charisma. If I hadn't been in the U.S. army in 1963 when Malcolm spoke at Michigan State University in January, I probably would have been there too. On that occasion, he addressed issues around the race problem. The campus NAACP sponsored the event with more than a thousand people in attendance, half of them white, according to one report.

Malcolm's strong and charismatic connection with Michigan was not limited to the state, but it also strung out to the African diaspora as he corresponded with African students at MSU. In his diaries Malcolm cited a letter that he had received a month before his departure for Africa in 1964 from Ayo Azikiwe, the second oldest son of Nnamdi Azikiwe, the first president of Nigeria. At that time Ayo was a student at MSU and had begun corresponding with Malcolm requesting his visit to campus to lecture to the African Students Association. Malcolm told Ayo of his planned trip and that he hoped to meet his father and other dignitaries in order to erect a "bridge of understanding . . . that will bring our people closer together. The philosophy of black nationalism is designed to do this." (Malcolm X 2014, 193). In a letter from Ayo, a date for Malcolm's appearance at the university was set for the end of January 1965. That never occurred. Ayo's admiration for Malcolm was very similar to mine and that of thousands of others, including the Henry brothers, Richard, Laurence, and Milton, all of whom were equally enthralled and soon, like few others, began to devote considerable hours of work and dedication to Malcolm's sojourn, and this was certainly true toward his final days in the NOI and the founding of his two organizations.

The Henrys and their cohorts hosted several of Malcolm's most famous speeches. In 1963, a two-day National Grass Roots conference, convened under the leadership of the Rev. Albert Cleage Jr., was held in Detroit at King Solomon Baptist Church. Rev. Cleage, journalist William Worthy, and Malcolm were the main speakers. This event was highlighted by Malcolm's "Message to the Grass Roots," one of the last notable speeches he would deliver before leaving the NOI.

Another unforgettable moment for Malcolm in Detroit occurred on February 14, 1965, a week before his assassination and only hours after his home had been firebombed in East Elmhurst, Queens. That he decided to keep his commitment to come to the city and to speak at Ford Auditorium was simply astounding given the terrible incident he and his family had barely survived. But as Milton Henry told a reporter, this was typical of Malcolm.

In the middle of that speech, Malcolm addressed the issue of benevolent colonialism or "dollarism" as he defined it.

> Immediately everything was Peace Corps, Operation Crossroads: "We've got to help our African brothers." Pick up on that: Can't help us in Mississippi. Can't help us in Alabama, or Detroit or out here in Dearborn where some real Ku Klux Klan lives. They're going to send all the way to Africa to help. I know Dearborn; you know, I'm from Detroit. I used to live out here in Inkster. And you had to go through Dearborn to get to Inkster. Just like driving through Mississippi when you got to Dearborn. Is it still that way? Well, you should straighten it out. (Malcolm X 1965b, 170–71)

At the end of his speech, Malcolm thanked the audience for coming out,

> Considering the blackout on the meeting. . . . Milton Henry and the brothers who
> are here in Detroit are very progressive young men, and I would advise all of you to
> get with them in any way that you can to try and create some kind of united effort
> toward common goals, common objectives. (Malcolm X 1965b, 177)

Malcolm effusively thanked the "brothers" for attending the rally, but there were a number of sisters who played a key role in welcoming him and making sure that his stay was without incident. One can safely say that no Detroit sister was more important in his life than his wife, Betty. A product of Detroit's school system, Betty Dean Sanders said she was born in Detroit, so there's no reason to dispute that. If not, she certainly came of age in the city, living with foster parents in several sectors from Black Bottom to the North End. She attended Northern High School and then went on to the Tuskegee Institute in Alabama where she majored in nursing. The future couple had several insignificant brushes as early as 1956, sustaining their friendship by Detroit commonalities of relatives and the NOI. By 1958, however, the love and adoration soon led to blood tests and a pair of rings in Lansing, and the Shabazzes had come full circle to marital bliss.

Another family circle was completed two years ago when Malcolm's grandson Malcolm Shabazz spoke at MSU at the invitation of the Muslim Students' Association. "I have some history here," he told a small audience. "My grandfather and his brothers and sisters grew up here . . . and a lot of people on campus don't know he grew up here, he was raised here" (Walid 2010). And a lot of people did not know about the tragic ending to his grandmother's life as a result of a fire that the younger Malcolm ignited. But perhaps like his grandfather, there is redemption for all the false steps, and maybe one day he too will find the roots of nourishment in the Michigan soil that was so richly a part of his family legacy.

It was wonderful to discover during a recent visit to Lansing that a historic marker is now in place at Malcolm's homesite at Vincent Court on Martin Luther King Jr. Boulevard, bringing the two American heroes to another junction, which is much more than Detroit has done to commemorate Malcolm's contribution to civil and human rights. As of writing, nowhere in the state is there a monument to Malcolm's memory, not a library or public plaza. Moreover, the Malcolm X Academy, a public school in Detroit, which has another illustrious American, Paul Robeson, as a co-name, was severely damaged by a fire on May 10, 2011. Nor is there any impressive presence of Malcolm in statuary or reliquary on Detroit's streets, but if you visit some of the museums his image exists in sculpture, paintings, photos, and T-shirts.

But it's in the hearts and minds of so many long-standing residents that the pulse of Malcolm is most evident. And the musicians, playwrights, and poets of the city were touched by Malcolm, so much so that their words and impressions had to be gathered under one cover at Broadside Press where Dudley Randall and Margaret Burroughs artfully stitched them into a glorious tapestry of metaphors and similes. There are also references to Malcolm that resonate in plays such as Pearl Cleage's *Hospice*, where two characters reminisce about Malcolm's assassination. "I don't need any statue or street name to keep the memory and the importance of Malcolm in my life," said Danny Aldridge, a veteran activist who grew up in New York and has lived in Detroit for more than a generation. "And though I had a chance to experience him in East Elmhurst where we were neighbors, Detroit will always be a special place for my and his development, and his influence" (Boyd 2013). *Notebook* contributor attorney Carl Edwards, dean of the People's Law School, wrote that "Through Malcolm we begin to see ourselves differently and to see Detroit and United States differently. We immersed ourselves in the history of the United States and its inhuman treatment of our forefathers and mothers" (Boggs 2009, xxvi).

When Malcolm was released from prison in the spring of 1952, there was little doubt in his mind about his destiny or destination. "My going to Detroit instead of back to Harlem or Boston was influenced by my family's feeling expressed in their letters" (Malcolm X 1965a, 220), Malcolm wrote in his autobiography. "Especially my sister Hilda had stressed to me that although I felt I understood Elijah Muhammad's teachings, I had much to learn, and I ought to come to Detroit and become a member of a temple of practicing Muslims" (Malcolm X 1965a, 220).

It has been said that geography is fate, and Malcolm's choice to take his liberated self to Detroit put him on the road to world acclaim, earning him a unique plateau of respect that few Black Americans—no, Americans—have ever achieved. The current volume by MSU editors, celebrating, interrogating, and theorizing—while chronicling—the lived experiences of Brother Malcolm particularly as these experiences relate to the state of Michigan, rightly serves to institutionalize Malcolm's legacy by way of the Black Studies discipline.

WORKS CITED

Boggs, James. *The American Revolution: Pages from a Negro Worker's Notebook.* New York: Monthly Review Press, 2009.

Boyd, Herb. 2013. Interview with Danny Aldridge.

Malcolm X. 1965a. *The Autobiography of Malcolm X.* With the assistance of Alex Haley. New York: Ballantine Books.

———. 1965b. *Malcolm X Speaks: Selected Speeches and Statements.* Edited by George Breitman. New York: Merit Publishers.

———. 2014. *The Diary of Malcolm X (El-Hajj Malik El-Shabazz): 1964.* Edited by Herb Boyd and Ilyasah Al-Shabazz. Chicago: Third World Press.

Strickland, William. 1994. *Malcolm X: Make It Plain.* Oral histories selected and edited by Cheryll Y. Greene. New York: Viking Press.

Walid, Dawud. 2010. "Malcolm Shabazz Speaks On His Grandfather Malcolm X." Blog. http://dawudwalid.wordpress.com/2010/07/06/malcolm-shabazz-speaks-on-his-grandfather-malcolm-x.

Preface

Greetings from Michigan State University's African American and African Studies. Welcome to our three-part, sixteen-chapter Black/Africana Studies *reader*—as that it is how we envision the current book's usage for you! The edited volume—entitled *Malcolm X's Michigan Worldview: An Exemplar for Contemporary Black Studies*— uses the biography of Malcolm to both interrogate key aspects of the Black world experience while contributing to the intellectual expansion of the discipline that the National Council of Black Studies calls Black/Africana Studies. As our title suggests, what follows in this rich and comprehensive anthology will be parallel investigation of key events and themes drawn from Malcolm's lived experiences. The purpose of the reader is to posit Malcolm's early life in Michigan to enunciate core themes of the Black Studies discipline. Implicitly, the reader's contributors attempt to sew together the two—Malcolm X *and* the Black Studies discipline—interweaving, intersecting, and interrelating our key subject and object of study in this regard.

Especially leveraging the enlivening of the dynamic and provocative debate over the "Malcolm legacy" that emerged after the publication of Manning Marable's *Malcolm X* in 2011, naturally our book also engages this topic. The discussion about Malcolm at the time raised several questions. How does Malcolm's early childhood experiences in Lansing, Mason, and Detroit, Michigan, shape and inform his worldview? What is Malcolm's legacy on contemporary public affairs? Was Malcolm a humanist or a Black nationalist? Was Malcolm a race man? Was Malcolm antifeminist? What was Malcolm's association with the Nation of Islam?

Additionally, however, and perhaps more importantly, our book is much more concerned with using Malcolm's iconography as a way to deepen our understanding of our experiences as *Africana* peoples through advanced research and disciplinary study. In this respect, as icon, in the current study, we present Malcolm as a Black Subject who represents, symbolizes, and associates meaning with our emerging discipline. The book interrogates Malcolm's extraordinary human experiences to contribute to the development of the continuous formulation, deepening, and thereby strengthening of the Black Studies discipline.

As editors we are grateful to a range of you who have supported the production of this book. As is our tradition, these things are always a collective effort with considerable support from loved ones, family, friends, students, and colleagues! You know yourselves; thank you again and again! Nonetheless, we'd like to dedicate the current preface to acknowledge—while also overviewing—the fifteen (besides our own contributed chapters) co-contributors and contributions to the volume. They are author-contributors who as passionate, creative, and savvy Black Studies scholars inspired and collaborated with us at MSU's African American and African Studies program to produce the current intellectual dialogue about Malcolm X in relation to the Black Studies discipline.

Of course, foremost gratitude should go to the late Manning Marable whose rich body of scholarships, especially his last book *Malcolm X*, indirectly inspired us—like him—to produce our own version of our experiences with and perspectives of Malcolm from a Michigan point of view. In this regard, we are appreciative of the inducements of our colleague here at MSU, Dr. Austin Jackson, who cornered me at our campus Starbucks cafe about three years ago and asked me if I had read Marable's book. I hadn't then, but I did tell Austin that I was following the reviews, especially the many "hot and testy" postings on Abdul Alkalimat's H-Net Afro-American Studies listserv. Given Malcolm's Lansing connection so illustratively narrated in the book, Austin recommended that we convene a conference at MSU on Malcolm X's Michigan legacies.

It was from this conference that the idea of applying core Black Studies themes and concepts such as discourse and representation, race and identity, and community and political struggle to biographical elements of Malcolm X's legacy and lived experiences in the state of Michigan was born. With select MSU-African American and African Studies core faculty colleagues as conference conveners, including Professors Curtis Stokes, Carl Taylor, Geneva Smitherman, and Austin Jackson, and with this first edited volume developed for MSU's Black Studies program, we would embark upon a research exploration of Malcolm's contribution to African diaspora self-consciousness.

After the volume's formative beginnings, our energies went to the recruitment of a formidable cohort of Black Studies teacher-scholars who would contribute to realizing our research objectives for the edited volume. The volume is divided into three major sections: "Malcolm as a Theoretical Framework," "Malcolm and Community Engagement," and "Malcolm and Black World Struggle." Within each part, we compile a rich and comprehensive anthology that serves as a parallel investigation of key events and themes drawn from Malcolm's lived experiences. Chapters leverage Malcolm's early life in Michigan to enunciate his extraordinary human experiences using a range of multidisciplinary prisms and themes including discourse, race, culture, religion, gender, politics, and community. These core Black Studies themes serve to elicit insights about the Malcolm iconography that contribute to the continuous formulation, deepening, and strengthening of the Black Studies discipline.

Our opening chapter, "Malcolm X from Michigan: Race, Identity, and Community across the Black World" critically reviews and applies core Black Studies themes and concepts, including discourse and representation, race and identity, and community and struggle, to biographical elements of Malcolm X's legacy and lived experience. The chapter lays out a theoretical schema to examine Malcolm's contribution to African American self-consciousness vis-à-vis a Black/Africana Studies philosophy. In "The Paradigmatic Agency of Malcolm X: Family, Experience, and Thought," Abdul Alkalimat poses and answers the question "Why Malcolm X?" Alkalimat posits Malcolm as both an icon and paradigmatic model for the Black Liberation Movement; thereby Malcolm, for him, was the essence of Black Power.

On the other hand, in "Reeducating the Afro-American: Malcolm X's Scholarly and Historical Pedagogy," Lenwood G. Davis identifies Malcolm as an organic intellectual, one who originates from among the people but with the ability to listen, interpret, and provide a progressive vision for the future. In this chapter, Malcolm is examined as an educator, but not like the typical college-educated intellectual. In "Malcolm X: Master of Signifyin," Geneva Smitherman exposes us to Malcolm as a great orator, the "master of signifyin," and a guru in the manipulation of language in an effort to construct an appropriate reality for the Black revolution. Through education and discourse, Smitherman underscores Malcolm's genius in social construction and as a progressive visionary.

In "If You Can't Be Free, Be Indignant: The Womanist Legacy of Malcolm X," Sheila Radford-Hill examines Malcolm as a womanist (communitarian and African-centered), not a feminist (informed by liberalism and individualism), arguing that neither Malcolm nor the women with whom he worked would have considered him a feminist. Genuinely progressive politics requires the sustained intervention of black women, especially if we are concerned about the global reach of oppression. Joseph McLaren argues, in "Malcolm-esque: A Black Arts Literary Genre," that the 1960s BAM, including in Detroit, is fundamentally indebted to Malcolm. McLaren highlights Malcolm's oratorical style as pivotal; poets and other artists have paid homage to Malcolm's legacy.

In the opening chapter of Part 2, "Malcolm X's Pre–Nation of Islam (NOI) Discourses: Sourced from Detroit's Charles H. Wright Museum of African American History Archives," Charles Ezra Ferrell presents a summary and overview of selected letters, mostly handwritten, and other documents detailing the fascinating early life of Malcolm in Michigan, notably Detroit. Doing so makes known additional aspects of Malcolm's religious and political views, as well as contributing to the further development of Black Studies. At the center of this project is Detroit's Charles H. Wright Museum of African American History. Edward C. Davis IV's chapter on "Liberation and Transformation through Education: Black Studies at Malcolm X College, Chicago" explores how Malcolm's teaching at Malcolm X College in Chicago has allowed him to witness the intellectual and political growth of students, and thereby the importance of Malcolm in the academy. In "Malcolm X: An Education of Positive Youth Development Challenged by Street Culture," Carl S. Taylor, Pamela R. Smith, and Cameron "Khalfani" Herman provide an assessment of the potential and active positive aspects of Malcolm's life and legacy on youth street culture; Malcolm's black nationalism, self-assurance, and independence are highly valued among our youth.

In "A Detroit Black Panther's Soldiering Journey with Malcolm X: Extract Memoirs from an X Heir," Ahmad A. Rahman presents the autobiographical and historical accounting of his role in the Black Panther Party, occurring between Detroit and Chicago. The chapter shows how for both revolutionary leaders, Malcolm and Rahman, COINTELPRO, the U.S. government program to subvert and destroy radical organizations and leaders, especially blacks, was ever-present, whether known or unknown, during their journeys. In "Malcolm X and the Black

Campus Movement: Shaping Academic Communities," Ibram X. Kendi examines the ways in which Malcolm impacted the Black Student Movement, noting that Malcolm was absolutely central to its development. An example of this impact was that *The Autobiography of Malcolm X* was a must-read book during the late 1960s for all black student activists.

Beginning Part 3, Zain Abdullah, in "Malcolm X, Islam, and the Black Self," examines the tension between two organizations created by Malcolm during his last year, the Muslim Mosque, Inc. (religious entity focusing on moral reform) and the OAAU (focusing on racial inequality), in order to highlight the "hypocrisy" in the Muslim world and "realities" of racism in the United States. Finding the appropriate balance between religion and politics was especially challenging for the global black community, as Malcolm understood; good reason to remember that Malcolm was a very complex individual, particularly during his final year. In "Malcolm X and the Struggle for Socialism in the United States," Curtis Stokes examines the black socialist tradition of the New Negro era, focusing on three representative radicals (Hubert H. Harrison, Cyril V. Briggs, and Claude McKay) as the basis for Malcolm's political thought during the final fifty weeks of his life. During this period Malcolm, though a revolutionary black nationalist, offers suggestively the alternative of socialism for capitalism to address the plight of blacks and the oppressed everywhere.

In "Malcolm X, Black Cultural Revolution, and the Shrine of the Black Madonna in Detroit," Errol A. Henderson examines Malcolm's call for a black cultural revolution and its relationship to the Shrine of the Black Madonna in Detroit, as well as its meaning for other late 1960s black radicals. Unlike the previous chapter's association of Malcolm with a possible socialist project, Henderson examines how Malcolm's recommendation of a black cultural revolution was to have Black nationalism at its core, which subsequently graduates into an overarching political revolution. Following these themes and related to them, in "Malcolm X and the Cuban Revolution," Ollie Johnson explores how and why Malcolm embraced the Cuban Revolution. The chapter examines the perspective of Afro-Cuban Carlos Moore's impact on Malcolm while considering important racial dimensions of the Cuban Revolution.

Finally, in "Malcolm Omowale X (Re)Turns to Africa: Pan-Africanism and the Black Studies Agenda in a Global Era," Rita Kiki Edozie concludes our Malcolm academic biography by contextualizing the global African liberation projects of the 1950s and 1960s before carefully exploring Malcolm's understanding of Pan-Africanism. In doing so, the chapter identifies three radical black moments that prefigured Malcolm's Pan-Africanism: Garveyism, the Nation of Islam, and racism in the United States.

The current volume could not have been possible without the contributions of our contributors and many more scholars who have helped us with the current research project. We are in deep debt of gratitude to our doctoral students El Ra Radney, Shanti Zaid, A. J. Rice, and especially to Emile Diouf, who was critical to the editing support of such an array of disparate chapter contributions. For example, while providing editing support for the volume, Emilie traveled to Senegal for a research conference. As we virtually collaborated on the rigorous and laborious task of copyediting this voluminous book, Emilie relayed a story about her uncle in Senegal who has never been to the United States. While Emilie was working on the book one day, her uncle asked her what she was doing. She replied "You would not know. It is about Malcolm X" in Sereer. Her uncle, who is in his late sixties, exclaimed, "Malcolm X! A great man, who was a source of inspiration for us during the Senegalese liberation struggle against France!" This exchange is the best evidence of Malcolm's impact on the Black world.

The African American and African Studies' graduate students at MSU have been critical in providing coordination, research assistance, and manuscript preparation. The volume is especially dedicated to their profiles—students in Africana Studies departments and programs across the world—who will themselves carry on the "Malcolm" exemplar to deepen and expand our discipline, as well as to better understand while facilitating the transformation of the Black world.

PART 1

Malcolm as a Theoretical Framework

Malcolm X from Michigan

Race, Identity, and Community across the Black World

Rita Kiki Edozie with Curtis Stokes

In defending the intellect of a first Black president—Barack Obama—who had come under caustic critique by some media channels for his policies, a December 2011 blog post article cited a quotation representative of the language, style, and poetry depicting, honoring, commemorating, and eulogizing Malcolm X. The blog cited Malcolm as stating, "What do you call an educated negro with a B.A. or an M.A., with a B.S., or a PhD?" The answer? "You call him a nigger, because that is what the white man calls him, a nigger" (DeVega 2012).

We begin this chapter with Malcolm's controversial (perhaps politically incorrect) quotation to underscore what has been a major grievance for Black intellectuals who have constantly had to prove their worth within the academy. For us, not only is Malcolm X an inspirational role model for his critical insights on Black life but, as the quote in the previous paragraph implies, he is an intellectual leader whose Black Studies *study* still lives through his public discourses. This is exemplified through Malcolm X's message of cultural pride, his self-study, his critical analysis, and his social protest against injustice, which all served as a pedagogical approach for the education of Black people that would foreshadow the Black Studies academic movement (Smallwood 2001).

It is in this regard that, in celebrating Malcolm's ninetieth birthday anniversary

3

memorial in 2015, our edited volume examines Malcolm X as a historic African American leader, a child and onetime native of Michigan, a master orator and sage, and a foremost Black nationalist and Pan-Africanist public intellectual. Given these many distinctive attributes of Malcolm, his life in Michigan, and the orientations and status of the Black/Africana Studies discipline in the millennium, a cohort of Black Studies faculty at Michigan State University has long been inspired by Malcolm's iconography as a multidimensional intellectual and community activist who connects local community activism to nationwide Black nationalism and to global Pan-Africanism. Malcolm's 1963 visit to MSU and his earlier formative lived experiences in the Michigan region have motivated the editors to publish the current volume that brings the Black world community and academic discipline together in ways that bell hooks has described as practice in conjunction with contemplation (hooks 2003).

In this vein, as transdisciplinary Black Studies scholars, we hope to act as advocates of hook's notion of praxis, considered as action and reflection upon the world in order to change it. We especially consider our operative base in Michigan at MSU and from the university's African American and African Studies major academic unit as distinctive community and academic spaces that will influence the way that we narrate our perspectives on Malcolm. In considering our narratives this way, the current book, titled *Malcolm X's Michigan Worldview: An Exemplar for Contemporary Black Studies*, uses Malcolm's Michigan location as a launching board to posit his life as an excellent model, an epitome, a paragon, a quintessence, or an exemplar, as we subtitle the book, to navigate the complex contours of our academic discipline.

Four key questions guide our objectives in this regard: What do Malcolm's lived experiences and politics tell us about Black world existence, being, consciousness, human predicament, expression and empowerment? How is this experience relayed in the state of Michigan and its distinct Black communities (of Detroit and in Lansing) as places from which Malcolm hails? What is the genre and legacy of Malcolm's leadership in the Black world vis-à-vis the ideological platforms of civil rights and Black Power, liberalism and nationalism, human rights and Pan-Africanism? How can the Black Studies discipline be used as an effective tool to discern insights from Malcolm's lived experiences and political practices, and in turn, how can these insights help to develop the intellectual tenets of the discipline?

Furthermore, the manner in which our contributors respond to these questions is captured by four general themes that guide the overall study. A first theme concerns the way that we strategically engage with the "Malcolm Debate," which in 2011 was revitalized by the publication of the late Manning Marable's highly acclaimed yet provocative volume on Malcolm, *Malcolm X: A Life of Reinvention* (Marable 2011). Leveraging this debate, though proceeding in a very distinctive direction from Marable and the plethora of academic responses to his book, our anthology examines Malcolm as an icon, an exemplar, a philosophical vehicle for navigating and interrogating Malcolm X's lived experience in relation to the study of the Black world. Graeme Abernethy's *Iconography of Malcolm X* (2013) uses imagery to explore Malcolm's visual prominence in the eras of civil rights, Black Power, and hip-hop through prisms of representation across a variety of media.

Though slightly differently from Abernethy, we present Malcolm's icon in the way described in James Tyner's *Geography of Malcolm X*. In that book, Tyner presents Malcolm as an intellectual who developed his political thought from a dialectical dialogue of lived experience and critical integration. Tyner contends that the dialogue that Malcolm exuberates represents a geographical imagining that he regards as a feature of the black intellectual tradition's radical hermeneutic of everyday experiences (Tyner 2006, 104). In *Malcolm X and African American Self-Consciousness* (2005), Magnus Bassey motivates us further in this light when he writes that more needs to be done to relay Malcolm's contribution to African American self-consciousness vis-à-vis an Africana philosophy. Bassey writes that Malcolm raised questions about African American existence, being, consciousness, hopelessness, helplessness, expression, human predicament, and empowerment. These are all elements of an Africana philosophy that situates the articulations and traditions of Africans and peoples of African descent collectively to engage in discipline forming, tradition defining, and/or tradition reconstruction. Bassey's notion of dialectical dialogue representations of Malcolm's lived experiences presented by our volume as Black political thought is core to our exposition, analysis, and arguments about the Malcolm X icon.

A second related theme examines Malcolm's icon through the prism of community. We do this by immersing our inquiries about what we refer to as "the Malcolm phenomenon," a term that we use to interrogate Malcolm's distinctiveness in relation to issues of race and African diaspora cultural community grounding. To do so we examine issues of space and place, particularly from the vantage point of Malcolm's experiences in the state of Michigan. In *How Racism Takes Place* (2011), George Lipsitz presents a thesis that explains how racism takes place by not only describing things that happen in history, but especially describing how social relations take on their full force and meaning when they are enacted physically in actual places. Lipsitz goes on to illustrate how, through community issues such as residential and school segregation, mortgage and insurance redlining, transportation and taxation policies, we learn how race is produced by space.

For our study of Malcolm, Michigan localities, including East Lansing, Lansing, Detroit, and Mason, constitute geographical spaces undergoing the kinds of community issues that Lipsitz writes about. The regional place that we will examine represents an important network of towns and cities in Michigan where Malcolm X grew up and developed some formative ideas that led him to action and prominence. We feel that the platform from which we stand at MSU and the community in which we live, the state of Michigan, are opportune regional communities to examine the Malcolm X lived experience and its relationship to Black Studies. This is true when one considers ways that Malcolm's speeches invoke several memories that elucidate the circumstances and intricate contours of his lived experience in these areas. For example, when Malcolm lived in Lansing, he recalled of East Lansing that, "In those days Negroes weren't allowed after dark in East Lansing proper. There's where Michigan State University is located" (Malcolm X 1992, 6).

We know that Malcolm's father was controversially killed in Lansing, revealing violent race relations linked to the Ku Klux Klan in the 1940s.The Lansing community has attempted to address its wrongs against the Little family. On October 12, 1975, a historical marker was dedicated to the Lansing legacy of Malcolm X at 4705 South Logan, Lansing, Michigan. The plaque, put up by the Michigan Department of State, marks the spot where Malcolm's boyhood home once stood. The marker reads, "Malcolm X, born Malcolm Little, lived on this site in the 1930s. . . . He developed an understanding of black hatred and came to see his years in Lansing as common to the black experience" (Michigan Historical Center 2007).

Of Detroit, the site of his first arrest for grand larceny in 1945 and where Malcolm had been known as "Detroit Red," he would later remember, "My life has been a mirror of what the Black Ghetto across America presents as a community of despair" (qtd. in Cunningham 2010).

And yet again, on MSU's campus, on January 23, 1963, Malcolm spoke at the Erickson Hall Kiva where he had been invited by the NAACP MSU Chapter and the African Students Association to speak to faculty and students about the "race problem." In what was then well known to be the eloquent discourse of civil rights America's most dynamic revolutionary and Black nationalist leader, Malcolm would commend the African American and African student unity at MSU for rising to the occasion to address race, which he referred to as the most serious problem of our time (Malcolm X 1963b).

In revealing Malcolm's iconic attributes in relation to his status as a community, national, and international Black leader of repute and his enormous positive impact in the realm of Black politics in relation to race and identity themes in communities of color, we arrive at our third guiding theme. This concerns the complicated dimensions and impacts that political leadership, Black nationalisms, and democratic struggles play in discerning the politics and political legacies of Malcolm. Diverse opinions exist about how Black leadership is defined and what constitutes the ideological worldviews and political practices of various Black leaders. The late Ronald Walters and Robert C. Smith in their book *African American Leadership* (1999) define Black leadership as the capacity of an individual to affect the attitudes and behavior of African Americans insofar as social and political goals and/or methods are concerned.

Walters and Smith's characterization of leadership augments the earlier work of James Wilson who, in *Negro Politics: The Search for Leadership* (1965), describes the Black leader to be a civic leader—a person who acted as if the interests of the race or community were their goal. Also underscoring the importance of race as a dimension of Malcolm's radical leadership, in *Dark Days, Bright Nights: From Black Power to Barack Obama*, Peniel Joseph reveals a distinctive political role that Malcolm embodies as a Black leader. Joseph locates Malcolm as one of two of the most daring and provocative activists emerging from Black America during the civil rights era who introduced Black Power as a new political landscape that permanently altered black identity. Joseph contends that this brand of politics scandalized race relations in the United States and transformed American democracy where leaders like Malcolm unleashed passionate debates and sparked enduring controversy over the very meaning of black identity, American citizenship, and the prospect of a social, political, and cultural revolution (Joseph 2010, 12).

All three themes aforementioned inform our fourth theme, which concerns our lenses and method for examining Malcolm's lived experience in relation to the Black Studies discipline. At MSU, the university's just over a decade old program in African American and African Studies acts as the vehicle through which to examine scholarly phenomenon of Malcolm X in this manner. We are reminded that the civil rights period through which Malcolm pioneered his genre of politics also marked an important landmark in the formative establishment of racial inclusion practices in higher education and the institutionalization of the Black Studies discipline. Occurring during a first-phase era of Black Studies' emergence, the successful establishment of Black Studies programs that have proliferated in higher educational institutions across the country today emerged as a result of protests and demonstrations initiated by Black university students similar to the groups that hosted Malcolm X at MSU in 1963. Ibram Rogers (2012) has described this Black Student Movement as the academic manifestation of Black nationalism.

With fifteen PhD programs in African American and African Studies of which MSU is one, fifty-one years after our campus hosted Malcolm in 1963, we find ourselves in the third stage of Black Studies. In celebration of that historic event, by using Malcolm's lived experiences to deepen our understanding of the discipline as well as contribute to the emergent discipline's formulation and strengthening, the current anthology is MSU's contribution to the discipline's intellectual development. In African American and African Studies at MSU, housed in a humanities college (the College of Arts and Letters), we approach our core curricular in Black/Africana Studies as a humanistic discipline in key dimensions of the human and social lived experience.

First, we are conceptually interdisciplinary, incorporating African language, literature, history, philosophy, the arts, and social science to reflect on diverse heritages, traditions, and histories of African descendants and to engage the relevance of these studies with the current conditions of national and international life. We also encourage qualitative research methods that underscore dialogue, historical and logical analysis, subject voices, and critical interpretation and scholarly investigation. Finally, we emphasize engaged scholarship to impact community transformation, thereby shaping both individuality and community and presenting opportunities to infuse day-to-day life with humanistic knowledge and vice versa.

No doubt, the discipline variably referred to as Black/Africana Studies continues to present various definitions of what it is and what it constitutes. Indeed, there are still some who insist that it is not even a discipline as of yet, but a conceptually interdisciplinary field of study that supplements traditional disciplines. Nonetheless, we affirm the disciplinary nature of the study, which we acknowledge is an interdisciplinary and multi-disciplinary, theoretical and methodological academic study, consisting of an existing-but-nascent body of systematically and critically derived knowledge about the political, economic, and socio-culturally lived experiences of African descendent and African peoples and communities around the world.

We reference the National Council of Black Studies definition of our disciplinary mission (also called African American and African Studies, Afro-American Studies,

Pan-African Studies, Black American Studies, and African Diaspora Studies). NCBS presents the discipline's domain of inquiry as part of a mission to advance and transmit broad knowledge of the histories, cultures, and linkages among peoples of Africa and their descendants in the New World, and to provide intellectual tools to analyze, understand, and address the significant social, political, economic, and humanist problems they face.

Given our four broad objectives, for this book on Malcolm, we use his exemplar to elucidate five conceptual areas that similarly illuminate the broad and deep contours of the discipline. Presented and analyzed in subsequent subsections of this essay, they are discourse and representation; race and the African diaspora experience, class, gender, and ethnic identity; political struggle; and community.

The Malcolm Debate: Discourse, Representation, Black Studies, and the Marable Biography

When in a 1965 speech Malcolm complained that "They use the press to project us in the image of violence" (qtd. in Tyner 2006, 106), to explain the statement, James Tyner argued that Malcolm demonstrated an understanding of the complex interactions of power, knowledge, and the representation of people, places, and events. Tyner continued that Malcolm understood the role that representation had in the construction of the African American identity. For example, Malcolm often deconstructed the use of the term "Negro" arguing that it had been an externally imposed term that functioned as a tool of discipline and domination by the U.S. media (Tyner 2006, 106). The example reveals the importance of the role that discourse and representation play as crucial elements of the Black world and its study. As forms of politics and the political, discourse and representation are the tools of our trade whose constituent parts Black Studies scholars interrogate.

Classically, Michel Foucault defines discourse and representation as ways of constituting knowledge that has been informed by social practices, forms of subjectivity, and power relations (Foucault 1972). The poststructuralist scholar showed us how discourses may be a conscious or a taken-for-granted range of knowledge within a given set of power relations that informs types of appropriate behavior (Weedon 1987, 108). According to Diamond and Quinby (1988, 185), they are also a form of power that circulates in the social field and can attach to strategies of domination as well as resistance. Discourse may also be seen as a form of "representation," which is a political phenomenon when it speaks for the needs and desires of somebody or something. In this regard, representation is a form of proxy as well as a portrait (Spivak 1990).

The Black Studies discipline is intricately structured and projected as a discourse of both resistance and inclusion, an alternative polemic to White supremacy, and an oppositional discourse to traditional disciplinary narratives of Blackness. Critical race theory (CRT), an engaged framework that increasingly underscores a methodology for the Black Studies discipline, is a good example of the way that Black Studies employs discourse and representation to both reveal and transform relationships among race, racism, and power. CRT's unique voice of color thesis (one of five features of CRT) especially illustrates this when it argues that, because of their different histories and experiences with oppression, black (and other people of color in the United States) writers and thinkers may be able to communicate matters that White and Western thinkers are unlikely to know otherwise (Delgado and Stefancic 2001).

Discussions and debates about what constitutes Malcolm's icon and how to interpret his discourses underscore the importance of the topics of discourse and representation as they relate to CRT. For example, the 2011 debate about Malcolm after the release of historian Manning Marable's book (Marable 2011) revealed the core precepts of the discipline this way. In debating Marble's book, scholars, students, journalists, activists, and members writ large in the Black community engaged in discussions of community, race, ideology, and Black leadership. The backdrop of this robust public debate surrounded Marable's controversial claims about Malcolm in his biography. As with previous nationally renowned biographies of Malcolm by Alex Haley and Spike Lee, Marable's book surged to the top of the New York Times bestseller list and also won a 2011 Pulitzer Prize. The book's fame and the special circumstances of Manning Marable's death a few days before *Malcolm X* was released in print added to the context for the national discussion about both the intentions of the biographer (Marable) and what were the most appropriate interpretations of the lived experience of the biographical subject—Malcolm X.

The debate demonstrated the deep political nature of Black discourses as, no more than a year after Marable's biography was released in print, Black Studies scholars and activists put out *By Any Means Necessary: Malcolm X: Real, Not Reinvented (BAMN)* (Boyd et al. 2012) by way of response to Marable. The editors of *BAMN* used the Third World Press publication to take on Marable's so-called humanist reinvention of Malcolm (Marable 2011). Of concern to many of *BAMN*'s editors and contributors were Marable's attempts to decenter Malcolm's politics by minimizing his role as a progenitor of the Black nationalist and Pan-Africanist agenda. Many of *BAMN*'s contributors accused Marable of reinventing Malcolm and reconstructing him as a humanist rather than positing Malcolm as the unapologetic, radical critic of White supremacy and symbol for human rights that he was for Blacks throughout the world. Critics were especially concerned about Marable's inclination to underscore speculative aspects of Malcolm's sexuality, including suggestions of infidelity and bisexuality, without using substantive scholarly evidence.

Not all contributors to *BAMN* have been critical of Marable's casting of Malcolm X. Nell Painter commended the book for helping the American public to understand the role that Islam plays in the world (2012). Imani Perry extolled the book for assisting in our understanding of resistance and revolution throughout the Midwest, Africa, and the Middle East (Perry 2012). Needless to say, however, biographies of Malcolm—also seen as discourses and representations—such as Marable's *Malcolm X*, inform dynamic historiographies for Black Studies issues, topics, and themes in many respects. Malcolm's own autobiography told to Alex Haley—first published in 1965 not too long after Malcolm's death—sustained the living memory of Malcolm during the U.S. civil rights era. Alex Haley was a controversial biographer in his own right, as many wondered about the editorial liberties Haley took in completing the book after Malcolm's passing. Nevertheless, Haley's book used Malcolm to solicit an important national discussion about civil rights, human rights, and a range of radical democratic oppositions, all issues that were variably and ideologically configured according to Black nationalisms, socialisms, or culturalisms. The *Autobiography* has been reprinted in more than forty-five editions and remains a national bestseller.

One also need not ignore the fact that there has been a flurry of books that contribute to the debate about Malcolm X by a range of scholars of African American studies since Haley's biography, including books and article biographies published by some of the current volume's contributors. Indeed, Candace Mancini has acknowledged that Alex Haley's biography was at variance with Malcolm's actual lived experiences but that this fact was not revealed until the 1991 publication of Bruce Perry's *Malcolm: The Life of a Man Who Changed Black America*. Distinctively, Perry's contribution was to present Malcolm's life as a series of dramatic confrontations with racism. As well, in 1992, Spike Lee's media biography—the film *Malcolm X*—yet again reintroduced the dialogue about Malcolm, positing the leader as a cultural icon, which suited a new wave of Black cultural production and consumption.

Both Spike Lee and Malcolm as the subject of study inspired a dynamic debate about the Black condition in the 1990s. In the 1970s, as cultural icon and in death, Malcolm X would become the symbol of the Black Arts Movement (BAM). In his classic book on the topic, *A Nation within a Nation: Amiri Baraka and Black Power Politics*, Komozi Woodard (1999, 59) underscores the role that Malcolm had in using mass media for black nationality formation through TV, radio, and newspapers. Woodard described Malcolm as the bridge between the old nationalism and the new whereby Malcolm would stress the need for ethical reconstruction and cultural revitalization of the Black community. Malcolm's cultural iconography according to Woodard stressed personal and moral integrity, a focus on the African personality, radical grassroots mobilization and organizing, and black music and discourse as creative philosophy and expression (Woodard 1999, 61). Malcolm's model became a major theme in the poetry, art, and plays of BAM. Woodard rightly asserts of Malcolm's influences,

> What began in the Black Arts as a critique of the white establishment's interpretation and evaluation of black music, poetry and drama, led to a thoroughgoing social challenge to racist and capitalist hegemony over the cultural life of the black community in the Modern Black Convention Movement. . . . Malcolm stood as a steadying force for this New Nationalism. (Woodard 1999, 62)

Dubbed the literary version of Malcolm, Amiri Baraka would himself embody such a role and icon as he carried forth the movement inspired by Malcolm to begin a wave of black arts institutions across the nation. Thus when in 2012 Bill Fletcher, a supporter of Marable's *Malcolm X*, suggests that the best way to honor Malcolm's memory is to use the book as a teachable moment in the study of contemporary Black issues (Fletcher 2012), drawing from the historical repertoire of the BAM with its politics and arts, its comparative, global, and diasporic regional reach, and its sustained expansion of modern Black nationalism, Fletcher is right. Literary Black nationalism embodied by Baraka in the shadow of Malcolm's legacy sparked the BAM. This movement has mobilized thousands of American artists and writers who simultaneously prepared the path for the politics of the Modern Black Convention Movement (Woodard 1999, 51).

Our own discourses and representations of Malcolm in the current Malcolm biography provide us with a way to navigate the world Malcolm X sought to traverse and to understand the bounds of his imagination (Madhubuti 2012). Through it we are able to see how the current Black Studies reader biography of Malcolm presents an opportunity to reexplore and reinterpret the vast scope of that world. The Malcolm biography provides us as scholars with a teachable moment to explore Black Studies' regenerative discourses and representations about the meaning of Malcolm's life in relation to politics, economics, societies, and cultures throughout the world. It is from this platform that we use the Malcolm biographical genre. We see how some of the most pertinent issues affecting the Black world today include the future of charismatic leadership and democratic organization among Black communities, Black political power in the era of Obama, understanding twenty-first-century Pan-Africanism and the Black freedom struggle, and issues of gender and the Black working class (Fletcher 2012).

Thereby, in investigating the impact of Malcolm X's lived experience on Black Studies, *Malcolm X's Michigan Worldview* seizes the moment of the lively arena of classic and recently acclaimed biographies of Malcolm to explore Malcolm's biographical range and diversity as a worthwhile subject of world history, politics, and society. In this regard, we hope to present Malcolm's value as a scholarly contribution to Black Studies disciplinary learning.

Signifying Intersecting Identities of Blackness: Race and Identity

Henry Louis Gates writes that inadvertently African slavery in the New World satisfied the conditions for the emergence of a new African culture, a truly Pan-African culture, fashioned as a colorful weave of linguistic, institutional, metaphysical, and formal threads. He continues that what survived this long freedom struggle emerged as "African American" culture, an African culture with a difference (Gates 1988, 4). Gates goes on to refer to the way that African American linguistic identities are embodied in racial and cultural identities of significance. The figure of the "Signifying Monkey," similar to the Esu-Elegbara figure of West African Yoruba tradition, serves as a principle of verbal expression in African American culture. Like Esu, the Signifying Monkey expresses the nature and function of interpretation and double-voice utterance; it occupies a trope in which several peculiarly black rhetorical styles are encoded (Gates 1988, xxi).

Examine Malcolm's own words drawn from an interview that he gave to *Playboy* magazine:

When I'm traveling around the country, I use my real Muslim name, Malik Shabazz. I make my hotel reservations under that name, and I always see the same thing I've just been telling you. I come to the desk and always see that "here-comes-a-Negro" look. It's kind of a reserved, coldly tolerant cordiality. But when I say "Malik Shabazz," their whole attitude changes: they snap to respect. They think I'm an African. People say what's in a name? There's a whole lot in a name. The American black man is seeing the African respected as a human being. The African gets respect because he has an identity and cultural roots. But most of all because the African owns some land. For these reasons he has his human rights recognized, and that makes his civil rights automatic. (Malcolm X 1963a, 62)

Born Malcolm Little on May 19, 1925, in Omaha, Nebraska, in 1952, after joining the Nation of Islam (NOI) in Chicago, Malcolm changed his surname to X. In changing his name, Malcolm might be seen to be signifying or otherwise engaging in what Gates and Smitherman have referred to as "black rhetorical tropes" (Gates 1988; Smitherman 1994). Malcolm's rhetoric is borne of the signifying discourse tradition that Gates famously documents. In his public discourses, we see how Malcolm's dynamic lived experiences, multidimensional identities, and expansive leadership scope embody the intersections that stream together signifying, race, identity, and community subjectivity and struggle.

In *Black Talk* (1994), Geneva Smitherman shows how Black language has emerged as a result of racial conditions in America. African American language has come to represent a lexical core of words and phrases that are fairly stable over time and are familiar to and/or used by all groups in the Black community. Smitherman argues that there is underlying resistance in the language that further embodies social critique. Smitherman demonstrates how words developed double meanings as their definitions shifted according to the situation and were infused with irony, metaphor, and ambiguity. Similarly, we see how Malcolm is "marking and testifying," as Smitherman characterizes the elements of African American language. For example, "X" is a way to dishonor the slave name inheritance—Little—and a way to mark its revision. "X" becomes a marker of representation, a purposeful tropological thought that is deliberately used to obscure and reject the slave-owning name, Little. "X" testifies to the unknown identity indicating Malcolm's dissatisfaction with being denied self-determined assertion of his heritage.

Malcolm's signification also reveals the multisectionality of language, race, and identity in the Black community. For example, Malcolm again renames himself as

Malik Shabazz. Here Malcolm takes the signifying genre further and pushes it into the complicated issue of identity. The notion of Identity as both a multidimensional theoretical prism through which to discern identity and as a political practice and statement is just as important to the Black Studies discipline. Identities are social markers of convergence and difference, but in Black Studies, identities are particularly recognized as sites of oppression and resistance. Identities conceptualized as race, ethnicity, gender, and religion provide significant epistemological assumptions and premises of knowledge about Black peoples' experiences. When Malcolm describes the attitudes of the White hotel clerks as the "'here-comes-a-Negro' look," he invokes race and class identities, underscoring the way that each exists in relation to the other and how their intersectionality has shaped the Black experience in the modern world. In Malcolm's discourses, we observe the relational attributes of race, seen as a continuous process of social positioning and identity construction where race becomes conscious through social, political, economic, and psychological practices (Ann Phoenix in Murji and Solomos 2005).

While the intersectionality of Black world identities and the diverse ways that their combination plays out in various settings are important elements of the African American experience, most Black Studies scholars would agree that race and racial identity constitute a core defining theoretical framework for interrogating Black peoples' experiences on their own terms. Glen Ford holds no doubt that Malcolm lived and died a "Race-Man," putting race first in his discursive activity (Ford 2012). Malcolm's speeches are replete with critiques of White supremacy, a political phenomenon described by Charles Mills (1997) as a political system of domination in which white people have historically ruled over nonwhite people.

Malcolm's radical critique of White supremacy and American racism distinguished his genre of civil rights agitation. His discourses sought to reconfigure and transform the racial identities of both African Americans and African descendants around the world by linking Black identities to their roots in Africa, as well as engaging their intersections and connections with Africans on the continent, through his pioneering positing of cultural Pan-Africanism. In *Racism in the Autobiography of Malcolm X* (2009), Candace Mancini has argued that, for Malcolm, racism was historic and systematized, pervading every segment of American society. Mancini maintains that Malcolm understood racism as socioeconomic and political, and that it was utilized through other forms of power to systematically act out ill will onto an entire race of people.

Race occupies a deeply embedded position in the Black world lived experience though it remains a vacuous concept in Black Studies. Famously, Murji and Solomos state that the only real consensus on race as a paradigmatic value of knowledge production is that definitions about race remain contested and ambiguously defined (Murji and Solomos 2005). In putting forth "racialization" as a preferred concept, the authors acknowledge the state of affairs whereby there exists a descriptive and analytical impasse that obviates incontrovertible racial meaning and understanding. After all, as a method of inquiry, race has been examined variably by a range of scholarships and disciplines for its positivistic value, epidemiological research, evolutionary history, social descriptor function, source of political motivation, and for its futility and discontinuance (Murji and Solomos 2005).

The disciplinary study of racialization covers these varied dimensions and thereby presents race as a useful vehicle for describing the processes by which racial meanings are attached to particular issues often treated as social problems. As such, racialization signals the processes by which ideas about race are constructed, came to be regarded as meaningful, and are acted upon. Seen for its role as a social descriptor and as a source of political motivation (Murji and Solomos 2005, points d and e), racialization consists of an important element for the Black Studies discipline. In their definition of race, critical race theorists (CRiTs) attempt to capture the complex iterations of race as they relate to the Black experience. CRiTs famously refer to the ordinariness of race as it pertains to whiteness and to the everyday experience of most people of color in the United States (Delgado and Stefancic 2001).

Though Michael Omi and Howard Winant are not CRiTs, their racial formation thesis (1994) provides an important prism and method for understanding the key importance of race to the African American experience. Omi and Winant consider race as an intractable and enduring feature of U.S. politics and society where racial formations are pervasive and shape individual identities and collective action as well as social structures. The thesis defines race as an unstable and decentered complex of social meanings constantly being transformed by political struggle. Omi and Winant contend that racial categories remain an organizing principle of social life in the United States while meanings of race can shift as they are produced by practices of various groups. Building on the work of V. P. Franklin (1992), Errol Henderson underscores the special circumstance in which race was manifest in the United States. He describes the national consciousness that fostered the emergence of Black nationalism. Black nationalism arose as a result of a common experience of racial oppression—White exploitation of Black labor through racial slavery for the Black majority in the south and racist discrimination for the Black minority in the north (Henderson 2012, 168).

On his visit to MSU in 1963, Malcolm's lecture topic was the "Race Problem" where he demonstrated his unique and sophisticated insights on race. The lecture was critical of the Detroit-based Black elite at the time who, Malcolm complained, had failed to address the deep layers of structural racism. Struggles over the "Race Question" also continue to permeate MSU's campus environment in the present. In the fall of 2011, MSU students—the Black Student Alliance and the Black Unity Movement—accused the university administration of presiding over a "racist culture" after a string of racial incidents occurred targeting Black students. In sympathizing with the students, the university's president at the time, Dr. Lou Anna Simon, resolved to address the issue proclaiming that she had fought this battle herself during the 1960s civil rights movement. One of twenty-two of the students' demands to rectify racial biases on the MSU campus was the erection of a Malcolm X dedication on campus.

Intersecting Racialized Identities: Religion, Ethnicity, and Gender

Racial identity is but one of many other identities that Malcolm's experiences elucidate. Other identities that have been prominent in Malcolm's experiences are religious identity (Islam), ethnic identity (African heritage), and gender relationships (Black feminism and Africana womanism). However, all three identities are intersected and racialized when experienced in the African American U.S. contexts where racial meaning is attached to African American religious, ethnic, and gender practices that have always operated in environments of racial oppression and resistance. Like racial identity on its own terms, religious, ethnic, and gender identities and practices continue to affect the social positioning and identity construction of African Americans.

Malcolm's lived experiences illustrate the intersectionality and racialization of identities and underscore an important theme in Black Studies. Malcolm's experiences with racism in Michigan led him to write, "I began to change inside.... If I hadn't left Michigan to go to Boston, I'd probably still be a brainwashed black Christian" (qtd. in Mancini 2009, 93). Malcolm's intersectional religious and ethnic identities are revealed when Malcolm states that he uses his Muslim name, Malik el-Shabazz, to command respect (the honorific designation "El-Hajj" would be added to his name after his pilgrimage to Mecca in 1964). Uniquely, he associates his Muslim name with his African-descendent ethnic identity and surprisingly underscores the sore contradictions of race and civilization in civil rights America. Malcolm uses the name Malik el-Shabazz to signify an "African, who has cultural roots," an identity that he claims is respected by the White hotel clerks. Asserting Africanness suggests an ethnic identity whereas claiming Islam is a religious one that for Malcolm embodies both cultural heritage in the continent of Africa and racial resistance against European Christianity.

Malcolm's Pan-African and Black religious identities represented by Islamic and African-centered sociopolitical practices in the Black communities of Chicago and Detroit and in Harlem, provide important contexts for Black Studies disciplinary analyses on the cultural politics of identity. We know that Malcolm's political consciousness was shaped through his membership with the NOI, which like the Black church, embodies an important element of Black politics and society in the United States. In *Black Muslim Religion in the Nation of Islam* (2006), Edward Curtis IV argues that the activities of African American Muslims were a form of identity making where identities were dynamic and negotiated, not stable or given, as in other religions. He goes on to argue that African American Muslims constructed their Islamic identities through intellectual and creative activity, and Curtis's book shows how the NOI movement combined certain elements of Afro-Eurasian Islamic traditions with African American traditions as a form of Islamic practice.

Religious identity formation among Black Muslims also has a racial function. Marable's *Malcolm X* reveals this fact when he illustrates the underlying concerns that motivated Malcolm and Elijah Muhammad in the NOI. Both men, he says, had constructed a dynamic organization that attracted the membership of tens of thousands of African Americans and the admiration of millions more not simply because it demonized White people but because it channeled the profound sense of alienation that already existed among working-class blacks, born of the reality of southern Jim Crow segregation and northern discrimination (Marable 2011). Malcolm would reflect this Islam-race identity intersection in a discussion that he had explaining his attraction to Islam.

> America needs to understand Islam, because this is the one religion that erases from its society the race problem. Throughout my travels in the Muslim world, I have met, talked to, and even eaten with people who in America would have been considered white—but the "white" attitude was removed from their minds by the religion of Islam. I have never before seen sincere and true brotherhood practiced by all colors together, irrespective of their color. (Malcolm X 1964)

Also as regards the ethnic identity, we see in several of his speeches that Malcolm's choice name of Shabazz and his founding initiatives in the Organization of Afro-American Unity (OAAU) classify him as Afro-centric and Pan-Africanist, both divergent but interrelated core themes of the Black Studies discipline. In connecting the religious, ethnic, and racial identity markers that Blacks experience, Haki Madhubuti points out that it was Malcolm X and the NOI that first popularized the using of "Black" as the correct designation for people of African ancestry in America and that it was Malcolm's OAAU that made a formative connection between Black people in the United States, in Africa, and elsewhere in the Americas (Madhubuti 2012). Of the OAAU, Malcolm would proclaim,

> The Organization of Afro American Unity shall include all people of African descent in the Western Hemisphere, as well as our brothers and sisters on the African continent. Which means anyone of African descent, with African blood, can become a member of the Organization of Afro American Unity, and also any one of our brothers and sisters from the African continent. Because not only is it an organization of Afro American unity meaning that we are trying to unite our people in the West, but it's an organization of Afro American unity in the sense that we want to unite all of our people who are in North America, South America, and Central America with our people on the African continent. We must unite together in order to go forward together. Africa will not go forward any faster than we will and we will not go forward any faster than Africa will. We have one destiny and we've had one past. (Taylor 1964)

The "Africa" ethnic factor of Malcolm's politics and identity represented a vehicle for U.S. Blacks to explore the reservoir of their African heritage, to retrace African historical connections, to identify African cultural linkages in diaspora cultures, and to realign transnational relations with postcolonial African peoples. Steve Sharra writes that when Malcolm visited the continent of Africa twice in the last twelve months of his life, he followed in the footsteps of Dr. W. E. B. Du Bois in demonstrating how the struggles of African Americans in the United States and those of Africans on the continent were "interlocked." Malcolm X's visits represented a significant moment in the history of Pan-Africanism as he saw the support of Africans on the continent as key to internationalizing the African American struggle against racial injustice and inequality in the United States. Projecting the ideal of Pan-Africanism, through his OAAU, Malcolm sought to mobilize a global consciousness of the struggle needed to liberate Africans on the continent and in the diaspora (Sharra 2006).

In addition to Black Studies' core concepts of race, class, language, religion, ethnicity, Malcolm X's lived experience contributes a dynamic case study to disciplinary interests in the identity trope of gender. Ossie Davis's poetic "praise-singing" of Malcolm underscores the Black Studies/Black feminism contention within the identity and the discipline when he proclaims,

> Malcolm was our manhood, our living, black manhood! This was his meaning to his people. And, in honoring him, we honor the best in ourselves. . . . And we will know then for what he was and is—a Prince—our own black shining Prince!—who didn't hesitate to die, because he loved us so! (qtd. in Bassey 2005, 19).

Davis's tribute to Malcolm is certainly befitting and appropriate in concert with our theme establishing Malcolm's leadership impact on Black communities. But Davis's reference to the statement that "Malcolm was our manhood, our living, black manhood" has raised concerns among an emerging Black feminist network that has become a powerful subfield in—and some would say contender with (Guy-Sheftall and Heath 1995)—the Black Studies discipline. For example, Guy-Sheftall and Heath have indicated that the quote's characterization of African American leadership in terms of "manhood" underlies a guised patriarchy in the discipline (Guy-Sheftall and Heath 1995).

Part of the controversy of Manning Marable's *Malcolm X* dealt indirectly with gender fissures within the Black Studies discipline and divergent ideological tracts between Black Studies and Black Feminism Studies. Marable's inference that Malcolm committed infidelity against Betty Shabbazz, a renowned civil rights icon in her own right and wife to his death, enraged many Black nationalists. Critics were further irritated by Marable's tendency to cast Malcolm as chauvinistic by suggesting that Betty, rather than a loving wife and powerful partner, was in fact a nuisance to Malcolm and the cause of his extensive travel to avoid her. Furthermore, the insinuation by Marable's book that Malcolm perhaps dabbled in homosexuality did not augur well for those who enshrined Malcolm in Black manhood and saw him as "our own black shining Prince."

Are Marable's critics dismissive of the book because it suggests that Malcolm is queer or may not have been as faithful to his wife as commonly thought? How must one analyze the interconnectivity between Malcolm's lived experience and

Black Studies in terms of gender relations? The patriarchy that pervades the Black Studies movement, well documented by Black feminists, has now become a central theme in Black Studies. One stream of this tension is manifest in the Black feminist and Africana womanist epistemological tussle. Black feminists have critiqued core Black Studies ideologies—Black nationalism, Afrocentrism, and Pan-Africanism—for having overly focused on a race-only analysis that eschews the painful ways that patriarchy has manifest in African American communities (Cole and Guy-Sheftall 2003). A Black feminist perspective would prefer to see a Black Studies discipline that produces and reproduces Black women's knowledge gained at the intersections of race, class, and gender (Collins 2000). Doing so perhaps would foster more prominent biographies written on Betty Shabbazz and other revolutionary Black women who have similarly changed the course of history in collaboration with civil rights and nationalist male heroes like Malcolm. Such a study would appropriately expose and assess gender tensions within the X family and appropriately reconstruct Black masculinity frames that analyze Malcolm and his community impact.

On the other hand, the Africana womanist track agrees that Black women—all over the world—have fought against sexual, race, and class discrimination and that they have particularly challenged Africana male chauvinism (Hudson-Weems in Philips 2006). Nonetheless, additionally, according to this view, Africana womanism stops short of eliminating Black men as allies in the struggle for liberation and family-hood. The Africana womanist seeks to align with the community, with family, and with its responsibilities (Hudson-Weems in Philips 2006). Regina Jennings (2006) suggests the importance of understanding the X family in a womanist context, not a feminist one. Jennings reminds us that for Betty, a woman who chose to join the Nation where she met and married Malcolm, it would be important not to view the civil rights couple's relationship as patriarchal despite private challenges. Ilyasah Shabazz, Malcolm's daughter, chooses to present her mother, Betty, as a womanist who cared for and supported her husband and his work but who must be credited for her own efforts in human rights activism and female empowerment as well (Shabazz 2012).

Perhaps the truth about gender questions and Malcolm might be found in Magnus Bassey's argument, which uses the work of Clenora Hudson-Weems (1994) to conclude that Malcolm's attitude toward women mirrored the changing circumstances of his life. In his late adolescence through to his early adult life, Malcolm's attitude toward women was negative, guided either by "pimpism" at first or by the NOI later. Nonetheless, after his conversion to Islam, Malcolm's attitude toward women began to change for the better as he increasingly saw them as partners and people to be loved rather than as threats and commodities. Bassey claims that after Malcolm broke away from the NOI and visited Africa and Mecca, he showed even more respect for women. For instance, he admired Ghana for its mass education of men and women equally as a great nation. By Malcolm's final days, he was in the forefront of the evolving sense of consciousness regarding women when he would say, "Educate a man and you educate an individual. Educate a woman and you educate an entire family" (Bassey 2005, 108–10).

Race and Class in Black Nationalism and Internationalism

The realist-economic or what some refer to as the determinist-materialist theory of race moves our Malcolm-Black Studies thesis away from the previous discussion on race and identity that appropriately holds that racism and discrimination are matters of thinking, mental categorization, attitude, and discourse with its focus on identity and social construction (Delgado and Stefancic 2001). Alternatively, Black Studies scholars apt to examine the Black experience from a political-economic perspective see race in terms of class. They view racialization and racism as concerns that need to be seen through processes of interest, material determinism, or racial realism, which represent a means by which society allocates privilege and status, including the best jobs, the best schools, and the most inclusive access to the prestigious society (Delgado and Stefancic 2001). CRT materialists further point out that anti-Black prejudice emerged during slavery with capitalists' need for labor. This they claim was the process whereby conquering Western nations began to universally dehumanize their subjects through a process of biological racist determinism to legitimize economic exploitation (Delgado and Stefancic 2001).

There is sometimes a tension between these two approaches to race—considered the race and class conundrum—which is often apparent in the position of strict economic determinists, who argue that the process of racialization takes place and has its effects in the context of socioeconomic class, economic inequality, and power relations of production. Class trumps race. Indeed seen this way the idea of race may not even be explicitly articulated in these processes, these scholars claim (Miles and Torres 1999, 33). Inequality is of importance as the social descriptor, not race, and inequality is caused by the perversions of capitalism. This perspective rejects CRT as well as Omi and Winant's racial formation thesis as overdetermining the role of race and racialization theory in the characterization of contemporary politics and society.

The race/class tension is pertinent to the Black Studies discipline and to understanding Malcolm's role and significance in this regard. From this tension there exist contending perspectives among scholars to Black nationalisms, community interests, and global Black world struggles. Delgado and Stefancic pose the question—Is racism a means by which Whites secure material advantages on the exploits of Blacks? Or does racism occur as a result of a culture of poverty that is defined by broken families, crime, unemployment, and a high educational dropout rate? A response to either question requires that a Black Studies discipline uses racialization theories to examine and understand the use of race as a means for political mobilization and economic interests to address historical racially discriminatory practices. This kind of racialization, argue Murji and Solomos (2005), is justified for groups' heightened awareness of—and their wish to reduce or remove—racial injustice and inequality. Various iterations of the race/class tension are reflected in the political-economic approaches and methodologies of Black Studies disciplinary perspectives, and they significantly contribute to a deeper understanding of Malcolm's lived experience and genre of political-economic mobilization. The tension also provides a way to understand the Black experience through Malcolm expressed both locally and globally.

In modeling the OAAU around Malcolm's observations and participation in the global struggles occurring in Africa, we can also see how race/class and political/economic tensions are also manifest in Malcolm's global struggles. For example, curiously, during Malcolm's first trip to Ghana in 1964, the race/class tension and its impact on Black nationalism and Pan-African politics raised its ugly head. Malcolm was criticized in the *Ghanaian Times* by exiled South African journalist H. M. Basner who charged that Malcolm had failed to recognize the *class* aspects of racism and instead was consumed by *racialism*. However, Julian Mayfield, an African American resident in Ghana who hosted Malcolm's trip, countered the criticism by explaining that while Malcolm had been reluctant to involve liberal whites in the struggle his argument did not exclude a Marxist approach of race at the time (Gaines 2006, 198–99).

A known critic of the liberal practice of civil rights, Malcolm would proclaim in 1963,

The entire civil rights struggle needs a new interpretation, a broader interpretation. We need to look at this civil rights thing from another angle—from the inside as well as from the outside. To those of us whose philosophy is Black Nationalism; the only way you can get involved in the civil rights struggle is to give it a new interpretation. The old interpretation excluded us. It kept us out. (Malcolm X 1990, 31)

The Ghana incident as well as Malcolm's critique of the liberal civil rights approach to struggle provokes a deeper reflection to examine the divergent interpretations that explained Malcolm's political ideology.

In his own critical analysis of Marable's *Malcolm X* (Asante 2012), Molefi Asante poses a set of questions that underscore the race/class debate. Was Malcolm merely an African Americanist with a strong sense of racial justice—like Marable—or is it more correct to view Malcolm as a revolutionary whose core issue was racial oppression because he believed that race was the key to the African American historical materialist condition? Both Black liberalism and Black nationalism are ideologies that have been variably accommodated and engaged by the Black Studies discipline. Revolutionary Black nationalism is more closely associated with Malcolm whereas community nationalism in the form of micropolitical organization of Black majority neighborhoods, cities, and towns acted as a vehicle for the evolution of Malcolm's distinctive genre of Black nationalism. Examine, for example, Malcolm's rationale for establishing the OAAU.

The Organization of Afro-American Unity will organize the Afro American community block by block to make the community aware of its power and its potential; we will start immediately a voter registration drive to make every unregistered voter in the Afro-American community an independent voter. We won't organize any black man to be a Democrat or a Republican because both of them have sold us out. We propose to support and organize political clubs, to run independent candidates for office, and to support any Afro-American already in office who answers to and is responsible to the Afro-American community. (Taylor 1964)

The race/class tension is similarly characterized when one compares Black Power as a product of Black nationalism that is seen as a different examination of civil rights. During the civil rights period, Black nationalism was characterized by seven interrelated but distinctive elements: Black pride, a political mobilization strategy that transitioned from rights to power and civil rights to human rights, a change from seeing African Americans as a minority to a recognition that they are part of a continental African and Third World majority, the identification of the conditions of

African Americans as one that would be described by domestic colonialism as well as racial and ethnic discrimination, the problematizing of the use of nonviolence as a tactic for liberation, the critique of the Black petty bourgeoisie and recognition of its distancing itself from the Black poor and working-class African American communities, and finally the critique of White liberals in the civil rights struggle and their interference in Black leadership (Ayers 2012, 61).

These touchstone principles that would soon propel the collective action of Black nationalist movements and institutions like the Student Nonviolent Coordinating Committee, the Black Panther Party, and other organizations and movements, such as the OAAU, were first given clear articulation in the early 1960s by Malcolm X. Malcolm's Black nationalism invoked a political organization and racial justice advocacy for liberation through a core set of principles, including self-determination strategies, land ownership, and the attainment of civil rights through human rights (Ayers 2012). Illustrating, also, the intersections of Black liberation among local, national, and international communities of color in struggle and solidarity throughout the world, Malcolm would proclaim,

> The same rebellion, the same impatience, the same anger that exists in the hearts of the dark people in Africa and Asia exist in the hearts and minds of 20 million black people in this country who have been just as thoroughly colonized as the people in Africa and Asia. (Malcolm X 2014)

Notably as well, this history of Black world struggle parallels the founding establishment of Black Studies programs born out of Black nationalist educational struggles and activist movements' efforts to reconstruct society (Little et al. 2006). In many ways, this explains why a core objective of Black Studies is to contribute to community by translating knowledge into a political practice that transforms. Black Studies has incorporated the liberatory tradition into its disciplinary method, a tradition that includes the deep and rich reservoir of the canonical voices of the Black intellectual tradition and the critical thought and perspectives of scholars of black America, Africa, and the Black diaspora (Little et al. 2006).

As Malcolm straddled the intersectional geographic spaces of regional, national, and global domains so has the Black Studies discipline recently organized around three ideological and disciplinary geographical perspectives of study characterized as Black nationalism, Pan-Africanism, and diaspora nationalism. Classical Black nationalism focuses on the national arena that sees African Americans as a distinct community where "Black" is associated with the American experience of struggle against racism and for self-determination, justice, and rights. Favoring a global emphasis, the Pan-African framework privileges historical and cultural continuities among African descendants in America, Africans on the continent, and other African descendants in the diaspora. The much more recent diaspora framework underscores the transnational intersections of an amalgam of historicized, culturalized, and political-economic local communities in an integrated, interconnected Black world arena (Little et al.).

As the Black Studies discipline evolves and develops, the importance of race and class to the historical Black liberation struggle, its legacies, and its local, national, and global solidarities and shared experiences cannot be underemphasized. The civil rights and Black Power movements of the 1960s fostered the struggle's transfer from community to campus as students across the country forced their respective institutions to establish Black Studies programs. The name Black Studies signifies the discipline's freedom roots in the context of this struggle. Black Studies became the term used to describe a new academic endeavor, which at the time of its initial creation focused primarily on the experiences of African Americans. However, most programs today have grown to become inclusive of every aspect of life and culture that was the Black experience everywhere (Reid-Merritt 2009). Yet it is through tensions between race and class and the ways that such tensions mobilized struggles for spaces that Black Studies became a discipline that emphasized the contemporary community emancipatory project and its attendant cultural, intellectual, and social dimensions (Karenga 2009).

Malcolm and the Detroit Community

Given its status as the largest majority black city in the nation, Detroit's bankruptcy declaration in 2013 presented a reminder of the depth of crises facing Black America in a post–Civil Rights era and the question of the existence of any political will to deal with this and similar crises in Black communities. Herb Boyd, a former Detroiter, has written about ways that Detroit played a seminal role in Malcolm X's development as a community activist and thinker, remarking that, "It was in Detroit where he began his liberated odyssey with the Nation of Islam. . . . No matter where he journeyed, Malcolm always had a deep and abiding love for this city and the city never failed to return that love and devotion" (Huffpost Detroit 2012).

As a Black leader, Malcolm X used his role to inspire Black people to address problems they faced in their communities (Smallwood 2001). Exhibiting this fact, in establishing the Organization of Afro-American Unity (OAAU), Malcolm stated,

> This organization is not responsible to anybody but us. . . . This organization is responsible only to the Afro-American people and community and will function only with their support, both financially and numerically. We believe that our communities must be the sources of their own strength politically, economically, intellectually, and culturally in the struggle for human rights and human dignity. The community must reinforce its moral responsibility to rid itself of the effects of years of exploitation, neglect, and apathy, and wage an unrelenting struggle against police brutality. (Taylor 1964)

When he established the OAAU, Malcolm X performed the role of a community organizer. The OAAU presented a radical community action plan for Black Power in the areas of crime and self-defense, educational control, and political representation. Malcolm organized Black people for positive social change, and the same local manifestations of Malcolm's community struggles in Detroit are still with us today. For example, a May 19, 2012, event commemorating Malcolm X's eighty-seventh birthday at the Charles H. Wright Museum of African American History in Detroit highlights ways that race, class, gender, religion, linguistic and ethnic identities, histories and cultures, and political-economic struggle all come together in a black community that valorizes Malcolm as its own hero. At the event, Jo Ann Watson, a member of the Detroit City Council who describes herself as an avowed "Xer" and Pan-Africanist, welcomed the audience to the "African city of Detroit."

Speakers and artists proclaimed Detroit as their home and reflected on both Malcolm's historic engagement with Detroit's cultural vibrancy (NOI) and his experiences with the city's challenges (Detroit Red) as an African American majority city. With regard to education, the contemporary relevance to the city of Detroit couldn't have been made clearer when Malcolm stated,

> Our children are being criminally shortchanged in the public school system of America. The Afro-American schools are the poorest run schools in the city of New York. Principals and teachers fail to understand the nature of the problems with which they work and as a result they cannot do the job of teaching our children. They don't understand us, nor do they understand our problems; they don't. The textbooks tell

our children nothing about the great contributions of Afro-Americans to the growth and development of this country. (Taylor 1964)

Detroit today, a city that is 85 percent Black, reinforces George Lipsitz's thesis that this chapter began with in *How Racism Takes Place*. Race and racialization explain the problems of the city that is bedeviled by economic crisis and a loss of democracy with the March 13, 2013, inauguration of an Emergency Manager law to govern the city and the city's public schools. While Malcolm's early childhood experiences in Detroit reveal the city's long history of racial rebellions (Darden and Thomas 2007), it is in today's community issues, such as residential and school segregation, mortgage and insurance redlining, transportation and taxation policies, that we see how race is produced by space. Unemployment for Black males in the city is 57 percent, and Detroit schools, which have a vibrant history of community control and African-centered curricula, are also under the control of an emergency manager.

Kevyn Orr, Detroit's emergency manager appointed in 2013 whose appointment replaces the electoral functions of the city's mayor, is an African American corporate liberal financier who claims that he will turn the bankrupt city around. Orr has the backing of big global capital and the support of wealthy neoliberal financiers like Dan Gilbert, a millionaire whose "Operation Detroit" seeks to reconstruct the Detroit downtown financial district by buying up and gentrifying many of its tallest skyscrapers to build a new Detroit skyline and downtown city center. Indeed, the tensions between race and class, localism, nationalism, and globalization, and Black Nationalist struggle versus liberal black politics couldn't be more insightfully manifest in the problems of Detroit in the millennium. On the merits of Gilbert's claim to want to rebuild Detroit, one news article warned, "The uncomfortable reality is that Mr. Gilbert is a white guy trying to change the choicest parts of a city that is 83 percent African-American. A white guy who lives in an affluent village about 20 miles from downtown" (Segal 2013).

Hosted by and held at the largest African American history museum in the United States, the Charles Wright Museum, Detroit's Malcolm X Day commemoration also held a special one-day exhibition that displayed original writings, letters, and other artifacts that dated back to Malcolm X's childhood. In the subsequent sections of the current volume, like the Charles Wright exhibition, we guide our attendees (in our case, readers) to see how Malcolm's ideas, political practices, and multiple identities are linked to aspects of the Black experience and political agenda. These events are embodied in our community and struggle themes which have similarly laced Malcolm's discourses and political-economic organization.

Conclusion

The convergence of our guiding thematic objectives and Black Studies' core concepts and themes identified and analyzed in this chapter present an intellectual table of contents for the current title, *Malcolm X's Michigan Worldview: An Exemplar for Contemporary Black Studies*. The themes that we have addressed in our opening essay—iconography and biographical storytelling, race, discourse, intersectional Black identities of culture, gender, and religion, and black politics at community, national, and global levels—are reflected variably in the chapters that follow. In these subsequent essays, we hope to provide an academic vehicle for our discipline to deliberate, debate, and resolve and shape foremost public policy issues and sociocultural transformations affecting contemporary Black world communities.

At the same time, the book will underscore the role that the Michigan community, with all its virtues and vices, plays in developing Malcolm's ingenuity and leadership by reviewing a historical analysis of the Michigan community context that shaped the Malcolm X persona. We examine this community history against the broader impact of Malcolm's leadership and legacy while using the relationship between Malcolm and Michigan to investigate the wider influence of Malcolm's genre of politics on Black world communities comparatively and globally. We use Malcolm's exemplar as a vehicle to further explore the significance of race, identity, discourse, community, and Black world struggle.

These themes will further serve to facilitate our navigation of an African American icon, Malcolm X, and the Black Studies disciplinary scaffolding while deepening its contributed body of literature. Our diverse chapter discussions will converge critical research inquiries against a platform for multidisciplinary and transdisciplinary (academic and community partnerships) research, scholarship, and teaching of pertinent issues occurring in the Black world.

WORKS CITED

Abernethy, Graeme. 2013. *The Iconography of Malcolm X*. Lawrence: University Press of Kansas.

Asante, Molefi Kete. 2012. "An Afrocentric Take on Manning Marable's *Malcolm X: A Life of Reinvention*." In *By Any Means Necessary: Malcolm X: Real, Not Reinvented: Critical Conversations on Manning Marable's Biography of Malcolm X*, edited by Herb Boyd, Ron Daniels, Maulana Karenga, and Haki R. Madhubuti, 51–59. Chicago: Third World Press.

Ayers, Rick. 2012. "Malcolm X Still Inspires Today." In *By Any Means Necessary: Malcolm X: Real, Not Reinvented: Critical Conversations on Manning Marable's Biography of Malcolm X*, edited by Herb Boyd, Ron Daniels, Maulana Karenga, and Haki R. Madhubuti, 60–67. Chicago: Third World Press.

Bassey, Magnus O. 2005. *Malcolm X and African American Self-Consciousness*. Lewiston, NY: Edwin Mellen.

Boyd, Herb, Ron Daniels, Maulana Karenga, and Haki R. Madhubuti, eds. 2012. *By Any Means Necessary: Malcolm X: Real, Not Reinvented: Critical Conversations on Manning Marable's Biography of Malcolm X*. Chicago: Third World Press.

Cole, Johnnetta Betsch, and Beverly Guy-Sheftall. 2003. *Gender Talk: The Struggle for Women's Equality in African American Communities*. New York: Ballantine Books.

Collins, Patricia Hill. 2000. *Black Feminist Thought: Knowledge, Consciousness, and the Politics of Empowerment*. New York: Routledge.

Crenshaw, Kimberlé, et al., eds. 1995. *Critical Race Theory: The Key Writings That Formed the Movement*. New York: New Press.

Cunningham, Jennifer H. 2010. "Lost Chapters from Malcolm X Memoirs Revealed." *The Grio*. May 20. http://thegrio.com/2010/05/20/lost-malcolm-x-memoir-chapters-reveal-leaders-soft-side/.

Curtis, Edward E. 2006. *Black Muslim Religion in the Nation of Islam, 1960–1975*. Chapel Hill: University of North Carolina Press.

Darden, Joe T., Curtis Stokes, and Richard W. Thomas. 2007. *The State of Black Michigan, 1967–2007*. East Lansing: Michigan State University Press.

Delgado, Richard, and Jean Stefancic. 2001. *Critical Race Theory: An Introduction*. New York: New York University Press.

DeVega, Chauncey. 2011. "What Do They Call a President Who Happens to Be Black? If You Are Fox News You Call Him a 'Ghetto Crackhead.'" Blog. http://www.chaunceydevega.com/2011/12/what-do-they-call-president-who-happens_27.html.

Diamond, Irene, and Lee Quinby, eds. 1988. *Feminism and Foucault: Reflections on Resistance*. Boston: Northeastern University Press.

Fletcher, Bill. 2012. "Manning Marable and the Malcolm X Biography Controversy: A Response to Critics." In *By Any Means Necessary: Malcolm X: Real, Not Reinvented:*

Critical Conversations on Manning Marable's Biography of Malcolm X, edited by Herb Boyd, Ron Daniels, Maulana Karenga, and Haki R. Madhubuti, 121–35. Chicago: Third World Press.

Ford, Glen. 2012. "Dragging Malcolm X to Obamaland." In *By Any Means Necessary: Malcolm X: Real, Not Reinvented: Critical Conversations on Manning Marable's Biography of Malcolm X,* edited by Herb Boyd, Ron Daniels, Maulana Karenga, and Haki R. Madhubuti, 136–44. Chicago: Third World Press.

Foucault, Michel. 1980. *Power/Knowledge: Selected Interviews and Other Writings, 1972–1977.* New York: Harvester Press.

Franklin, V. P. 1992. *Black Self Determination: A Cultural History of African-American Resistance.* 2nd ed. Brooklyn, NY: Lawrence Hill Books.

Gaines, Kevin K. 2006. *American Africans in Ghana: Black Expatriates and the Civil Rights Era.* Chapel Hill: University of North Carolina Press.

Gates, Henry Louis, Jr. 1988. *The Signifying Monkey: A Theory of African-American Literary Criticism.* Oxford: Oxford University Press.

Guy-Sheftall, Beverly, and Susan Heath. 1995. *Women's Studies: A Retrospective: A Report to the Ford Foundation.* New York: Ford Foundation.

Henderson, Errol. 2012. "A Toothless Pursuit of a Revolutionary's Truths: Marable's Malcolm X: A Life of Reinvention." In *By Any Means Necessary: Malcolm X: Real, Not Reinvented: Critical Conversations on Manning Marable's Biography of Malcolm X,* edited by Herb Boyd, Ron Daniels, Maulana Karenga, and Haki R. Madhubuti, 163–77. Chicago: Third World Press.

hooks, bell. 2003. *Teaching Community: A Pedagogy of Hope.* New York: Routledge.

Hudson-Weems, Clenora. 2004. *Africana Womanism: Reclaiming Ourselves.* Troy: Bedford Publishers.

Huffpost Detroit. 2012. "Malcolm X Day: Detroit's Charles H. Wright Museum Celebrates with Speakers, Performances, Special Exhibit." May 14. http://huffingtonpost. com/2012/05/14/malcolm-x-day-detroit-charles-h-wright-museum_n_1515447.html.

Jennings, Regina. 2006. *Malcolm X and the Poetics of Haki Madhubuti.* Jefferson, NC: McFarland.

Joseph, Peniel E. 2009. "The Black Power Movement: A State of the Field." *Journal of American History* 96, no. 3: 751–76.

———. 2010. *Dark Days, Bright Nights: From Black Power to Barack Obama.* New York: BasicCivitas Books.

Karenga, Maulana. 2009. "Names and Notions of Black Studies: Issues of Roots, Range, and Relevance." *Journal of Black Studies* 40, no. 1: 41–64.

Lee, Spike. 1992. *Malcolm X*. DVD. Burbank, CA: Warner Home Video, 2000.

Lipsitz, George. 2011. *How Racism Takes Place*. Philadelphia: Temple University Press.

Little, William A., Selase W. Williams, Irene Vasquez, et al. 2006. *The Borders in All of Us: New Approaches to Global Diasporic Societies*. Northridge, CA: New World African Press.

Madhubuti, Haki R. 2012. "Publisher's Statement: Actually an Obligation." In *By Any Means Necessary: Malcolm X: Real, Not Reinvented: Critical Conversations on Manning Marable's Biography of Malcolm X*, edited by Herb Boyd, Ron Daniels, Maulana Karenga, and Haki R. Madhubuti, xiii-xxii. Chicago: Third World Press.

Malcolm X. 1964. "Letter from Mecca: Malcolm X: April, 1964." malcolm-x.org. http:// malcolm-x.org/docs/let_mecca.htm.

———. 1963a. "Playboy Interview: Malcolm X: A Candid Conversation with the Militant Major-Domo of the Black Muslims." *Playboy*, 10, no. 5: 53–63.

———. 1963b. "Race Problems and the Black Muslim Religion and Its Ideas." Speech at Michigan State University, Erickson Kiva, East Lansing, MI. January 23.

———. 1964. "Letter from Mecca: Malcolm X: April, 1964." malcolm-x.org. http:// malcolm-x.org/docs/let_mecca.htm.

———. 1990. *Malcolm X Speaks: Selected Speeches and Statements*. Edited by George Breitman. New York: Grove Press.

———. 1992. *The Autobiography of Malcolm X*. With the assistance of Alex Haley. New York: Ballantine Books.

———. 2014. "Quotations." malcolm-x.org. http://malcolm-x.org/quotes.htm.

Mancini, Candice. 2009. *Racism in the Autobiography of Malcolm X*. Social Issues in Literature. Lawrence: Greenhaven Press.

Marable, Manning. 2000. "Black Studies and the Racial Mountain." *Souls* 2, no. 3: 17–36.

———. 2011. *Malcolm X: A Life of Reinvention*. New York: Viking.

Michigan Historical Center. 2007. "Malcolm X Homesite informational Site." http://www. mcgi.state.mi.us/hso/sites/6487.htm.

Miles, Robert, and Rodolfo D. Torres. 1999. "Does Race Matter?" In *Race, Identity, and Citizenship: A Reader*, edited by Rodolfo Torres, Louis Mirón, and Jonathan Xavier Inda, 3–38. Malden, MA: Blackwell.

Mills, Charles W. 1997. *The Racial Contract*. Ithaca: Cornell University Press.

Murji, Karim, and John Solomos. 2005. *Racialization: Studies in Theory and Practice*. Oxford: Oxford University Press.

Omi, Michael, and Howard Winant. 1994. *Racial Formation in the United States: From the 1960s to the 1990s*. New York: Routledge.

Painter, Nell Irvin. 2012. "Revising Perspectives on Malcolm X." In *By Any Means Necessary: Malcolm X: Real, Not Reinvented: Critical Conversations on Manning Marable's Biography of Malcolm X.*, edited by Herb Boyd, Ron Daniels, Maulana Karenga, and Haki R. Madhubuti, 238–40. Chicago: Third World Press.

Perry, Bruce. 1991. *Malcolm: The Life of a Man Who Changed Black America.* Barrytown, NY: Station Hill Press.

Perry, Imani. 2012. "A Review of Manning Marable's Malcolm X." In *By Any Means Necessary: Malcolm X: Real, Not Reinvented: Critical Conversations on Manning Marable's Biography of Malcolm X.*, edited by Herb Boyd, Ron Daniels, Maulana Karenga, and Haki R. Madhubuti, 241–43. Chicago: Third World Press.

Philips, Layli, ed. 2006. *The Womanist Reader: The First Quarter Century of Womanist Thought.* New York: Routledge.

Shabazz, Ilyasah. 2012. "On My Father." In *By Any Means Necessary: Malcolm X: Real, Not Reinvented: Critical Conversations on Manning Marable's Biography of Malcolm X.*, edited by Herb Boyd, Ron Daniels, Maulana Karenga, and Haki R. Madhubuti, 241–43. Chicago: Third World Press.

Smallwood, Andrew P. 2001. *An Afrocentric Study of the Intellectual Development, Leadership Praxis, and Pedagogy of Malcolm X.* Lewiston, NY: Edwin Mellon Press.

Reid-Merritt, Patricia. 2009. "Defining Ourselves Name Calling in Black Studies." *Journal of Black Studies* 40, no. (1): 77–90.

Rogers, Ibram H. 2012. *The Black Campus Movement: Black Students and the Racial Reconstitution of Higher Education, 1965–1972.* New York: Palgrave MacMillan.

Segal, David. 2013. "A Missionary's Quest to Remake Motor City." *New York Times.* April 13.

Sharra, Steve. 2006. "Malcolm X and Pan-Africanism Today." Afrika Aphukira. May 19. http://mlauzi.blogspot.com/2006/05/malcolm-x-and-pan-africanism-today.html.

Smitherman, Geneva. 1994. *Black Talk: Words and Phrases from the Hood to the Amen Corner.* Boston: Houghton Mifflin.

Spivak, Gayatri Chakravorty. 1990. "Practical Politics of the Open End." In *The Post-Colonial Critic: Interviews, Strategies, Dialogues,* edited by Gayatri Chakravorty Spivak and Sarah Harasym, 95–112. New York: Routledge.

Taylor, Quintard. 1964. "Malcolm X's Speech at the Founding Rally of the Organization of Afro-American Unity." blackpast.org. http://www.blackpast.org/1964-malcolm-x-s-speech-founding-rally-organization-afro-american-unity.

Tyner, James. 2006. *The Geography of Malcolm X: Black Radicalism and the Remaking of American Space.* New York: Routledge.

Walters, Ronald W., and Robert C. Smith. 1999. *African American Leadership.* Albany:

State University of New York Press.

Weedon, Chris. 1987. *Feminist Practice and Poststructuralist Theory*. Oxford: Blackwell.

Wilson, James Q. 1965. *Negro Politics: The Search for Leadership*. New York: Free Press.

Woodard, Komozi. 1999. *A Nation within a Nation: Amiri Baraka and Black Power Politics*. Chapel Hill: University of North Carolina Press.

The Paradigmatic Agency of Malcolm X

Family, Experience, and Thought

Abdul Alkalimat

There is something special about a topic of conversation and study that stays current in the flow of academic scholarship and the social movements over many decades. The life and legacy of Malcolm X is such a topic. But, one might ask, why? In this volume we propose a theoretical answer to this question, both in general and in particular relationship to Black Studies.

One model for our task was taken up by Max Weber in his discussion of the transition from charisma to bureaucracy (Weber 1968). The special features of a dynamic individual in a particular context can command loyalty and a mass following, but long-run sustainability relies on the routinization of key aspects of the movement into the routine of institutional functionality. A quite different approach was proposed by Thomas Kuhn (1996). Kuhn studied the history of science and theorized that the stability and coherence of science at any given historical period is because of a dominant paradigm that establishes the rules and assumptions for "normal science." Our study suggests interplay between these two frameworks in the search for an answer to our question: Why after almost fifty years are people still interested in Malcolm X? Is this merely misguided worship, or is it more dynamic and compelling? Our answer probes into Malcolm's life and legacy.

Our approach will be to focus first on Malcolm directly and then on how his legacy was foundational for the history of Black Studies. On the one hand (à la Weber) we argue that the meaning of charismatic Malcolm X was institutionalized or normed into Black Studies. In addition (à la Kuhn) we argue that Malcolm's ideas and practices personified a Black Power paradigm within which the Black Liberation Movement struggles and the Black Studies programs carry out their research and advocacy (academic excellence and social responsibility).[1] Further, we will demonstrate this in relation to several key historical developments in Black Studies over the last half-century.

The importance of this argument is over whether Black Studies and the Black Liberation Movement have a center of gravity, a common page to be on. Here we have to make a distinction between dogma and a paradigm. A text that is followed to the letter is a dogma, something to be memorized, requiring no thinking, just repetition. A paradigm is a set of assumptions people share, but in that context each acts under their own will and intention. Malcolm X was the great catalyst that sparked a paradigm shift from an integrationist consciousness to Black consciousness, from inside the box to outside the box (Alkalimat 1990). Within this conceptual framework debates raged throughout the world to find direction in each concrete place and condition, and in this way creativity is facilitated and in no way diminished. New work is always required to connect abstract thinking to concrete time, place, and condition. Malcolm X led to a renaissance of intellectual creativity.

The canonical text in Malcolm X studies is *The Autobiography of Malcolm X*. Our concern here is with the deep logic of Malcolm's experience, basically an unchallenged logic even by his most severe "humanizers." Also important are his speeches, our most direct documentation of Malcolm X, especially when we can combine sight (photos and video) and sound (audio) with text.

The framework we are using looks at Malcolm as a paradigm of the Black experience. Our first focus is on identity, including family influences as related to the radical Black tradition. We will then examine the stages of Malcolm X's life, his archetypal life cycle, from inside the society to outside as a critic and revolutionary activist. Next we take up a critical examination of the thought of Malcolm X by examining his most famous speech given in Detroit (November 10, 1963), "Message to the Grass Roots" (Malcolm X 1963). After this examination of Malcolm X as paradigm we examine how Malcolm X impacted Black Studies through its three stages as social movement, as academic profession, and as knowledge network.

The Paradigm of Family

The first paradigmatic factor is about family. Malcolm X was born with parents who represented a major convergence of the five critical elements of the radical Black tradition: Pan-Africanism, nationalism, liberation theology, feminism/womanism, and socialism. This is critical in that Malcolm X is carrying forward a historical tradition and should therefore never be regarded as a decontextualized genius.

Pan-Africanism is the belief that Africa and the African diaspora are linked with a common past and a common future, and therefore every freedom struggle should be linked to the total liberation of the entire African continent (Rodney 1989; Adi and Sherwood 1995). The movements of W. E. B. Du Bois and Marcus Garvey were about the liberation of the continent from direct colonization, while the movements of Kwame Nkrumah and Nelson Mandela faced neocolonialism. In all cases the actors were committed to knowing about and actively participating directly and indirectly in the African liberation struggles everywhere in the diaspora. This aspect of the Black Power paradigm involves fundamental assumptions:

1. IDENTITY: we are African Americans, descendants from Africa;
2. CULTURE: African cultural values and practices continue to inform the African American experience;
3. POLITICAL PERSPECTIVE: everywhere in the African diaspora that Black people fight for their rights is a common struggle.

Nationalism is the belief that Black people are a nationality and have the right to self-determination. This is an affirmation and is in contradiction with looking toward the mainstream for standards to be guided by while fighting for integration. The critical political and moral mandate is for Black unity. Within the United States, the greatest nationalist movements have been led by Marcus Garvey, Booker T. Washington, and Elijah Muhammad. Fundamental assumptions include the following:

1. IDENTITY: Black people are a distinct nationality in the United States;
2. CULTURE: while being impacted by African retentions and European, Latino, and Native American cultural influences, African Americans have reinvented themselves as improvisational blues people;
3. POLITICAL PERSPECTIVE: Black unity is the historical mandate for all Black political motion.

Black Liberation theology is the rethinking of Black religious activity as being a manifestation of the desire and struggle for freedom (Wilmore and Cone 1979). Both Christianity and Islam can be interpreted as being stories of people's historical development, against all forms of tyranny and oppression, with a codified set of moral principles and ritual practices that order the life of the community (Wilmore and Cone 1979). Religious leaders have been important guides in the freedom struggles, just as at times they are tools of ruling elites and are used to maintain control to keep exploited people docile and/or living in fear. Fundamental assumptions include the following:

1. IDENTITY: we are all children of a god and deserve the honor and glory due to all of god's creation;
2. CULTURE: we embrace Black culture, especially music, oratory, and food, and then we use this cultural power to celebrate god's glory;
3. POLITICS: racism and class exploitation are violations of all religious beliefs and practices.

Feminism/womanism is the thought and practice of women and men who oppose male supremacy in all its forms (Hull et al. 1982). This is important for Black women as it links them with men in a fight against racism and class exploitation, but with all women in opposing patriarchy and advocating women's rights. In sum, this is a position that focuses on the triple oppression of Black women: racism, class exploitation, and sexism. Fundamental assumptions include the following:

1. IDENTITY: women are equal to men;
2. CULTURE: transgenerational transmission and reproduction of culture has been a key role of women, including through the rearing of children, as well as gendered forms of cultural creativity;
3. POLITICS: women have been a fundamental organizational resource for all political work in the Black community, but a continuing struggle must take place for women to play an equal role in political leadership.

Socialism is the belief that capitalism is an exploitative system that must be replaced by one organized for the maximum social good and not the accumulation of wealth based on profiting off the labor of others. The theoretical magnum opus of the science of political economy concerning capitalism is *Capital* by Karl Marx.

However, independent of this scientific work, the values of a society organized for the benefit of the people have come forth from many places in society. People like Cedric Robinson, in his book *Black Marxism* (1983), have argued that there are cultural and historical reasons why Black people have trended toward sharing values that privilege family and community, that is, their own form and origin of socialism. Some fundamental assumptions include the following:

1. IDENTITY: the majority of humanity are workers and farmers, and they create the wealth on which the progress of society is based;
2. CULTURE: culture must be evaluated on the basis of which it honors the working people and not the rich and ruling elites;
3. POLITICS: state power of the capitalists must be replaced by the power of the workers and farmers, on the basis of class struggle.

Table 1 points to the many ways that the parents and siblings of Malcolm X were themselves extensions of this radical Black tradition to which Malcolm X made such great contributions. The aggregations of these ideological categories into a coherent tradition makes sense at an abstract level, but it must be recognized that in practice there is a great deal of diversity within these categories, and at times critical conflict that impacts the path of the struggle. The transgenerational continuity of these tendencies reaffirms that this is indeed a tradition that is sustained by the realities of Black people's lives. Malcolm's family was a cauldron of this tradition. He was molded as an apostle of this sacred path as his birthright. This is confirmed also by

TABLE 1. The Worldviews of Malcolm X's Family

IDEOLOGICAL TRADITION	FAMILY LEGACY
Pan-Africanism	Mother was born in Grenada, and both parents in the UNIA
Nationalism	Father a major community organizer for the UNIA
Black Liberation Theology	Father a Baptist minister and mother a devout Seventh Day Adventist
Feminism/womanism	Strong mother, sisters, and half-sister
Socialism	Father taught and practiced self-reliance and self-determination, including building one's own house and having a garden for food

the fact that his brothers were equally vested in the tradition. As Sly would say, it was a family affair.[2]

The Experience Paradigm

The second paradigmatic factor is about experience. The four major stages of Malcolm X's life constitute a mapping of the Black male experience, mainly outside of the mainstream box. Malcolm X was mostly outside the box. This is not an idealist "ideal type" categorization of reality but a summation of the actual path of Malcolm's experience. As is often the case in Black improvisational blues culture, people have a fluid name-identity, combining legal names, with conventional use, with family nicknames, street nicknames, and finally intimate names shared between partners for life. Malcolm was such a person as is demonstrated in Table 2.

One of the important aspects of this categorization is that there is a spatial aspect to it. Today this concentric circles model (from small to world) has been leveled as communication and transportation technology have cut any lingering cultural lag from the major cities to the countryside. The worst of everything gets everywhere really quickly these days. But the dialectic remains. Malcolm Little was in the box and Detroit Red was out of the box, and this is the dialectic we find in every Black community, urban and rural. Malcolm went through four stages of growth as "the little brother," "the Detroit gangster," the grown race man, and the globalist.

Malcolm Little: This little brother was born into a two-parent household with intelligent and politically active parents. This was a Black family with strong cultural norms and a very positive self-image, especially in opposition to the crude racism of the time. Malcolm got good grades, participated in sports, and was even elected class officer in the seventh grade. This brother could have been headed up into the box, but the forces of oppression put Malcolm outside the box—bam! Racism slammed the door of achievement through academics. A racist act of violence stole his father, and a racist state mental health institution stole his mother. "Malcolm, you are out of the box!"

Detroit Red: Many young Black men with no parents bouncing around in foster care end up seeking identity and some kind of love on the street. Plus, with criminal records and no regular job, people organize their lives around some kind of hustle to survive. And lots of this is not legal or legitimate. Malcolm did it all, was a negation of his family and the tradition. He became the avenging angel in the nightmare of the

TABLE 2. Malcolm X's Evolving Identity

NAME	SPACE	INSTITUTION	CRISIS	GENERAL TYPE
Malcolm Little *Chaps. 1–2*	Small Midwestern towns, small Black community	Family and school	Racism in school, murder of father, hospitalization of mother	Positive youth experiences
Detroit Red *Chaps. 3–10*	Large East Coast cities, large Black populations	The "street" and prison	Drugs, violence, and arrest	Negative youth experiences
Malcolm X *Chaps. 11–16*	National minister, travels nationally	Nation of Islam	Contradiction in the NOI	Born again religious convert, nationalist political activist
Omowale *Chaps. 17–19*	Global activist in Africa, Middle East, and Europe	OAAU and MMI	Conflicts with the NOI and global security forces	Revolutionary political activist and Sunni minister

Note: The chapters are references to *The Autobiography of Malcolm X.*

guilt-ridden racist who fears facing justice at the hands of those whom he has been oppressing. Thug, dope addict, sexual pervert, almost anything you can imagine. He became "satan."

Malcolm X: But there is always dark before the dawn. In the joint (prison) he was born again. He rediscovered his intellectual prowess and began to study. His family reconnected and led him to conversion to Islam. Prison was the end of someone created by the system and birth of a revolutionary who was threatening and challenging the system. And when Malcolm became an organizing force in the Nation of Islam (NOI) he was using his knowledge of the street gained from his experience as Detroit Red. This was indeed the negation of the negation (Engels 1940).

Omowale: With the Yoruba name given to him on a visit to Nigeria and other parts of Africa, Malcolm Omowale kept moving. The moral strength and ideological grounding that was reaffirmed within the NOI was transformed further by the historical forces of world revolution and Black liberation throughout the African diaspora. Malcolm left the authoritarian ideological dogma of the NOI and entered a new world of creative thinking and movement building.

Every person travels a path through life, and in most cases can hear another person's story and find similarities: similar things happen, similar choices have to be made, similar failures and/or successes. Some lives connect with most of us, and that makes them culturally useful. All of us are trying to make sense of our lives, and these special people give us a point of reference, sort of a lighthouse in the storms of living life. Malcolm became a Black everyman, with a transgenerational impact. *The Autobiography of Malcolm X* is the fourth great autobiography of Black history along with the autobiographies of Frederick Douglass, Booker T. Washington, and W. E. B. Du Bois.

The Thought Paradigm

The third paradigmatic factor is about thought. The most developed political teaching Malcolm X gave us was the speeches he made in Detroit at the height of the struggle in the 1960s. In this chapter we will concentrate on the first November 10, 1963, speech titled "Message to the Grass Roots." This speech is a central text in the collected work of Malcolm X. It can be read on at least four levels: political, historical, sociological, and philosophical:

1. POLITICAL: Malcolm X begins the talk by establishing political culture as the basis for Black identity and makes an argument for Black unity based on racist political violence;
2. HISTORICAL: Malcolm X grounds his argument in a review of seven cases of revolutionary change from 1776 to 1959, almost two hundred years. He focuses on political economy (land) and revolutionary strategy (bloodshed);
3. SOCIOLOGICAL: Malcolm X argues that the difference between the house slave and the field slave was being repeated in the current situation between the civil rights leaders and the militant masses of people (class struggle);
4. PHILOSOPHICAL: The logic of this argument is based on what actually happened in history (materialism) as a function of the struggle of opposites, for example, land owners versus the landless (dialectics).

We have to review this material and think for ourselves about these matters as Malcolm X would have encouraged us to do. The main thing is that we have what he said, and now we have to make sense of it based on our understanding fifty years after Malcolm X gave this speech.

When Malcolm X gave this speech we were facing the illusions and hypocrisy of the Kennedy administration after giving Kennedy 68 percent of the Black vote in 1960. But things have gotten better and worse at the same time. Black people gave Barack Obama, the first Black president, 96 percent of their vote in 2008. This was a blow against racism. Blinded by their hopes and aspirations that Obama was more than he could have in any way been, Black people have been sold a bill of goods that this is as good as it could have been. It's a good deal even if it's a raw deal! Malcolm would have targeted Obama as a house Negro trapped in a "white" house with no chance of any real change. Their message: "Stay for a little while, then get out so we can get back to business." It is important to read Malcolm X's speeches seriously, very carefully, because there are always multiple levels of meaning and ways of using these ideas today some fifty years later. So, what can we learn from Malcolm X's speech "Message to the Grass Roots"?

Black Identity and Political Culture

The first seven paragraphs speak to the issues of Black identity and political culture. The argument begins by noting that there are many differences in the Black community, but none is more important than the common experience of being exploited and oppressed by white racist oppression. He uses the phrase "catching hell" to represent racist oppression and states that differences based on religion, political party affiliation, and fraternal group membership do not explain why we catch hell. The main explanation is that there is a racist pattern and all Black people catch hell together. Those who catch hell are contrasted with those that came over on the Mayflower. This is the polarity he creates in his argument—the Pilgrims (of European origin) versus those that catch hell (those of African origin) by their hand.

He then takes us to an international example, an example he regards as a road map suggesting what African Americans should do. He discusses the Bandung Conference in 1955 when twenty-nine countries came together to plot a common strategy for Third World countries. His argument is that they had to deal with a fundamental contradiction that continues to be with us today, the former colonies versus the colonial powers, now the countries dominating global capitalism and those neocolonies that are being subordinated in this new system. He concludes by indicating that Black people in the United States are similar to the countries that met in 1955. Rev. Adam Clayton Powell was at the conference representing the anticommunist interests of the United States, while Richard Wright was there writing his analysis as an independent Black left critic. Wright subsequently published a book on Bandung called *The Color Curtain* (1956).

In sum, Malcolm X argues that it is the political culture of violence that has forced Black people into a common identity, a survival mode of uniting against a common enemy. Moreover, he argues that just as anticolonial unity was the precondition for the former colonies to shake off colonial rule, so a comparable unity would be necessary for Black people in the United States to get free from this form of exploitation and oppression.

Revolution

Malcolm X wants to make a clear distinction between the Negro and the Black revolution. He begins by indicating that the two fundamental issues are what it is for and how it is done. He says it is for "land," and it is done through "bloodshed." What did he mean by these simple answers to very complex questions?

Land is the physical environment for living, and that requires a social organization of people for all kinds of survival and reproduction. In every case what comes out of the land has been the basis for the economy, the production of food, clothing, and shelter. Our reading can be full and accurate only when we understand that he uses the word "land" to represent political economy, the basis for a people's survival.

There are four ways this happens:

1. Land as agriculture for domestic consumption, to grow the home market.
2. Land as production resource for export to world markets for hard foreign exchange.
3. Land as space for national unity.
4. Land as place for a state, either a national state or a multinational state.

Each way is a test for a revolution:

1. Can the revolution feed its people and provide for a high standard of living?
2. Can the revolution compete in the world market and maintain good trade relations?
3. Can the revolution end national oppression?
4. Can the revolution embrace the politics of democracy and social justice?

Bloodshed is the way Malcolm X refers to armed struggle in this speech. Armed struggle is a strategic weapon in any mass movement to seize political power for the purpose of taking control of a country to redistribute the wealth for the sustainable guarantee to a decent life for all the people and not simply a ruling class of elites. All other means of change must be exhausted and met with violent repression before armed struggle becomes an option. This is discussed by Malcolm X in the second great Detroit speech, "The Ballot or the Bullet." There are other strategic tools that are necessary preconditions to any successful armed struggle:

1. The development of an ideological and political line that defines friends and enemies, problems and solutions, a vision and specific goals;
2. The creation of an organization that can serve as a general staff of workers to keep the mass struggles coordinated and always combining action with study of the ideological and political line;
3. The mobilization of mass based battlefronts in which people fight for reforms to improve their day-to-day lives, while not losing sight of the ultimate goal of making a total revolution.

The degree to which this leads to a total moral denunciation of the status quo, the government, and the dominant corporations, and the extent to which there is a clear line that is backed by an effective revolutionary organization, with masses in action with little hope for reform, being met by violent repression, determines whether armed struggle becomes a necessary and viable alternative.

Malcolm X talks about and therefore calls for a study of the following revolutionary experiences:

1. American Revolution, 1776—capitalism
2. French Revolution, 1789—capitalism
3. Russian Revolution, 1917—socialism
4. Chinese Revolution, 1949—socialism
5. Cuban Revolution, 1959—socialism
6. Algerian Revolution, 1962—national liberation
7. Kenyan Revolution, 1963—national liberation

He guides us to study the issues of both political economy and the strategy and tactics of each of these different revolutionary experiences.

Class Analysis: House Slave versus Field Slave

Then Malcolm X turns to the African American experience and begins by examining the social organization of class forces within the Black community. He focuses on the polarity that existed during slavery, a polarity that places the origin of different class forces in relation to the experiences of the enslaved Africans within the United States. The house slaves identified with the slave master, appropriated the culture and consciousness of the slave owners, and were alienated from the masses of Black people. The field slaves were separated from whites, retained more of their African identity, and consolidated a culture around repudiating the culture and society of the white racist slave owners.

By interrogating this distinction we can open up the discussion and see how vital it is for understanding the full complexity of what we face today. How can we read this?

1. This is the difference between service work (house) and production work (field), blue collar and white collar.
2. This is the distinction between those connected to the mainstream and those who are socially isolated into the Black community, the Black suburbs, and the inner-city projects.
3. This is the distinction between highly educated Black people with high-paying jobs and Blacks with less than a high school education working for minimum wage or unemployed.

Malcolm leads us to study the class differences within the Black community, both the objective differences (house versus field) and the subjective differences (consciousness and identity). He speaks from the vantage point of the field and covers many issues of culture (food), psychology (hatred for "master"), and social organization (housing).

Malcolm X contrasted what he called the Negro revolution versus the Black revolution. He uses the language of land and bloodshed to make the contrast. He attacks the fight for integration of public accommodations as reformist, and the tactic of "suffering peacefully" as a betrayal of the right to self-defense. He makes an analysis of how the Negro leaders were not in the Black revolution but were being used by the white power structure to control the Black community. He begins his analysis by referring to what he considered the failure of the movement in Albany,

Georgia, and Birmingham, Alabama. After that he points to the emergence of militant grassroots leadership. He refers to the internal conflict over fund-raising by the national Negro leadership.

The main example he uses is the March on Washington, 1963. He said Kennedy told the Negro leaders to stop the militant march, but the Negro leaders said, "we can't stop it because we didn't start it." They were then bribed into a plan that removed the militancy out of the march and turned it into a rhetorical exercise without militant action (confrontation). Out of this process came a council for civil rights leadership and fund-raising, leading to a quick $1.5 million fund. He focuses on the ruling-class tactic of co-opting Black leadership.

In sum, Malcolm X became the personification of a liberated Black man, a paradigmatic ideological force:

1. His family was rooted in the Black radical tradition.
2. His path of life maps a personal journey of transformation.
3. His thoughts linked our struggle to world revolution.

Legacy in Black Studies

Malcolm X became the standard reference for people in Black Studies, as the movement emerged in the heart of a massive Black Power movement that connected intellectual work and activist practice in the movement. This became a force in all phases of Black Studies: social movement, academic profession, and knowledge network.

Black Studies as Social Movement

One of the clearest examples of how Malcolm X was a referent for the movement is when the students at Duke University joined with community activists to create Malcolm X Liberation University (Wilson 1965, 2). They fought for a Black Studies program and in the process seized the administration building, which led to a militant confrontation. The militant students were put off and decided to get out of the box.

In February 1969, fifty Duke University students occupied the Allen Administration Building and renamed it Malcolm X Liberation University. Among their list of twelve demands were the establishment of an Afro-American studies program, an increase in the enrollment of Black undergraduate students, and the reinstatement of Black students who had left the university because of poor treatment they had previously received. Instead of continuing their education at Duke, many of these students decided to establish a new, all Black, university, which was open until 1973. They did this because they realized that, "The existing system of education does not respond to the needs of the Black community; it does not provide an ideological or practical methodology for meeting the physical, social, psychological, economic and cultural needs of Black people. Malcolm X Liberation University is a direct response to this vacuum" (Wilson 1965, 2).

They pulled out of Duke and established an independent institution that lasted from 1969 to 1973. The movement carries forward an identity with Malcolm through annual events in February (death) and May (birth), as well as in course assignments and lectures. One outstanding example of his continued connection to the Black Liberation Movement is the Malcolm X Grassroots Movement that has organizational presence in many large cities, especially in the Black Belt South.

Black Studies as Academic Profession

Every organization and journal founded in the modern Black Studies movement used Malcolm X as a reference. This is especially true of the *Black Scholar*, and the National Council for Black Studies. Other examples include the naming of Black Studies academic institutions after Malcolm X such as Malcolm X College in Chicago (1969), Malcolm X Institute at Wabash College (1970), and the Malcolm X Academy in Detroit (1991).

Black Studies as Knowledge Network

Movements are dense social networks. Malcolm X planted seeds while alive so his memory and legacy has been kept alive by grassroots networks based in the Black Liberation Movement. The master of this is the founder of the Malcolm X Lovers Network, Preston Wilcox.[3] Brother Wilcox was the master of using the copying machine to make copies and send them out to over two hundred people on a regular basis. This kind of networking continued with a listserv created by F. Leon Wilson (1997–2001).[4] In addition there have been many web pages about Malcolm X and that included Malcolm X in related sites on the civil rights movement and issues dealing with Black liberation. The main site that has been carrying on in the spirit of Preston Wilcox is BrotherMalcolm.net.

So for all of the three stages of Black Studies there has been a connection to Malcolm X, with networks of people carrying on to expand the depth of the activists working in the Malcolm X–inspired Black Power paradigm.

Conclusion: Icon versus Paradigm

We are now in a position to summarize our answer to the question, Why Malcolm X? Of course the setting is the broad movement for Black liberation, the freedom movement. In this movement there have been many different kinds of leaders, but only very few are the revered martyrs. Probably the two most celebrated have been Martin Luther King Jr. and Malcolm X, but only Malcolm became the personification of Black Power and the fight for Black self-determination. So, when the Black Power slogan emerged in 1966 it was to Malcolm X that the movement turned for identity, and by so doing created an icon. Now while iconic images of Malcolm X have been prostituted in the pop culture market (i.e., turned into a commodity for pleasure and fun), there is a deeper issue here. So, why do we need Malcolm X as an icon?

The impact of racism turns Black people against themselves in favor of those who get approval from the very racists themselves, mainstream "white" America. When Black Power hit there was a need for Black he/roes and she/roes as demonstrated by such cultural actions as the mural movement we started in Chicago. A group of Chicago artists were organized by the Organization of Black American Culture in 1967 to paint a large wall with images of key people in all walks of life. It was called the Wall of Respect. The largest image was of Malcolm X. This was the visualization of historical memory and, yes, hero worship. This kind of cultural intervention was hoped to have great utility for mass education and cultural pride.

What's the difference between an icon and a paradigm? One is a static reference, while the other is a generalized intellectual and ideological framework within which one thinks and acts. Iconic reference can lead to dogmatism, but never with a paradigm. A paradigm is a framework within which you have to do something. A paradigm is shared diversity; iconic worship leads to conformity.

We began this essay with the question, why Malcolm X? Our basic answer is that he became both icon and paradigm for the Black Liberation Movement. Therefore the question one needs to ask is what do we mean by paradigmatic agency? This is when a movement for social change operates within a paradigm, and after the Black Power moment following Malcolm X's assassination this is what happened, and it continues today. This paradigmatic agency represents a broad diversity of actions by different actors that have a focused impact because they share a common paradigm. Our basic answer to the question, why Malcolm X? is that Malcolm X is the personification of the paradigmatic agency of Black Power, its theory and practice.

NOTES

1. This phrase was first used in a conference at the University of California–Santa Barbara and subsequently adopted as the motto of the National Council for Black Studies.
2. See this video: http://www.youtube.com/watch?v=CNQpYz1ztx8, and read the lyrics: www.azlyrics.com/lyrics/slythefamilystone/familyaffair.html.
3. We have posted a website to document his work: http://www.brothermalcolm.net/.
4. The site has been archived: http://web.archive.org/web/20011124200413/http://maelstrom.stjohns.edu/archives/malcolm-x.html.

WORKS CITED

Adi, Hakim, and Marika Sherwood. 1995. *The 1945 Manchester Pan-African Congress Revisited*. London: New Beacon Books.

Alkalimat, Abdul. 1990. *Malcolm X for Beginners*. New York: Writers and Readers Publishing.

Engels, Friedrich. 1940. *Dialectics of Nature*. New York: International Publishers.

Hull, Gloria T., Patricia Bell Scott, and Barbara Smith. 1982. *But Some of Us Are Brave: All the Women Are White, All the Blacks Are Men: Black Women's Studies*. New York: Feminist Press.

Kuhn, Thomas S. 1996. *The Structure of Scientific Revolutions*. Chicago: University of Chicago Press.

Malcolm X. 1963. "Message to the Grass Roots." Malcolm X: A Research Site. November 10. http://brothermalcolm.net/mxwords/whathesaid8.html.

———. 1992. *The Autobiography of Malcolm X*. With the assistance of Alex Haley. New York: Ballantine Books.

Robinson, Cedric J. 1983. *Black Marxism. The Making of the Black Radical Tradition*. London: Zed Press.

Rodney, Walter. 1989. *How Europe Underdeveloped Africa*. Nairobi: East African
Educational Publishers.

Weber, Max. 1968. *Max Weber on Charisma and Institution Building: Selected Papers*.
Edited and with an introduction by S. N. Eisenstadt. Chicago: University of Chicago
Press.

Wilmore, Gayraud S., and James H. Cone, eds. 1979. *Black Theology: A Documentary
History*. Maryknoll, NY: Orbis Books.

Wilson, James Q. 1965. *Negro Politics: The Search for Leadership*. New York: Free Press.

Wright, Richard. 1956. *The Color Curtain: A Report on the Bandung Conference*. Jackson,
MS: Banner Books.

Reeducating the Afro-American

Malcolm X's Scholarly and Historical Pedagogy

Lenwood G. Davis

Much has been written about Malcolm X as an African American nationalist, civil rights leader, minister of the Nation of Islam, spellbinding orator, Pan-Africanist, world traveler, intellect, as well as founder of the Muslim Mosque, Inc. and of the Organization of Afro-American Unity. Be that as it may, little has been written about him as an educator, scholar, and historian. Therefore, the purpose of this essay is to discuss Malcolm X as an educator, scholar, and historian.

An educator is a person whose work is to teach, train, enlighten, and empower others. An educator is a teacher who teaches and gives lessons or instructs someone (Malcolm X 1992a, 173) According to this definition, Malcolm X would qualify as an educator. In most of his speeches and writings he was teaching African Americans about Woodson's concept of miseducation—the need to rediscover African Americans' racial pride, respect for themselves and others, defending themselves against others, protecting their women, knowing their history, getting an education, establishing schools, and becoming entrepreneurs, etc. Indeed, unlike Woodson, Malcolm would not use the term "Negro" to describe Blacks in America. In reeducating Americans and the world, Malcolm would reenvision the "Negro" identity, renaming the citizenship category referred to this community of Americans as "Black" or "Afro-American."

No doubt, Malcolm X was not an educator in the traditional sense of having gone to college and earned a degree; as a matter of fact, he only went to the eighth grade. Malcolm was self-educated. In his autobiography, he states that, while he was incarcerated at the Massachusetts Norfolk Prison Colony, he taught himself how to read and write (Malcolm X 1992a, 146). Malcolm reveals that he read the dictionary from A to Z. He not only looked up the definitions of each word, but also wrote the definitions down and memorized them. Malcolm saw the dictionary as a miniature encyclopedia. The leader described his education as being homemade and declared that it had provided him with deep insights on the problems of Blacks in America (Malcolm X 1992a).

The current chapter examines the important role of Malcolm X as an educator who exposed to America and to the world the miseducation of the Negro; but more than that embodied the elements of a great teacher for his community—the Black world—throughout his short life. In the current chapter, we will see how Malcolm's role as educator and mwalimu ("teacher" in Swahili) varied from educator, to scholar, and to historian. Importantly, in this chapter, Malcolm's role in educating the Black world is assessed for its adeptness in bridging textual scholarship and community experiences thereby revealing the liberation style of Malcolm's education in formulating a model for the teaching of Black Studies.

A Flexible Teaching Style and School-to-Community Praxis

Malcolm X had the uncanny ability to convey information to his audience in a way that they could understand and use regardless of their educational background. Peter Bailey refers to Malcolm as a master teacher who acquired his college education through local community work. William Strickland agrees with Bailey's assessment of Malcolm X. He declared: "He (Malcolm X) was intellectually flexible, because his first priority was to *communicate* in order to instruct. He spoke to people in the language they understood, because he was a people's intellectual, not an intellectual's intellectual" (Strickland 1994). Malcolm X concludes: "Education is an important element in the struggle for human rights. It is the means to help our children and increase their self-respect. Education is our passport to the future, for tomorrow belongs only to the people who prepare for it today" (Malcolm X 1992a, 298). In his autobiography, Malcolm acknowledges that he had many shortcomings. He said that one of the things that he regrets in life is that he did not have an academic education.

The leader declared: "My greatest lack has been, I believe that I don't have the kind of academic education. I wish I had been able to get—to have been a lawyer, perhaps. I do believe that I might have made a good lawyer" (Malcolm X 1992a, 386).

He continued, "I have always loved verbal battle, and challenge" (Malcolm X 1992a, 386). Malcolm pointed out that even back then in 1965 as an adult, if he had the time, he would not be one bit ashamed to go back into any New York City Public School and start where he left off at the ninth grade, and go on through a degree. According to Benjamin Karim, an assistant minister of Temple No. 7 in New York City and close friend of Malcolm X, the leader loved three things the most: "truth," "knowledge," and "teaching" (Gallen 1992, 56). Toward the end of Malcolm X's life, he explained what he had been teaching as a Muslim minister when he declared that for twelve years in that role, he always taught so strongly on the moral issues that many Muslims accused him of being "anti-woman." He continued to point out: "I had taught that within the Nation of Islam, my own transformation was the best example I know of Mr. Muhammad's power to reform Black Men's lives" (Malcolm X 1992a, 298). Sonia Sanchez reaffirmed Malcolm's impact when she stated that

> Malcolm had no formal Ph.D; he had a Ph.D. in Malcolmism, he had a Ph.D in Americanism, in what had gone wrong with this country, and he brought it to you; and for the first time many of us began to look at ourselves again, and to say, "Hold it, it's possible to work at a job and not sell your soul. It's possible to walk upright like a human being." (Smallwood 1999)

Sanchez continued, "He taught me, and I'm sure a number of others, that you are indeed worthy of being on this planet earth" (Gallen 1992, 42). Sanchez surmised that Malcolm stirred the imagination of all Blacks.

> He stirred them to go back to their yearning [to say], "I want to be a lawyer, a doctor, an Indian Chief, but I also want to have my dignity." And he was saying it's possible. [Even if you had had] the experience [of an] educational system that hounded you that said, "yes, you have a degree, but you're inferior, yes, you're a doctor but you're still a nigger." (Gallen 1992, 112)

She continued: "[Malcolm said,] 'I can tell you how not to be a nigger in this country'" (Gallen 1992, 112).

Andrew P. Smallwood pointed out that Malcolm's public discourse on African

American life and society gave him the role of a nonformal educator who developed an ideology and praxis for educating African Americans. It was his intellectual curiosity and exploration that made him a student of life and Black History (Smallwood 2001). Smallwood delineated:

> This became an important asset that he utilized in his meteoric rise in the NOI's leadership hierarchy and led him to eventually become an international spokesman on the issue of racial justice and human rights. But because of jealousy, his education and intelligence also led to his demise. (Smallwood 2001, 357)

Kathryn Gibson heard Malcolm X speak and suggested that he taught by using his oratory skills. She declared:

> Malcolm could speak for hours and she never saw him use a note. And he never lost track of his point, even though people would jump up and yell [and talk back]. It was like the Baptist church . . . where you respond back to the minister, and as he is speaking, you say "yes" or "make it plain" or "teach," and people did that constantly and . . . it just sort of kept on pumping him and kept him going. He was so very dynamic; I don't know anyone who equals him, I really don't. (Gallen 1992, 105)

Malcolm X, like many great teachers, rarely missed the opportunity to teach, whether it was in a restaurant, mosque, ballroom, street, pool hall, or lecture hall. It was pointed out that, like the best teachers, Malcolm was equally willing and always eager to learn (Gallen 1992, 42). John Henrik Clarke noted that Malcolm "was the fastest leader of anybody I've ever known" (Gallen 1992, 42). Clarke was Malcolm's "history man"; if you wanted something on history, you turn to him—and once Malcolm had read it and analyzed it, he knew more than historian Clarke knew about it (Gallen 1992 42).

According to Minister Karim, Malcolm certainly did not tolerate ignorance at Temple No. 7. Malcolm X required his assistant ministers to attend public speaking classes. Karim recalled that Malcolm would give assignments that made a Harvard University student scared of learning (Gallen 1992). He also stated that the ministers had to read several newspapers, including the *New York Times*, the *New York Tribune*, the *London Times*, and the *Peking (China) Review*, newspapers from Indonesia, and many papers from other countries. The ministers also had to read *Time* and *Newsweek* magazines, as well as watch the TV news (Gallen 1992, 43).

They also studied geography and history, the history of the events in the news and how it led to a particular thing that was going on at the moment. Karim contended that "Malcolm was more of a teacher than he was the man the public thought he was" (Gallen 1992, 43). Malcolm X wanted his ministers to be well-versed historians in the news and other subjects, because when they spoke in public they represented him. He was an example of a person who was more or less self-taught and could hold his own and debate with even college professors who had PhDs.

Malcolm X understood his audience. When he spoke before students and professors on college and university campuses, he used a different language. He spoke on the campuses of some of the following institutions: Harvard University, Yale University, Queens College, New York University, the City College of New York, and the University of California at Los Angeles (Gallen 1992, 46–48). When he spoke before a less-educated audience, he used language that they could relate to. Clearly seen from the previous discussion of Malcolm X, he can be viewed as an educator because he gave lectures and instructions to others.

Prison Notes

Earlier in his life when Malcolm was in prison, he had time on his hands and began to take a correspondence course in English (Gallen 1992, 155). He subsequently started taking another correspondence course in Latin (Gallen 1992, 156). As well, he attended a variety of classes taught by instructors who came from such places as Harvard and Boston Universities (Gallen 1992, 174). There were also weekly debates between inmates. It was there that he sharpened his skills in speaking and debating that would serve him well when he got out of prison and began speaking in such places as coliseums, arenas, some of the greatest universities in America, radio and television programs, not to mention speeches given all over Africa and England (Gallen 1992, 185)

Little did he know that these courses would be most helpful to him, later in life, when he emerged on the national and international stage. While in prison, Malcolm started corresponding with Elijah Muhammad and joined the Nation of Islam, which exposed him to Muhammad's teachings. Malcolm also sharpened his skills in writing letters. He wrote many letters to Elijah Muhammad, Ella Little, Philbert Little, Reginald Little, and others (Gallen 1992, 174). While in prison, Malcolm began to accept the teachings of Elijah Muhammad. He asserted that "the teaching of Mr.

Muhammad stressed how history had been 'whitened'—when white men had written history books, the Black man simply had been left out" (Gallen 1992, 175). Malcolm stated that Mr. Muhammad couldn't have said anything that would have struck him much harder (Gallen 1992, 175).

It was while Malcolm was in the Norfolk Prison Colony that he starting teaching and telling the Black inmates about the glorious history of the Black man—things they never had dreamed of (Gallen 1992, 183). He told them many historical facts about Blacks even before they were brought from Africa to America. Malcolm surmised that a lot of the Black convicts still wouldn't believe what he was telling them unless they could see that a white man had said it. So, often, Malcolm read to the inmates selected passages from white men's books (Gallen 1992, 184). Malcolm stated that it was right there in prison that he made up his mind to devote the rest of his life to telling the white man about himself or die (Gallen 1992, 186).

Robert L. Jenkins (2002, 358) contended that Malcolm concentrated most of his energy on those who had professed no set religious allegiance when they first entered prison, apparently so as not to offend the more traditional Christian and Jewish prison ministry. Malcolm's outreach work quickly won influence among the population. Jenkins concluded: "Although he sought to convey his messages to the incarcerated as an extension of Muhammad, it was clearly Malcolm who left the greatest impression on the lives of those he encountered" (2002, 358). Little did Malcolm X realize at the time that his prison teachings would have a profound effect on the incarcerated. After many of the inmates were released from prison they converted to Islam and joined Malcolm's temple. Malcolm believed that nobody ever got more out of going to prison than he did. In fact, he said, prison enabled him to study far more intensively than he would have had his life had been different, or if he had attended college (Malcolm X 1992a, 181).

Malcolm believed that the education, or reeducation, of the Black people of this country was necessary for the building of a new mass movement capable of fighting effectively for human rights (Malcolm X 1990, 1). He therefore took every opportunity he could to get on television and radio, at press conferences, interviews, and public meetings to teach large or small audiences about the connections between various aspects of the freedom struggle and therefore "induce people to think for themselves" (Malcolm X 1990, 1).

Malcolm imagined that one of the biggest troubles with colleges is that there are too many distractions, too much panty raiding, fraternities, and boola-boola, and all of that. Malcolm asked the question: "Where else but in a prison could I have attacked my ignorance by being able to study intensely sometimes as much as fifteen hours a day?" (Malcolm X 1992a, 181) It must be pointed out that Malcolm was not against African Americans attending college. In fact he urged African Americans to go to college. Malcolm X argued that the Black college student will be very instrumental in the liberation of Black people in this country (Gallen 1992, 1).

In Malcolm's view, education bridged the river to liberation, and he urged young African Americans to learn (Gallen 1992, 1). As such he opposed African Americans who attended college but did not take their education seriously or did not use their time wisely because of prioritizing extracurricular activities and other things.

Malcolm the Black Studies Scholar

A scholar is a learned person or a specialist in a particular branch of learning. Malcolm X would qualify as a scholar if we accept the definition that a scholar is a learned person, and he developed his skills and profile as a scholar in prison where, while at the Norfolk Prison Colony, Malcolm read the entire dictionary and knew its definitions. Malcolm gave his opinion of a scholar when he declared: "A scholar in my opinion constitutes a guiding light in a revolutionary period and is the bond that unites the abstract and the concrete" (Malcolm X 1990, 40). It is undeniable that Malcolm X was well read, educated, and a learned person, a scholar.

Malcolm recalled that the prison had a library with thousands of books on just about any subject. He stated that the first set of books that impressed him was *The Wonders of the World* (Malcolm X 1992a, 175–76). Some of the books that Malcolm read were Will Durant's *Story of Civilization* and *Story of Oriental Civilization*, H. G. Wells's *Outline of History*, W. E. B. Du Bois's *The Souls of Black Folk*, Carter G. Woodson's *Negro History*, Harriet Beecher Stowe's *Uncle Tom's Cabin*, Aesop's *Fables*, J. A. Roger's three volumes of *Sex and Race*, John Milton's *Paradise Lost*, Gregor Mendel's *Findings in Genetics*, Pierre Van Paassen's *Days of Our Years*, Fannie Kimball's *Journal of Residence on a Georgian Plantation*, and Frederick Olmstead's *Journeys and Explorations in the Cotton Kingdom* (Malcolm X 1992a, 176–77, 186–87).

Malcolm read books on a variety of subjects including history, religion, literature, slavery, the Bible, China, India, Africa, music, philosophy, art, etc. He also read about the life and times of many individuals such as Herodotus, St. Paul, John Brown, Homer, King James, Nat Turner, William Shakespeare, Jesus Christ, Francis Bacon,

Dr. Louis S. B. Leakey, and Mahatma Gandhi. When Malcolm discovered philosophy, he tried to touch all the landmarks of philosophical development. Gradually he read most of the old philosophers, Occidental and Oriental. The Occidental philosophers were the ones that he came to prefer because, to him, most of its philosophy had largely been borrowed from the Oriental thinkers. It has been stated that Socrates traveled to Egypt and was initiated into some Egyptian Mysteries.

Malcolm did not have much respect for three well-known German philosophers: Arthur Schopenhauer, Immanuel Kant, and Friedrich Nietzsche. He contended these three laid the groundwork on which the Fascist and Nazi philosophy was built. He argued:

> I don't respect them because it seems to me that most of their time was spent arguing about things that are not really important. They remind me of so many of the Negro "intellectuals," so-called, with whom I have come in contact—they are always arguing about something useless. (Malcolm X 1992a, 181–82, 187)

I disagree with Malcolm X's assertion that these three laid the groundwork on which the Fascist and Nazi philosophy was built because that philosophy did not come into existence until World War I (1914–18), and those philosophers lived during the 1700s and 1800s. Schopenhauer was born in 1788, Kant in 1724, and Nietzche in 1844. I also question his conclusion that "most of their time was spent arguing about things that are not really important." These three philosophers had a profound effect on modern man's thinking. Moreover, they influenced some of the greatest minds the world has ever known such as Albert Einstein, Sigmund Freud, Richard Wagner, Leo Tolstoy, Thomas Mann, Carl Jung, Otto Rank, Ludwig Wittgenstein, and Jorge Luis Borges. One also has to take in consideration the time and the circumstances under which Malcolm X made these remarks. I am sure that as he grew intellectually, he probably changed his opinion about them and saw them in a different light.

James Jennings discussed "The Meaning of Malcolm X in the 1980s" before the Black Students Association at Harvard University in 1982. He mentioned that some observers have portrayed Malcolm X as a bit psychotic, angry, another loud Black man, and emotional (Gwyninge 1993, 35). He urged students to compare carefully the thoughts and writings of Malcolm X with some of his intellectual contemporaries. Jennings told them that they "will discover it was he [Malcolm] who was the scholar; the 'established' and 'credentialed' scholars were, for the most part, the emotional ones" (Gwyninge 1993, 36). He continued that

Malcolm X did not attend Harvard [University], he didn't have a PhD or even a BA, but he was an intellectual giant because of his insistence on true scholarship. This is the kind of scholarship that is not shackled by credentials or acceptable ideals; it is a free scholarship—based on an honest pursuit of Truth. . . . His thoughts and writings collectively, provide a rigorous standard of intellectual inquiry. (qtd. in Gwyninge 1993, 36).

John Henrik Clarke declared that some people labeled Malcolm X as a "hate-monger," "racist," "dangerous fanatic," "Black Supremacist," etc. In reality, according to Clarke, he was none of these things. Certainly he didn't preach "Black supremacy" (Gwyninge 1993, 39). Clarke concluded that Malcolm X preached and taught more about Black pride, Black redemption, Black reaffirmation, and he presented to the Black woman the image of a Black man that she could respect (Gwyninge 1993, 40). *The Autobiography of Malcolm X* is a classic in American literature. Kalamu ya Salaam argued that *Malcolm X on Afro-American History* is also a classic of our national literature (Gwyninge 1993, 50). Salaam delineated "but we must study not in fear to keep us cowering in our corner of the cage, but study like a runaway memorizing an escape route through enemy territory that has been temporarily drawn in the dust." He asserts, "Malcolm's books help us in all of this" (Gwyninge 1993, 51). According to Salaam, "unlike other leaders who were Malcolm's peers and who were great speakers but who left no written records of substance [this assertion is debatable], Malcolm X has gifted us with a legacy that stands as signposts in our development." He states that Malcolm's two books are part of the Third World literature of liberation and can rightfully be placed next to the work of Amílcar Cabral, Julius Nyerere, Ho Chi Minh, Ernesto "Che" Guevara, and others. Salaam believed that few others of our national leaders of the sixties meet that measure. Salaam concluded, "Malcolm challenged not just our actions but also our thinking, and in challenging us to think he inspired us in classic ways consistent with the best of African-American struggle. To be for Malcolm X is to be for us" (Gwyninge 1993, 51).

Robert E. Terrill believed "Because a person's sense of self emanates, in part, from their perception of the environment with which they interact, by altering his audience's perception of their environment Malcolm X was able to alter their perception of themselves" (Terrill 2010, 7). He was empowering his audience to read, and critique, the oppressive landscape in which they lived their everyday lives (Terrill 2010, 7). In addition to Terrill, Molefi Kete Asante has also shown that Malcolm consistently schooled his African American audience not only on the importance of Africa and the necessity to have pride in their African origins, but also in the assertion of their identity as people of African descent. Asante argued:

> Malcolm understood that knowledge of, and practice of, cultural traditions that reinforced his audience's African identity were a powerful source of resistance, and that his project entailed the reconstruction and maintenance of culture in the face of a domination that would negate that culture. (Asante 1992, 2)

When Malcolm X was in Africa and other foreign countries, he heard the local people speak languages that he could not understand: "there I was standing like some little boy, waiting for someone to tell me what had been said: I never will forget how ignorant I felt," recalled Malcolm (Malcolm X 1992a, 386). Because of that experience, especially in several African countries, he wanted to learn some African languages. He also stated that he wanted to learn Chinese, because, according to him, it looked as if Chinese would be the most powerful political language of the future. In 1965 Malcolm X prophesied that China would be the most powerful economic country in the world although its political language is not powerful outside of China. Chinese is taught in several colleges and universities in the United States nowadays. Malcolm also stated that he was beginning to study Arabic, which he thought would become the most powerful spiritual language of the future. Once again, Malcolm's prophecy was fulfilled. Islam is one of the largest and fastest-growing religions in the world, and a true Muslim must know Arabic in order to read their holy book, the Qur'an, which is written in Arabic.

Malcolm was a spellbinding orator and used his oratorical skills to preach and teach. As pointed out previously he used every opportunity to teach anyone who would listen to him. Malcolm X not only taught African Americans to have pride in their race, to respect themselves and others, to defend themselves against others, to protect their women, to know their history, to get an education, to establish schools, and to become entrepreneurs, he also wanted them to become critical thinkers and not believe everything that they read. Instead, he urged African Americans to examine and analyze in order to see how a particular piece of knowledge can help them become more productive human beings. "Without education, you're not going anywhere in this world" (Malcolm X 2014).

There is little doubt that Malcolm X was a scholar. He was well read and a learned person. He had a vast knowledge of many subjects such as history and religion, but also literature, music, art, philosophy, drama, world affairs, and several other fields. He was always seeking knowledge. In person or on the radio, he could talk extensively on a variety of subjects. When it came to debating, even with so-called educated scholars, Malcolm X could hold his own. He was so knowledgeable that he seldom used notes during debates. When asked why he wanted to know certain information, he said he never knew when he might use it.

Malcolm the Historian

A historian is a writer of history, as well as an author and a specialist in history. If we accept that definition of a historian, Malcolm X could be called a historian. He wrote several articles and a book on African Americans and their history as well as lectured extensively on that subject. He also penned a book entitled *Malcolm X on Af-ro-American History* (1967). Malcolm did extensive historical research while in prison.

In his autobiography he mentioned that the prison library had an extensive collection of books on almost every general subject. Malcolm X recalled that there were thousands of old books, and some of the books were in crates and boxes that had not been opened (Malcolm X 1992a, 174) According to Malcolm most of the books were on history and religion. As mentioned previously, he describes the different kinds of books he checked out and read. Malcolm read Herodotus, "the father of history," or rather, he read about him (Malcolm X 1992a, 174). He read the histories of various nations, which opened his eyes gradually, then wider and wider, to how the white men had indeed acted like devils, pillaging and raping and bleeding and draining nonwhite people (Malcolm X 1992a, 174).

Reverend Albert Cleage argued that Malcolm's single contribution to the Black struggle was to teach Black people the "first basic principle" that "the white man is your enemy." Based on that principle, Cleage contended that Black people can "build a total philosophy, a total course of action for the struggle" (Clark 1991, 21). Malcolm X argued that it's a crime, the lie that has been told to generations of both Black men and white men:

> Little innocent Black children, born of parents who believed that their race had no history. Little Black children seeing, before they could talk, that their parents considered themselves inferior. Innocent Black children growing up, living out their lives, dying of old age—and all of their lives ashamed of being Black. But the truth is pouring out of the bag now. (Clark 1991, 21)

In many of Malcolm X's speeches and writings, he alluded to the fact that African Americans must know their history. "We must recapture our heritage and our identity if we are ever to liberate ourselves from the bonds of white supremacy," stated Malcolm (Clark 1991, 183). Malcolm X contended that we must launch a cultural revolution to unbrainwash an entire people, and this cultural revolution will be the journey to our rediscovery of ourselves (Clark 1991, 57). According to him, history is a people's memory, and without a memory, man is demoted to the level of the lower animals. "When you have no knowledge of your history, you're just another animal; in fact, you're a Negro, something that's nothing" (Clark 1991, 55). He continued:

> The only Black man on earth who is called a Negro is one who has no knowledge of his history. The only Black man on earth who is called a Negro is one who doesn't know where he came from. That's the one in America. They don't call Africans Negroes. (Clark 1991, 55)
>
> You have to have a knowledge of history, no matter what you are going to do; anything that you undertake, you have to have knowledge of history in order to be successful in it. Armed with the knowledge of our past, we can with confidence charter a course for our future. Culture is an indispensable weapon in the freedom struggle. We must take hold of it and forge the future with the past. (Clark 1991, 56)

Michael Eric Dyson (1995, 92) tells us that Malcolm's unabashed love for Black history, his relentless pedagogy of racial redemption through cultural consciousness and racial self-awareness, meshes effortlessly with Black Americans' (especially Black youths') recovery of their African roots. As rapper KRS-One summarized, a crucial feature of Malcolm's legacy is that Black children will "Come to know that they come from a long race and line of kings, queens, and warriors," a knowledge that will make them "have a better feeling of themselves" (Dyson 1995, 92). Rapper Michael Franti also expressed the feelings of many people and gave the essence of Malcolm X when he said the thing that he gained from Malcolm X was not his symbol as a militant, but his ongoing examination of his life and how he was able to think critically about himself and grow and change as he encountered new information (Asante 1992, 12). That's where he felt that he gained strength, through constantly conquering his own shortcomings and questioning our beliefs. It can be argued that Malcolm X should be considered a historian because he was not only a writer of history, but he also specialized in trying to correct some of the inaccuracies in history.

Malcolm X was not only a writer of history, he also made history. While he was living, he wrote articles as well as a book on Afro-American history. Although he was knowledgeable in African American and Islamic histories, he also was a student of world history, including African history as being a part of world history. Malcolm X recalled that when he was in prison he read the histories of various civilizations, and their rise and fall. He constantly pointed out that in the past others have written the history of people of African descent and it was distorted, and now they must correct those distortions and write their own history.

Conclusion

Malcolm X's life was short; yet, his legacy even lives on today. His legacy is that of an African American nationalist, orator, leader, and Muslim minister. His legacy should also include him as an educator, scholar, and historian. In closing, Malcolm was relentless in his pursuit of education, which he attained primarily in prison. As he grew from teacher to scholar to historian, books and community became his reservoir for understanding the world. In Malcolm's own words, "Education is our passport to the future, for tomorrow belongs to the people who prepare for it today" (Malcolm X 2014).

WORKS CITED

Asante, Molefi Kete. 1992. "A Tribute to Malcolm X." Special issue, *Black Beat Magazine.*

———. 1993. *Malcolm X as Cultural Hero and Other Afrocentric Essays.* Trenton, NJ: Africa World Press.

Breitman, George. 1976. "Unanswered Questions." In George Breitman, Herman Porter, and Baxter Smith, *The Assassination of Malcolm X*, edited by Malik Miah, 49–64. New York: Pathfinder.

Cleage, Albert B. 1972. *Black Christian Nationalism: New Directions for the Black Church.* New York: Morrow.

Cleage, Albert, and George Breitman. 1968. *Myths About Malcolm X: Two Views.* New York: Merit Publishers.

Dyson, Michael Eric. 1995. *Making Malcolm: The Myth and Meaning of Malcolm X.* New York: Oxford University Press.

Gallen, David. 1992. *Malcolm X: As They Knew Him.* New York: Carroll and Graf.

Gwyninge, James B., ed. 1993. *Malcolm X: Justice Seeker*. New York: Steppingstone Press.

Jenkins, Robert L. 2002. "Malcolm at the White Colleges." In *The Malcolm X Encyclopedia*, edited by Robert L. Jenkins and Mfanya Donald Tryman, 352–53. Westport, CT: Greenwood Press.

Malcolm X. 1967. *Malcolm X on Afro-American History*. New York: Merit Publishers.

———. 1970. *By Any Means Necessary: Speeches, Interviews, and a Letter by Malcolm X*. Edited by George Breitman. New York: Pathfinder Press.

———. 1990. *Malcolm X Speaks: Selected Speeches and Statements*. Edited by George Breitman. New York: Grove Press.

———. 1991. *Malcolm X Talks to Young People: Speeches in the United States, Britain, and Africa*. Edited by Steve Clark. New York: Pathfinder Press.

———. 1992a. *The Autobiography of Malcolm X*. With the assistance of Alex Haley. New York: Ballantine Books.

———. 1992b. *February 1965: The Final Speeches*. Edited by Steve Clark. New York: Pathfinder Press.

———. 2014. "Quotations." malcolm-x.org. http://malcolm-x.org/quotes.htm.

Smallwood, Andrew. 1999. "Malcolm X: An Intellectual Aesthetic for Black Adult Education." In *Black Lives: Essays in African American Biography*, edited by James L. Conyers, Jr., 169–80. Armonk, NY: M. E. Sharpe.

Smallwood, Andrew P. 2001. *An Afrocentric Study of the Intellectual Development, Leadership Praxis, and Pedagogy of Malcolm X*. Lewiston, NY: Edwin Mellon Press.

Strickland, William. 1994. *Malcolm X: Make It Plain*. New York: Viking.

Terrill, Robert E., ed. 2010. *The Cambridge Companion to Malcolm X*. New York: Cambridge University Press.

Master of Signifyin

Geneva Smitherman

I firmly believe that it was . . . as you call it, the Judaic-Christian society, that created all of the factors that send so many so-called Negroes[1] to prison . . . it's a breeding ground for [a] more professional type of criminal, especially among Negroes . . . and . . . in America today . . . when they refer to the President, he's just another warden to whom they turn to open the cell door.

—Malcolm X, 1963

The mid-twentieth-century Black freedom struggle, dating roughly from the 1954 *Brown v. Board of Education* U.S. Supreme Court decision to 1980 and the beginning of the Reagan-Bush presidency, was an epic historical moment in the long sweep of the Black oratorical tradition. That period saw the emergence of an explosion of oratorical energy all across the United States. Local and national intellectual-activists, Black Arts poets and writers, and local and national leaders used their speechifying gifts to convey provocative ideas about and analyses of the Black condition, ofttimes leaving their audiences spellbound. Black rhetoric was used as a weapon of intellectual warfare, to awaken dead Black folk (the unconscious), to educate, arouse, and elevate Black people. It was the speaker's task—indeed his calling—to "defend

[Black] humanity, to agitate for minimal rights, and to soothe the raw emotions of [the speaker's] mistreated brethren" (Smith 1972, 295–96). Among the numerous Black orators of this period were such well-known activists as Stokely Carmichael (later Kwame Ture), H. Rap Brown (later Jamil Abdullah Al-Amin), LeRoi Jones (later Imamu Amiri Baraka), and of course, Dr. Martin Luther King Jr. But Malcolm X was in a class all his own when it came to verbal combat. He gave us a whole new discourse for talking about the Black condition in America. He was a master of speechifying, steeped in Black people's rhetorical tropes, our semantic and linguistic strategies. Sonia Sanchez, poetic master of Black people's language, noted: "I think Malcolm authenticated the use of Black Language. . . . He brought the cadence and rhythm of Black English, the rise and fall, the control of an audience. . . . His style of delivery was distinctly Black . . . [and] also humorous. We fell out laughing. He'd make us get angry, then he'd bring us back down to reality. . . . Malcolm brought to us a consciousness we knew already" (in Alim and Baugh 2007, 94).

In his landmark study of what he labeled the "rhetoric of black revolution," Arthur Lee Smith (now Molefi Kete Asante) asserted that "there has been no truly eloquent black revolutionist since Malcolm X" (1969, 16). Of all the Black orators of that era, he had a special, uncanny ability to read and vibe with his audience. For example, whenever he would mention to audiences that he had been in prison, he would sense their surprise and quickly react, noting that all Black people in the United States are imprisoned.

In his discourse, Malcolm manipulated language to create a new, fundamental "sociolinguistic construction of reality" (Smitherman-Donaldson 1989, 8). He not only spoke Truth, he delivered Truth in a way that made it hit home, that spoke to both the head and the heart. In the question-and-answer period following his 1964 speech "The Black Revolution," delivered to a New York audience described as "about three-quarters white, a mixture of radicals . . . and liberals," he responded to a question having to do with the role of "white radicals" in the Black Liberation Struggle:

> It is we who have fought your battles for you, and have picked your cotton for you. We built this house that you're living in. It was our labor that built this house. You sat beneath the old cotton tree telling us how long to work or how hard to work, but it was our labor, our sweat and our blood that made this country what it is, and we're the only ones who haven't benefited from it. All we're saying today is, it's payday—retroactive. (Malcolm X 1970a, 18)

Further, while white progressives and other allies might be useful and might even encounter some difficulties in the struggle, Malcolm was brutally clear about who was suffering as a result of systemic white racist oppression: "If I understood you correctly, you were saying that those white senators and congressmen there that are filibustering and other things have done whites as much harm as they've done blacks. I just can't quite go along with that. You see, it's the black man who sits on the hot stove. You might stand near it but you don't sit on it" (Malcolm X 1970a, 14).

As a member of the Black Power generation, a Black Studies O.G. (Original Gangster), and a linguistic scholar-activist, what I cherish and remember most about Malcolm X is his speechifying style, in particular, his mastery of the art of Signification, aka signifyin. He used this Black rhetorical strategy to powerful effect in simplifying complex issues and analyzing painful social realities for his people. This chapter will engage Malcolm's signifyin, using it to explore an important element of the Black Studies discipline.

"Signification is the Nigga's Occupation" (Black Folk Saying)

Signifyin is a form of verbal art in which a speaker puts down, talks negatively about, needles—that is, signifies on something or somebody—a person, action, event, state of affairs, etc. It involves discourse characterized by hyperbole, irony, indirection, deployment of the semantically or logically unexpected—and most importantly, humor. Signifyin crosses generations, is engaged in by Blacks from all walks of life, and can be heard in both the church and on the street. Like Old Skool Black preachers: "Eerybody talkin bout Heaben ain goin dere," signifyin on religious Whites condoning and/or practicing racism, or church-going, shouting Blacks who regularly break the Ten Commandments. Although tantamount to a "dis," signifyin is a well-known, long-standing verbal tradition, familiar and acceptable to those born under the lash. While Signification is sometimes done purely for fun or verbal play, it can also function as a form of social critique (Mitchell-Kernan 1972; Smitherman 1977).

Signification is a form of discourse couched in humor, but it can also be serious as a heart attack. Malcolm began his "The Ballot or the Bullet" speech with these words: "Mr. Moderator, Brother Lomax, brothers and sisters, friends and enemies" (Ethnic Records 1964; also reprinted in Malcolm X 1965). Here he employs the logically unexpected: one doesn't begin a speech by addressing one's enemies. Opening his speeches by acknowledging "friends and enemies" became one of Malcolm's rhetorical trademarks. With this signifyin, he deftly disarmed his enemies in the audience without a direct frontal attack, letting them know he knew they were out there. Simultaneously, he motivated his friends in the audience to reflect on the all-too-familiar pattern of Blacks being betrayed by other Blacks, traitors in their midst who ran and told the White folks what the brothas and sistas was talkin bout—and planning.

Humor, a critical sine qua non element of Signification, involves clever puns and plays-on-words employed by innovative speakers adept at oratorical showmanship. Malcolm was squarely located in this Black verbal tradition of "super-cools, doo-rag lovers & revolutionary pimps" (Lee 1969, 33). Using wry, ironic humor, Malcolm flipped the script on cultural symbols. This allowed him to present an alternative perspective on venerated cultural icons, exposing what he perceived as trickeration and manipulation of his people. He deplored the nonviolence strategy preached and practiced by Dr. Martin Luther King Jr. and other civil rights leaders and repudiated the labeling of the civil rights movement as a "revolution"—which Malcolm deemed anything but. Rather he contended that it was White America's way of simply placating Blacks and paying mere lip service to Black people's legitimate demands for equity and social justice (including that "retroactive" check). Critiquing the common practice of singing "We Shall Overcome" at civil rights rallies and marches, Malcolm frequently signified with this rhythmic pun: "In a revolution, you swinging, not singing." Irreverently dismissing King's Nobel Peace Prize in his 1964 speech at the homecoming rally of the OAAU, Malcolm sets forth the following argument, concluding with caustic verbal play on the word "peace":

> You can come talking that old sweet talk, or that old peace talk, or that old nonviolent talk—that man [White man] doesn't hear that kind of talk. He'll pat you on your back and tell you you're a good boy and give you a peace prize. How are you going to get a peace prize when the war's not over yet? (Malcolm X 1970a, 154)

In similar signifyin style, Malcolm presents a laughing-to-keep-from-crying perspective on America's Peace Corps.[2] In a 1965 speech at the London School of Economics, sponsored by the Africa Society, he decries America's involvement in propping up corrupt African leaders, concluding this line of reasoning with Signification that conveys what he views as the real mission of the Peace Corps:

> I come from a country that is busily sending the Peace Corps to Nigeria while sending hired killers to the Congo. [Audience laughter.] The government is not consistent;

something is not right there. And it starts some of my African brothers and sisters that have been so happy to see the Peace Corps landing on their shores to take another look at that thing, and see what it really is. [From the audience: "What is it?"] Exactly what it says: Peace Corps, get a piece of their country. (Malcolm X 1992, 53–54)

One of the charges that was persistently leveled against Malcolm X was that he was a "separatist," advocating different societies for Blacks and Whites. In a 1964 interview with Black Arts poet A. B. Spellman, Malcolm responds to this charge. Spellman poses the following question, "What is the program for achieving your goals of separation?" Malcolm answers, signifyin with his characteristic biting humor, and thereby ultimately causing Spellman to rephrase the question:

A better word to use than separation is independence. This word separation is misused. The thirteen colonies separated from England but they called it the Declaration of Independence; they don't call it the Declaration of Separation. . . . When you're independent of someone you can separate from them. If you can't separate from them it means you're not independent of them. So, your question was what? Spellman: What is your program for achieving your goals of independence? (Malcolm X 1970a, 9)

Malcolm's "Message to the Grass Roots"

"Message to the Grass Roots" was delivered in Detroit, Michigan, on November 10, 1963, at a public rally held at the King Solomon Baptist Church. It was a packed house. In the audience were Black people from Detroit and other parts of Michigan and Grass Roots national and local leaders who had been meeting for three days at the invitation of Group on Advanced Leadership to deliberate the future course of the Black Liberation Movement. I was there that day with my late grandfather, a proud, self-made man, who had only gone to school two or three years, and who was always preaching to us kids about a "nation rising from the East" and a "Black Messiah" who was going to lead us from our condition of oppression. When Malcolm X emerged on the national scene, Grandfather speculated that the Black Messiah just might be this "young boy talkin bout the rise of the Black man."

And hopefully also, the Black woman, I remember mumbling under my breath (in those days, you didn't talk back to yo Elders). For sistas growing up in that era, there were so many confusing, contradictory norms and messages about what and how to be a woman. Like, a "real" woman stays at home and takes care of her husband and raises her kids. But then what does that say about Black women, like my mother and millions of others, who, because of the economic oppression of Black men ("last hired, first fired"), were forced to hold down a job outside of the home to help their husbands feed the kids? Like, standards of beauty for Black females ("you blessed, mellow yellow, got dat off-good hair," as an Elder once told me), which nullified the skin color and hair of Black women. And don't get me started on those pre-Black linguistic politeness rules for sistas (no "cussin," no "breakin verbs," none of that "ignut nigga slang"). A lot was riding on this "young boy talkin bout the rise of the Black man." History records that indeed Malcolm had a deeply profound, monumentally positive impact on the men and women of my generation. (Because of Malcolm I proudly came to embrace the moniker my peeps conferred upon me: "signifyin mama.")

"Message to the Grass Roots" was one of Malcolm's most well-known, oft-quoted speeches. Back in the day, excerpts from this speech would often be played in restaurants and at rallies and meetings in the Black community. The speech was recorded by attorney Milton Henry, then of the Republic of New Afrika, "on a semi-professional Sony 600 tape recorder, supplemented by a Tandberg unit, fed by a Shure 55SW mike operated at low impedance" (from the album cover; album and cover part of my personal collection). It was recorded in LP format by Charisma Records of Detroit in 1970 and distributed by the All Platinum Record Company in Englewood, New Jersey. This is believed to be the last speech Malcolm made before being silenced by Elijah Muhammad. The excerpts discussed here are taken from the LP recording (Malcolm X 1970b), buttressed, where necessary for clarity, by the printed publication of the speech in *Malcolm X Speaks* (Malcolm X 1965).

A major discourse strategy in Malcolm's speechifying was to lay out a theoretical argument on a complex issue and situate it in history and historical events. Then he would drive home his point with everyday household metaphors and down home signifyin. This analysis will focus on three key issues in "Message to the Grass Roots," all of which reflect Malcolm's oratorical, signifyin style: (1) the nature of revolution; (2) class distinctions and other divisions in the Black community; and (3) the 1963 March on Washington.

The Nature of Revolution

Throughout the Black freedom struggle, a central debate that raged not only among Black leaders and intellectual elites, but also among everyday Black people, was the question of revolution and the road to revolution. Was it possible for the journey to be a nonviolent and bloodless one? Addressing this question, Malcolm first succinctly summarizes various revolutions throughout history, beginning with the American Revolution in 1776, the French Revolution, and the Russian Revolution. Then he moves on to the mid-twentieth century, to the Chinese Revolution, the Cuban Revolution, the Mau Mau revolt in Kenya, and the Algerian Revolution. He teaches that "revolution is based on land. Land is the basis of freedom, justice, and equality." Then he caps his argument about the nature of revolution with these words, signifyin throughout:

> So I cite these various revolutions, brothers and sisters, to show you that you don't have a peaceful revolution. You don't have a turn-the-other-check revolution. There's no such thing as a nonviolent revolution. The only kind of revolution that is nonviolent is the Negro Revolution.... It's the only revolution in which the goal is a desegregated lunch counter, a desegregated theater, a desegregated park, and a desegregated public toilet; you can sit down next to white folks—on the toilet....
>
> Revolution is bloody, revolution is hostile, revolution knows no compromise, revolution overturns and destroys everything that gets in its way. And you, sitting around here like a knot on the wall, saying, "I'm going to love these folks no matter how much they hate me." No, *you need* a revolution. Whoever heard of a revolution where they lock arms . . . singing "We Shall Overcome"? You don't do that in a revolution. You don't do any singing, you're too busy swinging.... A revolutionary wants land so he can set up his own nation, an independent nation. These Negroes aren't asking for any nation—they're trying to crawl back on the plantation.

Class Distinctions and Other Divisions in the Black Community

Malcolm deconstructs and makes plain the ramifications and implications of divisions in the Black community, emphasizing that unity is the key to Black people's liberation. In the opening of the speech, he dismisses Black religious differences, arguing that those are irrelevant to Black oppression. Then later in the speech, he takes on the issue of class distinctions, eschewing the classic Marxist analysis of the contradiction between the proletariat and the bourgeoisie. Rather, in his illustrative teaching, this complexity is simplified and adapted to the U.S. Black condition, with Malcolm drawing on the history of the field slave and the house slave. With a slashing, biting, caustic signifyin critique, he updates the field/house slave distinction to the twentieth-century sociopolitical context, casting the masses of Black people as metaphorical field slaves and "Uncle Tom" Blacks as house slaves trying to "make you nonviolent."

What you and I need to do is learn to forget our differences. When we come together, we don't come together as Baptists or Methodists. You don't catch hell because you're a Baptist, and you don't catch hell because you're a Methodist. . . . You don't catch hell because you're a Democrat or a Republican, you don't catch hell because you're a Mason or an Elk, and you sure don't catch hell because you're an American, because if you were an American, you wouldn't catch hell. You catch hell because you're a black man. You catch hell, all of us catch hell, for the same reason. . . . We're all black people, so-called Negroes, second-class citizens, ex-slaves. You're nothing but an ex-slave. You don't like to be told that. But what else are you? . . . You didn't come here on the "Mayflower." You came here on a slave ship, in chains, like a horse, or a cow, or a chicken. And you were brought here by the people who came here on the "Mayflower." You were brought here by the so-called Pilgrims, or Founding Fathers. . . . We have a common enemy . . . a common oppressor, a common exploiter, and a common discriminator . . . the white man. . . .

There were two kinds of slaves, the house Negro and the field Negro. The house Negroes lived in the house with master. They dressed pretty good, they ate good because they ate his food—what he left. . . . They loved the master. . . . They would give their life to save the master's house. . . . If the master said, "We got a good house here," the house Negro would say, "Yeah, we got a good house here." Whenever the master said "we," he said "we." That's how you can tell a house Negro. If the master's house caught on fire, the house Negro would fight harder to put the blaze out than the master would. If the master got sick, the house Negro would say, "What's the matter, boss, *we* sick?" *We* sick! . . . And if you came to the house Negro and said, "Let's run away; let's escape, let's separate," the house Negro would look at you and say, "Man you crazy. . . . Where is there a better house than this? . . ." That was the house Negro. In those days he was called a "house nigger." And that's what we call them today because we've still got some house niggers running around here. . . . This modern house Negro . . . wants to live near [his master]. He'll pay three times as much as the house is worth just to live near his master, and then brag about "I'm the only Negro out here." "I'm the only one on my job." "I'm the only one in this school." . . .

On that same plantation there was the field Negro . . . those were the masses. There were always more Negroes in the field than there were in the house. The Negro in the field caught hell. He ate leftovers. In the house they ate high on the hog. The Negro in the field . . . [only] got the insides of the hog. They call it "chitlin's" nowadays. . . . The field Negro was beaten from morning to night; he lived in a shack, in a hut. He wore old, cast-off clothes. He hated his master. . . . When the house caught on fire . . . that field Negro prayed for a wind, for a breeze. When the master got sick, the field Negro prayed that he'd die. . . . You got field Negroes in America today. I'm a field Negro. The masses are field Negroes. . . . [They] say "*The* government is in trouble." Imagine a Negro: "*our* government"! I even heard one say "*our* astronauts"! They won't even let him near the plant . . . that's a Negro that is out of his mind. . . .

Just as the slavemaster of that day used Tom, the house Negro, to keep the field Negroes in check, the same old slave-master today has Negroes who are nothing but modern Uncle Toms, twentieth-century Uncle Toms, to keep you and me in check, to keep us under control, keep us passive and peaceful and nonviolent. That's Tom making you nonviolent.

The 1963 March on Washington

In the popular imagination, the march on Washington, D.C., is remembered as the event when Dr. Martin Luther King Jr. delivered his now widely celebrated "I Have a Dream" speech. Malcolm soundly critiqued the 1963 march. In his view, it got diluted and co-opted by President Kennedy and White elites. He contends that Kennedy and "tricky" White men bought off national Black leadership. In his signifyin style, he compares it to coffee being "too black, too strong."

It was the Grass Roots out there in the street. It scared the white man to death, scared the white power structure in Washington, D.C. to death. I was there. When they found out that this black steamroller was going to come down on the Capitol, they called in Wilkins, they called in Randolph, they called in these national Negro leaders that you respect and told them, "Call it off." . . . Old Tom said, "Boss, I can't stop it because I didn't start it." I'm telling you what they said. They said, "These Negroes are doing things on their own. They're running ahead of us." And that old shrewd fox, he said, "If you all aren't in it, I'll put you in it. I'll put you at the head of it. I'll endorse it. I'll welcome it. I'll help it. I'll join it." . . . A philanthropic society headed by a white man named Stephen Currier called all the top Civil Rights leaders together at the Carlyle Hotel [in New York City]. And he told them, "By you all fighting each other, you are destroying the Civil Rights Movement. And since you're fighting over money from white liberals, let us set up what is known as the Council for United Civil Rights Leadership . . . and all the Civil Rights organizations will belong to it, and we'll use it for fund-raising purposes." Let me show you how tricky the white man is. As soon as they got it formed, they elected Whitney Young as Chairman, and who do you think became the cochairman? Stephen Currier, the white man, a millionaire, . . . Powell knows it happened. Randolph knows it happened. Wilkins knows it happened. King knows it happened. Every one of that Big Six—they know it happened . . . [the white man] gave them $800,000 to split up among the Big Six and told them that after the March was over, they'd give them $700,000 more. A million and a half dollars, split up between leaders that you have been following, going to jail for, crying crocodile tears for. And they're nothing but Frank James and Jesse James and the what-do-you-call-em brothers. . . . The news media began to project these Big Six as the leaders of the March. Originally they weren't even in the March. You were talking this March talk on Hastings Street . . . on Lenox Avenue . . . on Fillmore Street . . . on Central Avenue . . . on 32nd Street and 63rd Street. . . . But the white man put the Big Six at the head of . . . the March. . . . They took it over. . . .

It's just like when you got some coffee that's too black, which means it's too strong. What do you do? You integrate it with cream, you make it weak. But if you pour too much cream in it, you won't even know you ever had coffee. It used to be hot, it becomes cool. It used to be strong. It becomes weak. It used to wake you up, now it puts you to sleep. This is what they did with the March on Washington. They . . . didn't integrate it, they infiltrated it. They . . . took it over . . . [and] it lost its militancy, it ceased to be angry, it ceased to be hot, it ceased to be uncompromising. Why, it even ceased to be a March! It became a picnic, a circus . . . with clowns and all. You had one right here in Detroit—I saw it on television—with clowns leading it, white clowns and black clowns. I know you don't like what I'm saying, but I'm going to tell you anyway. Because I can prove what I'm saying. If you think I'm telling you wrong, you bring me Martin Luther King and A. Philip Randolph and James Farmer and those other three, and see if they'll deny it over a microphone. It was a sellout, it was a takeover. When James Baldwin came in from Paris, they wouldn't let him talk because they couldn't make him go by the script. Burt Lancaster read the speech that Baldwin was supposed to make. They wouldn't let Baldwin get up there because they know Baldwin is liable to say anything. . . . They told those Negroes what time to hit town, how to come, where to stop, what signs to carry, what song to sing, what speech they could make, and what speech they couldn't make, and then told them to get out of town by sundown. And every one of those Toms was out of town by sundown. . . . Now I know you don't like my saying this, but I can back it up. It was a circus . . . the performance of the year. Reuther and those other three devils should get an Academy Award for the best actors because they acted like they really loved Negroes and fooled a whole lot of Negroes. And the six Negro leaders should get an award too, for the best supporting cast.

Signing Out: "Be What You Is Instead of What You Ain't, Cause if You Ain't What You Is, You Isn't What You Ain't" (Black Folk Saying)

Malcolm X: master signifier, relentless truth-teller, visionary leader. He had a major impact on my sense of self. For me—and I'm sure, countless others of the Black Power generation—Malcolm made it okay to be yourself. Just because you get a lil edu-mu-cation, or even become "colleged," as Langston Hughes's Jess B. Semple put it, didn't mean that the core element of who you are had to be negated; didn't mean that you had to reject your family background, your roots, yo hood, and all that grounded you and become some fake imitation of a White woman (or man). Importantly, Malcolm made it okay to be yourself in an era of burgeoning Black pride and emerging iconic, Black symbols. It was not the Afro, the dashiki, the kufi, the often conformist faddishness, the bombastic rhetoric (which all too often was tantamount to sellin a woof ticket), the celebration of Kwanzaa, etc., etc. It was not the symbols and images of newfound Blackness (which, as it turns out, ended up filling the coffers of the consumerist, capitalist United States—check out the megabucks made off Kwanzaa, for instance). None of this made you a Black woman or man.

Malcolm himself never even departed from his Nation of Islam style of dress— conservatively cut suit and tie; low cut hairdo. As righteous poet Haki Madhubuti put it four years after Malcolm's assassination:

> he didn't say
> wear yr/blackness in
> outer garments
> & blk/slogans fr/the top 10 . . .
> u are playing that
> high-yellow game in blackface

> minus the straighthair . . .
> the double-breasted hipster
> has been replaced with a
> dashiki wearing rip-off
> who went to city college. . . .
>
> (Lee 1969, 33)

Malcolm's message was that what counts is your mind, your thinking (as the Black Power slogan put it, "Blackness is a state of mind"). It is your actions that make you Black, that make you an advocate for human rights and social justice. This is the legacy of Malcolm X.

NOTES

1. Malcolm never accepted the label "Negro," preferring "Black" and "AfroAmerican" and often drawing a political and cultural distinction between "Black" and "Negro." In this respect, Malcolm was way ahead of his time. Black people had been using "Negro" semantics ("Negro people," "Negro businesses," etc.) since the campaign of the 1920s, led by W. E. B. Du Bois, to capitalize "negro," which for several previous decades had been represented in the lowercase. The widespread semantic shift from "negro/Negro" to "Black" and the attendant political-cultural distinction in the Black community didn't occur until circa 1966, the year often cited as the beginning of this linguistic change. For more on the history of racial labels, see Smitherman, "'What Is Africa to Me?': Language, Ideology and *African American*" (Smitherman 2000).

2. The Peace Corps is a program created by President Kennedy in 1961, with the objective of using young volunteer college graduates "to serve, under conditions of hardship if necessary, to help the peoples of . . . countries and areas [typically, Africa, Asia, Latin America] in meeting their needs for trained manpower" (from the Peace Corps Act, Public Law 87–293). This laudable objective was viewed with skepticism by progressives at home and abroad, many accusing the United States of using the Peace Corps as a front for espionage and political destabilization.

WORKS CITED

Alim, H. S., and J. Baugh, eds. 2007. *Language, Education, and Social Change*. New York: Teachers College Press.

Ethnic Records. 1964. *Malcolm X Speaking.*

Lee, Don L. 1969. *Don't Cry, Scream.* Detroit: Broadside Press.

Malcolm X. 1965. *Malcolm X Speaks.* Edited by George Breitman. New York: Merit.

———. 1970a. *By Any Means Necessary: Speeches, Interviews, and a Letter by Malcolm X.* Edited by George Breitman. New York: Pathfinder Press.

———. 1970b. *Message to the Grass Roots: From Malcolm X.* Charisma Records.

———. 1992. "The Oppressed Masses of the World Cry Out for Action Against the Common Oppressor." In *February 1965: The Final Speeches.* Edited by Steve Clark. New York: Pathfinder Press.

Mitchell-Kernan, C. 1972. "Signifying, Loud-Talking, and Marking." In *Rappin' and Stylin' Out: Communication in Urban Black America*, edited by T. Kochman, 315–35. Urbana: University of Illinois Press.

Smith, Arthur L. 1969. *Rhetoric of Black Revolution.* Boston: Allyn and Bacon.

———. 1972. "Socio-historical Perspectives of Black Oratory." In *Language, Communication, and Rhetoric in Black America*, edited by A. L. Smith, 295–305. New York: Harper and Row.

Smitherman, G. 1977. *Talkin and Testifyin: The Language of Black America.* Boston: Houghton Mifflin.

———. 2000. *Talkin That Talk: Language, Culture and Education in African America.* New York: Routledge.

Smitherman-Donaldson, G. 1989. "'A New Way of Talkin': Language, Social Change and Political Theory." *SAGE Race Relations Abstracts* 14 no. 1.

If You Can't Be Free, Be Indignant

The Womanist Legacy of Malcolm X

Sheila Radford-Hill

Studying the life and legacy of Malcolm X as a masculinist enterprise, that is, entirely from a male perspective, misses key aspects of the politics of race and gender within the history of the black diaspora. The traditional gendering of Malcolm X as an *alpha male* reflects a global fascination with black masculinity but erases the importance of Malcolm X's political relationships with black women.[1]

Malcolm X has been culturally reproduced as the epitome of black revolutionary masculinity. His writings, photographs, video clips, speeches, and images establish the masculine as a revolutionary norm while marginalizing the role that black women played in the development of revolutionary consciousness. The positioning of black women at the margins of black radical thought subordinates their unique contributions to the Black Power movement and obscures the interlocking dynamics of race, gender, and identity in nationalist politics and progressive public policy. An analysis of Malcolm X's legacy that focuses on his political relationships with women clarifies his impact on feminist and womanist organizing and scholarship.

Although theorizing about the role of gender in social movements raises questions about the meanings of black feminism, African feminism, postcolonial feminism, transnational feminism, womanism, Africana womanism, etc., a discussion of these definitional complexities will not be attempted here. The historical trajectories and theoretical differences among black feminisms and womanisms are duly noted, but this essay focuses on the convergences among black feminisms and womanist thought especially as they relate to issues of gender inequality, discrimination, and oppression. The fact that black feminisms and womanist theories coalesce around issues of race, class, and gender does not mean that these terms can be used interchangeably. An analysis of the differences among these gender-specific theories, however, would involve tracing the history of each theoretical perspective—a project that is beyond the scope of this work. Nonetheless, this research supports the proposition that those who are interpreting the life and times of Malcolm X must include womanist and black feminist theoretical perspectives as part of their analysis.[2] Despite differences in history, standpoint, and style of practice, both black feminism and womanism are interrelated concepts. The feminist perhaps embodies more liberal and individualist values, while the womanist is more communitarian and African-centered.

In subsequent sections of the chapter, Malcolm X's work with the Organization of Afro-American Unity (OAAU) is used to demonstrate the diverse ways that black nationalism had womanist roots. The chapter shows how the OAAU was a product of Malcolm's evolution as a political strategist and as a man who was changing his views about black women's role in the freedom movement. It reveals the way that the emerging race, class, and gender dynamics within the OAAU were also echoed within the Student Nonviolent Coordinating Committee (SNCC) and became part of the response to gender inequality by black feminist organizations such as the Third World Women's Alliance (TWWA), the National Black Feminist Organization (NBFO), and the Combahee River Collective.

To begin with, we will see how exploring connections between the OAAU and black feminist organizations not only evidences the womanist roots of the OAAU but also provides a gender-relevant critique of Manning Marable's *Malcolm X: A Life of Reinvention*. The short title of the current chapter is a good place to begin a gendered critique.

If You Can't Be Free and the Marable X Biography

"If You Can't Be Free, Be Indignant" is based on Farah Jasmine Griffin's book on the life of Billie Holiday titled *If You Can't Be Free, Be a Mystery: In Search of Billie*

Holiday. While not a biography, Griffin's cultural reconstruction of Holiday's story is a provocative and penetrating gender-based analysis of her life and legacy (Griffin 2001, 15). Like Marable, Griffin is attempting to reposition an icon in our cultural imagination, but Griffin's point of departure for Billie's story starts from an entirely different intellectual place than does Marable's story of Malcolm X. Specifically, Griffin begins her work on Holiday with the same justification that Alice Walker uses in her quest to revive the legacy of Zora Neale Hurston.

Griffin uses the often quoted Walker admonition to guide her analysis: "We are a people; a people do not throw their geniuses away."[3] For Walker and Griffin, it seems that when you do not allow a people's genius to be forgotten and when you analyze that genius through the lens of gender, important insights occur.[4] In contrast to Griffin and Walker, Manning Marable envisioned his job as Malcolm's biographer to be that of amassing sufficient historical evidence to topple a cultural icon. As a historian and biographer, Marable was not concerned with explaining the genius of Malcolm X.

To be fair, Marable generally rendered historical interpretations by looking for contradictions, inconsistencies, and betrayals in the archival record. His approach to Malcolm X's life was therefore consistent with the one he used in all of his writings. Also, a comparison of Marable with Griffin and Walker should acknowledge that history and cultural criticism are different disciplines with different standards and practices. Such academic distinctions do matter, but they do not diminish the main point, which is that Griffin and Walker set out to assess the genius of their respective icons rather than to expose their shortcomings and contradictions. By looking for genius in the midst of myths, images, mistakes, and cautionary tales, Griffin and Walker present more nuanced views of Holiday and Hurston and shed light on the meaning and purpose of cultural iconography itself.

Farah Jasmine Griffin's reading of Billie Holiday's life is particularly relevant as her analysis occurs within a full-fledged womanist framework. Griffin's approach allows her to reveal Billie Holiday's resilient strength of character and to interrogate the racism she endured, which was as tragic as her personal mistakes. In short, Griffin's work explores aspects of Billie Holiday's life that have the power to explain black culture and the American experience of race, gender, and class. In contrast, Marable considered the iconic aspect of Malcolm's life as a cultural wrong that needed righting/writing (Marable 2011, 1–14). While Griffin probes the cultural production of Holiday's genius, Marable portrays Malcolm X's cultural genius as an enemy of historical truth.

Griffin documents the impact of racism and sexism on Holiday as both a black woman and an artist. She theorizes that the mystery surrounding Billie Holiday's life was a strategy that Billie developed to claim her own dignity and to operate in an oppressive society more on her own terms.[5] Marable documents Malcolm X's life in considerable detail but does not attempt to explain Malcolm's behavior in relation to how he struggled to live his life with dignity despite the racism he endured. Although Marable clearly respects Malcolm X, he assiduously avoids legitimizing him as an iconic figure (Marable 2011, 12). As a result, Marable provides detailed and even salacious information about Malcolm X's life but doesn't fully explore why he remains an international cultural icon or what his iconic status says about black cultural life, about America, about racial justice, or about human rights movements around the world. In essence, Marable reveals many details about Malcolm's life *but obscures his genius*. This problem occurs because Marable ignores the creativity and artistry that Malcolm used to create a measure of freedom in a racist society.

The imperative part of this essay's title, "Be Indignant," suggests ways that the genius of Malcolm X is relevant to contemporary politics. To justify his murder and to provide a rationale for ignoring the lessons learned by studying his political development, Malcolm X continues to be portrayed as an extremist whose failure to repudiate violence sealed his fate and placed him on the wrong side of history (Powell and Amundson 2002). Malcolm X has been branded as a hate-filled black demagogue in order to downplay his genius for political analysis, organizing, and mass mobilization (Boyd et al. 2012). But Malcolm X's ability to connect the social conditions of black people worldwide with race, gender, and economic subjugation is the source of his relevance to the politics of our time. Malcolm's revolutionary political thought also provides the rationale for one last critique of Marable's work.

Critics of Marable's biography have expressed anger about his depiction of Malcolm X, but few have been concerned about the fact that Marable downplays the role of black women in creating Malcolm X's legacy. In the numerous critiques of *Malcolm X: A Life of Reinvention*, Marable's portrayal of the women closest to Malcolm as jealous, self-centered, lonely, or mentally unstable has gone relatively unnoticed (Ball and Burroughs 2012). Yet in reconstructing the narrative of Malcolm's life, Marable often depicts black women as nuisances, petty criminals, long-suffering victims, or fornicators and adulterers. In this respect, black women come dangerously close to being Jezebels, gold diggers, and haters; they are portrayed as emotionally crippled, tragic, or opportunistic figures that deserve our pity or contempt. When it comes to black women, *Malcolm X: A Life of Reinvention* lacks the nuance and complexity that surrounds their lives and their relationships with the real Malcolm X.

Given Marable's profeminist stance and his significant scholarly achievements, the slighting of black women may seem like a minor oversight (Marable 2011). But Marable's failure to more fully explore Malcolm X's relationships with the black women who were critical to his political legacy is a serious omission; especially since it is so widely acknowledged that black women's contributions to the struggle for civil rights and black nationalism extended the promise of American democracy. For this reason, Marable's lack of attention to the role black women played in Malcolm's political development subverts his overall thesis. The real Malcolm X could not have reinvented himself without the advice and support of real black women. Those who take issue with Marable's depiction of Malcolm X but ignore the stereotypical treatment of women in his biography are also making the case for studying Malcolm X's life and legacy from a womanist perspective.

The Womanist Roots of the OAAU

The OAAU was modeled after the Organization of African Unity (OAU). Like the OAU, the OAAU was envisioned as an umbrella organization whose work involved supporting nationalist-inspired groups in their efforts to secure freedom for African people around the world. The OAAU wanted to become a coalition whose goal was to pursue social justice and safeguard political equality. What distinguished the OAAU from traditional civil rights organizations like the Southern Christian Leadership Conference and the Congress for Racial Equality (CORE) was that the OAAU's platform moved beyond the demand for desegregation and called for an end to the social, political, and economic injustices inflicted on the masses of black people. The OAAU was organized to attack the effects of racism through political organizing and direct action (Sales 1994, 133–64).

Malcolm X's speech at the Founding Rally of the OAAU outlines objectives that resemble those of the Cambridge Nonviolent Action Committee organized in Cambridge, Maryland, and led by Gloria Richardson. Richardson, who moved to New York and became active in the OAAU, was trained in organizing by the SNCC, the organization that ultimately embraced black nationalism and became part of the radical arm of the civil rights movement. Richardson's leadership of the Cambridge Movement influenced Malcolm's leadership of the OAAU as evidenced by the

OAAU's emphasis on organizing against injustices that black people endured on a daily basis including economic exploitation, inadequate education, and substandard housing.[6] The Cambridge Movement anticipated the OAAU's platform, and both organizations advocated for a holistic view of black liberation including self-defense, education, politics, economics, and self-determination.

The OAAU was an early expression of twentieth-century black nationalism, and black women were integral to its founding. For example, Lynn Shiflett was the organization's first national secretary and a charter member of the organization along with Sara Mitchell, who succeeded her as secretary, Muriel Gray Feelings, a well-known educator and author of children's literature, and journalist Alice Mitchell. Woman supporters of the OAAU included Yuri Kochiyama, the Asian-American activist, and Ella Baker, the SNCC activist who was directly connected to the OAAU through her friendships with Malcolm X and John Henrik Clarke, a principal author of the OAAU's statement of "Basic Aims and Objectives." Floryence Kennedy was also an active supporter of the OAAU who became an influential member of the NBFO, and Fannie Lou Hamer, leader of the Mississippi Democratic Freedom Party, was a featured speaker at an OAAU rally in 1964. Other black women who supported the OAAU included Ora Mobley, the founder of the Central Harlem Mothers' Association, authors Paule Marshall and Maya Angelou, and actor Ruby Dee.

On the issue of women's involvement in the OAAU, Russell Rickford, a biographer of Betty Shabazz, writes:

> Now seeking truth before dogma and struggling to imagine a society free of degradation, Malcolm rediscovered black women. . . . By late 1964, he had swapped revolutionary wisdom with activists such as the Mississippi Freedom Democratic Party's Fannie Lou Hamer, Gloria Richardson of Cambridge, Maryland, and Maya Angelou of the American expatriate colony in Ghana. . . . even before his return to Africa, he had enlisted a handful of educated, strong-headed women to help organize and operate his OAAU. (Rickford 2003, 203–4)

As a black nationalist–inspired organization in the United States, the OAAU promoted race solidarity and encouraged urban blacks to develop economic opportunities in their own communities. The international agenda of the OAAU involved building alliances with national independence movements whether they were operating through peaceful or military means. Malcolm X's growing understanding of the connections between African independence and the struggle against apartheid in the United States propelled him and the OAAU toward a nationalist ideology.

Malcolm X was still conceptualizing his nationalist principles at the time of his death, but the OAAU continued to envision black nationalism as a strategy to connect grassroots people with black intellectuals and with members of the black middle class, as well as with various allies at home and abroad. Through a consolidated voting bloc, the support of progressive coalitions at home, and strong international alliances abroad, the OAAU would achieve the credibility and the political power needed to secure the human rights of black people.

When Malcolm X left the Nation of Islam (NOI), his emerging political theory intersected with the organizing experiences of activist black women. Malcolm's travel and his work with these activists led to a shift in his thinking about the role of women in the Black Liberation Movement. As Malcolm incorporated an analysis of global capitalism into his nationalist philosophy he began to move away from the NOI perspective that limited black women to traditional gender roles.[7]

Under Malcolm X's leadership, black organizational norms that included gender segregation, patriarchal dominance, rigid hierarchies, and intolerance of criticism or debate began to shift toward a more participatory and egalitarian approach to organizational leadership. This aspect of the OAAU involved building black women's leadership by establishing their roles within the organization based on their skills, commitment, and dedication. The involvement of black women as leaders led the OAAU to an articulation of the human needs of black people and their communities.

Perhaps reading the philosophy of Ghanaian educator Kwegyir Aggrey, visiting progressive African heads of state, or talking with activist women like Maya Angelou, Vicki Garvin, and Shirley Graham Du Bois helped Malcolm X connect issues of national development, economic injustice, gender inequality, and human rights. But whatever the reason, in the last year of his life, Malcolm X was starting to understand that when societies discriminate against women, they pay a heavy price in terms of their ability to sustain economic development and attack poverty long-term. Malcolm X knew that if the women of any nation remained uneducated, neglected, and abused, the nation itself would be limited in its ability to grow its economy and to benefit its people (Kristof and WuDunn, 2009). The fact that Malcolm X recruited educated young black women to work for the OAAU suggests that his vision for the organization reflected his new thinking about the relationship between gender and black freedom.

Black Feminism and the Legacy of the OAAU

The OAAU represented a different way of conceptualizing the black American freedom struggle, and black women activists and intellectuals were as responsible for this
new direction as Malcolm X himself. The black women who assisted Malcolm X in
the development of the OAAU undoubtedly influenced black feminist organizations
that, in turn, established the foundation of black feminisms and womanist thought. In
essence, the OAAU was a precursor to the Black Power era, a movement that played
a significant role in shaping black feminisms. Beginning in the late 1960s through the
1980s, black feminist organizations waged war against racism, misogyny, patriarchy,
white feminist privilege, and homophobia. In the process, black women advanced
the theoretical foundation of black feminisms, developed womanism in response to
racism and cultural insensitivity within the feminist movement, and pursued effective
strategies to demand freedom, dignity, and gender equality.

The resurgent ideology of black nationalism became a dominant force in black
political organization (Van Deburg 1997). As Black Power began to affect SNCC,
CORE, and other civil rights groups, black women became leading nationalist
intellectuals within civil rights, nationalist, and women's organizations. Black
feminist organizations fought for social, political, and economic equality on behalf
of black women who were directly affected by poverty and economic exploitation;
at the same time, they built alliances with antiracist women groups and developed
programs to raise the political consciousness of young black women. Black feminist
organizations were an important part of the grassroots support for Black Power.

As organizations like the OAAU and SNCC declined in influence, black feminist
organizations adapted the pioneering organizing strategies of these groups in order to
pursue nationalist-inspired, gender-based approaches to ending racism and sexism.

In 1966, when Frances Beal returned from Paris to the United States after living
abroad for seven years, the OAAU was fading into obscurity, but its impact was
being felt as Frances returned to work at SNCC. Major developments with respect
to women's organizing within SNCC served as the foundation for black feminist
organizing. For instance, the initial analysis of black women's gender oppression is
most closely associated with Beal, who became a founding member of SNCC's Black
Women's Liberation Committee in 1968.[8] The Black Women's Liberation Committee
eventually became the Black Women's Alliance and subsequently joined with a group
of Puerto Rican women to become the TWWA.[9]

Organizing documents such as TWWA's *Black Women's Manifesto*, the NBFO's *Statement of Purpose*, and the Combahee River Collective's *Black Feminist Statement* extended Beal's insights to argue for gender equality from an antiracist, anticapitalist perspective.[10] These black feminist groups insisted on black empowerment and social justice in ways that echoed the OAAU and the nationalist SNCC. For early black feminists, nationalist principles of self-determination became a model for political empowerment and cooperative economics became the alternative to capitalist exploitation. Pan-Africanist ideology influenced black feminists to embrace blackness as a cultural identity.

Each of the major feminist organizations called for the immediate recognition of black women's contributions to radical movements for change. The TWWA was part of the feminist vanguard in its analysis of black women, civil rights, and Black Power.[11] TWWA challenged male chauvinism and embraced Third World politics.[12] The organization sought to bring black women together across their social, racial, and economic differences and to build effective multiracial coalitions.

In 1973, the NBFO adapted the National Organization for Women's liberal political perspective into a demand for black women's rights. In its *Statement of Purpose*, the NBFO demanded freedom for black women and called for direct action on behalf of their needs, goals, and aspirations. The NBFO held a press conference to officially announce its existence on August 15, 1973.[13] At that time, Margaret Sloan-Hunter, the first chairman of NBFO, invited black women to join the organization. By the next day, the organization had received over four hundred inquiries from interested women (Springer 2005, 150–64). The NBFO held its first national conference in December of 1973, and by February 1974 there were over two thousand NBFO members working in ten chapters across the country. For the original thirty founding members including Doris Wright, Margaret Sloan-Hunter, Flo Kennedy, Faith Ringgold, and Michele Wallace, this was a significant turn of events.[14]

Because the NBFO was unprepared to grow as quickly as it did, the organization faced significant internal challenges. Nonetheless, the NBFO gave black women a platform that they used to find each other, to protest their exclusion from the women's liberation movement, and to analyze their subordination within the Black Power movement. Despite problems with the organization's development, the NBFO *Statement of Purpose* constructed an influential critique of white liberal feminism and hypermasculinity in the Black Power movement.

The Combahee River Collective was founded by Barbara and Beverly Smith, Demita Frazier, Cheryl Clarke, Gloria Akasha Hull, Margo Okizawa Rey, and Sharon

Page Ritchie, among others. The collective began as a chapter of NBFO but left the organization to challenge heteronormativity among feminists and to develop a comprehensive definition of black feminism. Working together, members of the Combahee Collective defined what it meant to be black, female, poor, middle-class, feminist, and/or lesbian.[15] The organization was significant because its seminars, retreats, and publications encouraged black women to think of themselves as members of empowered communities rather than as individual victims of misogyny and homophobia.

An analysis of the organizing statements of the TWWA, the NBFO, and the Combahee River Collective suggests that these black feminist organizations expropriated the political space for social protest and used various strategies to achieve political power and gender equality. Through their work, feminist organizations developed grassroots political education, consciousness raising, and mobilizing campaigns for black women to advocate for themselves and their families. Like their philosophical predecessors, the TWWA, the NBFO, and the Combahee River Collective were short-lived, but taken together these organizations shaped black feminist theorizing in the following ways:

1. Extending the framework of the personal is political by recognizing and applying the cross-cutting dynamics of race, gender, and class to feminist social and cultural analysis.
2. Developing a sociocultural analysis of gender oppression that influenced standpoint theory, oppositional consciousness, critical race theory, and transnational feminism.
3. Enabling black women to embrace a national, racial, and cultural identity as the basis for their political aspirations and interests.
4. Influencing postmodern approaches to privilege and oppression, including feminist analyses of gender identity, expression, and embodiment.
5. Producing insightful critiques of gender stereotypes and heteronormativity.

Black feminisms obviously have deep historical roots in black nationalist organizations, leftist politics, women's groups, labor unions, service organizations, and the civil rights movement. However, black feminist organizations like the TWWA, NBFO, and the Combahee River Collective along with other lesser known groups also laid the foundation for women's gender oppression to play a central role in the development of black nationalism in the United States.

The Feminist Masculinity of Malcolm X

Black women's leadership within the OAAU began with a political decision by Malcolm X. Black nationalism, Pan-Africanism, Sunni Islam, and international critiques of global capitalism influenced Malcolm's political philosophy, but what explains his decision to foster gender inclusiveness? This question becomes even more relevant in light of sexist incidents throughout Malcolm's life, especially those reported by his biographer as having occurred in the hours before his death. In fact, the revelation that he may have spent the night before his assassination with Sharon 6X Poole, his eighteen-year-old secretary, suggests that Malcolm X's personal behavior toward women contradicted his emerging political beliefs (Marable 2011, 423).[16] Given his struggle with female relationships in his personal life, it is significant that Malcolm X was attempting to change the norms of masculine behavior within his organization. Although these changes were not uniformly accepted by men associated with the OAAU, Malcolm still decided to include women in the OAAU leadership. Why? After all, this decision certainly ran counter to the traditional belief that men should control women. It also demonstrated some skepticism on Malcolm's part about norms of masculine behavior that allowed men to downplay or undercut women's abilities on the basis of their perceived inferior status.

The models of manhood that Malcolm X knew best were patriarchal, that is, steeped in culturally constructed and racially inscribed notions of gender supremacy. Yet, as Malcolm X deepened his Islamic faith and developed his political philosophy, he began to foster a masculine identity that was more in line with his politics. A growing awareness of the political implications of his behavior toward women likely influenced Malcolm X's reliance on them as supporters and leaders of a new movement for black liberation (Wade 1996, 17–33).[17] The OAAU would not have been possible without Malcolm's willingness to transform his masculinity in this way.

The idea of feminist masculinity involves men who are willing to change their behavior toward women to promote gender equality (White 2006, 265–80). By shifting from practices of male dominance to behaviors that involved more egalitarian gender norms, Malcolm X signaled that gender relations were political and that, as such, they could and should change (Connell and Messerschmidt 2005).

Theorizing Malcolm X in terms of the concept of feminist masculinity does not excuse his sexism and misogyny; nor does it imply that the black feminist movement was somehow dependent on his change of heart. It would also be a mistake to interpret women's leadership in the OAAU as equal to that of Malcolm X himself. The main reason for considering Malcolm X's feminist masculinity is to highlight the role that men play in transforming patriarchy, especially those profeminist men who articulate the need for women's inclusion and equality and act to defy masculine norms of gender subservience. Interrogating Malcolm's political relationships with women provides insight into the development of profeminist men. Profeminists have analyzed the condition and position of women to deepen the understanding of patriarchy and the complexities of masculine gender construction. As a concept, feminist masculinity implicates hegemonic forms of masculinity as social forces that produce and sustain gender inequality, discrimination, and oppression.[18]

Neither Malcolm X nor the women he worked with would have defined him or even themselves as feminist. Nonetheless, the OAAU fostered black women's political action, and for decades after Malcolm X's assassination, black feminist organizations extended his ideas about black nationalism and Pan-Africanism into programs promoting social justice for black women, their families, and their communities. The black women involved with the founding of the OAAU personally experienced the historical moment when *race, gender, and social class* were recognized as the basis of gender domination and privilege. As leaders, activists, organizers, artists, and intellectuals, black women were discovering and naming patriarchy as the source of gender inequality and were responding by creating new opportunities for self-definition and empowerment.[19]

Conclusion: Be Indignant

In contemporary times, the majority of Americans aren't upset enough about the plight of millions of U.S. citizens. The idea that America is a unique and exceptional nation dedicated to democratic principles silences moral outrage concerning poverty and the vestiges of racial injustice. Too many Americans have little or no interest in discussions about the impact of racism on generations of black people brutalized by slavery, Jim Crow, poverty, urban violence, mass incarceration, income disparity, environmental injustice, and the commercial exploitation of black culture. Too many Americans ignore the new racisms that target Muslims, immigrants, women, and gay, lesbian, and transgendered communities.

Unlike the current conspiracy of silence about injustice that holds that, if we ignore its manifestations and effects, it will go away, Malcolm was never silent, especially when it came to racial injustice. He was incensed by government timidity and foot dragging when it came to protecting black Americans who were protesting racial discrimination by exercising their constitutional rights of freedom of speech and assembly. He was angered by public policies that were created to replace legal segregation and maintain a racial caste in America. He was upset by the political economy of the ghetto, which he saw as a form of colonization. He was, in essence, a strong advocate for justice. In contemporary politics, we need strong advocates for social justice.

Malcolm X's strident approach to eliminating racism elevated the urgency of action against all forms of injustice and fostered a politics of principled struggle as opposed to a politics of winner take all. Malcolm's advocacy on behalf of black people was not about rage. Although his advocacy was motivated by anger at the unjust treatment of the majority of African Americans, Malcolm X's indignation was calculated to move a degraded people beyond silence and complacency and a divided nation beyond inaction. Malcolm X's anger was, in fact, a call to action. Contemporary politics needs a clear call to action. There is an urgent need to support policies that address poverty, foster broad-based civic engagement, and transform a polarized nation into one that is committed to working together to make things better for everyone, not just for a few.

Writing about Barack Obama for the *Atlantic*, Ta-Nehisi Coates explores the dilemma of a black president who rarely mentions race and never does so without creating a maelstrom. In explaining President Obama's silence on race, Coates's article, titled "Fear of a Black President," describes the double bind of African Americans who are trapped by the myth of having to be "twice as good, and half as black" to be accepted in America. This myth of assimilation comes with a corollary myth that states that blacks cannot show anger toward the perpetrators of racism (Coates 2012).

Judging by the comments on Facebook and the almost three thousand online responses to the article, Coates seems to have struck a nerve. President Obama's dilemma resonated especially with African Americans because they are familiar with the consequences of these myths. Most black people know, for instance, that buying into the assimilation myth, however necessary, internalizes victimization and self-loathing. They know that buying into the docility myth comforts the majority but trivializes the racial grievances of African Americans and absolves the nation of any culpability for social injustice. No matter how fervently we support our country, we know that the majority of Americans aren't really concerned about the very real challenges in the black community. We know that the apathy, if not outright antipathy, for the black community expressed by all too many Americans is part of President Obama's dilemma.

In contrast to the myths Coates describes, the history of black women's organizing and theorizing about identity and injustice shows the value of moral outrage in the service of political action. Their work began with a commitment to define the problems of women in black communities as national problems. Their work continues with the goal of broadening economic, educational, and social opportunities for all of us who are at risk of being excluded from the American Dream.

Progressive politics need to embody black women's historic sense of urgency in order to engage the American people in finding solutions to the intractable social problems of the least of us. This is true because the problems of the least of us eventually affect all of us. Progressive outrage should start from this place of empathy and compassion. Outrage on the left and in the center should not imitate the race-baiting and combative hysteria of the right, but the rhetoric of indignation should not be abandoned. The nation is dangerously close to being lulled into submission by the myths of assimilation and docility. As we move forward, Americans cannot allow themselves to be misled or bamboozled into supporting public policies that promote income inequality, mass incarceration, educational disparities, and the rationing of health care based on one's ability to pay.

The genius of Malcolm X includes his ability to defy Coates's myth and lead a movement that gained national and global recognition. Malcolm's indignation led to a dynamic campaign for human rights that is now accepted as part of a worldwide struggle for peace and justice, including among women. Black women played an important role in this struggle, and their work continues. For those who organize for justice and who struggle to defeat poverty, disease, and injustice in America or anywhere else in the world, Malcolm X's indignant heart and political genius will continue to light the path of freedom.[20]

NOTES

1. Popular characteristics of the alpha male include dominance, confidence, and a take-charge attitude. To explore this fascination with black men, see Cose 2002, 17–38.

2. Clenora Hudson-Weems (2004) has argued that black women are not feminists preferring instead the term "Africana womanism" to distinguish black women's gender politics from black feminisms and from Alice Walker's poetic definition of womanism.

Black feminism has a history of demands for gender equality as well as for producing compelling analyses of gender oppression. It is historical fact that black feminism existed to connect black women's needs and aspirations to the broader struggle for political, social, and economic equality. Womanism advances this activist tradition by recognizing the primacy of black women's experiences and the centrality of these experiences to the production of cultural knowledge. See Philips 2006, 37–56.

3. "We are a people. A people do not throw their geniuses away. And if they are thrown away, it is our duty as artists and as witnesses for the future to collect them again for the sake of our children, and, if necessary, bone by bone." Walker 1983, 93.

4. Zora's muse continues to inspire. For instance, Melissa Harris-Perry (2011) uses Hurston's literary masterpiece *Their Eyes Were Watching God* as an extended metaphor for black women's struggle for dignity and recognition as citizens.

5. Mysteries surrounding Billie Holiday's life include when and where she was born as well as factual omissions and confusions surrounding her life that she herself created.

6. The OAAU's statement of "Basic Aims and Objectives" reads, in part: "Economic exploitation in the African American community is the most vicious form practiced on any people in America; twice as much rent for rat-infested, roach-crawling, rotting tenements. . . . The OAAU will wage an unrelenting struggle against these evils in our community There shall be organizers to work with people to solve these problems." Bassey 2005, 145–52.

7. Clayborne Carson argues that the NOI rules of conduct guided women into undemocratic and acquiescent modes of behavior. Yet these rules were not unique to the NOI; rather, they were cultural practices modeled on the patriarchal hierarchy of the African American church. When black political organizations embraced these traditional norms, women were often confined to lower-level tasks, and even when they advanced, they could not challenge the overall structure of the institution. See Carson 1994.

8. It is widely reported that Frances Beal was familiar with the work of Malcolm X and that she and Malcolm had met in Paris.

9. In November 1964, Mary King and Casey Haden developed the first SNCC position paper outlining the need for women to discuss how gender subordination affects their work for peace and justice. Schneir 1994. The analysis in the essay "Double Jeopardy" written by Frances Beal demonstrates significant refinements in the analysis of gender subordination. Beal uses an intersectional approach to explain gender oppression from black women's perspective. See Beal's essay in Guy-Sheftall 1995, 146–56.

10. Beal also became a contributing editor to the TWWA newspaper *Triple Jeopardy*. The newsletter informed the public about human rights and social justice issues of concern to women of color nationally and internationally.

11. According to the Women of Color Resource Center, women active in the TWWA included Cheryl Johnson, Vicki Alexander, Barbara Morita, and Melanie Tervalon. See Ward 2006.

12. The Women of Color Resource Center's online archival collection at the Duke University Library contains a collection of TWWA papers. The TWWA's *Black Women's Manifesto* (http://library.duke.edu/rubenstein/scriptorium/wlm/blkmanif) reads in part, "If the potential of the black woman is seen mainly as a supportive role for the black man, then the black woman becomes an object to be utilized by another human being. The black woman is demanding a new set of female definitions and recognition of herself of a citizen, companion and confidant, not a matriarchal villain or a step stool baby-maker. It is not right that her existence should be validated only by the existence of the black man. . . . That is a type of slavery that will not deliver us as a people. That is a form of bondage which is an integral part of the racist and capitalist system which black women and black men must work to oppose and overthrow." The group's identification with African, Latino, and Asian diasporas was expressed by the term "Third World."

13. The NBFO *Statement of Purpose* reads in part, "The distorted male-dominated media image of the Women's Liberation Movement has clouded the vital and revolutionary importance of this movement to Third World women, especially black women. The Movement has been characterized as the exclusive property of so-called white middle-class women and any black women involved in this movement have been seen as selling out, dividing the race, and an assortment of nonsensical epithets. Black feminists resent these charges and have therefore established The National Black Feminist Organization, in order to address ourselves to the particular and specific needs of the larger, but almost cast-aside half of the black race in Amerikkka, the black woman. . . . We must, together, as a people, work to eliminate racism . . . which is trying to destroy us as an entire people; but we must remember that sexism is destroying and crippling us from within" (National Black Feminist Organization Collection 1974/1975).

14. An inside look at the challenges of the NBFO is available online. See Wallace 1978.

15. The *Black Feminist Statement* developed by the Combahee Collective reads in part: "The most general statement of our politics at the present time would be that we are actively committed to struggling against racial, sexual, heterosexual, and class

oppression and see as our particular task the development of integrated analysis and practice based upon the fact that the major systems of oppression are interlocking." Sharpley-Whiting and James 2000, 261–70.

16. The evidence supporting this claim is in dispute.

17. Wade views masculinity as a social construct whose norms are reinforced within one's culture. He argues that black men are subject to very different sets of socializing influences than white men and suggests that racism creates gender role conflicts that can cause black men to struggle with constructing self-definitions of masculinity.

18. Noteworthy examples of profeminism are found in the work of Michael Awkward, Robin D. G. Kelly, and Kenneth Mostern. For a classic discussion of profeminism, see Lemons 1997.

19. When placing black feminist and womanist political action in a historical context, it makes sense to note that black feminist organizing builds on British and U.S. social movements for racial and gender equality in the nineteenth and early twentieth centuries, including the abolitionist, antilynching, suffragist, and Black Club Women's movements. See James 1999, 41–71.

20. The phrase "indignant heart" is taken from Charles Denby's 1978 memoir. Charles Denby was a member of the United Auto Workers union and the editor of the Marxist newsletter *News and Letters* from 1957 to 1983.

WORKS CITED

Ball, Jared A., and Todd Steven Burroughs, eds. 2012. *A Lie of Reinvention: Correcting Manning Marable's Malcolm X*. Baltimore: Black Classic Press.

Bassey, Magnus O. 2005. *Malcolm X and African American Self-Consciousness*. Lewiston, NY: Edwin Mellen.

Boyd, Herb, Ron Daniels, Maulana Karenga, and Haki R. Madhubuti, eds. 2012. *By Any Means Necessary: Malcolm X: Real, Not Reinvented; Critical Conversations on Manning Marable's Biography of Malcolm X*. Chicago: Third World Press.

Carson, Clayborne. 1994. "African-American Leadership and Mass Mobilization." *Black Scholar* 24 (fall). http://www.stanford.edu/~ccarson/articles/black_scholar.htm.

Coates, Ta-Nehisi. 2012. "Fear of a Black President." *The Atlantic*, September, 76–90.

Connell, R. W., and James W. Messerschmidt. 2005. "Hegemonic Masculinity: Rethinking the Concept." *Gender and Society* 19:829–59.

Cose, Ellis. 2002. *The Envy of the World: On Being a Black Man in America*. New York: Washington Square Press.

Denby, Charles. 1978. *Indignant Heart: A Black Worker's Journal.* Detroit: Wayne State University Press.

Griffin, Farah Jasmine. 2001. *If You Can't Be Free, Be a Mystery: In Search of Billie Holiday.* New York: Free Press.

Guy-Sheftall, Beverly, 1995. *Words of Fire: An Anthology of African-American Feminist Thought.* New York: New Press.

Harris-Perry, Melissa V. 2011. *Sister Citizen: Shame, Stereotypes, and Black Women in America.* New Haven: Yale University Press.

Hudson-Weems, Clenora. 2004. *Africana Womanism: Reclaiming Ourselves.* Troy: Bedford Publishers.

James, Joy. 1999. *Shadowboxing: Representations of Black Feminist Politics.* New York: St. Martin's Press.

Joseph, Peniel E. 2009. "The Black Power Movement: A State of the Field." *Journal of American History* 96, no. 3: 751–776.

Kristof, Nicholas D., and Sheryl WuDunn. 2009. *Half the Sky: Turning Oppression into Opportunity for Women Worldwide.* New York: Alfred A. Knopf.

Lemons, Gary L. 1997. "To be Black, Male and 'Feminist'—Making Womanist Space for Black Men." *International Journal of Sociology and Social Policy* 17, nos. 1/2: 35–61.

Marable, Manning. 2011. *Malcolm X: A Life of Reinvention.* New York: Viking.

National Black Feminist Organization Collection. 1974/1975. University of Illinois at Chicago Special Collections Finding Aids, University Library. http://www.uic.edu/depts/lib/specialcoll/services/rjd/findingaids/NBFOb.html.

Philips, Layli, ed. 2006. *The Womanist Reader: The First Quarter Century of Womanist Thought.* New York: Routledge.

Powell, Kimberly and Sonja Amundson. 2002. "Malcolm X and the Mass Media: Creation of Rhetorical Exigence." *North Dakota Journal of Speech and Theatre* 15.

Reed, Ishmael. 1999. Preface to *Soul on Ice* [1968], by Eldridge Cleaver, 1–11. New York: Delta Trade Publishing.

Rickford, Russell. 2003. *Betty Shabazz: A Remarkable Story of Survival and Faith Before and After Malcolm X.* Naperville, IL: Sourcebooks.

Sales, William W., Jr. 1994. *From Civil Rights to Black Liberation: Malcolm X and the Organization of Afro-American Unity.* Boston: South End Press.

Schneir, Miriam. 1994. *Feminism in Our Time.* New York: Vintage Books.

Sharpley-Whiting, T. Denean, and Joy James, eds. 2000. *The Black Feminist Reader.* London: Blackwell Publishers.

Springer, Kimberly. 2005. *Living for the Revolution: Black Feminist Organizations,*

1968–1980. Durham, NC: Duke University Press.

Van Deburg, William L. 1997. *Modern Black Nationalism: From Marcus Garvey to Louis Farrakhan.* New York: New York University Press.

Wade, Jay C. 1996. "African American Men's Gender Role Conflict: The Significance of Racial Identity." *Sex Roles* 34, nos. 1/2, 17–33.

Walker, Alice. 1983. *In Search of Our Mothers' Gardens: Womanist Prose.* New York: Harcourt, Brace and Jovanovich.

Wallace, Michele. 1978. "On the National Black Feminist Organization." *Documents from the Women's Liberation Movement: An On-line Archival Collection.* Special Collections Library, Duke University. http://library.duke.edu/rubenstein/scriptorium/wlm/fem/wallace.html.

Ward, Steven. 2006. "Third World Women's Alliance: Black Feminist Radicalism and Black Power Politics." In *The Black Power Movement: Rethinking the Civil Rights-Black Power Era*, edited by Peniel Joseph, 119–44. New York: Routledge.

White, Aaronette M. 2006. "African American Feminist Masculinities: Personal Narratives of Redemption, Contamination, and Peak Turning Points." *Journal of Humanistic Psychology* 46, no. 3: 265–80.

Malcolm-esque

A Black Arts Literary Genre

Joseph McLaren

Malcolm X has been the inspiration for numerous works of literature, and, especially during the 1960s, the Black Arts Movement (BAM) era, when African American expression through verse was especially pronounced, he became the subject for a unique body of poetic works, constituting an important subgenre of BAM poetry. He developed an iconic persona as gifted orator and spokesperson, not only for the Nation of Islam (NOI) and later for the Organization of Afro-American Unity (OAAU), but also for the larger African American community and perhaps the younger generation in particular.

The effectiveness of Malcolm X's oratory can be linked to African griot traditions that utilize various levels of rhetoric, argumentation, and black language styles. One of his most well-known speeches, "The Ballot or the Bullet," delivered in Cleveland on April 3, 1964, with other versions presented in New York and Detroit, displays a variety of oral rhetorical devices and arguments that can be classified as "Malcolm-esque": Malcolm's rhetorical style. Poet Ishmael Reed noted, "Malcolm made wolfing and jive into an art form, and though his battles were fought on television . . . and his weapons were words, he was a symbol of black manhood" (1999, 1). One of the aspects of Malcolm X's speechmaking might be called "black-chastisement," urging through well-crafted criticism, through a form of the "dozens," a reinvigoration of black consciousness. As George Breitman remarks, "The printed speeches do not convey adequately his remarkable qualities as a speaker, their effect on his audiences, and the interplay between him and them" (1989, vi).

The effect of Malcolm X's oratorical style on various poets can be attributed not only to his body language and performance skills, but to his argumentation, which Archie Epps calls "the logic of the way he presented the black predicament in America" (Malcolm X 1991, 2). As such, Malcolm's speeches, which were expressed in highly charged and concentrated language, influenced as well by Marcus Garvey, present a primary text of Malcolm's political and social ideas. In describing and examining Malcolm as a Black Arts Movement literary subgenre of the Black Studies discipline, the current chapter reveals Malcolm's impact on the literary and cultural productions of prominent African American and African poets. In examining their works, the chapter reveals Malcolm's own literary genius in formulating Black beauty and aesthetics, in expressing Pan-African unity and Black Power, and in engaging with community to transform.

All of these elements of Malcolm's literary genius inform the elements of the Black Arts Movement era in which Malcolm's own politics and arts reigned. The chapter examines ways that poets who are products of the movement have used Malcolm's iconography in their literary productions in very much the same way.

The Detroit Black Arts Movement

Influenced by Malcolm-esque language and style, the poetry depicting, honoring, commemorating, and eulogizing Malcolm X comprises a literary genre that can be traced as well to African griot and praise song traditions. The impact of Malcolm X on Black Arts Movement poets can be shown through an examination of the rare edition *For Malcolm X: Poems on the Life and the Death of Malcolm X*, published by Broadside Press two years after Malcolm's assassination. The collection was edited by Dudley Randall, the iconic Detroit poet who established Broadside Press, and visual artist Margaret Burroughs, a primary organizer of the National Conference of Artists and instrumental in the creation of Chicago's DuSable Museum of African American History and Art (Boyd 2003, 161).

Dedicated to Betty Shabazz, this first publication by the press shows one of the goals of the literary movement, to establish publishing outlets that were initiated and controlled by African Americans. Randall, who "created a publishing house free of aesthetic repression or profit constraints," published eighty-one books, the majority of which were poetry (Boyd 2003, 134, 3). At the Detroit Black Arts Movement convention held at the Central Congregational Church, "public celebration of Malcolm X, his politics, and his relation to the emerging Black Arts movement was made a centerpiece of the program." This activity was also brought about through the efforts of Vaughn's Bookstore, forum discussion groups, and the Inner City Organizing Committee (Smethurst 2005, 226). Malcolm X, who a week prior to his assassination was a speaker at King Solomon's Baptist Church in Detroit, was a major influence on the Black Arts Movement (Boyd 2003, 123–24). He also inspired Black Panther Party members, one of whom, Melvin E. Lewis, alludes to the influence of Malcolm X, among others, in "Once I Was a Panther": "Malcolm, Mao, Marx, Ché and Nkrumah / were my road markers" (1998, 111).

The Broadside collection shows how prominent and not so well-known poets of the day evoked Malcolm X; the included writers were considered "an honor roll of younger poets" (Randall and Burroughs 1967, xx). From the perspective of the twenty-first century, this collection is a reminder of the ways in which black literary arts were a component of the civil rights era as it related to Black Power, and as noted by one of the major Black Arts Movement spokespersons, Larry Neal, they expressed the "desire for self-determination and nationhood" (1968, 28).

The poets in the Broadside collection represent various styles and perspectives, from the older generation including Randall, Burroughs, Gwendolyn Brooks, Margaret Walker, and Robert Hayden to the younger and more militant poets such as LeRoi Jones (Amiri Baraka), Sonia Sanchez, Etheridge Knight, and David Henderson. The relationship between the various generations is significant since it can be argued that Randall, for example, a product of "the political and cultural world of the Great Depression, . . . did not really take off until the 1960s" (Smethurst 2005, 22).

Poetic Subgenres of Malcolm-esque and Hayden's "Dee-troit Red"

Black Arts Movement poets meant for their verse to be delivered orally, and like the speech style of Malcolm X, their poems often contained such devices as repetition, evident in Malcolm's speeches, which, as Benjamin Karim recalls, had "stirring energy" (1992, 123). The emphasis on repeated phrase patterns suggests the black preacher and the soapbox or street corner orator's techniques. The poets who helped create a subgenre were also diversified by gender and location, with a number of women poets, East Coast– and Midwest-based writers, expatriates, and African writers included. Many of these poets were inheritors of the legacy of Langston Hughes, and as Molefi Asante observes, "More so than Langston Hughes in poetry or Martin Luther King Jr., in civil rights, it was Malcolm who elevated the people's street language to a national style" (1993, 29).

It is certainly fitting, as Randall and Burroughs have done, to consider the poems written about Malcolm X as they relate to chronology—those praising him and celebrating his life, commemorating his death, and showing "the aftermath" of his assassination. However, the poems can also be examined in relation to social ideas, Muslim identity, oratory style and persona, relevance to the masses of African Americans, black masculinity, Pan-Africanism, and Malcolm X's overall political ideas, which, according to Neal, "touched all aspects of contemporary black nationalism" (Collins and Crawford 2006, 6).

Biographical in structure is Robert Hayden's long poem, "El-Hajj Malik El-Shabazz (Malcolm X)," subtitled "O masks and metamorphoses of Ahab, Native Son," with possible allusions to Herman Melville's *Moby Dick* (1851) and Richard Wright's *Native Son* (1940). Divided into sections reminiscent of Hayden's classic "Middle Passage," the poem uses imagery to retrace the biography of Malcolm, beginning with references to his mother and father:

The icy evil that struck his father down
and ravished his mother into madness
trapped him in violence of a punished self
raging to break free. (Hayden 1967, 14)

Closely echoing through striking imagery the facts of Malcolm's father's death and the mental unraveling of his mother, Hayden refers to other aspects of Malcolm X's life known from the *Autobiography*, such as his nickname of "Dee-troit Red," the fact that he "conked his hair and Lindy-hopped" as well as the name change after joining the NOI: "He X'd his name" (Hayden 1967, 14–15). While following a chronology, Hayden notes the Hajj, the "Hejira to / his final metamorphosis," the period when Malcolm's ideas of race underwent a transformation (Hayden 1967, 16). In *The Autobiography of Malcolm X*, which stands as a "crucial part of his political legacy" (Marable 2011, 352), Malcolm acknowledges "orthodox Islam which had given [him] the insight and perspective to see that the black men and white men truly could be brothers" (Malcolm X 1999, 398). This realization has an ironic relationship to John Henrik Clarke's interpretation of Malcolm X's ultimate political philosophy, that it was "a struggle between the white haves and the black have-nots; a struggle of the oppressor and the oppressed" (1990, xxiii).

Also addressing Muslim identity as well as Malcolm's persona is Larry Neal's "Morning Raga for Malcolm" developed with an Eastern tinge. It opens with a prayer-like call to Allah, "O Allah . . . receive him, a morning god / bursting springly in ascendant / colors of the sun," and emphasizes the physical power of Malcolm, the visceral impact of his presence as in the lines "the voice tears at blood / streaked faces." Neal's imagery also evokes in graphic terms the suffering of black people: "mangled bodies, ripped out guts spewed from piss pot / to armchair deaths" (1967, 19, 20). This latter image suggests those put to death through electrocution; another draws on Malcolm's appeal to the masses, "the unavenged" or "these hordes" (Neal 1967, 20). However, Joyce Whitsitt also points to the irony of race in Malcolm's assassination by combining racial imagery with the "black martyr," while noting Malcolm's having been "Cut down by black hands, / Held down by little white minds" (1967, 21), the latter implying a larger conspiracy.

Related to the assassination of Malcolm X, Etheridge Knight's "It Was a Funky Deal" focuses on the injustice of Malcolm X's death, but does so by using the black popular culture concept of "funky," which in this case refers to an incorrect, suspicious, or wrong action. The "deal" has a wide range of possible interpretations, including the killing of Malcolm X as a result of a larger conspiracy, as in "You rocked too many boats, man. / Pulled too many coats, man" (Knight 1967, 21). The other note of betrayal occurs in the reference to Judas and the link between the betrayal of Christ and that of Malcolm X. Also, other black icons, such as jazz saxophonist Charlie Parker, "Bird," and "that / Lil LeRoi cat," poet Amiri Baraka, are singled out because they "Saw through the jive" (Knight 1967, 21).

Poems discussing Malcolm X's death further evoke the martyr image without necessarily considering the dilemma of black assassins and the larger conspiracy argument. Margaret Burroughs, for example, takes a differing stylistic approach to praising Malcolm in "Brother Freedom," where the traditional quatrain and rhyme pattern is used to explore martyrdom or sacrifice of the "fallen warrior." The title itself shows the bond of brotherhood, emblematic of the nationalist feeling of the era. Here again there are echoes of the speechmaking style, "his flashing eyes" and "his trumpet voice," but only a generic allusion to the assassination, the act committed by an anonymous "They." Burroughs employs a phrase similar to the famous statement from Ossie Davis's eulogy, "shining black manhood," but instead of "manhood," Davis uses the "shining black prince" signifier. Davis's eulogy, however, also reiterates the image of Malcolm in masculinist terms: "Malcolm was our manhood, our living, black manhood! This was his meaning to his people" (Davis 1990, xii). Furthermore, Burroughs connects Malcolm to a line of black icons, including Toussaint L'Ouverture, Joseph Cinque, Denmark Vesey, Nat Turner, Gabriel Prosser, Patrice Lumumba, and Medgar Evers (1967, 22). By including Lumumba in the list, she draws attention to liberation struggles in Africa during the 1960s and especially the clandestine manner in which Lumumba was killed. Malcolm, who journeyed to Africa in 1959 and 1964, appealed to African leaders to join the cause of black liberation in the United States.

Poetry Retelling the Final Period: The African Worldview

Malcolm X's Pan-Africanist ideas, culminating in what William Sales has called "the final period in the development of his thinking" (1994, 61), included the global Black world—Europe, Africa, the United States, the Caribbean, and Latin America—and embodied the founding principles of the OAAU. Malcolm perceived the "awakening" African American as parallel to that of migrating Africans in Europe. In a Rochester, New York, speech titled "Not Just an American Problem, but a World Problem," delivered on February 16, 1965, he contrasted Blacks in Europe—now an emerging topic for international forums in such countries as Portugal and Spain—with those in the United States: "when they migrate to England, they pose a problem for the English. And when they migrate to France, they pose a problem for the French" (Malcolm X 1992, 146).

Another poem, Ted Joans's "True Blues for a Dues Payer," also praises Malcolm through allusions to his death but using jazz poetry stylistics, where the motif of "blowing," soloing or playing with intensity, is used to describe the poet's own jazz performance: "blew the second chorus of Old Man River," through an "old gold trumpet loaded with black jazz" (1967, 25). The poem is told from the perspective of Joans, a painter, jazz aficionado, and expatriate, who is informed of Malcolm's death by reading a "French-Moroccan newspaper." Avoiding generalized uncertainty about the perpetrators of Malcolm's death, Joans asserts with clear cynicism and anger that Malcolm was "killed by a / group of black assassins of blacker Harlems in the black / night of dark deeds." The poem also refers to Ralph Bunche, labeling him "Uncle

Ralph Bunche" and grouping him with "those black blue bloods / who attend the White House policy lunch" (Joans 1967, 25). In hindsight, Joans's placing of Malcolm X and Ralph Bunche, who was, ironically, born in Detroit, in diametrical opposition is somewhat overstated, in that Bunche can also be perceived as having been, in the 1960s, an advocate for civil rights although his role in the U.S. State Department and intelligence gathering on emerging African nations may have been problematic for critics of U.S. destabilization in Africa. However, Malcolm X also perceived Ralph Bunche negatively, as someone who "didn't know his history" (PBS.org 2013). Bunche, who rejected the positions of Garvey and the NOI, was categorized, as Charles P. Henry informs us, as a "model Negro" (1999, 228). Nevertheless, "Black Power was viewed by the aging Bunche as an essential defensive reaction necessary for survival" (Henry 1999, 249).[1]

Clarence Major, a novelist and painter, also addresses the legacy and death in "Death of a Man: For Malcolm," which indicts the white power structure and perhaps also the internal apparatus of the NOI. After Malcolm X's break with the NOI, he continued to consider race as a global issue that might have resolution at the United Nations, a point suggested by Major. Malcolm

> would bring his native land
> before a world court
> for redress for crimes for sins
> against humanity. (Major 1967, 26)

Malcolm X argued that African Americans represented a nation within a nation and as such could plead their case on a global level.

Jay Wright's contribution, "The Solitude of Change," also addresses the death of Malcolm X but in abstract imagery that is less politically or socially charged: "The cavity in your breast / is like a shadowed lake / where turtledoves splash echoes / in a taciturn valley." This impressionistic imagining of the shotgun blast that killed Malcolm is followed by descriptions of Malcolm's Islamic persona but through a broad representation of Islam and racial identity: "the eloquent Arab / who had come back / from the temples." Wright also recognizes Malcolm's evolving views concerning race: "you were growing / to tell the debility of color" (1967, 28).

Another concern of the poets, the community concept, was reflected as well in "The Ballot or the Bullet," which expresses "the importance of controlling the economy of our community" (Malcolm X 1989a, 39). Black community ideas are developed in Margaret Walker's "For Malcolm X," a praise poem, which refers to "All you violated ones with gentle hearts," mistreated members of the community. Unlike in Baraka's verse, Walker does not chastise the community for its inability to hear Malcolm X or to receive his message. Although her descriptions of community members are not necessarily flattering, they do point to the social inequities of class, resulting in addiction, "hooked children," and impoverishment, "bowery bums" (Walker 1967, 32). The poem also reminds us of the funeral of Malcolm X, where the community at large could "Gather round this coffin and mourn [its] dying swan." The image of the "swan" suggests the funereal white head wrapping, the "Snow-white Moslem head-dress." Walker also acknowledges Malcolm's vocal power in the phrase "sand-papering words" and in the visceral image "dug scalpels in our / brains" (1967, 32, 33). Walker's metaphor is expressed differently by Davis in the eulogy, where he acknowledges Malcolm's awareness of "the power words have over the minds of men" (1990, xi).

Although it is now considered somewhat politically incorrect to use the concept of "men" when referring to both genders, Davis's statement is still relevant. The designation of the male gender to refer to black people, expressed as the "black man," was widespread during the sixties. Expressed in this "gendered" manner is Malcolm's intention to transform the consciousness of African Americans, exemplified in Gregory Reed's *Lost Chapters: Decoding the Autobiography of Malcolm X*: "Today it is my mission to end the white man's continual enslavement and imprisonment of America's black man's mind" (Cunningham 2010).

Sonia Sanchez, another of the celebrated poets, also uses the death of Malcolm as a point of observation but cautions her audience not to "speak to [her] of martyrdom / of men who die to be remembered" (1967, 38). Like Walker, Sanchez refers to the vocal abilities, combining images of race and elocution as in the line "thick-lipped with words."[2] The poem relies on the natural world to situate Malcolm's impact: "He was the sun that tagged / the western sky," where "western sky" implies Western culture on the whole. This image contrasts with references to urban violence as in "and mourn / my gun-filled nights" (Sanchez 1967, 38).

More associated with romantic poetry, nature imagery is also used by Bobb Hamilton but with militant symbolic intentions. The phrases "Man-made lighting" and "Eclipsed a black sun" suggest the death of Malcolm X through violent means (Hamilton 1967, 43). As in Sanchez's poem, martyrdom is considered, but in relation to blues-like black women martyrs who "Moaned" about having "'lost our man again.'" Ironically, the concept of brotherhood is turned into an Orwellian trope, where "big brother" is imagined as having "brass-knuckled teeth" and "Blood-cankered talons" (Hamilton 1967, 43, 44).

Eulogizing Malcolm

One of the most extensive poems eulogizing Malcolm X is David Henderson's "They Are Killing All the Young Men," which offers a treatment of the assassination. As a thematic thread, the poem uses factual details concerning a New York Police Department "infiltrator," along with ironic allusions to media announcements. Subtitled "To the Memory and the Eternal Spirit of Malcolm X—1927–1965," it begins with the announcement of the assassination, when the poet is watching television (Henderson 1967, 46). The bulletin, "Malcolm X shot several times in Audubon Ballroom," is followed by the poet's imagining the white response: "Don't Negroes meet in the strangest places?" (Henderson 1967, 47). By interspersing ironic comments about radio media, Henderson creates a mood of satirical counterpoint. For example, the music played on "specialized radio," stations directed toward African Americans, includes Brenda Holloway's "I'll See You Again," which contrasts with the news of Malcolm's assassination. Most important, Henderson reveals the kind of information that would later become the subject of the assassination investigation and the dilemma for African Americans, the fact that Malcolm was "gunned down by Negro with / sawed off shotgun" (1967, 47).

However, the main thrust of the poem is a characterization of Raymond A. Wood, "the faceless Negro cop / the invisible man of New York City / and the Black Liberation Front" (Henderson 1967, 49). Wood has been identified elsewhere by Breitman as "a Black undercover agent of BOSS (Bureau of Special Services and Investigation—the New York 'red squad')" who allegedly uncovered a 1965 plot to "blow up the Statue of Liberty" (1976, 54).

Further noted by Breitman, "We already know that there were 'several' undercover police agents in the audience" and that the CIA was complicit in that "involvement"; that is, it "must have resulted from the decision and direction of the Government in Washington" (Breitman 1976, 58; Carson 1991, 451). The juxtaposition of images of Raymond A. Wood, the "rookie spy," and the "alleged" assassin of Malcolm X is used to conclude the poem where "invisible men," a variation on Ralph Ellison's symbolic character in *Invisible Man* (1952), suggests a broader, more complex conspiracy (Henderson 1967, 54).

Another of the women poets, Christine C. Johnson expresses her eulogy in "When You Died," which uses straightforward language that evokes the assassination: "They silenced you / With shots," but her poem does not consider the irony of a black assassin (1967, 71). However, like Walker and Brooks, she describes the vocal aspects of Malcolm X, the "ringing voice." In contrast to the focus on black communities, Johnson pursues a humanist approach beyond the black community when she asserts, "victims of man's / Inhumanity and barbarism" (1967, 72).

On the other hand, Lucille Clifton's homage offers few direct allusions to Malcolm's persona, voice, or speaking style, but instead uses his name as a metaphor, a symbol of the times in which "black women shaved their heads / black men rustled in the alleys like leaves." However, when the poet remarks, "prophets were ambushed as they spoke," the image of Malcolm and his assassination is evoked (Clifton 2004, 2033).

Gwendolyn Brooks, the most renowned black woman poet of the early generation, eulogizes Malcolm and also considers the power of his words and his physical representation. Dedicated to Dudley Randall, her poem, simply titled "Malcolm X," views Malcolm as an "Original," but also as "ragged-round," the alliteration suggesting something of his conflicted early life. In the second stanza, there are evident parallels to Walker's poem.

> He had the hawk-man's eyes.
> We gasped. We saw the maleness.
> The maleness raking out and making guttural the air
> And pushing us to walls. (Brooks 1967, 3)

The reference to Malcolm's eyes is verbal parallel to the numerous photographs suggesting, even beyond the eyeglasses, the degree of ocular concentration and focus.[3]

When Brooks refers to "maleness," she reminds us of the derogatory terms of the twentieth century used to diminish black men, most notably "boy," and asserts through masculinist terms that Malcolm presented an image that was in complete opposition to obligatory subservient roles, such as those Richard Wright describes in "The Ethics of Living Jim Crow" (1993). For Brooks, the emphasis on Malcolm's "maleness" is not meant to diminish black women, but to provoke the reader to consider gender definitions within the construction of maleness as it relates to subservience. As Randall and Burroughs observe, despite political affiliation or attitude toward Malcolm X in his day, a black man could experience "pride in his blackness when he saw or heard Malcolm take on all comers, and rout them" (1967, xxi–xxii). The closing stanza reiterates the effect of Malcolm as persona, speech maker, and political activist, by noting that he "opened us" and was in fact "a key" to unlocking a resistance consciousness related to black nationalism (Brooks 1967, 3).

Black Hearts and Echoes: Amiri Baraka and William Kgositsile

One of the most recognized black nationalist poets of the Black Arts Movement is Amiri Baraka, then LeRoi Jones, whose "A Poem for Black Hearts," originally published in *Negro Digest* in 1965, considers, like Brooks, the physical presence, the eyes in particular, but also other attributes of Malcolm's speech delivery. The poem, its title a pun on "arts," also alludes generally, not by race, to those who killed Malcolm, calling them "stupid animals" (Jones 1967, 62). The opening focuses on Malcolm's eyes presented as if "they broke / the face of some dumb white man." In the language of the sixties, "white men" are not only equated with the power structure but derided for their skin color. Especially important for Baraka is Malcolm's rhetoric, his ability to use words as weapons that "fire darts, the victor's tireless / thrusts, words hung above the world / change as it may" (Jones 1967, 61).

Words are also relevant to memory and the desire to imitate Malcolm's vocal style, in that his mode "clings to our speech" (Jones 1967, 61, 62). Baraka includes the wider social analysis by addressing urban black communities, which are called "our filthy cities"; however, there is the sense that Baraka is not "blaming the victim," but recognizing, in the context of the sixties, economic and environmental issues (Jones 1967, 61). The poem echoes Brooks's masculinist images, but Baraka's anger is also directed at black males, who should cease "stuttering and shuffling" or "whining and stooping," words meant as insults in the spirit of the dozens. Baraka concludes with a somewhat homophobic allusion in asserting that if black men fail to "avenge ourselves for his [Malcolm's] death," then "white men call us faggots till the end of / the earth" (Jones 1967, 62).

The anger expressed in Baraka's poem can be found in a somewhat muted form in the contribution of K. William Kgositsile, the South African poet exiled in the United States, who offers diasporic and Pan-Africanist dimensions. It should be noted that Malcolm X develops Pan-African conceptions in certain speeches and, after his 1964 journey to Africa, voices the desire for international connections between African Americans and Africans. In the February 15, 1965, Audubon Ballroom speech, he mentions his contact with African leaders, who helped him to "see the problems confronting Black people in America and the Western Hemisphere with much greater clarity" (Malcolm X 1992, 111).

Kgositsile, who joins African American civil rights issues with the antiapartheid struggle in "Brother Malcolm's Echo," combines such locations as Watts in California, the site of the Watts Riots of 1965, and Sharpeville, in what is now Gauteng, the location of the Sharpeville Massacre of 1960, where the police opened fire on passbook system protesters, killing sixty-nine black South Africans. Kgositsile's combination of sites where "riots" occurred shows the poet's Pan-Africanist ideas as they relate to resistance. The representation of anger and acts of protest are evoked in the lines "Translated furies ring" and "grinning molotov cocktails / replenishing the fire" (Kgositsile 1967, 55).

Kgositsile's joining of the two struggles is expressed in political terms in the *Autobiography*, when Malcolm argues for a "brotherhood" with African nations and notes the failure of African American leaders "to establish direct brotherhood lines of communication between the independent nations of Africa and the American black people" (Malcolm X 1999, 378). Most important, South Africa, which was not an "independent" black nation at the time, would become that African nation for whom African Americans in general and certain groups in particular, such as TransAfrica and the Congressional Black Caucus, would vigorously support through such strategies as divestment.

Conclusion

Overall, the poetry devoted to the legacy of Malcolm X constitutes a literary genre because it explores specific aspects of his character, influence, oratory style, and, especially, his political and social message during and after his association with the NOI. The origin of this genre was related to the tragic assassination, the causes of which are complex and still debated (Sanitsky et al. 2013). These poems show the way the sixties generation of black creative writers joined with their forerunners in a unified goal to praise and memorialize Malcolm X, who, because of his influence, was the motivation for this poetic development within the Black Arts Movement. Certain poets emphasized his personal characteristics, community involvement, and black nationalistic politics, while others focused on the assassination itself, and through imagery and poetic arguments vented individual and collective anger. It is evident that the strident and militant voices of the Black Arts Movement were a reflection of the way Malcolm X expressed his attacks against racism and oppression, in his use of uncompromising language and the black oral tradition.

Many of the poets were also aware that Malcolm X was not a static figure, often stereotyped as an exponent of militant action, but rather a complex individual who evolved in his views about race and the global predicament of people of African descent worldwide and their connection to a broader humanistic end. The Black Arts Movement poets visualized Malcolm X at the juncture between the civil rights movement in the United States and the rise of independent African nations, where Pan-Africanism and black nationalism were mobilizing political concepts. Were it not for his untimely death, this genre of black poetry may have had a different artistic realization.

NOTES

1. See William Greaves's documentary *Ralph Bunche: An American Odyssey* (2001). Greaves also produced a short documentary on Malcolm X, directed by Madeleine Anderson, entitled *Malcolm X: Nationalist or Humanist?*
2. The use of "thick-lipped" is ironic in that it might be considered a racial stereotype as used in Shakespeare's *Othello*. Sanchez uses it as a description of racial pride.
3. One photo that captures this intensity is the image of Malcolm holding his finger to his temple. This photo differs from that of the Malcolm X postage stamp, which shows him staring to the side. See the "Historical Photo Gallery," Malcolm X Official Website, http://www.malcolmx.com/about/photos.html.

WORKS CITED

Asante, Molefi Kete. 1993. *Malcolm X as Cultural Hero and Other Afrocentric Essays.* Trenton, NJ: Africa World Press.

Boyd, Melba Joyce. 2003. *Wrestling with the Muse: Dudley Randall and the Broadside Press.* New York: Columbia University Press.

Breitman, George. 1976. "Unanswered Questions." In George Breitman, Herman Porter, and Baxter Smith, *The Assassination of Malcolm X*, edited by Malik Miah, 49–64. New York: Pathfinder.

———. 1989. Foreword to Malcolm X, *Malcolm X Speaks: Selected Speeches and Statements*, edited by George Breitman, v–vi. New York: Pathfinder.

Brooks, Gwendolyn. 1967. "Malcolm X." In *For Malcolm: Poems on the Life and the Death of Malcolm X*, edited by Dudley Randall and Margaret G. Burroughs, 3. Detroit: Broadside Press.

Burroughs, Margaret. 1967. "Brother Freedom." In *For Malcolm: Poems on the Life and the Death of Malcolm X*, edited by Dudley Randall and Margaret G. Burroughs, 22. Detroit: Broadside Press.

Carson, Clayborne. 1991. *Malcolm X: The FBI File*. Edited by David Gallen. New York: Carroll and Graf.

Clarke, John Henrik. 1990. Introduction to *Malcolm X: The Man and His Times*, edited by John Henrik Clarke, xiii–xxiv. Trenton, NJ: Africa World Press.

Clifton, Lucile. 2004. "malcolm." In *Norton Anthology of African American Literature*, edited by Henry Louis Gates Jr. and Nellie Y. McKay, 2033. 2nd ed. New York: Norton.

Collins, Lisa Gail, and Margo Natalie Crawford. 2006. "Power to the People!: The Art of Black Power." Introduction to *New Thoughts on the Black Arts Movement*, edited by Lisa Gail Collins and Margo Natalie Crawford, 1–19. New Brunswick, NJ: Rutgers University Press.

Cunningham, Jennifer H. 2010. "Lost Chapters from Malcolm X Memoirs Revealed." *The Grio*. May 20. http://thegrio.com/2010/05/20/lost-malcolm-x-memoir-chapters-reveal-leaders-soft-side/.

Davis, Ossie. 1990. "Our Shining Black Prince." In *Malcolm X: The Man and His Times*, edited by John Henrik Clarke, xi–xii. Trenton, NJ: Africa World Press.

Ellison, Ralph. 1952. *Invisible Man*. New York: Random House.

Hamilton, Bobb. 1967. "For Malik." In *For Malcolm: Poems on the Life and the Death of Malcolm X*, edited by Dudley Randall and Margaret G. Burroughs, 43–44. Detroit: Broadside Press.

Hayden, Robert. 1967. "El-Hajj Malik El-Shabazz (Malcolm X)." In *For Malcolm: Poems on the Life and the Death of Malcolm X*, edited by Dudley Randall and Margaret G. Burroughs, 14–16. Detroit: Broadside Press.

Henderson, David. 1967. "They Are Killing All the Young Men." "For Malcolm X." In *For Malcolm: Poems on the Life and the Death of Malcolm X*, edited by Dudley Randall and Margaret G. Burroughs, 46–54. Detroit: Broadside Press.

Henry, Charles P. 1999. *Ralph Bunche: Model Negro or American Other?* New York: New York University Press.

Joans, Ted. 1967. "True Blues for a Dues Payer." In *For Malcolm: Poems on the Life and the Death of Malcolm X*, edited by Dudley Randall and Margaret G. Burroughs, 25. Detroit: Broadside Press.

Johnson, Christine C. 1967. "When You Died." In *For Malcolm: Poems on the Life and the Death of Malcolm X*, edited by Dudley Randall and Margaret G. Burroughs, 71–72. Detroit: Broadside Press.

Jones, LeRoi. 1967. "A Poem for Black Hearts." In *For Malcolm: Poems on the Life and the Death of Malcolm X*, edited by Dudley Randall and Margaret G. Burroughs, 61–62. Detroit: Broadside Press.

Karim, Benjamin. 1992. *Remembering Malcolm*. With Peter Skutches and David Gallen. New York: Carroll & Graf.

Kgositsile, K. William. 1967. "Brother Malcolm's Echo." In *For Malcolm: Poems on the Life and the Death of Malcolm X*, edited by Dudley Randall and Margaret G. Burroughs, 55. Detroit: Broadside Press.

Knight, Etheridge. 1967. "It Was a Funky Deal." In *For Malcolm: Poems on the Life and the Death of Malcolm X*, edited by Dudley Randall and Margaret G. Burroughs, 21. Detroit: Broadside Press.

Lewis, Melvin E. 1998. "Once I Was a Panther." In *The Black Panther Party Reconsidered*, edited by Charles E. Jones, 109–14. Baltimore: Black Classic Press.

Major, Clarence. 1967. "Death of a Man: For Malcolm." In *For Malcolm: Poems on the Life and the Death of Malcolm X*, edited by Dudley Randall and Margaret G. Burroughs, 26. Detroit: Broadside Press.

Malcolm X. 1989a. "The Ballot or the Bullet" [1965]. In *Malcolm X Speaks: Selected Speeches and Statements*, edited by George Breitman, 23–44. New York: Grove Weidenfeld.

———. 1989b. *Malcolm X Speaks: Selected Speeches and Statements*. Edited by George Breitman. New York: Grove Weidenfeld.

———. 1991. *Malcolm X: Speeches at Harvard*. Edited by Archie Epps. New York: Paragon House.

———. 1992. *February 1965: The Final Speeches*. Edited by Steve Clark. New York: Pathfinder.

———. 1999. *The Autobiography of Malcolm X*. With the assistance of Alex Haley. New York: Ballantine.

Marable, Manning. 2011. *Malcolm X: A Life of Reinvention*. New York: Viking.

Melville, Herman. 2007. *Moby-Dick* [1851]. Ed. John Bryant and Haskell Skinner. New York: Pearson Longman.

Neal, Lawrence P. 1967. "Morning Raga for Malcolm." In *For Malcolm: Poems on the Life and the Death of Malcolm X*, edited by Dudley Randall and Margaret G. Burroughs, 19–21. Detroit: Broadside Press.

————. 1968. "The Black Arts Movement." *Drama Review* 12, no. 4: 28–39.

PBS.org. 2013. "Ralph Bunche: The Scholar-Activist, Human Rights and Civil Rights." February15. http://www.pbs.org/ralphbunche/activist_rights.html.

Randall, Dudley, and Margaret G. Burroughs, eds. 1967. *For Malcolm: Poems on the Life and the Death of Malcolm X*. Detroit: Broadside Press.

Reed, Gregory. 2010. *Lost Chapters: Decoding the Autobiography of Malcolm X*. DVD. Detroit: Keeper of the Word Foundation.

Reed, Ishmael. 1999. Preface to *Soul on Ice* [1968], by Eldridge Cleaver, 1–11. New York: Delta Trade Publishing.

Sales, William W., Jr. 1994. *From Civil Rights to Black Liberation: Malcolm X and the Organization of Afro-American Unity*. Boston: South End Press.

Sanchez, Sonia. 1967. "Malcolm." In *For Malcolm: Poems on the Life and the Death of Malcolm X*, edited by Dudley Randall and Margaret G. Burroughs, 38–39. Detroit: Broadside Press.

Sanitsky, Larry, Mary J. Blige, Kendu Isaacs, et al. 2013. *Betty and Coretta*. New York: A+E Networks.

Smethurst, James Edward. 2005. *The Black Arts Movement: Literary Nationalism in the 1960s and 1970s*. Chapel Hill: University of North Carolina Press.

Walker, Margaret. 1967. "For Malcolm X." In *For Malcolm: Poems on the Life and the Death of Malcolm X*, edited by Dudley Randall and Margaret G. Burroughs, 32–33. Detroit: Broadside Press.

Whitsitt, Joyce. 1967. "For Malcolm." In *For Malcolm: Poems on the Life and the Death of Malcolm X*, edited by Dudley Randall and Margaret G. Burroughs, 20–21. Detroit: Broadside Press.

Wright, Jay. 1967. "The Solitude of Change." In *For Malcolm: Poems on the Life and the Death of Malcolm X*, edited by Dudley Randall and Margaret G. Burroughs, 28–29. Detroit: Broadside Press.

Wright, Richard. 1940. *Native Son*. New York: Harper.

————. 1993. "The Ethics of Living Jim Crow" [1938]. In Wright, *Uncle Tom's Children*, 1–15. New York: HarperPerennial.

PART 2

Malcolm and Community Engagement

Malcolm X's Pre-Nation of Islam (NOI) Discourses

**Sourced from Detroit's Charles H. Wright Museum
of African American History Archives**

Charles Ezra Ferrell

In August 2003, the (unpublished) Malcolm X Papers Collection was purchased by Christy S. Coleman, president of the Charles H. Wright Museum of African American History. Coleman paid $250,000 for the collection that she bought from James (Jimmy) E. Allen—an antique collector known as "the Southern Picker," and coauthor and editor of *Without Sanctuary: Photographs and Postcards of Lynching in America*—and his partner, John Littlefield. These papers were appraised for their authenticity by Wyatt Houston Day Bookseller of Nyack, New York, in July 2003 and reappraised on May 26, 2006, for insurance purposes. According to the museum's records, these papers were archived on September 28 and October 27, 2004.

Prior to the Malcolm X Papers Collection's arrival in Detroit, these primarily handwritten letters by Malcolm during his teenage and young adult years had been loaned, in 1999, to Emory University's Woodruff Library by Allen and Littlefield. That exhibition, managed by bibliographer Randall Burkett, received national coverage by CNN, the *Atlanta Journal-Constitution*, and various online news agencies. It also captured the attention of leading scholars such as James H. Cone and David Garrow. Cone, author of *Martin and Malcolm and America: A Dream or a Nightmare*, proclaimed, "They are quite unique. The only other known personal letters written by Malcolm X are in FBI files" (Roedemeier 1999).

Garrow, a distinguished research professor of history and law and author of *Bearing the Cross: Martin Luther King, Jr., and the Southern Christian Leadership Conference*, a Pulitzer prize–winning book about Reverend Dr. Martin Luther King Jr., stated,

> What's so impressive, even when you know the basic sketch of his life, is what a remarkably poetic, expressive writing ability Malcolm has as a teenager. This material shows what an immensely talented individual he was, even when he was twenty years old. . . . This collection makes crystal clear that Malcolm was someone of very impressive intellect long before he became a Muslim. (Garrow 1986)

Malcolm X is undoubtedly one of the most important political leaders of the twentieth century, yet he is largely misunderstood. Often, he is viewed simply as traumatized youth, shuffled between foster homes in Michigan and the home of his half-sister Ella Mae Little Collins in Roxbury, Massachusetts. He is also depicted as a misguided youth growing up in the streets of Harlem (New York) as "Detroit Red," swinging in and out of odd jobs, and falling into a life of drugs, crime, and incarceration. After that traumatic childhood experience, he is seen to be intellectually transformed under the tutelage of a fellow Charlestown prisoner, John Elton Bembry, and eventually through the teachings of the Nation of Islam (NOI) directed by Elijah Muhammad.

There exists a vibrant history of Malcolm's experiences in Detroit, archived at the Wright Museum. Recently purchased letters written by Malcolm during his childhood years in Michigan reveal a side of Malcolm that has not fully been addressed. This chapter is an expository of these elements and seeks to argue and illustrate how they inform the foundations of Malcolm's intellectual genius, spirituality, and dynamic leadership. Drawing from two of Malcolm's Wright Museum's archived letters, "Letter to Ella" and "Letter to Brother Raymond," with this chapter, we contribute yet another insight into Malcolm's political and spiritual leadership in ways that further enhance advanced research in the Black Studies discipline.

That is to say, while in his autobiography Malcolm retells important experiences of his youth, the Malcolm X Papers Collection at the Wright Museum sheds new light on Malcolm X's intellect, the depth of his spiritual understanding, and the strength of his leadership qualities during his youth. The papers certainly offer a glimpse into the early genius of Malcolm prior to his first meeting with Elijah Muhammad of the NOI in 1952.

For the current chapter, select extracts from the *Autobiography* as well as another sort of retelling through my authorship of Malcolm's life through the Wright Museum's collection of Malcolm's early childhood handwritten letters provides an occasion to fully comprehend Malcolm's youthful educational journey, which is central to the current volume. The papers provide us with a way to weigh the context out of which Malcolm's life emerged and the formidable challenges he experienced.

Retelling the Early Years through the *Autobiography*

The untold lynchings and burnings of African descendants in America by white racists were largely sanctioned by local, state, and federal law enforcement through their active participation and/or nonprosecution. This climate of sanctioned violence provided the foundation for the philosophical underpinning and raison d'être for Dr. W. E. B. Du Bois's activism and cofounding of the NAACP, the expansive growth of the Honorable Marcus Garvey's Back-to-Africa Movement and Universal Negro Improvement Association (UNIA) in the United States, and the justification to view the perpetrators of these crimes against Black people through the controversial dictum "the white man is the devil," propagated by separatist Elijah Muhammad of the NOI and broadly embraced by thousands of African descendants.

Earl Little, Malcolm's father, was born July 29, 1890, in Reynolds, Georgia. He was a six-foot-four-inch dark black traveling Baptist minister and a fearlessly devout Garvey evangelist and organizer. Malcolm recounts,

> Among the reasons my father had decided to risk and dedicate his life to help disseminate this philosophy (Garveyism) among his people was that he had seen four of his six brothers die by violence, three of them killed by white men, including one by lynching. (Malcolm X 1965, 2)

Coincidently, Elijah Muhammad, born October 7, 1897, in Sandersville, Georgia, who would later serve as a surrogate father for Malcolm, was also personally traumatized by the Maafa of lynching. Clegg in *An Original Man* put it this way,

> The unspeakable happened sometime around the winter of 1907, when Elijah, now ten, had first begun taking firewood to Cordele for sale. As he approached the African-American section of town, he encountered a large crowd of whites. He

moved closer to see what the crowd saw. There, for all who cared to see, the corpse of an eighteen-year-old black youth whom Elijah had known was "dangling from a tree limb." (Clegg 1997, 10)

In 1919, James Weldon Johnson coined the phrase "the Red Summer" for the bloody anti-Black violence that permeated southern and northern American cities during that spring, summer, and fall. It was apropos that Malcolm (El-Hajj Malik El-Shabazz) titled the first chapter of his autobiography "Nightmare." Prior to Malcolm's birth at University Hospital on May 19, 1925, white racists perpetuated terrorism on his family in Omaha, Nebraska. This unforgivable violence and disrespect was waged against his family by governmental agencies during his youth and continued throughout his life. Terrorism against African descendants was prevalent throughout America and visited Malcolm's family doorstep. Their home was set ablaze by white racists, causing them to move north to Milwaukee, Wisconsin. They would later move to Indiana Harbor (East Chicago), Indiana, and then to Lansing, Michigan.

Malcolm's earliest vivid memory occurred at age four, November 7, 1929, just one month after the crash of the stock market and the onset of the Great Depression. Young Malcolm was awakened by the terrifying sounds of repeated gunfire and shouting while their first Lansing home was burning down around him and his family. Unfortunately, being awakened in his home by a firebomb would take place on two more instances in Malcolm's life. His father tried to shoot the two escaping white arsonists. While his mother stood in horror holding his baby sister, white police and firefighters simply observed the destruction of their home at a visible distance, without coming to their aid. Their home incinerated into flying sparks, leaving them exposed and vulnerable (Malcolm X 1965, 3).

Malcolm enjoyed a close bond with his father. He believed his father regarded him as his favorite because he was the only child who accompanied his father to Garvey UNIA meetings. It was in such meetings that Malcolm witnessed his father's intensity, intelligence, toughness, and down-to-earth oratory. This was his first training in the powerful art of political articulation. In January 1928, Malcolm's parents purchased a house in a white neighborhood of Westmont, near Grand River Avenue and Waverly Road in Lansing. As in Omaha, his father continued to preach the Pan-Africanist teachings of Marcus Garvey at numerous home-based UNIA meetings throughout the Lansing area.

Based upon a decree—Chancery Case #14215—dated October 12, 1929, Circuit

Court Judge Leland Walker Carr, of the Ingham County Circuit Court, ordered Earl and Louise Little to vacate their home because it was located in a white neighborhood. Leland Walker Carr later served as a justice of the Michigan Supreme Court from 1945 to 1963 and held the position of chief justice in 1947, 1955, and 1962–63. Capital View Land Company, a corporation, and James W. Nicoli—who owned the Westmont subdivision—took Earl and Louise Little to circuit court. The company argued that, because the land contract stated only Caucasians could live there, Earl and Louise Little were in violation of the contract. The court ruled that Malcolm's parents must vacate their home. The decree stated,

> this land shall never be rented, leased or sold or so occupied by any other persons than those of the Caucasian race. It was admitted on the said cause as alleged in the bill of the complaint, that the parties Earl Little and Louise Little are each of African [*sic*] race, that is, he is a negro and she is a negress. That by virtue of the restriction placed in the said deed, This court holds as follows: This court does hereby determine that the said defendants, Earl Little and Louise Little are not of the Caucasian race but of the African [*sic*] race and that he, said Earl Little is a negro and that Louise Little is a negress and they are occupying the said premises described and the court does thereby order, adjudge and decree, that by virtue of the laws of this State, and the restrictions so made that said Earl Little or Louise Little or either of them shall not occupy the said premises.

On November 7, 1929, before their eviction could take place, the Little's home was set ablaze by white racist arsonists. Their home burned to the ground. No one was harmed. One month later, in December 1929, Malcolm's father built a new four-room home for their family on the outer boundaries of East Lansing, the current location of Michigan State University. In January 1931, at age five, Malcolm began kindergarten at Pleasant Grove Elementary School in East Lansing, Michigan. The school extended to the eighth grade level. According to Malcolm, his family was the first to integrate that all-white community.

Eleven months later, in December 1931, Malcolm's forty-one-year-old father was viciously murdered by members of the Black Legion (aka Black Legionnaires), a twenty to thirty thousand member racist paramilitary terrorist group, centered in Detroit and East Central Ohio, that grew out of the infamous Ku Klux Klan. Earl Little's skull was crushed on one side. His body was transported from the initial crime scene and laid across rail tracks at Detroit Street and East Michigan Avenue where a streetcar severed him up to his torso, nearly cutting him in half. Malcolm's father lived in that traumatized painful state for one hundred and twenty minutes. Malcolm was just six years old.

At thirteen, Malcolm was separated from his family by the state of Michigan. Malcolm asserted often painfully how his family was destroyed in 1937 (Malcolm X 1965). He was forced to live with the Gohannas family. Understandably, he began acting out in school. He placed a thumbtack on his teacher's chair, wore his hat into the classroom, skipped school, and was eventually expelled. He was sent to a detention home run by the Swerlins in Mason, Michigan, twelve miles from Lansing. Soon thereafter, Malcolm began the seventh grade at Mason Junior High School. There, he joined the debating society and was a member of the basketball team, while employed as a dishwasher after school.

The cumulative impact of these deeply traumatic and chaotic life experiences would *precondition anyone* for a life of sociopsychological underdevelopment. Yet Malcolm was able to weather these storms, and through the liberating power of disciplined self-education became a major contributory force for human justice in world history. In his landmark work, *The Souls of Black Folk*, W. E. B. Du Bois often refers to the character of the Black soul "whose dogged strength alone keeps it from being torn asunder" (1994, 2). Malcolm's life and educational strivings personified, in microcosm, the strength of will evident in Africans who endure the unjust weight of oppression.

Education in Michigan: Northern Injustice

English and history were Malcolm's favorite subjects. His mastery of these subjects would play a pivotal role in his effectiveness as a powerful revolutionary leader of historical significance. It is ironic that the two instructors of his endeared courses would severely disappoint him and crush his budding aspirations. Malcolm recalled the racist onslaught he was subjected to by his history instructor in the presence of his classmates.

> The one thing I didn't like about history class was that the teacher, Mr. Williams, was a great one for "nigger" jokes. One day during my first week at school, I walked into the room and he started singing to the class, as a joke, "Way down yonder in the cotton field, some say a nigger won't steal." Very funny. I liked history, but I never

thereafter had much liking for Mr. Williams. Later, I remember, we came to the textbook section on Negro history.

It was exactly one paragraph long. Mr. Williams laughed through it practically in a single breath, reading aloud how the Negroes had been slaves and then freed, and how they were usually lazy and dumb and shiftless. He added, I remember, an anthropological footnote on his own, telling us between laughs how Negroes' feet were "so big that when they walk, they don't leave tracks, they leave a hole in the ground." (Malcolm X 1965, 29)

On December 23, 1938, Louise Little, Malcolm's dedicated and hard-working mother, suffered a mental collapse. This nervous breakdown was due to the weight of her husband's unprosecuted murder, unjust employment practices, being swindled by insurance agencies who failed to pay the insurance policy death claim—deceitfully claiming her husband's death was a suicide—and dealing with state agencies' continuous threats to take and separate her eight children, while she attempted to adequately feed and care for them with little or no funds. She was declared legally insane. Malcolm's mother was committed to the Michigan State Mental Hospital in Kalamazoo where she remained for twenty-six years before being released, in 1963, into the care of his brother (Philbert) and their family.

Through his internal strength and focus, in spite of the immense obstacles life had dealt him, in the second semester of the seventh grade, young Malcolm achieved the third highest grades in his class and was elected class president. In the summer of 1940, Malcolm left Michigan for the first time to visit his half-sister Ella Mae Little Collins in Roxbury, Massachusetts. When Malcolm returned to Mason, his self-concept was transformed. He had experienced the warmth of Black life in Boston, lived under the unified strength and dominance of his "dark-skinned" half-sister, and felt reconnected to a unified family. Thus, from the beginning of the eighth grade (8-A), Malcolm's increased sense of Black identity led to a discomfort, a "restlessness," while in the presence of whites. Yet he remained a top academic performer.

Malcolm yearned to capitalize on his academic success to obtain the so-called American Dream. Mr. Ostrowski, his eighth grade English teacher, shattered his desire just as he was on the verge of transitioning to high school. Malcolm recalled,

It was just in his nature as an American white man. I was one of his top students—one of the school's top students—but all he could see for me was the kind of future "in your place" that almost all white people see for Black people. He told me, "Malcolm you ought to be thinking about a career. Have you been giving some thought?"

When Malcolm replied he would like to be a lawyer, Ostrowski leaned back in his chair, clasped his hands behind his head, arrogantly half-smiled, and devastated Malcolm's youthful aspiration, self-esteem, and sense of academic purpose by stating,

> Malcolm, one of life's first needs is for us to be realistic. Don't misunderstand me, now. We all like you here, you know that. But you've got to be realistic about being a nigger. A lawyer—that's no realistic goal for a nigger. You need to think about something you *can* be. You are good with your hands—making things. Everybody admires your carpentry shop work. Why don't you plan on carpentry? People like you as a person—you'd get all kinds of work. (Malcolm X 1965, 36)

This sense of ostracization for Malcolm deepened. He knew his classmates' aspirations, in large part, were simply to be farmers. Those whites who espoused loftier careers were encouraged by Ostrowski, in spite of the gnawing fact that nearly none of Malcolm's classmates were his academic peer. Although Malcolm's father was brutally murdered, his mother institutionalized, his siblings split up—living in three separate locations—and he was expelled from school, it is noteworthy that he regarded the Ostrowski incident as *the first major turning point* of his life. This statement underscores how intertwined his sense of self was with his career aspirations, or precisely, his need for self-determination. This incident, coupled with his recent experiences in Boston, fueled his withdrawal from the need for social inclusion in the white American mainstream.

Revelations and Early Genius: A Letter to Ella

The Malcolm X Papers Collection, archived at the Wright Museum in Detroit, reveals a blueprint, a path, and a trajectory into which Malcolm's life would eventually blossom. Table 1 is the true-to-form re-creation by the author of a career path chart contained in the Malcolm X Papers Collection. The original chart was apparently created during his eighth grade period. Although it is undated, it bears his signature: "Malcolm Little." One can extrapolate, with a high degree of accuracy, how each

TABLE 1. Malcolm's Career Path

CAREER PATH		
BASIC TERMINAL JOBS	**SUPPLEMENTARY TERMINAL JOBS**	**RELATED JOBS**
Lawyer District Attorney Politics	Banking Real Estate Politics Department of Justice	Orator Banking Real Estate Trust Company Department of Justice Capital View Land Company Police Magistrate Teacher of Law
INTERMEDIATE JOBS		
Clerk Apprentice Orator		
TRAINING JOBS		
Clerk Apprentice		

career path listed by Malcolm would later manifest itself in certain aspects of his adult life.

It is well documented that Malcolm was an extraordinary debater and orator, undoubtedly one of the world's best. These are the essential skills of a successful trial attorney, district attorney, and politician—all careers that Malcolm envisioned. In fact, most U.S. politicians are lawyers. Malcolm would play a significant role in expanding the NOI's real estate through opening temples, later referred to as mosques. He also oversaw the collections of monies to fill the coffers of NOI officialdom. Yet the overall thrust of his life's aspirations was to be a political leader who would achieve freedom, justice, and equality for African Americans—and all oppressed peoples of color—subjected to imperialistic white supremacy and any form of structural and systemic oppression.

After Malcolm achieved psychological independence from the politically restrictive philosophy of the NOI, he strongly advanced the need for African American self-respect, self-determination, political independence, global cultural awareness, and self-defense. Malcolm traveled throughout Africa and the so-called Middle East where he was welcomed and treated as a head of state. His mission, in part, during his international travels in 1964 was to garner diplomatic support to indict the United States before the world court of the United Nations for the criminal treatment of twenty-two million African Americans who, since their ancestors' brutal enslavement, were systematically lynched, disenfranchised, and denied their innate human rights. Malcolm encountered the Customs Department in France that denied his entry into that country. He would later acknowledge this denial was due to the manipulative handiwork of U.S. governmental agencies, most likely the CIA, in conjunction with the State Department.

Thus, the consistency of life patterns and issues that would later imprint Malcolm's adult life is intuitively revealed in the career path he mapped out as a teenager. All the major themes of Malcolm's later life are written there, most notably the crystallization of his goal to be a brilliant orator. His letters would support this fact. For example, one letter, written by Malcolm on December 14, 1946, while in Charleston Prison, provides rich insight into his purposefulness, warmth, intelligence, discipline, and demands for self-excellence (see Figures 1 and 2). It also reveals Malcolm's unquenchable thirst for knowledge through the developmental and transformative tools of reading and writing—independent self-education. The letter documented his singular reason for seeking a transfer from Charleston Prison to Norfolk Prison Colony, which he expressed three times in this correspondence. Malcolm wanted access to the best library in the prison system. It is not surprising Malcolm obtained his goal. Eventually, he was transferred to Norfolk Prison Colony in late March 1948, after a fifteen-month stay at Concord Reformatory.

At age twenty-one, he set the goal of writing a book and requested fountain pens as a gift from his half-sister, Ella Mae. This goal demonstrates his intellectual propensity. Malcolm wrote:

My Dear Sister,

I'm writing this to let you know what I want for Xmas. At least I'm blunt—hu[h]? I've worn my fountain pen completely out. That's what I need, a fountain pen and a pair of gloves (preferably mittens). You asked me two months ago what I wanted for Xmas, so don't go blowing your top, now that I've told you.

The pen, I need, because I still intend writing that book while I'm here. I've already started on it (several times) but I've had to destroy it because I wasn't satisfied with what I had accomplished.

I haven't written to you in a long time, because one day you mentioned something to me about my "faring [sic] letter," so now I write to you only when there is no other alternative. Jaci was over here to visit me last week. I wondered why you didn't come too. I also wondered if you were going to send me some more pictures. Reg said he left the ones I was asking about there. They can brighten up my smile.

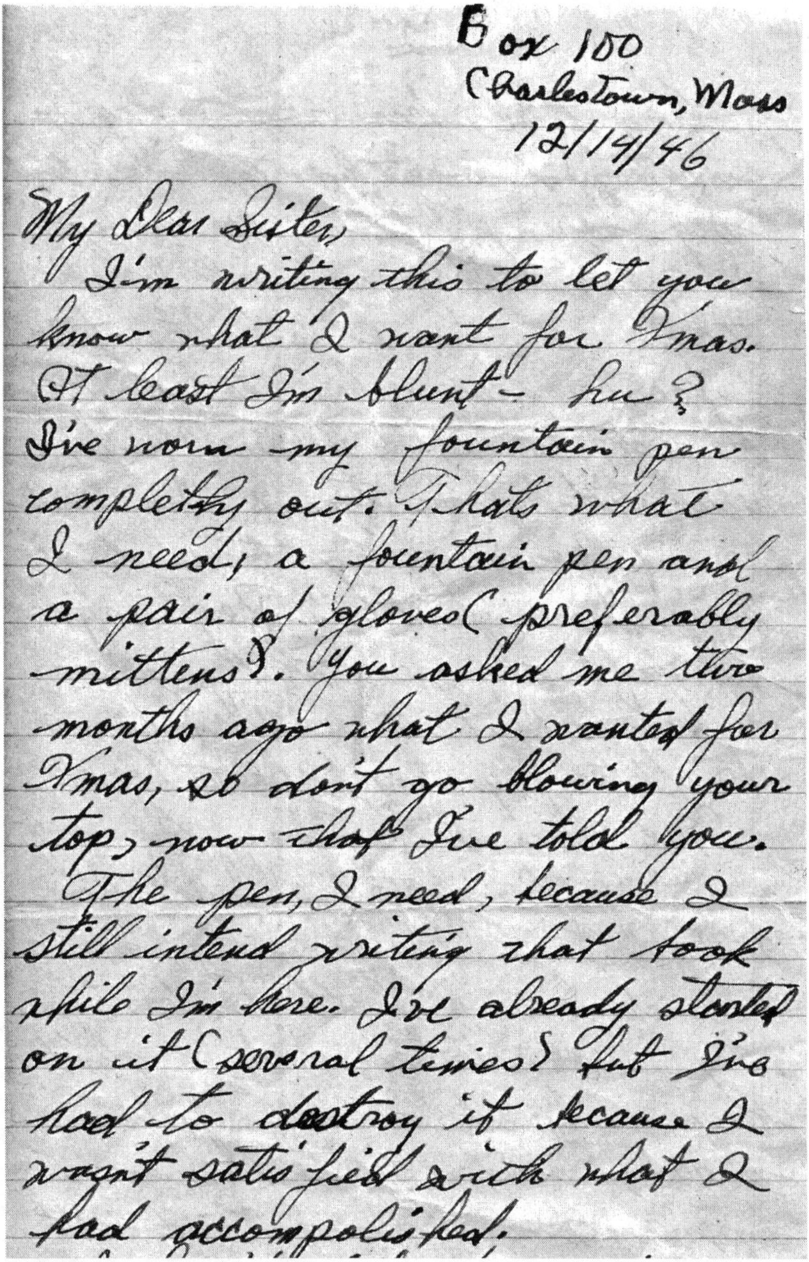

Box 100
Charlestown, Mass
12/14/46

My Dear Sister,
I'm writing this to let you
know what I want for Xmas.
At least I'm blunt— hu?
I've worn my fountain pen
completely out. Thats what
I need, a fountain pen and
a pair of gloves (preferably
mittens). You asked me two
months ago what I wanted for
Xmas, so don't go blowing your
top, now that I've told you.
The pen, I need, because I
still intend writing that book
while I'm here. I've already started
on it (several times) but I've
had to destroy it because I
wasn't satisfied with what I
had accompolished.

FIGURE 1. 14 December 1946 letter from Malcolm Little to Ella Collins, from The Wright Museum Archives Malcolm X Papers, MSS117. Courtesy of the Charles H. Wright Museum of African American History.

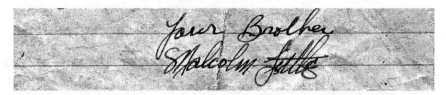

FIGURE 2. 14 December 1946 letter from Malcolm Little to Ella Collins, from The Wright Museum Archives Malcolm X Papers, MSS117. Courtesy of the Charles H. Wright Museum of African American History.

Are you still going to get me transferred to Norfolk? I'm working in the foundry now. The work is a little harder and very much dirtier, but I don't have any of the prejudices, narrow-mined instructors messing with me now. I almost broke my own code and lost my head last week. But I counted to ten and was transferred the next day. One good thing you learn how to do while you're in here and that is how to use a little self-control. If you get me transferred to Norfolk, I'll try and complete that whole book next year. They have a fine library down there and one can learn so many more different things. My only reason for wanting to go is the library alone.

Tell Kenny that Jimmy Williams is (or already has, I'm not sure which at present) moving to Los Angeles, California. Reggie will either go with him, or follow out later. My only other need, Ella is a pair of warm gloves. You already know how much cold weather . . . and I disagree. If I thought it would cost you too much, I wouldn't be asking you for anything.

You know me, [*sic*] if I don't get them I won't be disappointed. Will you be over here to see me this month? If this letter is boring, just remember that I'm writing it from behind these dark dreamy walls and there isn't very much of any particular interest that I could write about.

I only hope you don't stop trying to get me transferred to Norfolk.

Hoping to see or hear from you soon.

Your Brother,

Malcolm Little

Budding Spirituality: A Letter to Brother Raymond

In the following correspondence, penned by Malcolm while in Norfolk Prison Colony at age twenty-five, he reveals a spiritual sophistication that far exceeds his years.[1]

March 18, 1950

As Salaam Alaikum

My Most Dearly Beloved Brother Raymond,

May the All-Wise Allah be with you as I write, and may He bestow upon you Eternal Life.

Your beautiful words arrived last night and found me thirsty awaiting them. . . . Yes, what you say is true, all things come from Allah. It is he who gives us our thoughts and our words and it is to Him[2] that they return. That is why our thoughts and our words will one day soon be our Judge. Yes, he Loved us when we knew Him not. He was our First Love and He will <u>be</u> our Last. He has placed so many beautiful things in the <u>atmosphere</u> for us to grasp at will, if we only will.

Originals possess an abundance of intelligence, and I pray Allah one day soon we will all realize this and cultivate the beauty of our Intellect to the extent where all of our desire will <u>be</u> of a Spiritual Nature.

Most of us look forward in life to eventually obtaining wives and husbands, so we prepare ourselves in a manner we think will attract the opposite sex. Having become occcidentialized [*sic*], we concentrate on cultivating our physical make-up (an attraction that is, at best, <u>temporary</u>). This is where many make our mistakes and thus are not able to retain our mates once we've attracted them. . . . We don't have appreciation for real beauty.

The most beautiful thing in the world, and is a beauty that <u>forever</u> attracts, is that which is read in the depths of one's eyes. . . . therein lies the essence of one's' [*sic*] Soul . . . the Book of Allah . . . for it is the deep unfathomable work of Nature that forever leaves the onlooker mute with silent admiration.

People who possess this look of 'far-awayness' are very <u>deep thinkers</u> . . . and are often classed as "Dreamers." The Dreamers are never sad, for they remain not in this wicked world of sadness . . . they live in the "Within" . . . they can climb to the "Heights," and abode in Worlds of their own . . . and the earthy creatures who are bound by material desires, gaze into depths of the In-dwellers' Dreamy eyes and become enslaved by the captivating Mystery of that Soul lost so deeply within Itself . . . and the Way-Beyond. Long ago the Brothers of our Black Nation knew and practiced the Art of the True Beauty . . . and <u>they were perfectionists</u>.

. . . Ah my Brother, if we could only more fully realize the importance and power of thought and thinking. It is the most inspiring Force in the universe . . . for it is truly composed of the essence of Allah . . . just think of our Words . . . Words that we speak cause vibrations that increasing traverse the entire universe . . . but our

thoughts are of greater importance still, because, because we <u>speak</u> as we <u>think</u> . . .
but deeper yet are our <u>Feelings</u>, for we only Think <u>as we feel</u>, our feelings controlling
our thinking . . . and the atmosphere we are in affects and effects our feeling . . . but
the atmosphere itself is comprised and controlled by the vibrations of our words,
the vibrations of our thoughts, and the vibrations of our feelings . . . <u>All</u> being of the
Same Essence and comprising that Holy Spirit that moves the Universe. . . . All are
One . . . All in All . . . Allah! For one to control one's thoughts and feelings, means one
can actually control one's atmosphere and all who walk into its sphere of influence.
This we know to be True.

It is your own thoughts that are generated into the universe by your beautiful
mind, and picked out by me, of the atmosphere, that are producing this letter. Am
I not writing that which you most desire to hear? Does it not come from your very
own Heart?

. . . So your father is a Preacher? Mine was also, that's why he is dead today . . .
he didn't preach according to "Hoyle." He was a devout Garveyite; in fact Marcus
Garvey lived with us much of the time. He was a Muslim, you know. My mother
was very close to him, having come from the Islands too. There is much more that I
know today concerning that affair that I didn't know before because my youth and
dead mind. (My mother taught us Islam from birth, but we never realized it. They
put her in an asylum in 1938. You can imagine why). In 1931 my father was "placed"
under a street car . . . again, you can imagine why. We children were all too young
to fully ever know what was going down. . . . I have tried to get a librarians job, but
having never had a black librarian here, conventions are like steel bars to crack. This
library here is famous as a prison library.

. . . So you went to college? I must seem quite dumb to you then (in a way). I
only finished eighth grade, but I've always been all eyes and ears (and even all nose)
on the side. One can pick up some bits of knowledge here and there that way. . . .

As Salaam Alaikum

Sincerely, Your Brother in Truth Malcolm X

This excerpt was transcribed by the author due to the rare insights it reveals
about a dimension of Malcolm's self, rarely known. This letter is a testament to
Malcolm's phenomenal self-development. Malcolm understood that one could
evolve through reading, writing, debating, and oratory. His self-developed brilliance
elucidates the inherent weakness and destructiveness of the American educational

curriculum that fosters self-hate among non-Europeans and/or mass ignorance of the broader populace through its distorted views of history, and thus reality.

Throughout Malcolm's thirty-nine years, he constantly evolved and transformed himself through all forms of education, including travel. At twenty-five, Malcolm understood the importance of being the "dreamer," striving for perfection, and going deep within oneself to commune with the Divine. Yet he learned through his life struggle that political activism shaped by spiritual discipline were required prerequisites to fight injustice on behalf of African people oppressed by a structurally racist and materialistic system. Historians and political scientists, in particular, will find of great interest Malcolm's assertion that the Honorable Marcus Garvey lived with his family for a period of time.

Conclusion

The Malcolm X Papers Collection found its way back to Michigan where Malcolm grew up as a child and received his so-called formal education. According to James Allen, he acquired the Malcolm X Papers through a third party individual. Allegedly, that individual purchased them from a neighbor who acquired them from the home of Ella Mae Little Collins when she was in dire health. Allen said he was heavily weighted while in possession of these papers and felt they should rightfully reside in the place where Malcolm had lived.[3]

It is the mission of the Wright Museum, the largest museum devoted to African American history in the world, to promote youth-focused education. There is no better model regarding the transformative power of education than the life of Malcolm X. The Malcolm X Papers Collection attests to the brilliance of—and drive for excellence by—Malcolm, even in his early developmental years. Through the current volume on Malcolm X, educational Black Studies institutions also play a role in promoting Malcolm's young genius to contemporary Black youth.

NOTES

1. Excerpted from a letter to "Raymond," a friend (at that time) and fellow Muslim.

2. The underlined text, capitalization, and the majority of the ellipses are Malcolm's.

3. Http://www.emory.edu/WELCOME/journcontents/archive/art/malcolmxHUM.

WORKS CITED

Allen, John. 2000–05. *Without Sanctuary: Photographs and Postcards of Lynching in America*. http://withoutsanctuary.org/main.html.

Carson, Clayborne. 1991. *Malcolm X: The FBI File*. Edited by David Gallen. New York: Carroll and Graf.

Clegg, Claude Andrew, III. 1997. *An Original Man: The Life and Times of Elijah Muhammad*. New York: St Martin's Press.

Dray, Philip. 2002. *At the Hands of Persons Unknown: The Lynching of Black America*. New York: Random House.

Du Bois, W. E. B. 1994. *The Souls of Black Folk* [1903]. New York: Dover.

Garrow, David J. 1986. *Bearing the Cross: Martin Luther King, Jr., and the Southern Christian Leadership Conference*. New York: Vintage Books.

Malcolm X. 1965. *The Autobiography of Malcolm X*. With the assistance of Alex Haley. New York: Grove Press.

Roedemeier, Chad. 1999. "Early Letters Give New Picture of Malcolm X Teen Writes about Girls, Dancing, Becoming Lawyer." *Florida Times Union*, September 8.

Liberation and Transformation through Education

Black Studies at Malcolm X College, Chicago

Edward C. Davis IV

Black Studies scholar Maulana Karenga suggests "one of the most important achievements of black studies scholars is to have put forth contestation in Africana studies as a fundamental mode of understanding self, society, and the world . . . seek[ing] to create a space and process for students to recover, discover, and speak the truth and meaning of their own experience, to locate themselves in social and human history" (2000, 167). Reflecting upon the global history of self-liberating social movements of the past sixty years, one must not overlook or ignore the role of Malcolm El-Hajj Malik El-Shabazz as a monumental transformative figure in the formation of ontologies of Blackness, of self, and of communities in an era of racial segregation and globally imposed legal technologies and epistemologies of inferiority, such that persons of African descent globally became classified by the Hegelian myth as being nonpersons separate from human history and from the human race.

The powerful rhetoric of Malcolm X remains a key force of the civil rights and Black Power liberation movements of the second half of the twentieth century, providing Black people around the world with a sense of pride and rehabilitating sense of humanity. Without Malcolm X, the discipline of global Black/Africana Studies would lack core elements of critical adult learning (andragogy), as well as a legacy of transformative empowerment. Teaching Black Studies at Malcolm X

College (MXC) in Chicago, I apply my own unique transformative adult learning theory in the classroom and through my curriculum in an effort to empower students to reimagine reality, their world, their communities, and themselves. This praxis of liberation and transformation through education follows a long tradition of andragogy and self-emancipation through Malcolm X the leader, the legend, and the learning environment.

In 1972, during his tenure as the first president of MXC, Dr. Charles Hurst, in his book *Passport to Freedom: Education, Humanism, and Malcolm X*, prescribed his plan for combating the challenges of providing a transformative postsecondary education to African American adult learners in the city of Chicago. The liberating humanistic education Hurst outlined reflected the transformative andragogy proposed by critical social theorists such as Frantz Fanon, Paulo Freire, bell hooks, Malcolm Knowles, Henry Giroux, and Edward Taylor. In *The Wretched of the Earth* (1963), French Caribbean psychoanalyst Frantz Fanon described the emancipatory healing elements of constructing a national culture in postcolonial spaces, such that lived experiences of the poor masses diffuse throughout the country in lieu of reproducing the oppressive social mores of the dominant foreign colonial bourgeois elites. Writing at the dawn of African liberation in 1960, Fanon foresaw the self-perpetuating neocolonialism that would come to shape the worldview and social terrain of the postcolony situated primarily in the educational systems left behind by European colonial regimes.

Jean-Paul Sartre's preface to *The Wretched of the Earth* reiterates the call for the oppressed to "cure himself of colonial neurosis" (Fanon 1963, 21). The cure comes through a rehabilitating humanistic traditionalism. Crucial reading during the Black consciousness movement of the 1960s, the writings of Fanon established the framework toward psychological liberation from the mental clutches of colonial oppression, setting the stage for cultural revolutions rooted in resurrecting indigenous traditional institutions, preserving ancient knowledge formation, and resuscitating dying epistemologies that might serve as the cultural anchors of national consciousness.

In 1970, Brazilian educator and philosopher Paulo Freire continued the intellectual discourse outlined before him in the groundbreaking work *Pedagogy of the Oppressed*. As Freire examined the conditions of the poor in Brazil, he clearly established a correlation between oppression and the educational system controlled by the oppressor. Freire established that the banking model of education assumed that the oppressed constitute empty vessels, or a tabula rasa, into or upon which the cultural knowledge of the dominant class could be infused or written. By depositing knowledge into an empty vessel, the banking model of education ignored the preexisting humanity and endogenous epistemologies of poor persons, whereby relegating the masses to the margins of society. Thus, the educational philosophy for the adult masses consists not of an emancipating andragogy (educational practice for leading or teaching self-sufficient adults). Instead, marginalized adult learners are prescribed an oppressive pedagogy (educational practice for leading or teaching children).

For as Freire notes, "The banking approach to adult education, for example, will never propose to students that they critically consider reality" (Freire 2000, 74). A transformation of this nature undermines the system of oppression, which relies upon an oppressed mass of people to sustain inequality. Instead, the existing educational structure reifies oppression, marginality, and social exclusion by suggesting ways of integrating and incorporating the masses within the oppressive structure for the benefit of the elites and not for the purpose of transformative and liberating self-education for the benefit of one's own personhood. As such, one might conclude that institutions must be rebuilt in order to rebuild persons, self-identities, and communities.

In her groundbreaking work, *Teaching to Transgress: Education as the Practice of Freedom* (1994), bell hooks extends the intellectual postulations of Fanon and Freire as she navigates the terrain of socioeconomic oppression within a poststructuralist, feminist, antiracist critique. As she traces the intersections of race, class, and gender in the marginality of others, she touches upon the critical issue of self-expression in the praxis of critical andragogy in her chapter "Language: Teaching New Worlds/New Words." Here, hooks poses a rarely articulated question, as she ponders how her African ancestors must have been terrified by the strange utterances of English, and of European languages in general, aboard the slave ships during the Middle Passage, upon the auction block, and on the plantation. With the strange utterances of European languages came the crack of the whip and the piercing sting of oppression, as each generation of Africans in the Americas become ever more alienated from the languages, thoughts, customs, and traditions of their ancestors.

Bell hooks postulates that a culture of resistance emerged out of the remnants of African language and tradition, which we now find in popular African American culture. In the hush harbors of the plantation, in the traditions of the maroons, and in the hybrid creole languages of diaspora communities throughout the Americas, a culture of resistance has existed for hundreds of years. Sadly, however, the memory and present reality of the oppressed remains within the linguistic imagination of the oppressor, since masses of colonized peoples around the world have lost their indigenous languages in the name of progress and education. Strangely, marginalized groups must express their marginality in the language of the oppressor in order to communicate with each other, and in order to liberate themselves from the oppression imposed upon them.

Influenced by hooks, Freire, and Fanon, Henry Giroux continues the conversation on critical pedagogy and andragogy in his work *Border Crossings: Cultural Workers and the Practice of Education* (2005). Although Giroux does not distinguish pedagogy (leading children) from andragogy (leading adults), he does strongly suggest that educators must not deposit knowledge into the minds of learners. Instead, educators are cultural workers engaged in the active pursuit of leading critically engaged learners in the construction of their own realities as actors and agents, instead of as passive beings who serve the aims and agendas of the elites. Giroux notes the essential role of "a politics of voice" that gives power to learners who are critically engaged in "issues regarding the construction of the self" related to "questions of history, culture, community, language, gender, race, and class" (2005, 73). As such, Giroux's critical pedagogy must be a source of liberation and unification through coalition building that crosses the boundaries of epistemologies, worldviews, linguistic limitations, and social identities.

Within the body of adult learning theory, Malcolm Knowles remains legendary in his call for a uniquely separate mode of instructional design where andragogy and pedagogy remain distinct from one another. Assuming that children lack schema and preestablished knowledge and life experience, adult learning theory and andragogy require leading students toward a constructivist educational model in order to become active agents in their own life-long learning as social transformers. Edward Taylor reassembles previously constructed theoretical debates on transformative learning theory from Malcolm Knowles, Jack Mezirow, bell hooks, and Paulo Freire. Taylor notes a long tradition of psychocritical discourse, which gives birth to transformative learning theory in adult education, such that education becomes a self-reflective process leading toward transformation, discovery, and social emancipation. Taylor notes several critical principles and components that are essential to actualizing a Freirian emancipatory transformative learning experience. Transformative learning theory must provide adult learners with the rediscovery of power rooted in critical reflection toward agency to transform one's own life and community, while fostering a liberating metacognitive approach to learning that moves away from the banking approach and that establishes a horizontal relationship between teacher and student that moves away from hierarchal educational models (Taylor 2008, 8).

In 1911, Crane Junior College became the first community college in the city of Chicago; however, by 1968 student movements led to a campaign to rename the institution Malcolm X College and to construct a new campus on Chicago's West Side. Consistent with our volume objective, the current chapter analyzes the unique role of MXC within the Black metropolis of Chicago, the nation, and the world. Formerly housed within Crane High School, adult learners at Crane Junior College evoked the self-emancipatory image of Malcolm X as a unifying figure for community development and individual self-transformative learning. As such, they chose to move outside of the deteriorating high school building that served as a site of oppressive pedagogy into a new structure where critical andragogy provided a passport into a world of transformative adult learning.

Noting the intersections between the Black Power, Black Studies, and Black Campus Movements vis-à-vis the current era of so-called colorblind postracialism, this chapter uniquely situates MXC as a site of critical metacognitive educational and identity formation for the public community at large. Drawing upon the multidisciplinary traditions of Black Studies, we use the chapter to examine the presence of the field within the college, in addition to teacher-student engagement within the framework of resistance, transformation, and empowerment. With an emphasis on andragogy and adult education in the Black community, we will present student and faculty reflections upon the learning and teaching experience at MXC as a privileged space for critical andragogy and as a sacred site for global Black Studies.

Piecing together primary sources from the MXC library, coupled with interviews from teacher-student pioneers in the early days of MXC, mixed textual and ethnographic data within a theoretical framework of historical institutionalism and constructivist theory in education, through the Black Studies lens, will be used. The emergence of the Illinois chapter of the Black Panther Party and the tumultuous citizen uprising of 1968 will be examined within the historical context of the civil rights movement in Chicago at the end of the Great Migration, paying close attention to the different and similar agendas of the Black Power and Black Campus Movements.

Conceptualizing the assassinations of Malcolm X and Dr. Martin Luther King Jr. as transformative moments in Black consciousness formation, this chapter will explore antecedents to the global protests of 1968, which fueled the emotional fires that energized the Black Campus Movements of the late 1960s and 1970s. We use these movements to examine the transformation of the Crane Junior College to

Malcolm X College, uncovering the foundational curriculum, which became essential to the process of critical transformative teaching for adult and community learners situated within the walls of the new campus. We use this method to evaluate the varied experiences of former and present faculty, including my own experience, coupled with the insightful contributions of students who have benefited from the privileged space and transformative education that takes place at MXC on the West Side of Chicago. As the college's first professor of African American Studies, my own insights and perspectives play a crucial role in narrating the research study.

Transforming Public Space: Creating Malcolm X College from Crane Junior College

In August 2010, I began teaching at MXC, one of the City Colleges of Chicago. Soon, I became the first full-time faculty member hired to teach African American Studies in the history of the institution. When Mrs. Betty Shabazz attended the dedication ceremony of MXC in May 1971, the curriculum of the institution provided a series of socially reparative, community-building courses taught as sociology, anthropology, literature, history, economics, and psychology. Budget cuts and political transitions of the 1980s, 1990s, and 2000s slowly eroded and altered the foundational curriculum of the institution in favor of a Social Sciences Department of two full-time faculty members, and a limited set of course offerings in the area of Black/Africana Studies. As the Social Sciences Department grows, my efforts continue to develop the Black/Africana Studies curriculum with the hope of establishing a framework that can provide generations of adult learners with liberation and transformation through education at MXC.

Several months into my new position, an older gentleman walked into my office. As we began to speak, he informed me that he had served as president of the Malcolm X College Alumni Association and had a story he wished to share with me. Beginning with tales of his days as a student of the college in 1968, he recounted a familiar history of protest and triumph. As one knows, the 1960s may constitute one of the most tumultuous decades of the twentieth century. Following the assassination of Malcolm El-Hajj Malik El-Shabazz in 1965, Stokely Carmichael (Kwame Ture) and Charles Hamilton penned their groundbreaking text *Black Power*. Within one year, the Black Panther Party was founded in Oakland, California, when Huey P. Newton, Bobby Seale, and Eldridge Cleaver protested the absence of Black Studies and African-centered curriculum at Merritt Community College. Ibram H. Rogers (2012) refers to these uprisings as *Black Campus Movements*, which sprung up all around the country following the assassination of Malcolm X.

As the former president of the MXC Alumni Association confirmed, 1968 proved to be a violent year around the world. On April 4, 1968, Dr. Martin Luther King Jr. was assassinated in Memphis, Tennessee, causing Chicago and the world to erupt in riots. In May 1968, protests erupted in Paris, France, over that country's involvement in its former colony of Indochina (Vietnam). The assassination of Bobby Kennedy in June 1968 led to collective trauma and widespread civil uprising that set the country on fire. Shortly thereafter in August 1968, Chicago was set ablaze again when the Democratic National Convention assembled in the city. In the summer of 1968, a young Fred Hampton, future chairman of the Chicago chapter of the Black Panther Party, would graduate from Proviso East High School and enroll at Crane Junior College, the oldest City College of Chicago (Williams 2013, 56–59).

With Fred Hampton and a collection of young people energized in this globally transformative year, a powerful movement was developing on the West Side of Chicago. Before the end of 1968, a group of students at Crane Junior College, including Hampton, would lead their own Black Campus Movement. In October 1968, as they demanded a campus housed outside of the crumbling walls of Crane High School, as they demanded a Black Studies curriculum, and as they demanded improved educational opportunities for themselves and for future generations of West Siders, the students of Crane Junior College declared their autonomy and renamed their campus Malcolm X College. In 1969, City Colleges of Chicago officially recognized the name change and created the only education institution in the world named for Malcolm X.

From the intensely segregated, racially divided socioeconomic margins of Chicago, the students of the new MXC created "homeplace," which bell hooks refers to as "the construction of a safe place where black people could affirm one another—and by so doing—heal many of the wounds inflicted by racist domination" (1990, 42). Hooks further notes "we could not learn to love and respect ourselves in the culture of white supremacy, on the outside; it was there on the inside, in that 'homeplace,' most often created and kept by black women, that we had the opportunity to grow and develop, to nurture our spirit" (1990, 42). While hooks notes that homeplace is a space created by women, we see that in the 1960s and 1970s, women and men created the homeplace of MXC on the West Side of Chicago together. Today, however, women have become the overwhelming majority among students, instructors, and administrators at MXC, causing one to question greater social changes, which Augusta Del Zotto (2004) refers to as a historical social and literal elimination of African American men, or gendercide.

Along with Fred Hampton, many other active Black Panthers in the Illinois chapter included future Congressman Bobby Rush, who also assisted in educational efforts in the city of Chicago. Thus, with the efforts of several student-led protests, the first campus of City Colleges of Chicago founded in 1911 became Malcolm X College before former Crane Junior College students moved into the modern black glass MXC campus building in 1971. In December 1969, Fred Hampton was murdered in his sleep by the Chicago Police Department (Williams 2013). The anger over his assassination further united the community to organize for the creation of a safe educational space where Black West Siders and socially and economically marginalized Chicagoans as a whole could feel safe to learn and transform their lives.

Campus in Limbo

Following the assassination of Fred Hampton, newly appointed college president Dr. Charles Hurst Jr. immediately set out to create a physical location for a campus in spatial limbo. When students stormed out of the dilapidated Crane High School, refusing to be educated as college students within the walls of a high school, the new MXC found itself a campus without borders. An administrative office was housed near the Rush University Hospital, Cook County Hospital, and University of Illinois medical district. Another facility for teaching and instruction was located near what is today part of University of Illinois–Chicago (UIC) circle campus near the Maxwell Street flea market district. Buses shuttled students between locations.

In March 1970, *Black World/Negro Digest* and *Ebony* magazine (both Johnson Publications) featured articles on the foundational education underway at MXC (Poinsett 1970; Buresh 1971; Hurst 1970). These separate pieces written by Poinsett and Hurst laid out the problems the young MXC faced. A new building was under construction at 1900 West Van Buren; however, Dr. Hurst was left with the responsibility of overseeing the construction of a campus while building a curriculum from scratch. In *Passport to Freedom*, Dr. Hurst further details his agenda and vision for a college campus on the West Side of Chicago with the purpose of eradicating the educational and socioeconomic inequities many African Americans in the city of Chicago had endured for decades.

Centuries of slavery and segregation had left the generation of the Great Migration and their descendants in similar predicaments as their enslaved and sharecropping forefathers and foremothers. When Mrs. Betty Shabazz dedicated the college on May 19, 1971, the community felt empowered in a college where no one would be allowed to fail; however, the curriculum would have to repair the cultural erasure that American hegemonic forces had created with respect to the truthful histories of Africa, Black America, and the diaspora. Furthermore, Dr. Hurst set out to assemble staff, faculty, and students engaged in a project of andragogy for self-liberation and community development.

Duke Jenkins, Willie Johnson, and Perry Williams

Who made up the student body, faculty, and support staff following the inaugural opening of MXC? While there are countless figures too numerous to name, key individuals helped lay the educational foundation of the college and continue to carry a sense of pride in their association with the foundational legacy of MXC. Though he passed away in 1996, Dr. Ulysses "Duke" Jenkins was a foundational educator in the areas of anthropology, African studies, and theater. After completing his doctorate in Germany, Dr. Jenkins returned to the United States and chose to teach at MXC as a founding faculty member. As early as 1971, Dr. Jenkins created and taught courses such as the following:

- Anthropology 202: Cultural Anthropology
- Anthropology 204: Cultures of Sub-Saharan African
- Anthropology 219: Remnants of Africa in the Diaspora
- Anthropology 220: Black Theater

The courses Dr. Jenkins taught fit well within Dr. Hurst's agenda for college-wide Black Studies–focused curricula, coupled with a desire to reconstruct Black hope through reading Black books. Perry Williams studied under Dr. Jenkins in 1972. To this day, Mr. Williams expresses how the classes he took with "Duke" changed his life. During and after the classes he took with Dr. Jenkins as a young nineteen- or twenty-year-old adult learner, Mr. Williams began to develop his own Black Studies library based on the works of Cheikh Anta Diop, Anténor Firmin, John Mbiti, W. E. Abraham, Lloyd Fallers, C. L. R. James, Jomo Kenyatta, Kwame Nkrumah,

Frantz Fanon, Malcolm X, and many other great scholars from the 1800s to the present, mostly focusing on African indigenous political and religious philosophy, social organization, cultural knowledge, and the diaspora. Many of these authors contributed to a canon of Black Studies literature essential to Dr. Jenkins's Black anthropology courses taught at MXC in the early 1970s.

Although Perry Williams graduated from UIC and became a broker and later an accountant at the U.S. Postal Service, now in his retirement, he reads intensely as he did in his youth as a student at MXC. He credits the anthropologist Dr. Ulysses Duke Jenkins with planting the seed of knowledge that continues to grow in him today. Although Dr. Jenkins left MXC to become a professor of anthropology and dean of diversity at Northwestern University in Evanston, Illinois (O'Brien 1996), his impression lives on in the students within the MXC Alumni Association who remember his courses with great precision. Dr. Jenkins was credited with establishing study-abroad programs to Africa and to areas of the African diaspora for students who completed his Anthropology 204 and Anthropology 219 courses. These experiences cannot be forgotten given the life-changing nature of travel to Africa and to various corners of the diaspora outside of the United States for a marginalized young person of color living on the West or South Sides of Chicago.

Today, study-abroad options to Africa and various locales in the diaspora no longer exist at MXC; however, students remain interested in these opportunities. My own research and efforts to reoffer and design Anthropology 204 and Anthropology 219 had demonstrated intense student interest not only to study Africa and the diaspora deeply beyond survey level courses. Students understand that, like Malcolm X, they must travel outside of the boundaries of Chicago in order to experience firsthand the sociocultural and geographic spaces of Black consciousness and African historiography in order to fully transform their visions of self, community, and world.

Like Dr. Ulysses Duke Jenkins, Willie Johnson came to MXC as the building opened its doors. As the first African American librarian to be hired at MXC, Mr. Johnson told me how difficult times were in the early days of the college. Born in Montgomery, Alabama, Willie Johnson worked for Chicago Public Schools as a librarian until transitioning to the newly opened MXC in 1971. Discrimination among his peers was quite intense; however, Willie Johnson held his ground and became the longest serving librarian at MXC when he retired in 2000. Mr. Johnson admitted that he hadn't been very versed about Malcolm when he first arrived at the College. He admitted that, given that he had grown up in Montgomery, he'd been much closer to the ideas of Martin Luther King. (Williams 2013). All the same, Johnson learned a great deal about the legacy of Malcolm X and become proud to be part of assembling the foundational curriculum Dr. Hurst promoted and designed based on eradicating institutionalized racism and ignorance of Black heritage, regardless of one's ethnic origin (Hurst 1972).

As history appears to repeat itself, Mr. Johnson noted how former students now come to him thanking him for his help. Many of them may be teachers for Chicago Public Schools or for City Colleges of Chicago. The protocol during the early days of MXC, according to Mr. Johnson, required faculty members and staff to be always ready to answer any student's questions about Black history, Black culture, education, social issues, social inequality, and social justice. Mr. Johnson was influential in creating the Black Books Club, which Dr. Hurst mentions in *Passport to Freedom*. The library was also the focal point for courses on institutionalized racism. Mr. Johnson believes that the mostly white administration of City Colleges of Chicago in the downtown central offices "frowned upon Black Studies"; however, he noted that the College still managed to foster an environment of global Black awareness in spite of the bureaucratic restraints in the racial politics of Chicago in the 1970s and 1980s.

Although the Council Wars proved difficult, Mr. Johnson notes that the administration of Mayor Harold Washington (1983–87) brought a great deal of funding to MXC. He further noted that in the 1970s and 1980s, the hallways were so crowded with students that enrollment appeared to exceed ten thousand students each semester. Like many Black Chicagoans, Mr. Johnson makes an effort to visit MXC during the annual Kwanzaa festivities in December, which has become one of the largest Kwanzaa celebrations in the world. Since retiring, however, Mr. Johnson noted that he does not feel the same spirit of vibrant, engaged students. Perhaps these issues are not local but reflect a number of issues affecting global Black communities, which Cornel West (2001) refers to as the nihilistic threat.

Empowerment through Critical Student Learning:
The Malcolm X College Student Experience

Why do students choose to attend MXC in postracial America? Most students of the college clearly comprehend the realities of race in America, understanding the legacy of Malcolm X as the scholar-activist-political thinker whose personal experiences resemble their own lives as socioeconomically marginalized residents of the global city of Chicago. Some students passionately admit "I wanted Malcolm X's name on my diploma." Others believe that the professors at the College "care more" than professors at other colleges or at four-year universities due to the ideology of transformative empowerment associated with the person of Malcolm X.

For some students MXC serves a purpose as an affordable, local place to earn "credentials of economic value." Still other students share Malcolm's experience of incarceration, autodidactic empowerment, and self-improvement. In April 2013, I assembled a small focus group and conducted short interviews with current and former students from MXC. Most students in the focus group had previously taken courses with me in African American studies, anthropology, or general social sciences. Two students were current African American studies students, two were current anthropology students, and one had never been a student in any of my classes or in any social sciences classes at MXC.

Among seven of my former students, four have graduated from MXC. One student currently attends Columbia College as a BA candidate in African American studies and communications, another attends UIC as an African American studies major, and two other MXC graduates are not currently enrolled in any institution but plan to earn bachelor's degrees in education and geography/urban planning. Three of my former students who participated in the focus group have pending transfer offers to National Louis University and UIC, while one has transferred to a four-year institution without earning an associate's degree from MXC. Nine of the students were African or African American, while three students in the focus group identified as Mexican American.1 Questions asked in the focus group included the following:

· Why did you choose to enroll at Malcolm X College?
· What connects you to the life and legacy of El-Hajj Malik El-Shabazz?
· Did you attend Malcolm X College because of a particular educational program, location, or because of the character/name of the college?
· How has your education at Malcolm X College empowered or transformed you and your life?

D.H., a wife, mother, and grandmother from the Austin neighborhood, confessed that her first exposure to Black/Africana Studies came in elementary school when her seventh grade teacher covertly taught the students Black history in his literature class. As an African American studies major at UIC, D.H. felt empowered by the extensive curriculum African American Studies 101 and Anthropology 202 exposed her to. Part of the minority of students to earn a grade of A in both classes, D.H. feels

confident she will succeed at UIC and be able to teach future generations in Black/
Africana Studies. If nothing else, she wants to be properly equipped to educate her
African American adult children, her grandchildren, and the children of her church
and Austin community.

J.H., a wife, mother, and grandmother, also from the West Side of Chicago, hopes
to continue her career as an educator. Although she had decades of experience, she
did not have the degrees. As a result, she has returned to school to earn her associate's
in applied sciences in early childhood development, her BA/BS in education, and her
MA/MS in education. While she began studying at Harold Washington College, J.H.
believes that the instructors at MXC "care more with a teaching style that encourages
students." She also mentioned how her own experience as a parent and grandparent
are nurtured at MXC in her capacity as a mentor to younger students. While J.H.
feels her child development classes have been helpful, she credits knowledge gained
in African American studies and anthropology as opening her mind to theoretical
perspectives and different modes of thinking, which allow her to see the world
through the lenses of others. Her hope is to start her own school and day care center
with her daughter, an education major who just completed her bachelor's degree.
They both plan to earn MEd degrees together.

K.H. and K.S. are both West Siders and recent graduates of MXC. Although
they have not enrolled in BA programs, they plan to study geography and urban
planning, as well as education, respectively. K.H. came to MXC because it is close
to home and because of the name, prestige, and idea of having a diploma with the
name of the great civil rights leader and speaker. After years of military service, K.H.
came to MXC with a great deal of anger for white people given years of discrimination he experienced over sixty years. He credits African American studies and
anthropology courses for helping him to see the humanity in us all and for easing
his anger. He now works through his aggression and finds that it helps him to get
things done more effectively. Furthermore, the lack of geography courses at MXC
led him to take both African American studies and anthropology. His knowledge
of global geography and city, urban, and rural development has greatly improved.
Unlike K.H., K.S. is a young mother in her early thirties working in a school as a
classroom assistant. Like J.H., she needed to earn her associate's degree in child
development to remain on her job.

This West Side single mother struggled through the murder trial of her brother
to finish up her degree at MXC. Her hard work and determination paid off. During
the focus group, she revealed that she feels as though her options are limitless, if

she tries her best. She plans to enroll in a BA/BS program, but she is uncertain what step to take next. She credits African American studies with opening her eyes to the world around her. African American studies "built more self-worth, to be more proud and confident," which she says allows her "to make history by studying at an historical campus."

J.V. identifies as a young twenty-year-old Mexican American student who barely passed high school. When hearing J.V. describe his troubled academic and behavioral history in high school, I was quite shocked. J.V. was a former student in my anthropology course who thrived. While nearly every student considers this course to be difficult due to theoretical perspectives, reading and writing requirements, and the geographic regions covered, J.V. easily earned the highest grade in the class. He credits his success at MXC to a change in mentality. As a North Sider, when J.V. finished his neighborhood high school with a C- grade point average, he chose not to attend Wright College with his friends. His father told him to work for the Chicago Fire Department and to get a certificate at MXC in the EMT program.

When he enrolled at MXC, J.V. not only pursued the paramedic program, he thrived in all subjects and became a super star in Phi Theta Kappa. He believes his high school teachers just did not care about him and racially profiled him. Likewise, he subconsciously lived up to socially constructed stereotypes. J.V. credits anthropology as opening his eyes to the realities of social constructs, whereby he was able to break the mold and live up to his true potential. He thanks MXC for giving him a chance and for not seeing him as just a statistical demographic.

A.M. is an artist and student who has taken a nontraditional route toward earning a bachelor's degree. After spending more than three years as an undergraduate at an out-of-state Big Ten school, she returned home to Chicago without her BA. She enrolled at MXC to earn a few credits that could be transferred back to her Big Ten school once she has the financial means to do so, or she may complete her BA at a university in the Chicago area. A.M. studies because she wants to learn as much as she can. In her twenties, she is not pressured to complete her degree and get a job as much as she feels she needs to learn how the system works in order to change it.

During the focus group, A.M. and K.S. expanded on their reading of Michelle Alexander's *New Jim Crow* (2010) citing references to the school-to-prison pipeline, police monitoring in our public schools, high drop-out rates of Black and Latino high school students, and the dismantling of community bonds that build stable neighborhoods and strong families. A.M. has transferred to a suburban four-year college and hopes to complete her BA soon; however, she is truly grateful for the time she spent pursuing African American studies at MXC. She believes she could have never learned as much about her own Black heritage in the cornfields at her Big Ten out-of-state university.

U.S. was born and raised in Nigeria. After completing anthropology and other courses at MXC, he has been accepted into a BA program in a related applied social sciences program. He began in fall 2013. C.C. grew up living between Mexico and the United States, working as a farmer and English teacher before settling in Chicago. Both U.S. and C.C. are about forty years old with a great deal of global knowledge. They easily earned grades of A in a difficult anthropology course. C.C. chose to come to MXC because of her conversion to Islam and her repeated readings of *The Autobiography of Malcolm X*. While C.C. lives near Daley College, she chose to come to MXC because of the name of the great civil rights leader. C.C. feels a great deal of responsibility to the world around her to be an agent for change. U.S. and C.C. were able to use their years of experience and deep knowledge as group leaders in their Anthropology classes. They both expressed disappointment as brilliant college students who had to work with students who refused to read for the group assignments.

They both revealed that they feel some of their group members are lazy, do not know how to think critically, and are not serious students. C.C. and U.S., as students who pay out of pocket, feel that students on financial aid who do not study disgrace the name of Malcolm El-Hajj Malik El-Shabazz. C.C. realizes that the problem is systemic and begins with structural changes to the American educational system, which marginalized and gave up on J.V. because of his Hispanic heritage. U.S., D.H., J.H., K.S., and A.M. believed the structural problems we see in the American educational system begin at home with parents teaching their children how to read, write, and value education.

T.P., C.H., and T.F. are gifted students who took African American studies at different times. A young man in his thirties, T.P. expressed that he was wrongfully incarcerated and went through a personal transformation while in the penitentiary. He became an autodidact who read three books every day. He told me his regime of reading one book for one hour, transitioning between texts each hour. At the end of the week, all three books had been read cover to cover, and he could check out three new books from the prison library. T.P. proved to be the top student in his section of African American studies, often finding himself bored by the slower pace of most students. C.H. is now finishing her BA in African American studies and public relations and communications at Columbia College. As the top student in her section of African American studies, C.H. became fascinated with African American studies.

C.H. credits Black Studies with giving her the confidence to move forward in her early thirties, while giving her the knowledge often denied in the public city and suburban schools she attended from kindergarten through twelfth grade. T.F. shares C.H.'s belief that knowledge is hidden from African Americans in order to "keep us from succeeding in this system." Like most others, she chose to attend MXC because of the dedication of the instructors and because of the name of the legendary leader. T.F. became emotional when she revealed she has been cheated from knowing her Black heritage. If she had known better, she admits she could have "taught my children and my grandchildren better." In her fifties, T.F. is a strong and determined student who took African American studies to educate others about Black heritage. Her dedication was contagious in the classroom; the same can be said of C.H. and T.P.

Finally, M.R., a nineteen-year-old Mexican American female student, admits that she has not taken any courses in social sciences but plans to pursue African American studies or anthropology in the future. She hears many positive reports from peers about these courses and how they come to broaden students' thoughts about the world. She realizes that while racial politics dominate Chicago's neighborhoods, she needed to move beyond nearby Daley College, where many of her high school friends attend, in order to study at MXC. In high school, M.R. wrote a paper on the Black Panther Party and felt empowered after doing her research. This activity left an impression, which she feels led her to enroll at MXC after high school. She embraces the diversity of the campus and loves working with "professors who actually care about you. They are so great! I am so blessed. This [attending MXC] was the greatest decision of my life."

Conclusion: Teaching at Malcolm X College

In the three years that I have been fortunate to teach African American studies, anthropology, and social sciences at MXC, I have come to form my own unique style of critical teaching and learning, building upon the philosophies of Paulo Freire, bell hooks, Henry Giroux, Ngugi wa Thiong'o, Frantz Fanon, and others. In my efforts to cross borders and teach for critical transformation, my teaching philosophy involves a metacognitive engagement with great Black books that produce deep thinking. As students offered during the focus group, and often in classes, my own engaged teaching method connected to critical texts empowers students who come to possess schema that can be activated in daily life for transformation of self and community. Reconnecting with one's ancestry, history, traditional cultural knowledge, and epistemologies empowers the individual and adult learner systematically marginalized within hegemonic ontologies of domination and exclusion. Overall, I can say that I am thankful for the chance to contribute to the legendary homeplace of Malcolm X College, as a transformative cultural worker breaking down barriers and building minds for future generations of community agents, actors, learners, and leaders.

NOTE

1. Students gave their permission to have their names used in this report; however, I chose to only use their initials.

WORKS CITED

Alexander, Michelle. 2010. *The New Jim Crow: Mass Incarceration in the Age of Colorblindness*. New York: New Press.

Buresh, B. 1971. "The College Where Failure Isn't Allowed." *Boca Raton News*. September 2.

Del Zotto, Augusta. 2004. "Gendercide in a Historical-Structural Context: The Case of Black Male Gendercide in the United States." In *Gendercide and Genocide*, edited by Adam Jones, 157–71. Nashville: Vanderbilt University Press.

Fanon, Frantz. 1963. *The Wretched of the Earth*. Translated by Constance Farrington. New York: Grove Press.

Freire, Paulo. 1970. *Pedagogy of the Oppressed*. Translated by Myra Bergman Ramos. New York: Continuum.

Giroux, Henry A. 2005. *Border Crossings: Cultural Workers and the Politics of Education*. 2nd ed. New York: Routledge.

hooks, bell. 1990. *Yearning: Race, Gender and Cultural Politics*. Boston, MA: South End Press.

——. 1994. *Teaching to Transgress: Education as the Practice of Freedom*. New York: Routledge.

Hurst, Charles G., Jr. 1970. "Malcolm X: A Community with a New Perspective." *Negro Digest* 19, no. 5: 30–38.

——. 1972. *Passport to Freedom: Education, Humanism, and Malcolm X*. Hamden, CT: Linnet Books.

Johnson, Willie. 2013. Interview conducted by Edward Davis. April 23.

Karenga, M. 2000. "Black Studies: A Critical Reassessment." In *Dispatches from the Ebony Tower: Intellectuals Confront the African American Experience*, edited by Manning Marable, 162–70. New York: Columbia University Press.

O'Brien, Dennis. 1996. "Ulysses Duke Jenkins, Retired Assistant Dean at Northwestern." *Chicago Tribune*. September 10. http://articles.chicagotribune.com/1996–09–10/news/9609100011_1_mr-jenkins-ife-african-american-church.

Poinsett, Alex. 1970. "Dr. Charles G. Hurst: The Mastermind of Malcolm X College." *Ebony*, March, 29–38.

Rogers, Ibram H. 2012. *The Black Campus Movement: Black Students and the Racial Reconstitution of Higher Education, 1965–1972*. New York: Palgrave Macmillan.

Taylor, Edward. 2008. "Transformative Learning Theory." In *New Directions for Adult and Continuing Education: Third Update on Adult Learning Theory*, edited by S. Merriam, 5–16. San Francisco: Jossey-Bass.

wa Thiong'o, Ngugi. 2009. *Something Torn and New: An African Renaissance*. New York: BasicCivitas Books.

West, Cornel. 2001. *Race Matters*. New York: Vintage Books.

Williams, Jakobi. 2013. *From the Bullet to the Ballot: The Illinois Chapter of the Black Panther Party and Racial Coalition Politics in Chicago*. Chapel Hill: University of North Carolina Press.

An Education of Positive Youth Development
Challenged by Street Culture

Carl S. Taylor, Pamela R. Smith, and Cameron "Khalfani" Herman

In 1997, Robert Little, Malcolm X's brother, addressed issues concerning African American youth in urban environments. This discourse was during a meeting about how to best provide positive youth development especially for young African American males. Mr. Little, who was an executive administrator in the Michigan Department of Social Services, reflected on Malcolm X's opinion that the gender-separate education model for the Nation of Islam (NOI) Schools was a good model for African American communities in Detroit. The contents of their model underscored a positive youth development application tailored specifically for youth in urban environments.

Robert Little had not been a member of the NOI; however, he was in agreement that the NOI did have an applicable model for urban youth. He stated that Malcolm did not want him to join the religion as some of his siblings were members. This discussion was purely about being able to meet the dangerous lure of the street life that Malcolm experienced during his early life (Taylor 1997). El-Hajj Malik El-Shabazz (formerly Malcolm Little, and aka Malcolm X) was a symbol of positive youth development that emanated from his engagement with a deep history and sociology of the distinctiveness of black American community in his life's work. Malcolm especially focused on the underclass, working class, middle class, and youth.

In his autobiography he underscored the importance of youth development in the African American community. With a focus on street life, his biographical analysis provides an understanding of the ecological environment, a critical component in addressing the needs of the urban community. His bountiful knowledge of the history and mores of African Americans played a key role in his life's work. Malcolm experienced the plight of African Americans in rural, suburban, and urban black communities early in his life. He knew of the mosaic landscape that both black scholars and writers have revealed so well. Alice Walker's *The Color Purple* (1982), Langston Hughes's poetry (Hughes and Bontemps 1970), W. E. B. Du Bois's *The Souls of Black Folk* (1968), Kenneth Clark's *Dark Ghetto: Dilemmas of Social Power* (1989), and Richard Wright's *Native Son* (1969) all vividly describe a black community's challenge in America. The conflict between street life and youth culture depicted in these Black Studies scholarly works is not new.

Historically, African American youth have been entangled with street life. Malcolm considered the ghetto, slums, and red-light district to be a Third City, a term that we use to represent the underground and underworld fusion that manifests itself in micro and macro socioeconomic networks. Third Cities of the genre that Malcolm grew up in are societies that African Americans utilize to survive unfair and discriminatory treatment by the dominant culture. Within the definition of the Third City is the concept of street (i.e., a place outside of the traditional culture), which is part of both underground and underworld social and economic networks.

Then—and now—the Third City offered an oasis, refuge of relief, humanity, and self-government for the people who were unable to receive these benefits from the governing society. Within the subculture/substructure of street life, street entertainment is often marginalized by crime. The mainstream society is not the determining voice inside the communities plagued by poor housing, low wages, and other aspects of poverty. Voices are based on third city values and beliefs from the perspective of those living, working, and creating a life outside the mainstream.

Though never using the term himself, in his autobiography, Malcolm X warned America about a Third City. Malcolm spoke of a ghetto filled with injustice, un-employment, and resentment toward the mainstream society (Malcolm X 1965). Malcolm understood what many American leaders, including other Negro leaders, failed to understand about the ghetto. It is the neighborhood communication system, the means by which the enslaved African was able to be human on his/her terms, that gave a slave the ability to engage in a sense of choice, freedom, and humanity during those times. It is where Africans from different nations, villages, and tribes learned to forge a life to exist and resist the rage against the inhumanity of their daily existence in an alienated and isolated foreign land.

The Midwest—especially Michigan—framework of Malcolm's early childhood shaped his understanding of what African Americans faced in American society (Malcolm X 1965). Malcolm's family—the Little family—suffered the social and economic realities of being African American in the twentieth century. During Malcolm's childhood, adolescence, and young adult life, he experienced the double standards forced on his family, friends, and blacks in general by White America (Malcolm X 1965). Thousands of black families found their lives complicated by racist policies that were instituted by a nation that had yet to fully transition from slave ownership to accept African blacks as American citizens (Morris 1984).

Grounding its analysis in the context of the Third City, the current chapter illuminates Malcolm X's advocacy for African American youth development, black community improvement, and overall more humane treatment of black people. Our objective is to demonstrate how it is that many African Americans in Malcolm's experience continue to be anchored in daunting social and economic conditions creating unattractive behavior, attitudes, and practices not in accord with the strong southern Christian tradition typical of that era.

Critical by nature, Malcolm understood the shackles of being labeled delinquent early in his childhood (Malcolm X 1965). The proverbial good versus bad was attached to the tradition of the "good Negroes versus bad Negroes" syndrome, and even worse was the troubling problem of the African race that carried the striking burden of being considered a less than desirable malcontent. At a time of losing his father, the family was dismantled, and being placed in a detention center did little for his self-esteem. The depth of poverty was great for the Little family after Rev. Earl Little died mysteriously.

The revelation of Malcolm struggling as a young boy just to have food connects too many people in the world and America. Unfortunately, today many black youth are driven toward a hard, resentful reality of hopelessness, poor education, and criminality by the same oppressive treatment from society at large (CDF 2007). Families and children like Malcolm find themselves outside of society due to an array of events and circumstances, which are predicated by race, class, and gender, as exemplified by Louise Little. Her sudden change of life impacted her mental health.

Without her husband her life became excruciatingly painful and difficult. While traditional youth developmental theories addressed white youth, there were no such theories that considered youth of other ethnic backgrounds. The social worker rationalized the decisions of the Little family as anomic after Rev. Little died. What authorities saw was a young mother overwhelmed by her social circumstances, with young children that were severely handicapped by the family's misfortunes. Life in the greater Lansing area proved hard for the Little family, much like many other Negro families across the nation at that time.

It is noticeable as Malcolm spoke of hardships that he is able to pinpoint when he found his survival in delinquency that led to his removal from his female-headed household. Louise Little was a strict disciplinarian for her children. The rules that governed the Little family correlated to traditional African American life founded in the tenets of black southern Christians. While life was challenging with Earl Little as the family patriarch, it was his death that made everything worse for his family. The disintegration of black families proved to be particularly difficult for children and served as a contention within Malcolm's protest.

The state of Michigan provided a variety of experiences for Malcolm, who spent his childhood and adolescence in Mason, East Lansing, and Lansing, and additionally in Kalamazoo to visit his mother in an institution for the mentally ill. He identified Michigan social services as the culprit for wrecking his family's stability (Malcolm X 1965). His life experiences, in particular his early childhood, troubled adolescence, and incarceration as a young adult, contributed to his ascension into an iconic spokesperson for the NOI and further development as an African American, Pan-African activist and leader (Malcolm X 1965). Today, the conflict of street culture and youth in the black community can be reviewed by a great deal of Malcolm El-Hajj Malik's analysis. In his role as spokesperson for the NOI, Malcolm X knew the pitfalls of street life and its perils for blacks.

The current chapter explores the challenges of "street culture" that has always presented a force to recognize, respect, and reject for many blacks. The streets have been a symbolic alternative to the more traditional, black Christian values and belief system. Malcolm Little's transformation into Malcolm X began in prison. Closer examination reflects upon a road that still exists today in America for many African American youth with dysfunctional families, poverty, foster care, inferior education, and crime. Minister Malcolm's life questioned how the traditional black community engaged with or ignored youth culture unless it fit with the black majority Christian value system (terms). During the course of this analysis of Malcolm's influence and impact on the Black community, the traditional youth development role of good boy and good girl finds defiance by the street codes that include crime.

This chapter explores the complexity and mixed messages within black life during Malcolm Little's human development including what influenced him early on and how his life was shaped beginning in Omaha in 1925. Before he became Detroit Red, Satan, Malcolm X, and El-Hajj Malik El-Shabazz, growing up in Michigan, Malcolm Little encountered W. E. B. Du Bois' notion of a duality of consciousness (DuBois, 1968). The puzzlement of being Negro, Nigger, colored, good, bad, American, and hustler confounded Malcolm as it did many at that time.

The chapter is divided into four sections that evaluate how Malcolm's life experiences shaped his message for young black Americans: (1) Street Roots, an in-depth look at the dichotomy of Malcolm's upbringing in rural and urban areas; (2) Street Transformation, Incarceration, and Youth, on Malcolm's time in foster care and juvenile detention after his father's death; (3) Female: Street versus Nation, Good Girl versus Bad Girl; and (4) a concluding section on Cultural Factors Divided by Generations.

Street Roots: Collective, Individual, Country, and City

Southern black youth learned from the assault on the black community, known as segregation—a phenomenon punctuated by Jim Crow laws—that they were to obey, fear, and respect. Youth development in the African American community was extended beyond the nuclear family to include community folks. The Negro church historically spearheaded this leadership (Morris 1984). Malcolm Little learned early of that leadership with his father, Earl Little, a Baptist preacher. His autobiography begins with early memories of the Ku Klux Klan terrorizing his then pregnant mother in Omaha, Nebraska. That incident of horror influenced Malcolm's idea of segregation. In his autobiography the memories of how poorly African Americans were treated in America became reality for Malcolm as a young child. The premise of full, equal citizenship in a democracy was untrue for countless Negro families in the United States in 1925. The Little family left Nebraska and relocated briefly to Milwaukee before finally landing in Michigan (Malcolm X 1965).

Ironically, in 1920, Michigan had the largest Ku Klux Klan membership in America. Malcolm learned as a child, like many African American youth and their families, of the challenges that African people had suffered since their arrival in America (Malcolm X 1965). While Malcolm's childhood was in the 1920s and 1930s, a time of segregation and racial injustice, his father left a strong impression on his son. Today, the concept of "street" is usually compared, defined, and applied to urban communities. Over the years, in literature, the word "street" has shared different perspectives (Anderson 1990; Oliver 2006). The cultural strain of being acceptable and worthy of American citizenship was upon the black community with the proclamation of freedom by President Lincoln.

Historically, there were many codes, laws, ordinances, and policies that were designed primarily to control African Americans (Dinnerstein and Jackson 1987). Blacks suffered an inferior status with the exception of a few free Africans upon the birth of the United States. The Black Codes, Jim Crow, *Dred Scott* ruling, voting tolls, and a separate movie house served as daily reminders of the unwritten rule for black folks not to forget your place in America (Morris 1984). Later, as a national spokesman for the NOI, Malcolm X would give the story of the house nigger versus the field nigger to dissect the divided conflicts of being a slave on a plantation.

The early days of slavery also left a deep psychological scar on many Africans in the Americas. This concept of good Negro versus bad Negro arose out of the life of slaves, some obedient and some disobedient during their captivity. Slave scholarship displayed how rebellious slaves and antisocial behavior manifested itself with some leading to serious uprisings, violence by insurgents seeking revenge, and freedom from an oppressive slave system (Styron 1967). Their captors, unlike slavery in Asia, Africa, and Europe, went out of their way to assure the dismantling of all former cultural collectiveness, individual homeland connections that slave owners feared could lead to uprisings, coups, rebellions, and even large-scale revolution by their African slaves.

To reconstruct their lives in America, Africans mixed cultures and languages to form a new system of communication. The invasion of Christianity was only the beginning of being assimilated by their new masters in America. All Africans were burdened with knowing their slave owners' culture first and foremost (Davis 2006; Thomas 1997). For the purpose of their survival, necessity gave way to finding other means to create a culture that would allow them to endure the hideous inhumanity provided by their slave masters. The birth of another culture under the suspicious and watchful eyes of the slave owners was nearly impossible (Davis 2006; Thomas 1997). While most slaves seemed obedient, ruled by fear and brutality, there were others who learned to meet in the secretiveness and darkness away from the dominant culture. Slaves became resourceful in their ability to create a sense of social life under the guise of entertainment for their masters. Many so-called good slaves formed lines of communication, with intelligence about their owners. It is here that an underworld and underground network took root to allow the slaves some sort of independence. Taskmasters managed slaves; some slaves were used as enforcers, working as interpreters of the different tribal cultures that existed even after the cultural cleansing. Political actions of slave owners would label some slaves as troublemakers from their deeds within the slave circle of networks.

The term "country" described an African who was colorful, a bit of an outlandish type with a demeanor of emulating what he/she believed to be fashionable yet missing the mark of being acceptable by a more conservative black tradition. House servants were taught to dress better, with hand-me-down clothing from the owners. An automatic elitism came with the social divide, labeling house versus field slaves. Those in servitude in the house would be exposed to better conditions compared to the harsh physical conditions of fieldwork, which included brutal overseers who used violence as a tool to keep the slaves in order. The field slaves were cast as Philistines (Davis 2006; Thomas 1997). The class divide found the field workers dressed in shabby, torn clothing that allowed field hands to look upon the well-dressed house servants with both envy, resentment, and jealousy. The field servants ate whatever the plantation management provided, which was rather substandard compared to the leftovers from the table of the slave owners. The house servants had a unique connection within the infrastructure of the plantation/slave system.

The casting of the country Negro began in those days of slavery, remained as the slaves became free, and followed into the network of survival of the African American community. American society had its own interpretation for the label "street" that seemed to parallel the segregated world of colored folks. Author Alice Walker in her profound, controversial story of fiction *The Color Purple* brought the postslavery days into light with the remaining struggle of male versus female roles in the Negro southern Christian tradition. Walker gave an excellent account of the struggle and divide within the African American Christian southern value system. The character of Suge Avery shed light on the country versus city images that shaped blacks historically leaving the south for a better life up north. Suge Avery is a controversial character that exemplifies the attraction of the Jezebel image, trademarked by a rowdy, unchristian lifestyle that the urban fast life portrayed. The juke joint image painted a portrait of liquor, sex, and profanity secluded in the privacy of the woods due in part to the mores of the Christian church, closely guarded by the pastor.

While black preachers promised an afterlife of reward, the devil promised an immediate reward in the juke joints and nightclubs up north. In many ways it was the classic war of good versus evil (Walker 1982). Youthful Malcolm Little was drawn to the streets much in the way that black youth are still attracted to the streets in more current times. Zoot suits, illicit sex, smoking cigars and cigarettes, drinking hard liquor, playing numbers, gambling, and participating in the underworld was the work of the devil according to the moral base of black Christians. America had its early boomtowns and mining camps in which racial lines were well drawn for not only blacks but also other minority groups such as Asians, Latinos, and Europeans. Yet none of these other ethnic minority groups that entered America had the inhumane experience as a slave that Africans did. Self-esteem, self-worth, and more are part of the whole question of images that arose from their hellish appointment in North America (Davis 2006; Thomas 1997).

Historical issues of how blacks had internal conflict, poor education, isolation, and neglect due to slavery were revealed in different academic reports (Davis 2006; Thomas 1997). E. Franklin Frazier discussed the internal conflicts in *The Black Bourgeoisie* (1997), along with Carter Woodson's *Miseducation of the Negro*, which underscored the struggles black folks found after slavery (Woodson and Cummings 1996). The term "city" was cast as the counterpart to "country" in the Black southern Christian tradition. During an interview with a group of elders in Detroit, the discussion about country versus city slick paralleled that of the good Christian versus a risqué, adventure-seeking sinner. The pastor was the spokesperson in most matters during slavery and postslavery days in the south. Malcolm's father was a pastor and avid Garveyite. The black church's rhetorical fire and brimstone coupled with the self-determination of the Garvey Movement was the bed of Malcolm Little's childhood.

The comparison of country living and city life often found its way into popular culture as it was incorporated into the messages of artists in various genres. In the controversial musical *Porgy and Bess* the images were outlined clearly in the story, with the character Sporting Life depicting the slick city hustler type compared to the more innocent, naïve, country boy of Porgy vying for the love of Bess. Iconic musical genius Stevie Wonder's song "Living for the City" is a story of how innocent blacks from the southern tradition were tricked upon entry into New York City (Wonder 1973). It is here that the image of the city player took root in the south.

Early on we see Malcolm Little transforming as he was influenced by the streets of New York, Boston, and Detroit. Urban centers shared street culture within the complexities of separate worlds of blacks and whites where an unequal social and economic condition in the colored neighborhoods was the fabric into which America was sewn together (Brown 1999; Wright 1969). Malcolm's early childhood days in East Lansing, Lansing, and Mason, Michigan, may have contributed to his image, influenced by his "country" disposition, which was akin to being somewhat unsophisticated. It was clear in his autobiography that he was acutely aware of the status of clothing, hairstyles, and materialism that working allowed individuals to have. His story, depicting the difference between New York City, with a strong cultural presence of music, sports, and nightlife, and other black communities cast the divide of country versus city dwellers in the black community (Malcolm X 1965).

Filmmaker Spike Lee captured the visual of a young zoot suit–wearing Malcolm in his mode as Detroit Red in the cinema depiction of *Malcolm X* (1992). In one encounter Malcolm, wearing the loud-colored full regalia of suit, two-tone colored shots with a big rim hat, bumped into a bar patron who was dressed more in black mainstream tradition. The man was enraged and went on to curse Malcolm including a description of Malcolm being a "country nigger type." This encounter exploded violently with Malcolm rebuking the man's assertion that he was a country bumpkin. Furthermore, Malcolm reprimanded him with a violent burst to never talk of his mother in a disrespectful manner.

Reflective of the autobiography of Malcolm's experience, the challenge, isolation, and rage of a young black male allowed Malcolm X the Muslim spokesperson a street connection to black youth. He understood Harlem youth; he knew the language, symbols of street hustling, and street science. Malcolm's childhood, adolescence, and young adult life had exposed him to the juxtaposition of small rural towns like Mason, Michigan, to Lansing/East Lansing, which fell in between rural and urban, and larger cities such as Boston and Detroit. Both race and class in midsized cities like Lansing segregated all of his early experiences. "Negro" status regulated itself within a social infrastructure that whites, mainstream America, knew little about. The duality in which blacks developed began in that necessity to survive upon entering this nation as slaves. Black life found street (outlaw) culture and language as a means to live and communicate without their oppressive masters knowing that street life was a world where dignity, status, and independence existed despite the masters' world of slavery, denigration, and misery (Brown 1999; Malcolm X 1965).

Street Transformation, Incarceration, and Youth

The street is the communication system where many disconnected African Americans live daily. It is the social institution where families, youth, and many adults historically make their lives since mainstream society has marginalized their existence. Malcolm Little as a young boy discovered a drastic change in his life with the death of his father (Malcolm X 1965). Louise Little, Malcolm's mother, found herself with a young family in need until a harsh state welfare ruling dismantled her family (Malcolm X 1965). The dilemma of many African American youth historically has been in the intermixing of juvenile detention, foster care, and incarceration (Taylor 1996). While Louise Little's life unraveled upon her husband's death, the myriad of challenges with her being thrown into the role of head of the family and single motherhood failed to take into account that a young Malcolm's sudden behavioral problems were rooted in his drastic family change. As he began acting out, by cheating, stealing, and fighting, there were obvious signals that Malcolm was attempting to express his grief and call out for help.

Malcolm was taken out of his family home and placed in a juvenile detention facility that was a large home run by a family. The Little siblings were not all taken from the home, which may have been puzzling and punitive for a young boy who would still see his siblings in different homes in the same community. His description of how he was treated as a young boy leading into his adolescence provided an all too common story in America for young black boys. The incarceration system begins early with juvenile detention in the guise of youth homes. For many, incarceration begins early on with confinement in youth homes. This systemic routing is the foundation of a gateway into adult prisons (Edelman and Smith 1980; CDF 2012; Taylor 1996). Malcolm Little's transition into Detroit Red was propelled by the lessons he learned early from the dominant culture. Here, he watched as good citizens—"good Negroes"—struggled for position and status within the mainstream society.

That struggle underscored a lifelong battle that culminated in the civil rights movement (Morris 1984; Malcolm X 1965). In general, the black community was encompassed in second-class citizenry, which was higher in social standing than any low-wage members of the Third City. In prison Malcolm's rebirth was facilitated by his transformation into the NOI.

The NOI, under the leadership of Elijah Muhammad, became the lone beacon for many incarcerated men and women. Ironically, the transition of Malcolm Little to Detroit Red to Malcolm X reveals the role of religion and the manifestation of new relationships with other religions besides the southern Christian that was led by the Baptist and A.M.E. churches. This new relationship connected to youth culture played a significant part in youth development, while Islamic values and mores of the NOI based on similarity was equally identical to black southern Christian values (Taylor 1997).

El-Hajj Malik El-Shabazz, aka Malcolm X, often reflected on his youthful days that included incarceration as a juvenile and adult and poignantly sought to address young people as critical members of the black community. This point is important even today as urban youth are still disproportionately represented in both juvenile detention and adult penal institutions (CDF 2012). There are socioeconomic issues such as violence, teen unemployment, homelessness, dysfunctional families, and inferior public education plaguing urban communities and youth today as they did when Malcolm chronicled them in his autobiography. The warnings and analysis about the significance of street life is part of the legacy of his leadership.

Female: Street versus Nation, Good Girl versus Bad Girl

Various voices of leadership in Harlem spoke of urban youth over the years. Malcolm X addressed the different dimensions of the strain created by the traditional good versus evil divide in black youth culture in Harlem. One dimension was the racial divide of white versus black underscored by the unprecedented youth involvement during the civil rights movement's fight for just social conditions. Malcolm had the innate ability to sense racial inequality because he knew race well, but there was a class divide within black families that was blurred by black Christian leadership that had women in secondary roles such as the Negro Housewives League of Detroit, so aptly described by historian Darlene Clark Hine (1997).

Black female leaders existed in select positions, and Malcolm was part of the male leadership that dictated the roles that black women were allowed to fill. Malcolm knew Harlem youth, but it was essentially black male youth that were on the verge of defying the traditional black leadership in politics and the church. Ironically, there is not a great deal of information about the role of black females in Harlem when Malcolm spoke of the tension between different factions, mainstream Negroes and black youth. Male dominance anchored both formal and informal structures including street culture.

Black girls and women were in the center of the good girls versus bad girls debate.

They were acceptable as mothers, teachers, a few businesswomen, and nurses, such as Betty Shabazz prior to marrying Malcolm (Hine 1997; Rickford 2003). On the other hand, there were the street images of prostitutes, exotic dancers, drug addicts that were indeed bad girls, fast girls, "hoochie coochie" females, as they were called in song by iconic black entertainer Cab Calloway (Calloway and Rollins 1976; Shipton 2010). Theologian-scholar James Cone discussed the era of the black women's role for both Rev. King and Minister Malcolm in his classic *Martin and Malcolm and America: A Dream or a Nightmare* (1991). Both men despite their religious differences shared similar views about the role of women in the community.

The role of black women in black leadership was emphasized by the likes of Ida B. Wells, Mary Bethune Cook, Daisy Bates, Ella Baker, and Fannie Lou Hamer, with Rose Graggs in Detroit having a personal relationship with the first lady, Eleanor Roosevelt (Capeci and Wilkerson 1991; Hine et al. 1990; Ransby 2003). This critical leadership of black women did little to tell us what the role of black female youth was in those heated, tense moments when Malcolm encouraged black youth not to riot in their protest and unhappiness against the injustice of white America.

Later we find the female protest against black male domination from the likes of Black Panthers Elaine Brown (1992) and Kathleen Cleaver (Cleaver and Katsiaficas 2001), writer Alice Walker (1982), and writer Michele Wallace (1990). In the NOI the role of females existed with Clara Muhammad who headed the education and social grooming of Black Muslim girls and women (Rickford 2003). The big question was Malcolm's understanding of urban youth and how that included or isolated black female youth. When he spoke of the deadly hustler from the ghetto in his autobiography, where, if it existed, was his thinking about women and black female adolescents?

Malcolm's mother shaped his view of women early in life, as she struggled with domestic violence, racial injustice, mental health, poverty, and the death of her husband. After his mother faced the dilemma erected by his father's murder, he found a multidimensional challenge in the dissolution of his family. Malcolm had his older half-sister to guide his life during his transition from Malcolm Little to Detroit Red to Malcolm X, and finally to El-Hajj. His viewpoint on good girl versus bad girl was given depth due to his association with the dark side of street culture. Malcolm's experiences with pimping, number running, and interracial relationships and his familiarity with street women shaped his outlook later in life as a Muslim man. The encounters young Malcolm had with street women combined with his knowledge about the Muslim faith identified the qualities he believed to be womanly and appropriate. He held the belief that a woman, especially a Muslim woman, should dress, speak, and act a certain way in order to best represent herself, her family, and her faith. Beyond his ideas of a woman's general behavior, it is apparent that Malcolm did not shun women from participating in the movement, but he did limit their involvement. In fact his wife, Betty Shabazz (formerly Betty Sanders), met him after attending several of his lectures and later joined the Nation before building a family with Malcolm.

It appears as though Malcolm valued the role of women in the home, as mothers, wives, and caregivers, a concept that could be traced back to his own experiences with his mother. One could argue that he believed a family's strength was in part greatly dependent on the female's ability to nurture. In search of Malcolm's message for young black women, the answer may indeed lay in his relationship with his own wife and six daughters.

Concluding . . . Today? Cultural Factors Divided by Generations

Hip-hop is a dynamic and evolving form of cultural expression that attempts to describe the experiences and struggles of a generation of marginalized urban youth (Chang 2006; Clay 2003; George 1998; Kitwana 2002; Rose 1994). During his tenure as a black leader, Malcolm X was able to use the knowledge he gained in the streets of Detroit and Boston to heighten his ability to relate and connect with young blacks. Part of his aptitude for reaching young audiences was Malcolm's familiarity with the cultural and artistic movement that often manifested itself in the music of the times. The bebop tunes of the 1940s jazz movement provided the musical accompaniment to Malcolm's days as Detroit Red in Harlem and Boston before his incarceration. Malcolm was an avid fan of musical artists like Billie Holiday, Sonny Greer, and Lionel Hampton whose music played in Boston's Roxbury dance hall where he worked as a shoe shiner during his teenage years (Malcolm X 1965). Hip-hop enthusiasts today recognize the impact of bebop on the rhythm and rhyme style of rap music.

One can find a variety of bebop sampled throughout the hip-hop genre. Malcolm X understood the significance of cultural movements found in art and music as they paralleled the social movements in the surrounding communities. Black youth have traditionally had a strong connection to the music of their generation; whether it is bebop or hip-hop, the spirit of the music reflected the spirit of the people. Malcolm was able to use his knowledge of this connection to reach a younger audience with his messages about social change beyond his religious platform. Although a significant part of Malcolm's legacy is his role in the spread of Islam throughout the country, he was also responsible for influencing youth in various dimensions.

Malcolm's teachings of Black nationalism, independence, and superiority led to a positive rise in the self-esteem of black youth. Malcolm's legacy continued in popular culture, solidifying his messages and image as a black leader for decades after his assassination. The iconic image of Malcolm X emerged again in the late 1980s and early 1990s in connection with such hip-hop artists as Public Enemy and the film adaptation of his autobiography, *Malcolm X* (Lee 1992). His influence on the youth population did not end with his death; Malcolm's teaching continued to impact young people across the world as the youth of his era became the leaders of today.

WORKS CITED

Anderson, Elijah. 1990. *Streetwise: Race, Class, and Change in an Urban Community*. Chicago: University of Chicago Press.

Brown, Claude. 1999. *Manchild in the Promised Land*. New York: Touchstone.

Brown, Elaine. 1992. *A Taste of Power: A Black Woman's Story*. New York: Pantheon Books.

Calloway, Cab, and Bryant Rollins. 1976. *Of Minnie the Moocher and Me*. New York: Crowell.

Capeci, Dominic J., and Martha Frances Wilkerson. 1991. *Layered Violence: The Detroit Rioters of 1943*. Jackson: University of Mississippi Press.

CDF (Children's Defense Fund). 2007. "America's Cradle to Prison Pipeline® Report." Washington, DC: Children's Defense Fund. http://www.childrensdefense.org/child-research-data-publications/data/cradle-prison-pipeline-report-2007-full-lowres.pdf.

———. 2012. "Portrait of Inequality 2012: Black Children in America." Washington, DC: Children's Defense Fund. http://www.childrensdefense.org/child-research-data-publications/data/portrait-of-inequality-2012.pdf.

Chang, Jeff. 2006. *Can't Stop, Won't Stop: A History of the Hip-Hop Generation*. New York: Picador.

Clark, Kenneth B. 1989. *Dark Ghetto: Dilemmas of Social Power*. Middletown, CT: Wesleyan University Press.

Clay, Andreana. 2003. "Keepin' It Real: Black Youth, Hip-Hop Culture, and Black Identity." *American Behavioral Scientist* 46:1346–57.

Cleaver, Kathleen, and George N. Katsiaficas, eds. 2001. *Liberation, Imagination, and the Black Panther Party: A New Look at the Panthers and Their Legacy.* New York: Routledge.

Cone, James H. 1991. *Martin and Malcolm and America: A Dream or a Nightmare.* Maryknoll, NY: Orbis Books.

Davis, David Brion. 2006. *Inhuman Bondage: The Rise and Fall of Slavery in the New World.* New York: Oxford University Press.

Dinnerstein, Leonard, and Kenneth T. Jackson, eds. 1987. *American Vistas.* New York: Oxford University Press.

Du Bois, W. E. B. 1968. *The Souls of Black Folk: Essays and Sketches.* New York: Johnson.

Edelman, Marian Wright, and Paul V. Smith. 1980. *Portrait of Inequality: Black and White Children in America.* Washington, DC: Children's Defense Fund.

Frazier, Edward Franklin. 1997. *The Black Bourgeoisie.* New York: Free Press Paperbacks published by Simon & Schuster.

George, Nelson. 1998. *Hip Hop America.* New York: Viking.

Hine, Darlene Clark. 1997. *Hine Sight: Black Women and the Reconstruction of American History.* Bloomington: Indiana University Press.

Hine, Darlene Clark, Beverly Guy-Sheftall, Adrienne Lash Jones, Beverly Washington Jones, Dorothy C. Salem, Mildred I. Thompson, and Vicki L. Crawford. 1990. *Black Women in United States History.* Brooklyn: Carlson Publishing.

Hughes, Langston, and Arna Wendell Bontemps, eds. 1970. *The Poetry of the Negro, 1746–1970.* Garden City, NY: Doubleday.

Kitwana, Bakari. 2002. *The Hip Hop Generation: Young Blacks and the Crisis in African American Culture.* New York: BasicCivitas Books.

Lee, Spike. 1992. *Malcolm X.* Warner Bros. Pictures.

Malcolm X. 1965. *The Autobiography of Malcolm X.* With the assistance of Alex Haley. New York: Ballantine Books.

Morris, Aldon D. 1984. *The Origins of the Civil Rights Movement: Black Communities Organizing for Change.* New York: Free Press; London: Collier Macmillan.

Oliver, William. 2006. "'The Streets': An Alternative Black Male Socialization Institution." *Journal of Black Studies* 36, no. 6: 918–37.

Ransby, Barbara. 2003. *Ella Baker and the Black Freedom Movement: A Radical Democratic Vision.* Chapel Hill: University of North Carolina Press.

Rickford, Russell John. 2003. *Betty Shabazz: A Remarkable Story of Survival and Faith before and after Malcolm X.* Naperville, IL: Sourcebooks.

Rose, Tricia. 1994. *Black Noise: Rap Music and Black Culture in Contemporary America.* Hanover, NH: University Press of New England.

Shipton, Alyn. 2010. *Hi-de-ho: The Life of Cab Calloway*. New York: Oxford University Press.

Styron, William. 1967. *The Confessions of Nat Turner*. New York: Random House.

Taylor, Carl S. 1996. "Growing up Behind Bars: Confinement, Youth Development, and Crime." In *The Unintended Consequences of Incarceration: Papers from a Conference Organized by the Vera Institute of Justice*, 40–65. New York: Vera Institute of Justice.

———. 1997. Author (Carl Taylor) Interview with Robert L. Little at Kellogg Hotel, East Lansing, Michigan.

Thomas, Hugh. 1997. *The Slave Trade: The Story of the Atlantic Slave Trade, 1440–1870*. New York: Simon & Schuster.

Walker, Alice. 1982. *The Color Purple: A Novel*. New York: Harcourt Brace Jovanovich.

Wallace, Michele. 1990. *Black Macho and the Myth of the Superwoman*. London: Verso.

Wonder, Stevie. 1973. "Living for the City." *Innervisions* (album). Detroit: Tamla (Motown).

Woodson, Carter Godwin. 1996. *The Mis-Education of the Negro*. Grand Rapids, MI: Candace Press.

Wright, Richard. 1969. *Native Son*. New York: Harper & Row.

A Detroit Black Panther's Soldiering Journey with Malcolm X

Extract Memoirs from an X Heir

Ahmad A. Rahman

My story shadows Malcolm's. I was a leader in the Black Panther Party in Detroit and sent to prison in 1971 after an FBI investigation. A victim of COINTELPRO, I spent twenty-one years behind bars, earning my bachelor's degree and becoming the first prisoner ever admitted to a graduate program at the University of Michigan–Ann Arbor. Having earned a PhD in history, I am now an associate professor of history at the University of Michigan–Dearborn. I write through the current chapter a snippet of an autobiography of my own to reveal how Malcolm's journey was my own. Like Malcolm's, it was a journey of discovery to consciousness of the Black condition; it is a story that illustrates my resistance to White supremacy. Most importantly, my story parallels Malcolm's as an example of liberation through defiance to racist systemic oppression. Like Malcolm's, my own mini autobiographical extracts selected for this important volume documenting my hero's legacy straddle between Detroit and Chicago's urban Black communities and histories.

My path to prison began with Malcolm X and what I had heard he had said black people should do after the Ku Klux Klan bomb murdered the four little girls in the 16th Street Baptist Church in Birmingham, Alabama, on Sunday, September 15, 1963. If posttraumatic stress syndrome colors a life thereafter, post–Birmingham bombing anger colored mine. I was twelve years old, in the same age group as

Addie Mae Collins (age fourteen), Carol Robertson (age fourteen), Cynthia Wesley (age fourteen), and Denise McNair (age eleven). I had spent the very same Sunday morning in my family's Antioch Baptist Church on Chicago's South Side. These girls likely enjoyed riding bikes, going to school, and playing in parks just like I did. They were me.

When the *Jet* magazine my mother bought detailed their slaughter, I searched it for strong statements from black leaders that offered something more forceful than prayer to prevent more Sunday morning bombings. As usual, Dr. King had called for us to remain nonviolent and not lose faith in the white man. We could only defeat hate with love. Hate could never defeat hate, he said. When my friends and I got together soon after the bombing, for the first time we talked about something other than baseball, football, and child's play.

This was also the first time that I had ever disagreed with Dr. King. He was a living saint to everybody I knew. I remember saying that I thought that only monsters could blow up those girls and monsters deserved a stake in their hearts. My playmates, all Baptists like the four murdered girls, nodded in agreement. Like me, they kept seeing themselves in that church blown up with those girls. Some of us even had nightmares and woke up scared and sweaty. Dr. King's soft words left me feeling helpless and vulnerable. I never saw a black leader on TV who believed, like us, that Dracula deserved the stake.

Then one day my mother's friend, Miss Toni, came to visit. While my mother fiddled in the kitchen, the nut-brown-skinned, blond-haired Miss Toni sat on the couch with me on one side of her and my older brother Eddie on the other. She told us that she had attended a meeting at the Nation of Islam (NOI) Temple in Hyde Park in Chicago, Illinois. There she had seen a man named Malcolm X. He said that since the government would not protect our children from being blown up in churches and our people from being murdered by the Klan, it was time for black people to form their own army. That army should go south to protect our people from KKK murderers. Hearing her say this made me almost feel like crying. At last some black leader had said what I wanted to hear.

Malcolm X had told her that our black army should not go south singing and marching, as if the songs would hurt the racists' ears and marching would hurt Klan feet. No, we should go south with the intent to fight fire with fire. And then we would see that anybody who would bomb a church and murder four innocent children was nothing but a low-down coward. We made these cowards look strong by our acting weak. Show them the true strength of the black man and they will run like roaches in the light. I felt the same way, but did not have the ability to say it like Miss Toni said Malcolm X had. I saw black people on TV getting spat on and having dogs attack them without fighting back. I saw them act as if the song "We Shall Overcome" contained magic words that would turn real bloodsucking vampires like Bela Lugosi human. I did not believe it.

Now I knew a leader who did not believe it either. I swore that day that whenever Malcolm X formed his army, I would march in their ranks. I did not care if they only let me carry water or stir grits. I would run away from home, school, baseball, and all that was my childhood to march in that army. In my mind, only the Army of Malcolm X would save black children from KKK murderers and Alabama Governor George Wallace's curly lipped hate. I would rather die fighting in Malcolm X's army than helplessly and nonviolently accept them treating black people worse than dogs in the south.

Convincing Me Who Had Killed Him

On February 21, 1965, the evening TV news announced that gunmen had shot Malcolm X dead at the Audubon Ballroom in Harlem. My mother paused to stand and stare at the image of Malcolm on the screen. It was the worst photo of him I had ever seen. It looked like they had doctored the photo to make him almost look like a monkey. The background was so dark and gray that his dark gray skin on the black-and-white TV almost blended into the background. "I knew they'd kill him," Mom said. Who "they" were I assumed was The Man, the Ofay (pig Latin for foe), the devil, the antichrist, the anti-Muslim, the proracism, the pro–Vietnam War. I assumed immediately that his killers were white men. For no black man could have gunned down our commander. He had dedicated his life to uplift his people, and none of his people would, could, kill our champion.

Later newscasts announced that New York policemen had arrested members of the so-called Black Muslims for the murder. I still could not believe black men could have pulled a trigger against Malcolm X. So thoroughly did he dedicate himself to his people that to kill him would be akin to killing one's own brother or father. A white man surely killed him. But little misgivings started leaking into my mind when I remembered a conversation with my father more than a year before. Over delicious greasy hamburgers at my dad's favorite restaurant, he looked around to make sure nobody was listening and began. "I know you are interested in the Nation of Islam. I see you not wanting to go to church." "Uh oh," I thought. "I gotta pay for this burger by listening to a sermon." But sermonizing was not Dad's way. He taught by example. He was known as a good-humored, generous Christian gentleman, and he liked that description. When he walked down the street, bums in the neighborhood would race to reach him first to ask for the change in his pockets. "Dad, why give a wino a quarter for his next bottle?" I asked once. The bums had nicknamed him "Easy," because of how easily he gave handouts without preaching or questioning.

Dad looked around the restaurant to make sure nobody could hear him. Then over cheeseburgers and fries, he confided in a low, secretive voice, "You know that one of my partners from the old neighborhood is a high up captain in the Nation of Islam." Whenever Dad mentioned a friend from the old neighborhood I knew he meant a member of the gang that he had led before World War II. They still gathered now and then to rehash war stories from the Chicago streets and the battles against Hitler and Hirohito. The fight against Germany and Japan was *The War*. To me, instead of B.C. and A.D. they marked time by BW and AW—before World War II and after it. America had fought in Korea, and now fought in Vietnam, but for them the war they helped win was the only war. Every one of them had served in the army when they said colored soldiers had to watch their backs because white soldiers hated them and watch their fronts because enemy bullets loved them. Over beers at one of their old hangout taverns, the high up captain had confided this to my dad, "Elijah Muhammad's got his followers not getting any poontang, but he's getting all the young girl poontang in the world. He's got some of his secretaries knocked up. Nobody knows it. But stuff could leak out and hit the fan."

I knew Muslims were not supposed to drink. But Black Muslims didn't always do what they were supposed to do. I reasoned that people called them Black Muslims because they practiced a separate Islam that Allah had designed exclusively for Black people and not Arabs. Hence Dad's descriptions of his beer-drinking meetings with his old friends who were in the NOI never disturbed me. But I did not think the Messenger of Allah, the Honorable Elijah Muhammad, would be climbing out of the same escape hatch that relieved the pressure on Christian ministers. I carried a higher image of Mr. Muhammad. He was Allah's (not Jesus's) chosen champion to lead the so-called Negro out of four hundred years' wandering in the wilderness.

If ever there were a black Superman, he was the Honorable Elijah Muhammad. He was pure of all that was afflicting the black man and woman. He only ate one meal every day or one meal every other day. He did not drink or smoke. His superhuman, divine intelligence elevated him as the example of what we would become when we left the white man's world and joined the lost-found Nation of Islam. When everybody else in Black America wanted to answer to "colored," or "Negro," he boldly asserted that we were Black. He proclaimed that no other name was more noble than Black man and Black woman. In his book *Message to the Blackman* he taught us about the true Good Samaritan:

> The so-called Negroes fell into the hands of the slave-masters, who have robbed, spoiled, wounded and killed them. The Good Samaritan here would be the Mahdi (Allah)—God in Person, as He is often referred to by the Christians as the "the second coming of Jesus," or the Son of Man to judge man. This one will befriend the poor (the so-called Negroes) and heal their wounds by pouring into their heads knowledge of self and others and free them of the yoke of slavery and kill the slave-masters, as Jehovah did in the case of Pharaoh and his people to free Israel from bondage and the false religion and gods of Pharaoh. (Muhammad 1965, 27)

Dad's words stung. Surely he was just saying this to keep me Christian. I ran to the Messenger's defense. "But, Dad, Muslims can have more than one wife." "Hah! Wife? He isn't married to but one woman. Those other women are girlfriends, you know, poontang on the side." I finished my greasy, cheesy burger, and Dad asked me if I was full or wanted another. We agreed to split one. Dad switched conversations while we waited for the third burger to finish cooking. We talked about the Chicago White Sox and the Cubs' stars Ernie Banks and Billie Williams and what great seasons they were having. I have forgotten what else we discussed. But I never forgot what Dad said about Mr. Muhammad. Therefore, when my mother said she knew "they" would kill him, I halted the mental train that rushed pell-mell to blame the monolithic white man.

Now I read in the newspapers and heard on the news about Minister Malcolm's split with Elijah Muhammad. All the accused assassins were members of the NOI's quasi-military Fruit of Islam. They had been soldiers in the official Army of Malcolm X while I was still waiting for Malcolm's army to go south to join. People questioned why the captured assassins killed him. Apparently, as my dad predicted, news about Mr. Muhammad's other women had spread in the media because Minister Malcolm had turned against the Honorable Elijah Muhammad. Nevertheless, I had stuffed my life so full of adolescent pursuits of skirts, getting high grades in school, playing football and baseball, and the growing excitement of gang life that I had totally missed hearing or reading anything about the Messenger's sex scandal.

I occasionally bought a *Muhammad Speaks* newspaper from the bow-tied NOI members. Even still, I had never read a word about Minister Malcolm splitting from the Nation and the Messenger. My commander's death blindsided me, as did the ensuing public discussion about his being on the outs with the Messenger. Before Minister Malcolm's death, to me the NOI was a domain of complete goodness. Malcolm's death made it a domain of complete confusion.

When I bought a Qur'an I searched in vain for the holy words describing the black man as God and the white man as the devil, as the Messenger taught. Neither did I locate Yacub's test tubes where he created by an ancient grafting process the white man from the black man. I bought the book *Malcolm X Speaks* and, for the first time, began to read Malcolm's actual speeches. I could track his development from "Old Testament" separatist, nationalist Malcolm, who repeated all the teachings of Mr. Muhammad, to "New Testament" internationalist, revolutionary Malcolm. Alex Haley's *Autobiography of Malcolm X* crowned my Malcolmist education. Nevertheless, brutal police beatings and killings of black men continued in the north. Attacks on churches and civil rights activists continued in the south. This unchecked violence made me believe more than ever in Malcolm X's vision of a black army to protect our community. We needed this army for self-defense. Even though he was no longer alive, I still regarded myself as a soldier in the Army of Minister Malcolm X.

I Am a Malcolm X Soldier Now

Mama Irwin walked through her backyard tossing handfuls of corn to her chickens. Aunt Dilla had driven off in her orange car on an errand. I searched the kitchen drawers for the shotgun shells. I found them in a box in the pantry. I took five shells, one for each Klansman and an extra if I missed. I hid them in two white socks in the dresser in my bedroom. The news that evening was full of the violence of some Jewish establishment bombed and civil rights workers assaulted. These victim reports had become the norm for my Mississippi relatives. They only made them sigh and affirm the social healing and protective power of Jesus. My faith was in the knife that I slept with in my fist. I awoke myself in the middle of the night and ran to the front porch and grabbed the shotgun. Cub Scouts and Boy Scouts had taught me that practicing is a higher level of preparation. I aimed the shotgun from my hip through the porch screen and blasted Klansmen before their cocked arms could throw firebombs and dynamite. I practiced reloading and blasting them again as they rushed toward the porch to "Emmet Till" me. I shot them till their hawk faces burst into flames.

Satisfied with my war preparations, I returned the shotgun to its place on the porch. I tossed in bed, changing from each uncomfortable position until I fell asleep with my mind alert for an engine or voice telling me that the Emmet Tillers were back. After all, if Mama Irwin and Aunt Dilla would not protect the house, then the duty fell upon me as the only Malcolm X soldier present. Besides, their small town southern smarts were neither a match for the KKK's murderous intentions nor capable of detecting my war plans. They would not know till the shooting started that not Jesus but five shells, a shotgun, a knife, and a Malcolm X soldier protected this house.

My faith was in a gun and a knife that I believed would cast Ku Klux Klan demons into hell where they belonged. Anyway, my relatives were country and I was city. Geography preset my ability to think a step ahead of them. They could continue following Dr. King. I would continue my secret gun preparations, beyond their knowledge, as a soldier in the Army of Malcolm X. I expected the Klan to return because they knew they had failed to scare Aunt Dilla into stopping the presses. I expected that next time they would not just stare. When nobody was around, I rehearsed attacking the Klansmen as soon as they drove up. I strategized to hit them before they could light their firebombs or dynamite. I practiced blasting them before they had time to fire their guns.

Days later I heard the shrill, alarmed voice of Mama Irwin. "Ronnie!" My heart leapt. Was it the Klan or chicken hawks? I rushed to the dresser to grab my five shells out of the drawer. The two socks I had hidden them in were stacked neatly. They were empty. I clutched my knife in my pocket to make sure it was there. "Ronnie come shoo these hawks away from my chickens. Git some rocks and chuck em at em." Shoo? Rocks? Chuck? As I hustled out the screen door I glanced over my shoulder. The shotgun was gone, too. My great-grandmother stood by the side of her house with her hands on her hips watching me. I didn't see any chicken hawks. "Oh, that's okay, baby, they gone." But chicken hawks did not move out of sight that fast. They swooped higher in wider circles. How could they have flown away before I ran to the yard? And what happened to the shells and the gun? I walked past Mama Irwin back into the house. I noticed her half smirk, as if something funny had occurred and she was trying not to laugh. I scanned the four corners of the porch. No shotgun. I returned to my bedroom and opened the dresser drawer. I ransacked it for the shotgun shells. Nothing.

Confusion, bewilderment, fear, anger—all these feelings and more tried to rush through the door of my mind and got bunched up at the opening. All the mental and emotional space was already filled with wonder at how Mama Irwin and Aunt Dilla had discovered my plans. I also wondered why they never mentioned the shells. I waited for Mama Irwin to take her afternoon nap. Making sure Aunt Dilla and no civil rights workers were near the kitchen, I opened the pantry door to see if the shells were still there. Some square cans of cream of tartar, nutmeg, and black pepper, and round cans of baking power now filled the space where I had found the shells. During the next couple days I searched the whole house with a stealth and thoroughness that would have impressed a cat burglar. I never found shotgun or shells. My great-aunt and great-grandmother never mentioned them and neither did I. That made me feel as outwitted and cornered as the chicken that ran into a corner in the coop to escape a neck wringing.

I did not, however, accept defeat. I took seriously my duty to protect the house, even if they only wanted divine protection. Aunt Dilla assigned me the job of mowing the lawn. One day I poured some of the gasoline meant for the lawn mower into an RC Cola bottle. I stuck a rag in the top of the bottle. I hid a box of matches beside the bottle in a corner of the chicken coop behind a wooden crate the chickens roosted on. Now at night I mentally rehearsed running to the chicken coop, lighting the Molotov cocktail, and flinging it at the Emmet Tillers' car. I would set them aflame so they entered hell already burning. For the remainder of the sizzling, scorching hot Mississippi summer, whenever Mama Irwin called the Malcolm X soldier to chuck rocks at chicken hawks or fetch eggs, he responded, "Yes, ma'am," in his most obedient, mannerly, and respectful voice. But he did not pour the gas out of the pop bottle into the lawnmower until the day before he caught the New Orleans train back to Chicago.

In Chicago, We Are the Heirs of Malcolm

Back in Chicago, teenage friends and I came to conclusions about America. *They* were flooding our communities with cheap dope to kill our freedom struggle. The comedian Dick Gregory said *They* pushed birth control pills on our women to genocide us now that we didn't want to be their slaves, but when we were their slaves they wanted us to produce a million babies for them to sell. We agreed. *They* shipped thousands of our brothers off to Vietnam to get rid of the aggressive and fearless black man. *They* sought to leave in America only a bunch of Negro sissies who would follow their passive puppet, Martin Luther King Jr. *They* would use every medicine to keep him alive to keep black people practicing nonviolence in the United States while, as Malcolm X taught, we inflicted the utmost violence overseas in wars against brown people who never lynched us. *They* promoted Dr. King as their hand-picked Negro leader.

Yvette Stevens (later Chaka Khan) and my friend Fudd (called that because his head was shaped like that of the cartoon character Elmer Fudd) brought back word to our neighborhood that followers of Malcolm X had formed a branch of the Black Panther Party in Chicago. The leader's name was Fred Hampton. His charisma and fearless dynamism drew me into the work of the party in Chicago as a community worker. I started selling the *Black Panther* newspaper and feeding children free breakfasts in church basements and socal halls. I read through the Panther reading list. There I engaged the ideas of Karl Marx, Vladimir Lenin, Mao Tse-tung, Frantz Fanon, Kwame Nkrumah, Che Guevara, and Amílcar Cabral. Reading these revolutionaries, after studying black history and literature, honed my view of the whole world.

I saw Huey P. Newton and Bobby Seale, the cofounders of the Black Panther Party, as the best examples of the living legacy of Malcolm X. Self-defense was our policy as nonviolence was the policy of the late Martin Luther King Jr. His assasination in April 1968 told us all that whether we were for self-defense or were nonviolent, the forces that hated us wanted us dead. Our stance on violence was not as important as the ideas we promoted that challenged the triple-headed monster of capitalism, racism, and imperialism. Huey P. Newton had written our tribute to Malcolm in his essay "In Defense of Self Defense." Huey wrote:

> In our time, Malcolm stood on the threshold with the oppressor and the endorsed spokesmen in a bag that they could not get out of. Malcolm, implacable to the ultimate degree, held out to the Black masses the historical, stupendous victory of Black collective salvation and liberation from the chains of the oppressor and the treacherous embrace of the endorsed spokesmen. Only with the gun were the Black masses denied this victory. But they learned from Malcolm that with the gun they can recapture their dreams and make them reality. (Hilliard and Weise 2002, 41)

Fellow Detroit Panthers elected me to the detail that protected Huey when he came to Detroit in November 1970. I felt greatly honored by their confidence in my abilities to assure that no harm came to our leader. In a hotel room in Ann Arbor, Huey and I briefly discussed Malcolm's influence on his and Bobby's founding of the party. Surprisingly Huey did not speak of ideology. He did not mention any of Malcolm's speeches. He spoke first of family. Malcolm X did not have any sons; he had six beautiful daughters. We were his sons. That is what he meant when he referred to us as the "heirs of Malcolm X." We were the heirs of Malcolm's ideas, his courage, his implacable spirit, his fearless embrace of the gun. The same gun the white man loved so much that he had a whole association, the National Rifle Association, just to worship the gun.

Once Huey got to going, his mouth was a waterfall for words. Black people had been forbidden to bear arms to protect themselves as slaves. Then Reconstruction laws forbade them to protect themselves from killer night riders. Most black people accept being victims of white racist gun violence from the police and any other person who is white. "Shoot them in the ass and they will turn the other butt cheek and take a bullet in it too," he said. I laughed. Black men were expert marksmen overseas when they wanted us to shoot their enemies. But when confronted by racist pigs in America, we were afraid to touch the gun like Superman is afraid to touch kryptonite. Malcolm overcame that fear. Like the great Robert F. Williams in Monroe, North Carolina, he showed us that only our fear fuels our enemies' courage. Now our courage fuels their fear.

My conversation with Huey ended sooner than I wanted. I had to stand guard in the hallway to make sure no police knocked down the door and murdered Huey like they did comrades Mark Clark and Fred Hampton in Chicago. Before enemies reached Huey they would have had to get past me and comrades Nine Millimeter and Thirty-eight Special.

I Am Detroit Red

1970: I walked out of the office of the National Committees to Combat Fascism on Mack and Baldwin Streets in Detroit. I balanced on my shoulder a painfully heavy box containing over one hundred copies of our newspaper, *The Black Panther*. I remembered after I walked three blocks toward the bus stop that I had left my wallet behind. I stopped. My wallet held my draft card. Walking down the street without it during the Vietnam War was evidence I had defied the government threat of years in prison and a hefty fine by not registering for the draft. I had registered, except that under the question about whether I am a homosexual I had written that I am both a homosexual and a lesbian. I also proclaimed membership in the nonexistent "Communist Black Revolutionary Viet Cong." I hoped this nonsense would keep me out of the draft without my having to go underground or flee the country. Muhammad Ali spoke for me too when he refused entry into the army because no Viet Cong ever called him nigger.

The police had no computers in their cars back then to check a computerized database that did not yet exist either. Without the draft card, the police could arrest me on the probable cause of the federal crime of draft evasion. They could keep me locked up until, at their leisure, they called the selective service system for confirmation of my draft registration. I never walked out of a house or office without that card. I had seen the police stop young people of all races just to finger through their wallets for their draft cards. Not having it gave them an extra excuse to hassle you. By 1970 the selective service was not so selective. It controlled the draft that fed the future dead into the Vietnam meat grinder. They selected most men who were poor, working class, not in college or politically connected, and had a pulse. Many war resisters burned their draft cards. Scores of thousands of resisters escaped to Canada, Sweden, France, and other countries that welcomed them. I never saw any black men burning their draft cards. Our skin color already gave cops probable cause to hassle us for breathing while black. It was foolish for us to not carry a draft card and give them evidence we were actually committing a federal felony. I debated whether to return to the office and get my card. The box of papers was awfully heavy and I was nearly at the bus stop. So I kept walking. As I was about to cross the street to the bus stop, a police squad car pulled up to the curb in front of me, blocking my path. Two cops got out of the car and demanded a search. I set down the box on the sidewalk and let one of the cops pat me down. Before he had even finished feeling all my pockets, he asked with a grin, "Where's your draft card?" I could not conceal my surprise at the question. I immediately wondered if he knew that I did not have my wallet. I wondered how he could know. Surely the police had not planted an agent in our office who informed them so quickly that I had left my wallet behind.

"You're under arrest for violation of the Selective Service Act," the cop said, as he racked the handcuffs closed on my wrists behind my back. No right to remain silent. No talk about an attorney being provided for me if I could not afford one. TV police give Miranda rights. In real life police rarely tell black men of their rights. After they get incriminating evidence from black men, though, cops will routinely testify in court that they read them their Miranda rights as soon as they touched them. The relationship between white authority and black males is loaded with baggage both have carried since the first white authorities abused black men on African shores. This relationship falls under the same laws that governed command and obedience during the Middle Passage—none. Cops and black men know that they dwell together in a zone of lawlessness. Most Americans watch TV cops act heroic and compassionate toward black people and think this behavior reflects reality. They do not know that words like justice and truth do not exist in many police minds when they confront black men. Police only think control, control, control. The Black Panther Party advocated resistance, resistance, and resistance.

I jerked my head down toward the box of Panther papers. A picture of Huey P. Newton looked up from the box. "My papers," I said. "Shut up," the cop said as he pushed me onto the backseat of the squad car. Then he got in beside me. This was unusual and rarely seen. Both cops routinely stayed in the front seat. I knew then I might be in for what Panther gallows humor called "a good time." The cop behind the steering wheel turned around and stared at my eyes. "We've caught us a red-eyed nigger," he said. My eyes were indeed red from lack of sleep and a bottle of apple wine. Basic self-defense required our never letting the foe get away with calling us niggers without responding. That slur was a punch in our brains. We had to counter that punch to ward off the intended mental damage. "And you are a gray-eyed oink!" I spat out the last word so forcefully that I actually sounded like a pig.

The cop beside me took out of his pocket a hand-sized flapjack. That was a piece of lead stitched in a leather pouch with a handle. He flapped the lead down hard on my knee. Sparks of pain shot through my entire leg. "Here's some more power to the people," he said, lifting the flapjack to hit me again. I jerked my leg down to try to take the blow on my thigh. The pain was just as bad. "Power to the people!" he shouted with a laugh. I remember feeling strangely thankful that he did not knock out my teeth with the flapjack. Detroit cops were notorious for bloodying defiant black mouths. They wanted their victim to regret not submitting to white power for the rest of his life every time he gummed or dentured his food.

At the next stoplight the driver turned around again. Perhaps he felt the flames of anger shooting from my red eyes. Maybe he knew that I had just left an office that stored an arsenal including sniper rifles with scopes and large-caliber hunting guns that could drop huge deer. He might have heard that we had boxes of armor-piercing bullets. Possibly it dawned on him that he had to continue patrolling this neighborhood when and if I got out of jail. He ordered Officer Brutality to stop the beating.

"That's enough," he said. "He's gonna wind up dead or doing life anyway." They both laughed. They booked me in the Gratiot Avenue police station lockup. One thing about going to jail always was the same for me. It allowed me to catch up on my sleep. Within a few minutes I was snoozing on the cold iron bed.

It likely was around 3:00 or 4:00 A.M. when the sound of white male voices jerked me awake. Two men in dark suits, white shirts, and dark ties stood in front of the cell. They told the guard, "He's the one. Bring him to the room." The guard nodded. I sat up in the bed. Were they going to beat me to death? Were they going to work the old tried, true, and bloodless—hanging the black man with his belt and testifying that he committed suicide? Half a dozen scenarios swirled in my mind and made me start sweating. Each scenario ended with me dead. I had felt for weeks a premonition of oncoming disaster. No. They were taking me out of the cell. If they meant to strangle the hated Black Panther they would likely use my belt in the cell. Maybe they planned to claim I attempted to escape, which forced them to shoot me.

The guard told me to stick my hands through the bars. He squeezed the handcuffs as tight as he could. He searched my face for pain. I stared into his eyes without wincing from the sting of steel smashing my flesh against my bones. He ordered me to walk in front of him toward a room at the end of a hall. The two white men in suits awaited me. They were as fresh and well groomed as if they had just showered, dressed, and started their day. The strangely tiny room was painted a bright, white color that was not relaxing. A claustrophobe would have panicked when he sat down. He might have submitted to their demands just to get some breathing space. They flashed badges that said "Department of Justice," not "FBI" like we see in the movies. They dropped a sheet of paper in front of me on the tiny table that they said stated that I had been informed of my rights. "Read it and sign it," the older agent commanded. His authoritative voice must have been accustomed to quick compliance. His tone left no room for disobedience.

"I am a black man in America and I know I have no rights," I said, shoving the paper back across the table without reading or signing it. They paused a moment and looked at each other. The older agent must have passed a signal for the younger one to begin the interrogation.

Concluding . . . Reflecting . . . Still Living the Defiant
Symbol of Malcolm

Years later I would discover that their success rate recruiting informers and agent provocateurs justified their certainty. We learned about COINTELPRO too late to save dozens of Panthers from prison and death via the plots of the FBI and their black $75-a-week traitors. If they had slapped me I doubt that I would have felt as insulted as this proposition made me feel. They thought I was a slave they could buy for a measly seventy-five bucks a week. They wanted me to fight with them against Malcolm, Denmark Vesey, Gabriel Prosser, Nat Turner, David Walker, Frederick Douglass, Harriet Tubman, Sojourner Truth, W. E. B. Du Bois, Ida B. Wells-Barnett, Marcus Garvey, Kwame Nkrumah, and Dr. Martin Luther King Jr. They wanted me to sell my own people down the river of bondage. They wanted me to serve them in the big house like a house nigger. They wanted me to snitch on slaves who had the courage to escape. They wanted, no, *expected* me to switch sides. I felt anger welling up in my chest. I just shook my head and said, "I will *never* work for you!"

The Black Panther Party defiance that was now my nineteen-year-old second nature spouted spontaneously, without any conscious reflection, like an uncontrollable geyser, these words that I would have many years to reflect on as the seal of my fate: "*I* will know. And I don't think I can live with the thought of myself as a coward." This statement flew from my mouth quickly and without thought. It came up from some unconscious part of myself I had never before examined. I had never told myself I could not live with the self-image of a coward. When the sun rose that morning the two agents started the ruthless process of labeling me a top-level threat to U.S. national security. First they branded me in the FBI's files. Then they spread this lie as my official image to the Secret Service, Michigan State Police, Detroit Police Department, and other secret police agencies I could not decipher on blacked-out pages.

I had no inkling that choosing death before dishonoring the Army of Malcolm X marked me in all their files as more dangerous than a Russian Communist spy. Their files claimed I was as dangerous as a terrorist saboteur who sought to destroy the U.S. Constitution by force and violence. Neither I nor they said a word about the president in that room. That did not stop them from convincing the Secret Service to classify me as a dangerous potential assassin of Richard Nixon and of all future presidents. To this day if a president visits anywhere near where I live or work, I suspect that I get watched and followed until he has flown away.

In that little white room I did not know how vengeful the devil gets when he invites your soul to his party and you refuse his invitation. Despite the decades of heavy prices I would pay for following Malcolm's example of being implacable to the ultimate degree, not for one second have I ever regretted my refusing to dance with the devil. In the movie *The Shawshank Redemption*, the Morgan Freeman character went before the parole board decades into his sentence and repudiated the dumb kid he was when he went to prison. I went before the Michigan Parole Board decades into my life sentence and I was proud of what I stood for as a teenager. I repudiated nothing.

WORKS CITED

Hilliard, David and Donald Weise. 2002. *The Huey P. Newton Reader*. New York: Seven Stories Press.

Muhammad, Elijah. 1965. *Message to the Blackman in America*. Chicago: Muhammad Mosque of Islam No. 2.

Malcolm X and the Black Campus Movement

Shaping Academic Communities

Ibram X. Kendi

George Breitman, editor of *Malcolm X Speaks*, gave a lecture at a memorial meeting sponsored by the Militant Labor Forum in New York on February 11, 1966. It was almost a year after Malcolm X was assassinated. At one point, Breitman revealed the segment of society in which Malcolm's ideas were "taking root." They were budding "especially among the young people," he disclosed, "those in their twenties and late teens, and younger even than that" (Breitman 1967, 151–52). In 1968, an unidentified white faculty member at Tougaloo College, a historically black Christian college in Mississippi, told a reporter, "Malcolm X is more popular than Jesus Christ here. The students actually worship him" (*The Reflector*, March 19, 1968). By 1969, Malcolm's ideology had blossomed into the booming Black Power Movement, striking "a responsive chord among black people in general, but particularly black youths," Betty Shabazz informed *Ebony* (Shabazz 1969, 173). Two years later, Malcolm still held the mantle as "probably . . . the most quoted of all modern black spokesmen . . . among black leaders of high school and college age," as surmised by *Chicago Tribune* columnist Vernon Jarrett (*Chicago Tribune*, February 21, 1971).

In the late 1950s and early 1960s, Malcolm X, as the national spokesman for the Nation of Islam (NOI), became a national figure through his marathon organizing of NOI mosques, his constant and forceful ridiculing of the southern-oriented, desegregationist, nonviolent civil rights movement, his lambasting of whites as "devils," and the 1959 CBS documentary "The Hate that Hate Produced." He impressed students with his fiery speeches, quick wit, striking analogies, glorification of black people and Africa, and down-to-earth yet scholarly expressionism. However, they were not attracted in mass to his ideology since it was wrapped in NOI theology, which deified Elijah Muhammad, shunned activism, preached a strict moral code, espoused whites as inherently evil, and demanded complete separation of the races.

As each year passed in the 1960s, Malcolm's rhetoric became more secularized and matured politically—with remnants that previously intoxicated students coming to the fore. Consequently, with each year, his appeal to students skyrocketed. In 1964, he not only left the NOI, after a prolonged suspension and life-changing experience in Mecca, dropped NOI theology, became an Orthodox Muslim, and founded the Muslim Mosque, Inc. and the Organization of Afro-American Unity (OAAU), he also began developing and sharing his ideas of black national and international unity, self-determination, self-defense, and cultural pride. The boldness still jumped out of his rhetoric. The logic continued to emanate from his sayings. The love of black people and justice remained. His authenticity and his honesty were as obvious as ever. This fresh ideology struck that responsive chord among black students, particularly after Malcolm's death.

Over the last forty years, the literature on Malcolm X has been saturated with similar assessments about his powerful and lasting impact on black student activists in the late 1960s and early 1970s. In one of the first and few studies on black student activism, Anthony Orum (1968, 80–81) classified Malcolm as one of the originators of the movement. Black student activism was "spurred by the rise of Malcolm X and his assassination," Nathan Hare (1969) asserted. James Turner, a former Northwestern black campus activist, situated Malcolm as "perhaps the single most important influence on black students" (Turner 1969, 135). Malcolm X "greatly influenced the activity of black students," Frederick Harper (1975, 9) wrote. Jeffrey Ogbar addressed Malcolm's impact on "many young people" (2004, 136), and Alphonso Pinkney discussed his "widespread" appeal "among Afro-Americans, especially the youth" (1976, 64). Malcolm's words were reflected in "a younger generation of Black Power militants," Peniel Joseph (2006, 92) ascertained. "Black college students used Malcolm X's ideas as ideological reference points," Donald Cunnigen (1993, 32) posited. Donald Alexander Downs (1999, 4) and Richard P. McCormick (1990, 5) both recognized Malcolm's impact on black campus activists at Cornell and Rutgers, respectively.

Wayne Glasker described the activists at the University of Pennsylvania as the "ideological children of Malcolm X" (2002, 38), while William W. Sales postulated that "by 1967–68, on previously all-White northern and southern campuses, a Black Student movement was born, consciously identified with the thought of Malcolm X" (1994, 169). Even William L. Van Deburg explained that members of Black Student Unions were "greatly influenced by the writings of Malcolm X" (1992, 71).[1]

None of these scholars, however, specifically explored Malcolm's remarkable contribution to black student ideologies during the late 1960s and early 1970s. In other words, this idea of Malcolm's impact has become a generally accepted historical reality, even though there is little in the historiography of Malcolm X that provides an organized base of research for this historical assessment. The scholarship on Malcolm's role in inspiring black students is scattered in a series of studies on a myriad of other topics.

This chapter synthesizes the extant historical literature and, with supplementary periodical and primary research, provides a thorough disclosure of Malcolm's function in the configuration of the ideologies of black students. It divulges the scattering of Malcolm's ideological seeds into the minds of black students through his speaking at numerous colleges and universities in the early 1960s. Malcolm's ideological seeds blossomed during the Black Campus Movement in the late 1960s.

Although the ideas of Frantz Fanon, Dr. Martin Luther King Jr., Mao Tse-tung, Robert F. Williams, Karl Marx, Albert Camus, James Baldwin, and W. E. B. Du Bois, among others, played a role in formulating the ideologies of black students, Malcolm X was the ideological father of the Black Campus Movement. For the duration of the Black Campus Movement, which began in 1965 and ended by 1972, thousands of black students requested, demanded, and protested for a relevant learning experience. Black students crusaded for diversity at more than five hundred colleges and universities in every state except Alaska.

At historically white and black colleges and universities, black campus activists formed politically and culturally progressive black student unions (BSUs) and gained control of some student government associations (SGAs). They utilized these pressure groups to advocate for a range of campus reforms, including an end to campus paternalism and racism and the addition of more black students, faculty, and Black Studies courses and programs. Their ultimate aim was to diversify and thus racially reconstitute higher education (Rogers 2012).

Scattering of Malcolm's Ideological Seeds

Malcolm purposefully sought to impress upon black students his developing ideas by speaking at numerous colleges and universities across America and other sites with student crowds. In the last few years of his life, he forecasted that black youngsters would be in the forefront of any radical mass black rebellion, and by the time of his death they were beginning to make him a prophet. In an interview after he left the NOI on March 19, 1964, Malcolm expressed his "accent will be upon youth" (Malcolm X 1965, 21). Malcolm and his associates by this time had already issued a call for college students around the nation "to launch their own independent studies of the race problem," so an "action program geared to their thinking" could be devised (Spellman and Malcolm X 1964).

At variance with traditional Marxist thought that considered the working class as the faction with the most revolutionary potential, Malcolm positioned black students as the chief change agents. In his speeches, he articulated at least two main arguments for this position. First, Malcolm contended that this "new generation" had less of a stake than adults "in this corrupt system and therefore can look at it more objectively" (Malcolm X 1970, 6). To Malcolm, "adults" in part signified the ostensibly older and conservative civil rights establishment. Second, Malcolm consciously sought to ideologically nurture this "new generation of black people who have come on the scene" because they were "disenchanted" and "disillusioned over the system," and "willing to do something about it." They had reached the point of no return "out of frustration and hopelessness," Malcolm said in April 1964 (Malcolm X 1965, 76).

After traveling to Africa that year, where he was personally and ideologically welcomed by throngs of students at African universities, Malcolm internationalized his pitch to students on November 29, 1964 in the first OAAU rally. "The students all over the world are the ones who bring about a change; old people don't bring about a change" (Malcolm X 1979, 142). According to Malcolm, black students were aggravated and desperate, discontented and cynical, crucially objective, and ready to produce radical change. Deciding to ideologically adopt and nurture this burgeoning mass of rebellious youth, Malcolm embraced as many opportunities as possible to speak to students at colleges and universities in the late 1950s and early 1960s.

He was the second most requested speaker on college and university campuses in the last year of his life behind only Barry Goldwater (Malcolm X 1991, 161). White students too clamored to hear Malcolm X. These hundreds of lectures were critical in the ideological formation of black students, as none of the other thinkers whose ideas shaped their thoughts spoke to them as often as Malcolm X. He reasoned with the students. They were eager to listen. Malcolm served in his most comfortable role as a master teacher, and he "appealed to their sense of justice." As Benjamin Karim, Malcolm's assistant minister, noted, "He invited them to open their minds, to think, to call upon their knowledge and logic in order to see the fallacies of America's past and to imagine its future possibilities" (1992, 128).

Black nationalists and radicals, and those critical of civil rights methods, seeking a new line of thought, were enrolled in America's colleges and universities in the early 1960s. This small but growing band of activists, who would soon reach a critical mass during the Black Campus Movement in the late 1960s, could be found jockeying for clout in SGAs at black colleges, campus chapters of civil rights organizations, and the mainly sociocultural black student groups that by 1966 were politicized. There were also some Black nationalist student groups, particularly those affiliated with the Revolutionary Action Movement. Students were able to use these organizational bases to invite Malcolm X to their campuses.[2] Like BSUs and SGAs in the late 1960s, these early 1960s student groups used their meager funds to bring relevant voices to campus, voices that would arouse, edify, and thrill their peers—voices that would fill seats. Other than James Baldwin or King, who busied himself leading protests and congregations, no voice attracted students more than Malcolm X in the early 1960s.

The "wretched condition" of the seventeen million colored Americans "is the by-product of the hypocrisy which is skillfully cloaked in the disguise of Western Democracy," Malcolm said at the University of Southern California on March 23, 1958 (*New York Amsterdam News*, April 5, 1958). According to Queens College student Gay E. Plair, Malcolm facilitated a "challenging and stimulating discussion" there in 1960, and gave an encore in 1961.[3] In a May 1961 talk at the University of California–Berkeley, Malcolm addressed a multiracial crowd that included Donald Warden and other black students who within a year organized the Afro-American Association—"California's first indigenous Black nationalist organization" that "laid the intellectual foundations for the West Coast Black Power Movement," Donna Murch explained (2010, 71–72).

At the Harvard Law School Forum on March 24, 1961, Malcolm lectured to a record-breaking crowd in the university's largest auditorium. "As your colleges and universities turn out an ever-increasing number of so-called Negro graduates with education equal to yours, they will automatically increase their demands for equality in everything else," Malcolm reasoned, forecasting the coming Black Campus Movement (*New York Amsterdam News*, April 8, 1961). He lectured at New

York University in early 1962, stimulating "countless corridor conversations," and the African American Club asked him to come back later in the year.[4] Malcolm accepted an invitation in 1962 to speak at Michigan State University from Ayo Azikiwe, the leader of the school's African Students Association and the son of the future Nigerian president Nnamdi Azikiwe.[5] Students asked Malcolm to speak, and he usually accepted. So in 1962, he spoke at Harvard, Columbia, MIT, Williams College, the University of Pennsylvania, and Smith College, among other institutions.[6]

Malcolm probably lectured to more black students in 1963 than in any other year.[7] At UC–Berkeley that year, Malcolm indicted white liberals for their "hypocrisy" (*Afro-American*, November 2, 1963). He fielded appeals to inculcate at the University of Chicago, the University of Connecticut, Cornell, and Columbia in 1964.[8] "May I stress how much we would like to have you come and address the union," wrote future presidential candidate and Yale student John F. Kerry to Malcolm. Henry A. Kissinger produced the invitation for Malcolm's speech at Harvard that year.[9]

Many of Malcolm's speaking engagements at colleges and universities in the early 1960s were debates, allowing him to lean on debating skills he had enhanced in prison. In 1962, Malcolm matched up with NAACP National Youth Secretary Herbert Wright for the second time in successive years at City College in an event hosted by the campus NAACP. About three hundred people—seventy-five of whom were black—showed up to hear Malcolm famously declare "it'll take more than a cup of tea in a white restaurant to make us happy" (*New Pittsburg Courier*, March 10, 1961). Malcolm "outclassed" Professor Neal Brown at Rutgers in a debate in 1961 hosted by its NAACP and "awakened and delighted the apathetic and sleeping among us," expressed Rutgers student Edwin Stevens (*Afro-American*, November 18, 1961). Malcolm faced off with historian August Meier at Morgan State on March 28, 1962—an "occasion," student G. Fraser Williams said, that "will surely be recorded as one of the most memorable ones in the history of our . . . campus."[10]

Malcolm's most influential debate was against Bayard Rustin on October 31, 1961 at Howard's Crampton Auditorium. With the fifteen-hundred-seat auditorium filled to capacity, there were five hundred black students outside hoping for extra space. Sociologist E. Franklin Frazier moderated the debate, titled "Integration or Separation." The school's student government and the Nonviolent Action Group (NAG), a Howard organization affiliated with the Student Nonviolent Coordinating Committee (SNCC), hosted the event. "The black man in America will never be equal to the white man as long as he attempts to force himself into his house," Malcolm argued at one point. "The real problem is that the anemic Negro leader, who survives and sometimes thrives off of gifts from white people, is dependent upon the white man whom he gives false information about the masses of black people." Malcolm's captivating performance permanently etched itself in the minds of many attendees. "To this very day, whenever—and wherever—I meet people who were at Howard with us, that is what they seem to remember first," Stokely Carmichael, a member of NAG, explained decades later. For Carmichael, it was a decisive moment in his ideological development. At the time, a "European theoretical context" anchored his political worldview. But what "Malcolm demonstrated that night . . . was the raw power, the visceral potency, of the group our unarticulated collective blackness held over us. I'll never forget it." Malcolm's storied impact led one unidentified professor to tell reporters, "Howard will never be the same. I feel a reluctance to face my class tomorrow" (Carmichael and Therwell 2003, 253, 259–60).

In the last few months of his life in particular, Malcolm increased his rhetorical overtures to black student activists, specifically in the south. At the Hotel Theresa in Harlem on December 31, 1964, Malcolm shared his thoughts with a delegation of thirty-seven teenaged SNCC activists from McComb, Mississippi. Malcolm urged the students not to follow the inactivity of his generation who "sat around like a knot on a wall while the whole world was fighting for its human rights." According to Stokely Carmichael, Malcolm made "a hell of an impression" on these students. "The youth came back elated, just elated, talking about nothing but Malcolm" (Breitman 1990, 137, 139, 145; Carmichael and Thelwell 2003, 440).

On February 3, 1965, Malcolm X spoke to three thousand students at Tuskegee. "I believe in religion, but a religion that includes political, economic, and social action designed to eliminate some of these things, and make a paradise here on earth while we're waiting for the other" (Malcolm X 1992, 22). After leaving Tuskegee, Malcolm traveled over to nearby Selma, Alabama, where members of SNCC had invited him to speak. Malcolm lectured to three hundred young civil rights fighters at Brown Chapel A.M.E. Church, elucidating his famous house Negro and field Negro dichotomy (Malcolm X 1992, 27).

On February 18, 1965, three days before Malcolm was killed, he spoke to about fifteen hundred students from Barnard and Columbia—his last major speech before his ideological children. Malcolm conveyed the fearlessness, the commands for justice and equality, and the flexibility of tactics that all dominated Black Power student activism. "I would rather be dead than have someone deprive me of my rights," he bellowed. Blacks "must take any means necessary to secure his full rights as an individual human being. Our demands are just, and we will use any means to get them" (Malcolm X 1992, 177–78).

Before his death, Malcolm had every reason to believe he had succeeded in one of his final goals—the conscious production of a radicalized mass of black students. He told a Vassar College administrator, C. H. L. Pennock, in 1962 that student groups throughout the U.S. had shown a lot of interest (Malik Shabazz to C. H. L. Pennock, March 22, 1962). In his correspondence with young people, they incessantly noted their allegiance to his views. Robert Johann, a twenty-one-year-old from New Jersey, who had just been diagnosed with an incurable illness, wrote Malcolm, "You have always been a great admirer of mine. I mean every word of this."[11] When he decided to leave the NOI and organize the Muslim Mosque, Inc. and later the OAAU in 1964, students notified him about their willingness to stand with him.[12] Michigan State's Ayo Emeka Azikiwe, who had stayed in touch since Malcolm spoke at his school in 1962, gave Malcolm his "blessing in your new move to uphold the dignity of the black mind."[13]

Effects on the Black Campus Movement

Nothing proved more indicative of the flowering of Malcolm's ideas among black students in the late 1960s than the development of two colleges in his honor— Chicago's Malcolm X College and Malcolm X Liberation University (MXLU) in Durham, North Carolina. The former was renamed after the Black Power pioneer in 1969 and is still in operation as a community college. Malcolm X College, which showcased Malcolm's shiny black Oldsmobile, was established to "serve as a catalytic agent to synthesize the varied components of the community into a viable force for liberation"(Van Deburg 1992, 71, 80–81). Likewise, MXLU formed after black students in North Carolina realized their schools could not address their concerns for a relevant education (*New York Times*, September 14, 1969).

Painted in black on a peach-colored wall just inside the door of the new building for MXLU glistened a Malcolm saying that read this was a school for members of "a new generation of black people who have become disenchanted with the entire system and who are ready now and willing to do something about it." The college opened with fifty-nine students in the fall of 1969 as "a nation-building school, a school for people who want to build an independent African nation and who want to be doing things right now," said Howard L. Fuller, its director (*New York Times*,

October 28, 1969). Malcolm stressed the imperative of "doing things right now," but he was not able to be there physically with the students to aid them in their activism. It would be an understatement to say black students were saddened when Malcolm X was assassinated on February 21, 1965. As Bobby Seale, a Merritt College student at the time of Malcolm's death, begins his memoir:

> When Malcolm X was killed in 1965, I ran down the street. I went to my mother's house, and I got six loose red bricks from the garden. I got to the corner, and broke the motherfuckers in half. . . . Every time I saw a paddy roll by in a car, I picked up one of the half-bricks, and threw it at the motherfuckers. I threw about half the bricks, and then I cried like a baby. I was righteously crying. I was pissed off and mad. (Seale 1991, 3)

Like scores of black students across the country, Andrea Coaxum of Boston University wept as well when Malcolm X died (*Bay State Banner*, September 5, 1968). To deal with their grief, many black students held services and rallies in Malcolm's honor, including at Southern Illinois University and San Francisco State College (*Chicago Daily Defender*, February 25, 1965; Barlow and Shapiro 1971, 84).

With the Civil Rights Act of 1964 and the Higher Education Act of 1965 providing the pressure, black students, some still reeling from Malcolm's death, flooded into America's colleges and universities in the latter half of the 1960s (Hine et al. 2003, 562). These drones of black students were welcomed by the initiators of the Black Campus Movement who enrolled in the early 1960s. Therefore, many of the pioneers of the Black Campus Movement—those students who organized BSUs, radicalized existing black student groups, or took leadership positions in SGAs in 1965 and 1966—were underclassmen when Malcolm went on his collegiate speaking tour, shaping black students' ideologies. For example, Gwen Patton, who became Tuskegee's SGA president in the fall of 1965 and led her student body in demanding and protesting for a relevant education, was moved by Malcolm's speech at Tuskegee in February 1965 (telephone interview, May 16, 2010).

These pioneers and the critical masses of black campus activists forced the diversification of higher education using tactics gleaned from the teachings of Malcolm X. The first tactic of organizing a separate body—a Black Student Union—that could unite black students, advocate, and support their own interests was derived to some extent from the ideas of Malcolm X (Malcolm X 1965, 41). The second decision to call this new organization "black" or "Afro-American" came in part from Malcolm.

The nation's first BSU formed at San Francisco State College in the spring of 1966. James Garrett, one of the organizers of this BSU and a former member of SNCC, remembered he and his comrades specifically chose the term "black" to harness a particular wave of consciousness spreading across America at that time—a wave unleashed by the teachings of Malcolm X. "There was a national consciousness that was developing and consolidating," Garrett said. "Blackness was the new consciousness or the consolidation of a consciousness that came from Malcolm X" (Rogers 2009, 32). Hundreds of student groups in the next few years formed BSUs or renamed existing groups with the term "black" or "Afro-American."

After they organized themselves using "black" or "Afro-American" in new names, many groups issued lists of *demands* to their administrations, particularly at the height of the movement from King's assassination to the end of the spring 1969 semester. "The philosophy of Malcolm X" was "inherent in" the black students' demands, noted Frederick Harper (1971, 401). Many were nationalistic in nature. These students demanded "separate facilities in which to conduct alternative educational and cultural activities," Van Deburg explained. These separate facilities included black living, dining, and meeting areas and autonomous departments of Black Studies to go along with demands for more black students, faculty, coaches, players, administrators, and resources (Van Deburg 1992, 72).

When administrations did not give in to their list of demands, the black campus activists usually in varying degrees decided to "fight for it"—usually the fourth tactical occurrence, again somewhat inspired by Malcolm who said in a speech in London, "If something is yours by right, then you fight for it or shut up. If you can't fight for it, then forget it" (Malcolm X 1992, 53). In their fight, they took over buildings, organized strikes—whatever they could do to force the hand of the administration. The aura of Malcolm X was ubiquitous during these social combat efforts. In one of the first protests of the Black Campus Movement at Howard University in April 1965, black campus activists, compelled by the death of their ideological father, marched on their administration building to protest the autocracy of Howard administrators.

As Jerrold Roy, a chronicler of the Howard movement, explained, "Malcolm X's impact on the Howard student movement loomed larger after his death than when he was alive" (2000, 104–5). In November 1967, Central State's Unity for Unity boycotted classes and picketed in support of the college's nonacademic workers striking for pay increases and life insurance. The students also protested for black history courses with credit and required reading lists, and demanded for Malcolm's autobiography and *Malcolm X Speaks* to be added to the library's collection (*New York Times,*

November 15, 1967; *New York Amsterdam News*, December 2, 1967). In March 1968, when more than twelve hundred Howard students took over their administration building, they gained control of the university switchboard and blasted speeches by Malcolm X and read his autobiography (*New Republic*, April 13, 1968). Days before King's assassination, Cheyney State students, in their demands to change the college "from a Negro institution to a black one," called for "more emphasis on writers like W.E.B. DuBois, James Baldwin and Malcolm X, than Shakespeare and [Henry Wadsworth] Longfellow" (*Philadelphia Tribune*, April 2, 1968). During the infamous Columbia building takeovers in April 1968, black students hung posters of Malcolm and a cardboard sign proclaiming "Malcolm X University, Founded 1968 A.D." outside the main door of the seized Hamilton Hall (*New York Times*, April 29, 1969).

In October 1968, twelve black campus activists at UC–Santa Barbara barricaded themselves inside North Hall, renaming it "Malcolm X Hall," and refused to come out until their eight demands for a more relevant education were met. Also that fall of 1968, when the BSU at San Francisco State held a press conference in early November before its four-and-a-half-month student strike—the longest student strike in higher education history—BSU chairman Ben Stewart credited "Brother Malcolm X, by his courageous life and character," for laying the "foundation for the struggle." In January 1969, sixty-four black students at Brandeis barricaded themselves inside a building, issued their demands, and then draped a huge sheet from a second-story window that displayed a photograph of Malcolm, declaring the building to be part of "Malcolm X University." When they walked out of the building eleven days later, they sported Malcolm X buttons (Karagueuzian 1971, 92–93; Vargus 1977, 105–25).

Down the eastern seaboard a few months later, seventy-five black campus activists, armed with guns and knives, took over the administration building at Voorhees College in South Carolina, and proclaimed the historically black college "the liberated Malcolm X University," plastering the walls with posters of Malcolm and issuing a list of demands, including the establishment of a Black Studies department (*New York Times*, April 29, 1969). In February 1969, more than one thousand students boycotted classes to support a demand for a new college at UC–Santa Cruz to be named after Malcolm X. Later that month, in the early morning at Duke, forty-eight black students entered the administration building, walked to the central records section, told the clerical help it had to leave, nailed the doors shut, threatened to burn university records if the police were called, and renamed the area "Malcolm X Liberation School" (Harris and Honcharik 1969, 30; Kornberg and Smith 1969, 107–9). In 1970, a group of armed black student activists at Columbia seized an abandoned ROTC office and renamed the space Malcolm X lounge. Meanwhile, black campus activists seized an administration building at West Virginia State after college officials refused to name a dormitory after Malcolm X (*Washington Post*, May 7, 1970).

These spaces seized by black students symbolically represented their bold rebelliousness—their displeasure with their irrelevant education. Malcolm X was their personified symbol of bold rebelliousness. Therefore, it made sense they would name these occupied spaces after Malcolm X. It was a tribute to their ideological hero whose words inspired them to claim those spaces to demand a better educational life.

Black Studies became the center of this improved educational life. But before the courses and departments were institutionalized, black students were reading Malcolm in college programs and on their own time. In the summer of 1966, there were 220 government-financed Upward Bound programs to develop their academic skills. In these programs, students read *The Autobiography of Malcolm X* (*Bay State Banner*, August 13, 1966). That fall of 1966, at Wesleyan, black students founded a reading group that peered through *The Autobiography of Malcolm X* (Young 1988, 21–22). In the spring of 1967, his autobiography circulated as one of the two most read books by black students, along with Claude Brown's *Manchild in the Promised Land* (*New York Times*, February 26, 1967).

When black campus activists started winning Black Studies courses in 1967, they used them to systematically study the speeches and *The Autobiography of Malcolm X* (Harper 1975, 10). Black campus activists at schools like City College in New York even read excerpts from his speeches during their meetings (Dyer 1990, 83). If they were not studying his words, then, like their younger brothers and sisters in high school, they were participating in tributes to Malcolm on his birthday or death-day or looking at his posters hung in bedrooms and dorm rooms across America. In 1968, Holy Cross freshman and future U.S. Supreme Court Justice Clarence Thomas became one of the many students to line his wall with an image of Malcolm X (*New Yorker*, September 27, 1993).

Conclusion

Since assassins killed Malcolm X only about a year after he left the NOI, Malcolm did not have enough time to implement his ideas that were so awe-inspiring to students. Through remembering their past encounters with Malcolm, hearing

Malcolm's continuous enunciations of the "new generation" poised to rebel, and reading Malcolm's speeches and autobiography, black students, like other Black Power activists, did execute what they considered to be Malcolm's ideas. They were his "natural constituency" when he was alive and became his constituent legacy in his death. Malcolm X became the ideological father of the Black Campus Movement. When Black nationalism and blackness was king, Malcolm sat on its rhetorical throne. During a time when students regaled authenticity and boldness, they deemed Malcolm the most genuine, the boldest. In an era of standing up to white America and standing for black love, no one appeared to stand higher and stronger than Malcolm X.

For the disaffected, disillusioned, dissatisfied black youngsters across the ideological spectrum, Malcolm draped as their primary mirror for boldness, honesty, confrontational behavior, fearless dedication, unvarying defense of self, black pride, the veneration of Africa, black unity, and the ultimate ability to sacrifice as a martyr. To the youth, no other black ideological formulator could boast so strikingly of *all* of these qualities. "Malcolm was the only figure of that generation, the only one, who had the natural authority, the style, language, and charisma, to lead and discipline rank-and-file urban youth," Kwame Ture said. "The only one who commanded that kind of respect" (Carmichael and Thelwell 2003, 441).

NOTES

1. Also see *Sun Reporter*, December 27, 1969.
2. Some students were denied the ability to bring Malcolm, though. For example, see *Afro-American*, May 20, 1961; *Washington Post*, February 14, 1961.
3. Gay E. Plair to Malcolm X, September 8, 1961, box 3, folder 17, Malcolm Collection; Gay Plair to Malcolm X, September 24, 1961, box 3, folder 17, Malcolm Collection.
4. H. Lawrence Ross to Malcolm X, February 8, 1962, box 4, folder 3, Malcolm Collection; Audrey Johnson to Malcolm X, August 31, 1962, box 3, folder 17, Malcolm Collection.
5. Malcolm X to Ayo Azikiwe, November 10, 1962, box 3, folder 3, Malcolm Collection.
6. See the following letters in the Malcolm Collection: Gerald M. Harris to Malcolm X, September 17, 1962, box 3, folder 8; John Hartman to Malcolm X, February 12, 1962, box 3, folder 17; J. Haywood Harrison to Malcolm X, March 13, 1962, box 3, folder 17; Arthur Lipman to Malcolm X, April 9, 1962, box 3, folder 17; Maher Kamel to Malcolm X, May 17, 1962, box 3, folder 17; Maher Kamel to Malcolm X, July 31, 1962,

box 3, folder 17; N. J. Block to Malcolm X, August 21, 1962, box 3, folder 17; Malcolm J. Arth to Malcolm X, August 27, 1962, box 3, folder 17; Thomas F. Burke Jr. to Malcolm X, September 24, 1962, box 3, folder 17; Robert A. Spivey to Malcolm X, September 27, 1962, box 3, folder 17; Charles Richter to Malcolm X, October 13, 1962, box 3, folder 17; Alexandra Corman to Malcolm X, December 18, 1962, box 3, folder 17.

7. See the following letters in the Malcolm Collection: Hugh Hawkins to Malcolm X, January 29, 1963, box 3, folder 18; Oliver Fein to Malcolm X, February 6, 1963, box 3, folder 18; Edward Pearlmutter to Malcolm X, n.d., box 3, folder 18; Pamela Young to Malcolm X, box 3, folder 18; Sylvester Murray to Malcolm X, April 13, 1963, box 3, folder 18; Richard Fernandez to Malcolm X, April 17, 1963, box 3, folder 18; Mike Thelwell to Malcolm X, July 16, 1963, box 3, folder 18; Robert A. Osofoky to Malcolm X, August 27, 1963, box 3, folder 18; Joseph V. Aprile to Malcolm X, September 1, 1963, box 3, folder 18; Ron Jameson to Malcolm X, September 2, 1963, box 3, folder 18; Morroe Berger to Malcolm X, September 18, 1963, box 3, folder 18; William J. Jacobs to Malcolm X, September 21, 1963, box 3, folder 18; Anthony S. to Malcolm X, September 25, 1963, box 3, folder 18; Phil Brown to Malcolm X, October 3, 1963, box 3, folder 18; Carolyn S. Ensor to Malcolm X, October 9, 1963, box 3, folder 18; E. Boundzeki to Malcolm X, October 10, 1963, box 3, folder 18; William Shedd to Malcolm X, October 18, 1963, box 3, folder 18; Lawrence F. Hull to Malcolm X, October 29, 1963, box 3, folder 18; Anne Donaldson to Malcolm X, October 30, 1963, box 3, folder 18; Robert Coults to Malcolm X, October 30, 1963, box 3, folder 18; Donald A. Goldsmith to Malcolm X, October 31, 1963, box 3, folder 18; Irving Kirsch to Malik Shabazz, November 8, 1963, box 3, folder 18; Christine A. to Malcolm X, October 18, 1963, box 3, folder 18; Joseph R. Washington Jr. to Malcolm X, January 23, 1963, box 3, folder 19; Douglas Harris to Malcolm X, September 23, 1963, box 4, folder 4; Kathryn Edmonds to Malcolm X, October 2, 1963, box 4, folder 4.

8. See the following letters in the Malcolm Collection: Malcolm X to Charles Keil, March 21, 1964, box 3, folder 4; Richard Levinson to Malcolm X, January 8, 1964, box 3, folder 19; William L. England to Malcolm X, March 10, 1964, box 3, folder 19; Jeffrey Cohlberg to Malcolm X, August 14, 1964, box 3, folder 19; Charles J. Graham to Malcolm X, August 18, 1964, box 3, folder 19; Clara Henning to Malcolm X, November 24, 1964, box 3, folder 19.

9. John F. Kerry to Malcolm X, August 15, 1964, box 3, folder 19, Malcolm Collection; Henry A. Kissinger to Malcolm X, June 5, 1964, box 3, folder 19, Malcolm Collection.

10. Meier, August. "The Black Muslims: A Critique," n.d., box 4, folder 3, Malcolm Collection.

11. Robert Johann to Malcolm X, March 15, 1964, box 4, folder 5, Malcolm Collection.

12. Joseph B. Axenroth to Malcolm X, September 23, 1963, box 4, folder 4, Malcolm Collection; Malik Shabazz to Martin Miller, December 6, 1963, box 3, folder 4, Malcolm Collection.

13. Ayo Emeka Azikiwe to Malcolm X, March 25, 1964, box 3, folder 3, Malcolm Collection.

WORKS CITED

Barlow, William, and Peter Shapiro. 1971. *An End to Silence: The San Francisco State College Student Movement in the '60s.* New York: Pegasus.

Breitman, George. 1967. *The Last Year of Malcolm X: The Evolution of a Revolutionary.* New York: Merit Publishers.

Carmichael, Stokely, and Ekwueme Michael Thelwell. 2003. *Ready for Revolution: The Life and Struggles of Stokely Carmichael.* New York: Scribner.

Cunnigen, Donald. 1993. "Malcolm X's Influence on the Black Nationalist Movement of Southern Black College Students." *Western Journal of Black Studies* 17, no. 1: 32–43.

Downs, Donald Alexander. 1999. *Cornell '69: Liberalism and the Crisis of the American University.* Ithaca, NY: Cornell University Press.

Dyer, Conrad M. 1990. "Protest and the Politics of Open Admissions: The Impact of the Black and Puerto Rican Students' Community (of City College)." PhD diss., City College of New York.

Glasker, Wayne. 2002. *Black Students in the Ivory Tower: African American Student Activism at the University of Pennsylvania, 1967–1990.* Amherst: University of Massachusetts Press.

Hare, Nathan. 1969. "Statement By Hare: New Role for Militant Educator." *Sun Reporter,* December 27.

Harper, Frederick D. 1971. "The Influence of Malcolm X on Black Militancy." *Journal of Black Studies* 1, no. 4: 387–402.

———. 1975. *Black Students: White Campus.* Washington, DC: APGA Press.

Harris, Daniel, and Joseph Honcharik. 1969. *Staff Study of Campus Riots and Disorders, October 1967–May 1969.* Prepared for the Permanent Subcommittee on Investigations of the Committee on Government Operations, United States Senate. Washington, DC: Government Printing Office.

Hine, Darlene Clark, William C. Hine, and Stanley Harrold. 2003. *The African-American Odyssey.* Vol. 2. Upper Saddle River, NJ: Prentice Hall.

Joseph, Peniel E. 2006. *Waiting 'Til the Midnight Hour: A Narrative History of Black Power in America*. New York: Henry Holt.

Karagueuzian, Dikran. 1971. *Blow It Up! The Black Student Revolt at San Francisco State College and the Emergence of Dr. Hayakawa*. Boston: Gambit.

Karim, Benjamin. 1992. *Remembering Malcolm*. With Peter Skutches and David Gallen. New York: Carroll & Graf.

Kornberg, Allan, and Joel Smith. 1969. "'It Ain't Over Yet': Activism in a Southern University." In *Black Power and Student Rebellion*, edited by James McEvoy and Abraham Miller, 100–122. Belmont, CA: Wadsworth Publishing.

Malcolm Collection. Papers, 1948–1965. Schomburg Center for Research in Black Culture, New York Public Library, New York.

Malcolm X. 1963. "Race Problems and the Black Muslim Religion and Its Ideas." Speech at Michigan State University, Erickson Kiva, East Lansing, MI. January 23.

——. 1967. *Malcolm X on Afro-American History*. New York: Merit Publishers.

——. 1968. *The Speeches of Malcolm X at Harvard*. Edited by Archie Epps. New York: Morrow.

——. 1969. *Malcolm X Talks to Young People: Speeches in the U.S., Britain, and Africa*. Edited by Steve Clark. New York: Pathfinder Press.

——. 1970. *By Any Means Necessary: Speeches, Interviews, and a Letter by Malcolm X*. Edited by George Breitman. New York: Pathfinder Press.

——. 1990. *Malcolm X Speaks: Selected Speeches and Statements*. Edited by George Breitman. New York: Grove Press.

——. 1991. *Malcolm X: Speeches at Harvard*. Edited by Archie Epps. New York: Paragon House.

——. 1992. *February 1965: The Final Speeches*. Edited by Steve Clark. New York: Pathfinder Press.

McCormick, Richard P. 1990. *The Black Student Protest Movement at Rutgers*. New Brunswick, NJ: Rutgers University Press.

Murch, Donna Jean. 2010. *Living for the City: Migration, Education, and the Rise of the Black Panther Party in Oakland, California*. Chapel Hill: University of North Carolina Press.

Ogbar, O. G. Jeffrey. 2004. *Black Power: Radical Politics and African American Identity*. Baltimore: Johns Hopkins University Press.

Orum, Anthony M. 1968. *Black Students in Protest: A Study of the Origins of the Black Student Movement*. Washington, DC: American Sociological Association.

Pinkney, Alphonso. 1976. *Red, Black, and Green: Black Nationalism in the United States*.

Cambridge: Cambridge University Press.

Rogers, Ibram H. 2009. "Remembering the Black Campus Movement: An Oral History Interview with James P. Garrett." *Journal of Pan African Studies* 2, no. 10: 30–41.

———. 2012. *The Black Campus Movement*. New York: Palgrave MacMillan.

Roy, Jerrold. 2000. "Student Activism and the Historically Black University: Hampton Institute and Howard University, 1960–1972," PhD diss., Harvard University.

Sales, William W., Jr. 1994. *From Civil Rights to Black Liberation: Malcolm X and the Organization of Afro-American Unity*. Boston: South End Press.

Seale, Bobby. 1991. *Seize the Time: The Story of the Black Panther Party and Huey P. Newton*. Baltimore, MD: Black Classic Press.

Shabazz, Betty. 1969. "The Legacy of My Husband, Malcolm X." *Ebony*, June, 172–82.

Spellman, A. B., and Malcolm X. 1964. "Interview with Malcolm X." *Monthly Review*, March 19.

Turner, James. 1969. "Black Students and Their Changing Perspective," *Ebony*, August, 135–40.

Vargus, Ione D. *RevivalofIdeology:TheAfro-AmericanSocietyMovement*. San Francisco: R &E Research Associates.

Van Deburg, William L. 1992. *New Day in Babylon: The Black Power Movement and American Culture, 1965–1975*. Chicago: University of Chicago Press.

Young, Alford A. 1988. *Revolt of the Privileged: The Coming Together of the Black Community at Wesleyan University, 1965–1976*. Middletown, CT: Wesleyan University Press.

PART 3

Malcolm and Black World Struggle

Malcolm X, Islam, and the Black Self

Zain Abdullah

In traditional African societies, spiritual beings intrude into the daily lives of the earthly bound (Reed 2003, 1–3). And within the African American religious tradition, various forms of belief have been integral for producing courageous, disciplined, and hope-filled human beings against the tyranny of Jim Crow segregation in the south and social degradation in the north. For many Black religious traditions, there is no separate place for secular things and another for the sacred. There was no separation of religion and politics, for example, when Denmark Vesey, trembling with saintly desire, led a violent slave revolt in 1822.

The divine spirit also tore into Nat Turner a decade later, inducting him and his coconspirators into the ways of insurrection and rebellion. Sojourner Truth and Harriet Tubman knew no such division during their fight against the American system of slavery. God spoke directly to them in transcendent fits and starts or what we call "visions" and "dreams." By the late nineteenth century, Henry McNeal Turner prophetically proclaimed that "God is a Negro," fiercely striking out against racism and discrimination in the pews and at the polls. African Muslims were also there, and many strictly guarded their religious precepts as a viable force against the dehumanizing effects of slavery.[1]

Yet, besides this entry of the sacred into the public domain, one could argue that religion fundamentally provides African Americans with the chance for some sort of divine communion, leaving all other aspects of their mundane lives to the social realm.[2] The view that God fights on the side of the oppressed therefore is certainly not commonly held, nor is the idea that Black religion should be inherently concerned with protest. Black religious nationalism, however, conflates civil disobedience with the search for divine transcendence.[3] Malcolm X was conceived and brought before the world as one nurtured by this tradition. His was the world of Denmark Vesey, Harriet Tubman, and Henry McNeil Turner—a realm where the spiritual answers the existential call of the political. It was a world in which the presumed division between religion and politics not only had no place, but this way of excluding the sacred from the profane made no sense for disenfranchised Blacks, people with virtually no real equal access to the larger society. The spiritual and the political constituted a single domain, and this was the world Malcolm X and countless others inhabited.

This chapter intends to remind readers that religion mattered in the life of Malcolm X, and that Islam in particular mattered in a very specific way. But religion does not operate in our lives as a static entity. It moves us; it is shaped by us—at times with devastating effects. Our religious proclivities are in varying degrees shot through with other desires, attempts to reconcile our social, political, or cultural needs with our spiritual sensibilities. For members of the Nation of Islam (NOI), or what many refer to as the "Nation," race and religion were not mutually exclusive, and neither could they be for Malcolm. At the same time, this doesn't mean that race and religion ceased to be strange bedfellows. They were certainly a dilemma for Malcolm, especially after he split from the Nation, forcing him to found two distinct organizations to address separately the racial and religious concerns of his followers. His attempt to reconcile this tension is largely what this chapter explores. During the latter part of his life, for example, his college lectures primarily addressed huge crowds of white students, often with a contingent of immigrant Muslims. And in this setting, his ideas about both race and religion or Islam were hotly contested.

The atmosphere of Malcolm's college talks around the country were often described as tense yet electric. Maya Angelou noted in her reflections about him that in "the presence of powerful people, the air crackles with energy" (Alexander 1998). Much of this excitement was generated by the controversy that followed him. Malcolm's speech at Michigan State University on January 23, 1963, was one of many he had given on campuses across the country. More than one thousand people came out, mostly white students with local NOI members dispersed in the audience. The event was cosponsored by the African Students Association and the campus chapter of the NAACP. Standing before the crowd in preparation, Malcolm eased the tension by tugging on the mic cord around his neck, stating how he became nervous when "noose like things" were hanging this close to him, drawing laughter from the assembly (Alexander 1998).[4]

His MSU talk, however, was unique in several respects. First, the public response to these college talks resulted in negative press for the NOI, and their leader, the Honorable Elijah Muhammad, ordered Malcolm to decline any subsequent invitations (Jenkins 2002). This injunction gave Malcolm less than one year to address college students while a minister in the NOI. By December, Malcolm would face a ninety-day suspension from public speaking for remarks he made about President John F. Kennedy's assassination, calling it a case of "the chickens coming home to roost" (Tryman 2002).[5] He was never reinstated, and on March 8, 1964, he officially announced his departure.

The second distinctive feature about the MSU lecture was its content. Malcolm and Nation ministers would typically not preach NOI theology like Yacub's History, their mythic narrative about the origin of the races and the nature of Black divinity and white wickedness. The college talks were more secular in tone, even though they still spoke of the apocalyptic fall of America. These speeches also included Malcolm's explanation of Muhammad's program for "self help and black pride" (Terrill 2010, 97). They also contained one of his most notable oratorical conventions—his distinction between the house Negro and the field Negro, a metaphorical device to explain the divide between Black integrationists and separatists and the rise of Black radicalism around the world (Malcolm X 1989, 26–27). Departing from the Nation's appellation that Blacks are Asiatic, Malcolm proclaimed that all Negroes are Africans (Malcolm X 1989, 24).

This single assertion marked a public break from the Nation's brand of racial determinism and religious millenarianism, particularly as it was designed to explain the solution for Black liberation. This shift begins Malcolm's search for a way to reconcile racial and religious solutions to Black degradation. This chapter explores two aspects of his journey: (1) mythopoesis or his attempts to negotiate the Nation's mythmaking and his concern for Black liberation, and (2) orthodox Islam and the resulting tension between it and his ongoing struggle for racial justice. Although these two sections occur one after the other, they actually represent two aspects of a single struggle. That is, while the chapter is divided into two categories, the two phases are not meant to reflect any sort of continuum in terms of his spiritual or intellectual development. While they may have occurred at different times, these two challenges often overlapped or intersected with one another. They were just played out within different contexts and resulted in a unique response. But his goal remained the same. Each category, then, reveals his efforts to manage the twin forces of race and religion and bring them into the service of the Black liberation struggle.

Mythopoesis: Yacub's History and the Souls of Black Folks

Mythopoesis or the process of mythmaking has long been an essential feature of the human condition. Still many think that mythology is the realm of make-believe, fabricated stories invented by the much less initiated. In politics, however, myths have another purpose altogether. While the 1908 *Oxford English Dictionary* described myth as "a purely fictitious narrative," the 1976 supplement quotes the *British Journal of Sociology* as stating, "We use myth in a sense a little different from the popular one. To us it does not mean an untrue or impossible tale, but a tale which is told to justify some aspect of social order or of human experience" (Thompson 1985, 7; Barany 1981, 348). Plato advocated political mythology or what he called the "royal lie" to foster solidarity among the citizenry (Thompson 1985, 18). Myths then are not about how narratives measure up against naked facts. They are much more about how we have responded to those facts in creative and imaginative ways. "The truth of the myth," George Barany noted, "is a function of its pragmatic and dramatic effectiveness in moving men [and women] to act in accordance with typical, emotionally charged ideals" (1981, 354).

The Nation's mythic narrative of Yacub's History and how Malcolm grappled with it reveals much about his ideas on Islam and racial justice. While some may claim that the NOI was an apolitical organization, Yacub's History provided members with a counterdiscourse of the present state of affairs, overturning white supremacist notions of the world and crafting a new script about the outcome of western civilization.[6] I am not suggesting that every single Muslim in the Nation fully subscribed to the myth of Yacub. I actually argue much to the contrary elsewhere (Abdullah 2012). But the ideals presented in Yacub's History produced strong emotions that not only allowed thousands to alter their thoughts about themselves, but also inspired them to change how they responded to the racism around them. Many of the themes in Yacub's History were not new. Calling whites "devils," for instance, was already practiced during the Chinese Boxer Rebellion. In the early 1900s, their political rallying cry was "Kill the foreign white devils!" (Malcolm X 1999, 181; Bickers 2011). Enslaved Africans characterized their plantation masters in similar ways. Harriet Jacobs, born a slave in 1813, became an abolitionist and an author. She employed biblical imagery to depict her former master as a creature who "walked to and fro upon the earth," which is a reference to the devil in the book of Job (Lowance 1991, 321). Slave narratives often referred to slaveholders as beasts and likened them to diseases. Slave writings also depicted their masters as pigs, dogs, worms, and other creatures considered despicable. One wonders if the word "Yacub," an Arabic word for "Jacob," could possibly have some reference to Harriet Jacobs and her use of a similar approach.

In the MSU speech of 1963, Malcolm had already begun to publicly move away from certain religious and racial precepts found in Yacub's History. His proclamation that Negroes were "Africans" deviated sharply from the Nation's mytho-religious narrative that Blacks originated from the continent of Asia. In fact, Malcolm would later claim that Elijah Muhammad did not promote any sort of African consciousness, challenging his audience to "find one word in his direct writings that's pro-African" (Malcolm X 1989, 134). At MSU, he also called for African unity, and this clearly signaled a shift in his racial politics. In the Nation, race was intimately tied to religion and Islam was believed to be the "natural" faith of all Blacks (Hartnell 2008). It was not that Africa eclipsed Asia as a religious site. Africa was included as the rightful designation for what he defined in this speech as the New Negro. But the "new type," he announced, "rejects the white man's Christian religion" (Malcolm X 1989, 36). While the Nation had increased their efforts to demonstrate their connection with the Muslim world, Malcolm stressed the added importance of an international perspective and urged Blacks to join hands with their "brothers and sisters in Africa, in Asia, in the East" (Malcolm X 1989, 33). This change also forced him to rethink his previous ideas, not just concerning race but also religion. In fact, the ideological adjustment in his 1963 speech constitutes one in a series he made to reconcile his religious commitment to Islam and his petition for racial justice.

In 1963, the MSU talk in January and the "Message to the Grass Roots" lecture delivered on November 10 were two of Malcolm's last speeches as a minister in the NOI. While both speeches included heavy criticism of white racism and a call for Black unity, they also included sharp attacks on Christianity. Both talks, however, were titled for their political agenda and completely ignored their religious implications. The MSU speech, for example, is usually titled, "The Race Problem in America." Manning Marable, however, deviated from this convention, referring to the talk as the "Black Muslim and the American Negro" (Marable 2011). Malcolm X and the NOI, journalist and activist Tariq Ali asserted, were "winning recruits by arguing that Christianity was the religion of the slave-owners. The fact that most of the churches were segregated underscored their message" (2011, 155–56). But the NOI was also in defiance of traditional Islamic approaches to religion. In contradistinction to orthodox Islam, the Nation catered its message to directly address Black pain and suffering, even if it failed to conform with Middle Eastern versions of religiosity. The historian and associate of Malcolm, John Henrik Clarke, commented on it in the following way:

> Malcolm X and Elijah Muhammad's message made a whole lot of people feel whole again, human being again. Some of them came out and found a *new* meaning to their manhood and their womanhood. Had Elijah Muhammad tried to introduce an orthodox form of Arab-oriented Islam, I doubt if he would have attracted five hundred people. But he introduced a form of Islam that could communicate with the people he had to deal with. He was the king to those who had no king. He was the messiah to those some people thought unworthy of a messiah. (Strickland 1994, 99, emphasis added; see also Bagwell 1993)

The "new" meaning Blacks found in the Nation and the "new" Negro of which Malcolm spoke in his MSU speech are accounted for by way of their change in political consciousness, which was typified in his narrative about the house slave and the field slave. However, the religious transformation this New Negro undergoes, a point punctuated throughout the speech, is rarely discussed. "So again," Malcolm says at one of these moments at MSU, "this new type, as I say, he rejects the white man's Christian religion. You find in large numbers they're turning toward the religion of Islam. They are becoming Muslims" (Malcolm X 1989, 40). In "Message to the Grass Roots," Malcolm pilloried what he called "these old religious Uncle Toms," associating Christianity with Black suffering (Malcolm X 1990, 12). Islam, in contrast, is "a good religion," Malcolm continued. Characterizing Islam as the natural religion of Black people, he went on to say, "In fact, that's that old-time religion. That's the one that Ma and Pa used to talk about" (Malcolm X 1990, 12). As a minister in the Nation, Malcolm clearly saw the problem of Black suffering in both religious, or in this case Islamic, and social terms.

Malcolm also tried diligently to dispel doubts that the Nation was not accepted by the Muslim world. As early as 1959, he had been commissioned by Elijah Muhammad to embark upon a tour of Europe and Muslim countries (Marable 2011, 165–66). In a letter written from abroad, Malcolm articulated his new insight about

"Islam and Afro-Asian solidarity" (Marable 2011, 167). He promptly realized that the Nation's "sectarian concepts and practices, such as Yacub's History, might have to be abandoned," Manning Marable wrote, "and the assimilation of orthodox Islam would need to be accelerated" (Marable 2011, 168). By this time, Malcolm, as national spokesman for the NOI, had responded to scores of letters from Muslim outsiders criticizing their core tenets (Marable 2011, 300). His glib reply to Muslim critics, both in writing and at public addresses, about what were considered heretical aspects of the Nation was to rebuke immigrant Muslims for their failed efforts at converting Black Americans to Islam. During his Harvard address on March 24, 1961, for instance, Malcolm mocked questions about the notion of a Muslim "orthodoxy" and ridiculed foreign Muslims for their ineffectiveness in gaining recruits:

> There are probably one hundred thousand of what you (whites) call orthodox Muslims in America, who were born in the Muslim world and who willingly migrated here. But despite the fact that Islam is a propagating religion, all of these foreign Muslims combined have not been successful in converting one thousand Americans to Islam. On the other hand, they see that Mr. Muhammad by himself has hundreds of his fellow ex-slaves turning eastward toward Mecca five times daily giving praises to the great God Allah. No true Muslim in his right mind would denounce or deny this meek and humble little black man, born in Georgia. (Malcolm X 1968, 125)

By the following year, a foreign Muslim student at Dartmouth, Ahmed Osman, attended one of Malcolm's sessions at Temple No. 7 in Harlem. The result was a heated exchange during the question-and-answer period. While seemingly no compromise was made, Malcolm welcomed the Islamic literature sent to him by Osman, materials acquired from the Islamic Centre in Geneva, Switzerland (DeCaro 1996, 201).

In 1963, Malcolm made further adjustments to align NOI teachings with the broader Muslim *ummah* (global community). Appearing on the Chicago television program *At Random*, for example, Malcolm altered the stated premise in Yacub's History that "white devils" are evil by nature and innately bad. Instead, he stated that the Qur'an stipulated that "you judge a man by his conscious behavior . . . [and] anyone who intentionally or consciously carries into practice the attributes or characteristics of the devil is a devil" (DeCaro 1996, 162). Yet two months later, while on a radio show in Washington, D.C., Malcolm returned to the Black man's "natural" propensity toward goodness, but he also admitted that the Muslim world maintained a color-blind ideology (DeCaro 1996, 162). Malcolm obviously understood the difference between the two perspectives on race. This recognition, however, did not obviate his defense of the Nation's position on separation, nor its right to be a legitimate Muslim organization. During the question-and-answer session at MSU, he argued that when "the Algerians refused to integrate with the French, did that . . . mean that they weren't Muslims? When the Arabs refused to integrate with the Israelis, does that mean they're not Muslims? When the Pakistanis refused to integrate with the Hindus, does that mean they're not Muslims?" (Malcolm X 1990, 51).

After explaining how other Muslims were engaged in their own political struggles to liberate themselves from their opponents, he concluded by stating that "when we accept Islam as our religion, that doesn't mean that we are religiously wrong to reject the man who has exploited us and colonized us here in this country" (Malcolm X 1990, 52). Since Malcolm was a minister in the Nation, Islam (no matter how he was forced to redefine it throughout his career) was certainly a major concern for how he thought about the Black liberation struggle. And it was equally important for how he was forced to negotiate its various meanings while championing Black rights, even after his expulsion from the Nation.

"Orthodox" Islam and the Black Freedom Struggle

Many assume that Malcolm X outgrew the Nation, and that this would summarily explain his departure from the group. He had an epiphany, they claim, either on his Mecca pilgrimage or shortly after his announcement to leave the NOI. Even Malcolm himself at times made similar statements, arguing that the separation was a result of his exposure to "true" Islam. A month before his assassination, however, he gave an interview and responded to a question about his break from the NOI. "I didn't break," he said, "there was a split. The split came about primarily because they put me out, and they put me out because of my uncompromising approach to problems I thought should be solved and the movement could solve" (Malcolm X 1992a, 158). Karl Evanzz, a biographer of Malcolm X, referred to FBI files detailing numerous phone calls to Elijah Muhammad in which Malcolm made earnest pleas for reinstatement after his ninety-day suspension was completed (1992, 211). It finally occurred to him that his long-standing affiliation with the Nation had come to an end. He made his official break with the NOI on March 8, 1964. "Internal differences within the Nation of Islam forced me out of it," he said before reporters at the Teresa Hotel. "I did not leave of my own free will. But now that it has happened, I intend to make the most of it" (Malcolm X 1992b, 210). Still, the complete break for Malcolm was much more gradual, a process that had begun some time before his actual departure.

As mentioned earlier, while a minister in the Nation, he had already begun to change his thinking, especially regarding NOI theology and its biological views on race. He slowly began to float ideas about race as a matter of social behavior rather than some sort of innate or natural determinism (Marable 2011, 310). Eleven days after his public declaration to leave the group, he gave an interview in which he explicitly rededicated himself to Elijah Muhammad and his message. "I am a follower of the Honorable Elijah Muhammad," he remarked. "I believe in the Honorable Elijah Muhammad. The only reason I am in the Muslim Mosque Inc. is because I feel I can better expedite his program by being free of the restraint and other obstacles I encountered in the Nation" (Malcolm X 1992a, 5).[7] A major source of friction, though, was the Nation's policy of noninvolvement in American politics, which included the civil rights struggles. In spite of this, Malcolm possessed a strong desire for direct action as a solution against racism and Black suffering. But the Nation preached a millenarian philosophy and prophesied about the coming apocalyptic change that would reverse the status quo. Nation followers were to remain steadfast to this belief and uphold the principles of Black self-sufficiency. Malcolm felt this strategy placed the Nation in a religious and political "vacuum," and he found it extremely difficult to abide the group's lack of action toward social change (Malcolm X 1989, 166–67).

This tension between the NOI and Malcolm became particularly telling when the 1963 March on Washington for Jobs and Freedom occurred. Elijah Muhammad had forbidden NOI members from supporting the march in any way. Malcolm, however, informed members at Mosque No. 7 that he had managed to obtain Muhammad's special permission to attend (Marable 2011, 256). In fact, there was no way if at all possible Malcolm would miss it. "Whatever black folks do," he said, "maybe I don't agree with it, but I'm going to be there, brother, 'cause that's where I belong" (Carson 1991, 69). This was Black mobilization at its highest level, and Malcolm wanted to be where the action was. During his interview with A. B. Spellman on March 19, 1964, just after his split, Malcolm stated that he believed that Muhammad still had the best solution to solve the race problem. By solution, we can assume he was referring to Muhammad's program of separation. "I felt I could best . . . expedite his program better," Malcolm remarked, "by remaining out of the Nation of Islam and establishing a Muslim group that is an *action* group designed to eliminate the same ills" (Malcolm X 1992a, 4, emphasis added).

One month before his death, Malcolm continued to talk about the Nation as a movement that was "dragging its feet" for which he wanted some sort of redress (Malcolm X 1992a, 158). Now that he was out, and with just under a week before his demise, Malcolm announced before a crowd in Harlem's Audubon Ballroom that he was "trying to get something organized that will enable us to take a *direct action* against the forces that have been holding us back" (Malcolm X 1989, 143, emphasis added). By adopting a program of "direct action," he had clearly rejected the Nation's position for solving the race problem through divine intervention. This is not to suggest, however, that he rejected their belief regarding race-based separation, which he felt was not the same as segregation.[8] And while he had major problems with the nonviolent approach of Martin Luther King Jr., they both shared a commitment to direct action and the social gospel or, in Malcolm's case, a kind of Islamic liberation theology.[9]

Malcolm, though, argued for the need to work toward a Black liberation that was rooted in the right to self-defense. King, of course, rejected any sort of violent resistance whatsoever. But from the very first days after his split with the Nation and until his death, Malcolm consistently remarked that he remained a Muslim. But being a Muslim without a viable religious organization backing him posed a real problem, especially since he deeply felt that Blacks needed not only a resolution for social and economic reform but moral rectitude as well. His journey into the Muslim world was a possible solution. He had already been studying traditional Islam for some time, and he was even attending their Islamic centers for prayer and instruction before going to Mecca (Morrow 2012, 16–17).

Still, even before Malcolm joined the movement, Elijah Muhammad had "always insisted that his ministers present his creed as part of a global community of Muslims" (Marable 2011, 117). Elijah Muhammad's teachings, however, were both supported and ridiculed by "foreign" Muslims, as some had even worked in their parochial schools, the University of Islam, and others were employed as editorial staff for their newspaper (Essien-Udom 1962, 80 n. 45, 317–19). In April of 1958, for example, Malcolm spoke at the Third Pakistan Republic Day gala in Los Angeles. He urged "Arabs, as a colored people" to reach out to the "colored peoples" of America who "would be completely in sympathy with the Arab cause!" (Lincoln 1994, 169; Evanzz 1999, 185–86). By 1962, Malcolm was already responding to public attacks by immigrant Muslims, and he was using classical sources like the Qur'an to defend the Nation's teachings (DeCaro 1996, 156–58).

Malcolm's foray into the traditional world of Islam, then, could not have been, as his autobiography claims, based on an epiphany he experienced at the annual *hajj* pilgrimage in Mecca. In fact, one of his major biographers and confidants, Louis Lomax, believed that his Pauline awakening at Mecca was his "way to publicly state, and philosophically justify, that which he had known from the onset of his career with the Black Muslims and Elijah Muhammad." Lomax continued, saying that "King Faisal bluntly tells Malcolm that he has been preaching a false concept of Islam—as if Malcolm didn't already know it" (1968, 130). However, I don't believe it is a matter of Malcolm knowing or not knowing that he was following a "false" version of Islam. Malcolm rebuked in no uncertain terms any religion that was either unwilling to or incapable of addressing the desperate plight and poor conditions of Black people in America.

Shortly after leaving the Nation, he delivered his "The Ballot or the Bullet" speech at King Solomon Baptist Church in Detroit on April 12, 1964. He urged his audience to keep "their religion at home, in the closet, keep it between you and your God. Because, if it hasn't done anything more for you than it has already, you need to forget it anyway" (Ellis and Smith 2010, 8). Seven months later, Malcolm was more resolute about the need for Black people to embrace a pragmatic religion, one that would speak directly to Black need and oppression. "I believe in a religion that believes in freedom," he remarked at an Organization of Afro-American Unity (OAAU) Homecoming rally. "Any time I have to accept a religion that won't let me fight a battle for my people," he surmised, "I say to hell with that religion" (Malcolm X 1992a, 140).

Even his semi-Arabic name, El-Hajj Malik El-Shabazz, which some claim marked his conversion into orthodox Islam, had long been adopted by him and was already on his passport while he was a Nation minister (DeCaro 1996, 132). At a press conference after his pilgrimage to Mecca in 1964, a reporter asked him how long he had planned to keep Malcolm X, given the new public awareness of his Muslim name. "I'll probably continue to use Malcolm X," he replied, "and I'll probably use it as long as the situation that produced it exists," he said, pausing to chuckle and maintain a prolonged grin.[10] For Malcolm, embracing traditional Islam was not only about his "legitimacy and acceptance as a Sunni Muslim and international black leader," especially not for himself alone (Curtis 2002, 233). His effort to internationalize the Black struggle, however, meant that thousands of African Americans could be ushered into the worldwide community of Islam where they would achieve a much broader platform.

This link with the Muslim world, he believed, was not exclusive to converts alone. In a letter written from Lagos, Nigeria, in 1964, Malcolm declared that the

"Muslim world is forced to concern itself, from the moral point of view in its own religious concepts, with the fact that our plight clearly involves the violation of our *human rights.*" As he had become accustomed to employing Islamic sources when chiding Muslim critics when he was a minister, he continued to invoke the Qur'an as proof that traditional Muslims had a religious duty to fight oppression "no matter what the religious persuasion of the victims is" (Malcolm X 1990, 61). In the same letter, he stated his desire that his pilgrimage would "officially establish the religious affiliation of the Muslim Mosque, Inc., with the 750 million Muslims of the world of Islam once and for all" (Malcolm X 1990, 61). For Malcolm, orthodox Islam had a major role to play in the Black struggle. The dilemma, however, was whether Black people and the Muslim world would feel the same way.

Even as an orthodox Muslim, Malcolm continued to believe that solving the race problem would require some type of moral "reform" for Blacks along with a new social contract with the state (Malcolm X 1992a, 25–26). This moral reformation, he stated in March of 1964, would eliminate "the vices and other evils that destroy the moral fiber of the community" (Malcolm X 1992a, 5). For Malcolm, true independence was related to an ethical system that would "awaken" Blacks to a higher spiritual awareness, a role Islam would play in making them "morally more able to rise above the evils and the vices of an immoral society" (Malcolm X 1992a, 9). He maintained this belief just six days before his death. Reminiscing about the early days of the Nation, he told an Audubon Ballroom audience that as "long as that strong spiritual power was in the movement, it gave the moral strength to the believer that would enable him to rise above all his negative tendencies" (Malcolm X 1989, 127).

He argued that the confluence of both spiritual and political forces would be necessary to improve the Black condition. The MMI and the OAAU were founded for that purpose. Through organizational unity, he had hoped that the MMI would "give us direct ties with our brothers and sisters in Asia and Africa who are Muslims," and the OAAU would "set out on a program to unite our people on this continent with our people on the mother continent" (Malcolm X 1989, 125). In this way, the "minority" status of Black people in America would be overturned, and the struggle for human rights, undergirded by a moral authority that was international and a direct action agenda that was global, would gain majority support. Malcolm, however, expressed serious doubts about the desire of Blacks to enter Islam and that traditional Muslims would involve themselves in sustained activism against oppression.[11] Toward the end of life, however, his ideas were in flux. And we cannot be certain which direction he would have taken. We do know, on the other hand, that for his entire public life, Malcolm X was a man fully engaged in both the secular and sacred worlds. And he struggled to bring both to bear on the liberation of Black people.

Conclusion: On the Search for Brother Malcolm

On a cold Saturday morning in February, Malcolm lay in repose six days after his assassination.[12] Ossie Davis eulogized him with some of the most exquisite words ever spoken. At the center of the tribute, he rebuked those who would have us "flee, even from the presence of his memory" (Ellis and Smith 2010, 29). Our polite response to such delusions, Davis remarked, would be a graceful smile with perhaps a simple query: Did you ever "know" Brother Malcolm? The answer to this question, however, is anything but simple, as each of us recounts the "Malcolm" we have chosen to know.

Yet I believe that this is the kind of question that speaks volumes about who *we* are today more than who Malcolm was in 1965. But perhaps this appropriation of him is acceptable, particularly when we consider how "often what is most important about the past is the present-day perception of it" (Bestor 2004, 16). Manning Marable, for example, viewed Malcolm's life in terms of reinventions. Herb Boyd, along with several contributors to his edited volume, envisions a Malcolm who is "real" and not reinvented at all. Still, Alex Gillespie, an author of another volume on Malcolm, argues that "instead of asking which identity is the 'real' Malcolm X, we should be focusing upon the tensions between these different facets of his complex personality" (2010, 33).[13] Whether the approach is based on deconstruction, realism, or conflict, Malcolm X has been an elusive figure to capture.

Two years after Malcolm's death, a Detroit forum was held to address misconceptions about him, and a booklet was published as *Myths About Malcolm X: Two Views* (Cleage and Breitman 1968). The two speakers headlining the event were Rev. Albert Cleage, an African American, Black nationalist preacher, and George Breitman, a white American and founding member of the Socialist Workers Party.[14] Cleage and Breitman were both astute purveyors of Malcolm, despite their respective tendency to define him according to their nationalist and socialist beliefs (Cleage and Breitman 1968, 5, 22). But is it possible to avoid the trappings of this kind of self-projection? Malcolm Gladwell, a *New Yorker* magazine journalist, cautioned writers about the limitations of their craft. The few hours we spend interviewing a subject, he said, or the months and years spent digging in the archives, cannot compare to the entire expanse of a life that will inevitably escape us (2007, 74).

In Malcolm's autobiography, Alex Haley recounted how he had gathered some of Malcolm's scribbles that read, "My life has always been one of changes" (Malcolm X 1999, 411). In the same Epilogue, Haley included a letter from Malcolm that in part stated: "With the fast pace of newly developing incidents today, it is easy for something that is done or said tomorrow to be outdated even by sunset on the same day" (Malcolm X 1999, 413–14). During his final days, his thoughts were in rapid transition and he admitted to a reporter, "I am man enough to tell you . . . that I can't put my finger on exactly what my philosophy is now, but I am flexible" (Lomax 1968, 230). Yet what amazes me is how quick we are to state with stunning clarity who Malcolm X was or was not. "The real Malcolm X," Jan Carew argued, "was far more complex than the millions of empty words written about him" (1994, vii).

Writers would do well to capture as much of this complexity about Malcolm as possible. To be clear, I am not advocating for more salacious tidbits about his life, which is often employed to increase book sales. Rather, Malcolm was clearly a man of great faith, and he witnessed its impact on his life and that of others.[15] But we rarely find this Malcolm, the one constantly wrestling with how one lives a moral life in what can be considered at times an evil world.[16] We do find, however, myriad texts and materials espousing what they believe identified his politics, something even he was reluctant to do.[17] But even a cursory look at his speeches (before or after the split) will reveal the absolute prophetic nature of his message—a vicious harangue on the passionate encounter between his God and the inhumanities of this mundane world.

For him, it was the place where religion and politics entered into a deep and traumatic embrace over the existential and precarious nature of our human condition. This was the moral and ethical universe from which he sprang, and its foundational heritage is quite complex. This is not to discount the more dominant approaches already circulating in the public sphere for how we understand his meaning and legacy. I do want to suggest, however, that it is time for more complex thinking about the life of Malcolm X, and grasping more of his religious experience is one way to begin. These insights can increase our knowledge not only about the man himself but, more instructively, the world he inhabited as well.[18]

I first began to think seriously about Malcolm X and Islam in the spring of 1995. I was a graduate student in Manning Marable's seminar at Columbia University, which was open to us New School students by way of a consortium agreement. In the fall of 1996, I also took a course with Leith Mullings, Marable's widow, at the CUNY Graduate Center. All of this occurred more than a decade after my return from studying in Saudi Arabia, and some time after my former life as a Muslim chaplain in various correctional facilities. I had also given one or two community talks on Malcolm in the early nineties. A year before taking Marable's seminar, I worked with Malcolm's widow, Dr. Betty Shabazz, at Medgar Evers College in Brooklyn, where she was appointed director of institutional advancement and public affairs and where I worked as an academic counselor in the Worker Education Program.[19]

This was a wondrous time. I consider it my induction into a passionate regard for Malcolm and his legacy. Professor Marable embodied what it means to wear what I call the cloak of a scholar, and his deep commitment to his craft, his insatiable thirst for knowledge, and his willingness to speak truth to power were exemplary. Dr. Shabazz, Sister Betty, shared with me, at times, her intimate thoughts about Brother Malcolm, and no works of poetry or exposition could speak about him the way she could. But when we peer into the maze of works on Malcolm, we find an apparition of a different sort staring back at us. The poet Maya Angelou agonized over our portrayal of Malcolm and its impact on future generations, arguing that it would be "dangerous" to lose sight of his "wonderful sense of humor" (Strickland 1994, 227). Most important, Malcolm urged young people especially during his latter days to adopt the value of "thinking for themselves."[20] And this is a much-needed side of him that we must grasp.

Malcolm recorded some of his final thoughts in a two-part, written response to the editors of *al-Muslimoon*, a monthly magazine published by the Islamic Centre in Geneva, Switzerland. In his reply on February 14, 1965, the night his house was firebombed, he declared that his "first responsibility" was to African Americans "who suffer the same indignities because of their color" that he faced. He continued by saying, "I don't believe my own personal problem is ever solved until the problem is solved for all . . . of us" (Malcolm X 1992b, 252). Malcolm's Islam was clearly not the apolitical version of the Nation or the color-blind ideology of traditional Muslims. He strongly believed that the Muslim world had much to offer the Black struggle, an argument Edward Wilmot Blyden gave over three quarters of a century earlier, and a fact we can assume was not lost on Malcolm.[21] He chastised the Muslim world, however, for ignoring "the problem of the Black American" (Malcolm X 1992b, 252) And he explained how his main intention for traveling throughout the Muslim world and Africa was to gain a better grasp of Islam and African societies and to educate them about the plight of Blacks in America.

On the night before Malcolm's assassination, for example, his final response urged the Muslim world to uphold their full responsibility, since Islam represented "brotherhood" and "unity" for the human family (Malcolm X 1992b, 255). At the same time, he wrote that Africa was his "fatherland" and he was "primarily interested in seeing it completely free" (Malcolm X 1992b, 255). From the time he joined the Nation until his final day as a traditional Muslim, Malcolm struggled to reconcile what he felt was a divide between Islam and the Black world. "Despite his genuine conversion to orthodox Islam," Manning Marable wrote, "his spiritual journey was linked to his black consciousness" (2011, 481). And perhaps our recognition of this double-sided journey, which could conceivably represent a new kind of Black religiosity or prophetic Islam, will provide vital clues about Malcolm X beyond what we already know. Or, more importantly, it might just be that a deeper look will reveal something crucial about ourselves and, thus, a discovery of the reasons we find ourselves so beguiled by him.

NOTES

1. For a more extensive discussion on enslaved African Muslims in Early America, see Austin 1984; Austin 1997; Diouf 1998; Gomez 1998.

2. Anthony B. Pinn briefly discusses the fact that it is incorrect to assume that all Black religion is of the protest variety. For a basic overview of Black religion, see Pinn 2013.

3. There are numerous works on Black religious nationalism. A classic study is Wilmore 1983. More recent works include Hucks 2012.

4. For reference on "noose like things," see the blog comment by Bob Lurie, who attended the lecture, at http://detroitred.tumblr.com/post/3877595871/malcolmology-101-19-malcolm-x-speaks-at-michigan. Tension was equally high when Malcolm spoke at one of the historically black colleges and universities, since administrators saw Malcolm as an anti-integrationist and hate-monger. Personal communication with Lenwood G. Davis, Dept of English and Foreign Languages at Winston-Salem State University (December 1, 2011).

5. The statement "the chickens coming home to roost," was made just a week after President John F. Kennedy was assassinated (which occurred on November 22, 1963) when Malcolm X spoke at a Muslim rally in New York City. He was silenced for a period of ninety days beginning in December.

6. The entire narrative of Yacub's History is not located in a single volume. However, most of it can be found in Muhammad 1965.

7. During the official announcement of his breakup with the Nation, Malcolm had also stated that he had founded a new organization named Muslim Mosque, Inc. (MMI).

8. Malcolm talked about the difference between separation and segregation, and he disapproved of the latter, which he described as Black disenfranchisement as opposed to self-determination for Blacks. See his early discussion of it in 1963: Malcolm X 1989, 35–36.

9. In his famous speech "The Ballot or the Bullet," delivered on April 3, 1964, at the Cory Methodist Church in Cleveland, Ohio, Malcolm talked about how the MMI will be committed to "action" saying that "After our religious services are over, then as Muslims we become involved in political action, economic action and social and civic action." See Malcolm X 1990, 38.

10. Many believe that Malcolm adopted the name El-Hajj Malik El-Shabazz because of his second conversion to Sunni (orthodox) Islam. Ryan Williams LaMothe, for example, holds this assumption when he states, "The trips abroad had a profound impact on Malcolm X's religious subjectivity, which is reflected in his decision to change his name to El-Hajj Malik El-Shabazz" (2011, 534). However, Malcolm stated in a press conference after his return from the *hajj* that, while he always had the Arabic name, he only used it in the Muslim world. To listen to a video clip of this part of the press conference, go to http://www.youtube.com/watch?v=fdSXtnBqPBA.

11. In the *Autobiography*, Malcolm stated his uncertainty about the appeal of Islam to most in Black America, and he harbored serious concerns about Arab Muslim apathy. For African Americans joining Islam, Malcolm stated the following: "And I had known, too, that Negroes would not rush to follow me into the orthodox Islam which had given me the insight and perspective to see that the black men and white men truly could be brothers. America's Negroes—especially older Negroes—are too indelibly soaked in Christianity's double standard of oppression" (Malcolm X 1999, 371). As for Arab apathy, Malcolm said, "I saw that the Arabs are poor at understanding the psychology of non-Arabs and the importance of public relations. The Arabs said '*insha Allah*' ["God willing"]—then they waited for converts" (Malcolm X 1999, 351).

12. Malcolm X was assassinated on February 21, 1965, and his funeral services were held on February 27.

13. For these three recent approaches to the legacy of Malcolm X, see Marable 2011; Boyd et al. 2012; and Terrill 2010. For another written critique of Marable's notion of reinvention, see Ball and Burroughs 2012.

14. For major works written about Rev. Albert Cleage and George Breitman, see Ward 1969 and Allen and Lovell 1987.

15. A week before his death, Malcolm delivered a speech in which he discussed the role of faith in his life, referring to the word four times within a few sentences: "It was faith in what I was taught that made it possible for me to stop doing anything that I was doing and everything that I was doing. And I saw thousands of brothers and sisters come in who were in the same condition. And whatever they were doing, they would stop it overnight, just through faith and faith alone. And by this spiritual force, giving one the faith that enabled one to exercise some moral discipline, it became an organization [the NOI] that was to be respected as well as feared" (Malcolm X 1989, 127).

16. In terms of full biographies, one major exception that considers the role religion or Islam played in the life of Malcolm X is DeCaro 1996.

17. In the final scene of the documentary "Malcolm X: Make It Plain," a white reporter, after asking Malcolm to explain the "ultimate end" of his political philosophy, raised a question about how he viewed himself: "Do you consider yourself radical?" Malcolm smiled almost shyly and replied, "I consider myself Malcolm." See Bagwell 1994.

18. Edward E. Curtis, for example, views the period of Malcolm's full entry into classical Islam as a critical moment. "Malcolm converted to Sunni Islam," he says, "at what was arguably the most important moment in the history of Muslim missionary activity, or *da'wa*, in North America." See Curtis 2002, 230.

19. The Worker Education Program at Medgar Evers College is now called the Center for Professional Education. Dr. Edison O. Jackson, the president of Medgar Evers College at the time, sponsored a series of symposia on spirituality at the school. The second symposium was entitled "Symposium on Spirituality: An Islamic Perspective," which included a panel with Imam Talib Abdul-Rashid from the Mosque of Islamic Brotherhood, Professor Margarita Samad-Matias, poet and activist Aliyah Abdul-Karim, myself, and Amir Al-Islam as moderator. The event was held on Wednesday, March 23, 1994, and Dr. Betty Shabazz attended. I essentially delivered a sermon on the notion of faith in Islam. Sister Betty was genuinely engaged in the talk and the program as a whole. However, I believe her engagement speaks to a much larger issue. Despite her unfortunate experiences with the Nation, her attendance and support of the event reveals her abiding interest in Islam as a faith tradition. As Malcolm considered his own shift and endorsement of traditional Islamic practices, he talked about Sister Betty's undying support. "The first letter was, of course, to my wife, Betty. I never had a moment's question that Betty, after initial amazement, would change her thinking to join me. I had known a thousand reassurances that Betty's faith in me was total. I knew that she would see what I had seen . . . a new insight into the true religion

of Islam, and a better understanding of America's entire racial dilemma." See Malcolm X 1999, 345.

20. Malcolm X spoke to young civil rights activists in Mississippi on January 1, 1965. The title of this message was, "See for yourself, listen for yourself, think for yourself." See Malcolm X 1969, 48–82.

21. Edward Wilmot Blyden was a Pan-Africanist and Presbyterian minister who suggested that Islam could serve as a unifying force for Black people. See Blyden 1887.

WORKS CITED

Abdullah, Zain. 2012. "Narrating Muslim Masculinities: The Fruit of Islam and the Quest for Black Redemption." *Spectrum: A Journal on Black Men* 1, no. 1: 141–78.

Alexander, Brett, dir. 1998. *The Real Malcolm X*. VHS. Terre Haute, IN: Columbia House Video Library.

Ali, Tariq. 2011. "Leaving Shabazz." *New Left Review* 69 (May/June): 152–60.

Allen, Naomi, and Sarah Lovell, eds. 1987. *A Tribute to George Breitman: Writer, Organizer, Revolutionary*. New York: Fourth Internationalist Tendency.

Austin, Allan D. 1984. *African Muslims in Antebellum America: A Sourcebook*. New York: Garland Publications.

———. 1997. *African Muslims in Antebellum America: Transatlantic Stories and Spiritual Struggles*. New York: Routledge.

Bagwell, Orlando, dir. . 1993. "Malcolm X: Make It Plain." *The American Experience*. Boston: Roja Production & Blackwell.

Ball, Jared A., and Todd Steven Burroughs, eds. 2012. *A Lie of Reinvention: Correcting Manning Marable's Malcolm X*. Baltimore: Black Classic Press.

Barany, George. 1981. "On Truth in Myths." *East European Quarterly* 15, no. 3: 347–55.

Bestor, Theodore C. 2004. *Tsukiji: The Fish Market at the Center of the World*. Berkeley: University of California Press.

Bickers, Robert A. 2011. *The Scramble for China: Foreign Devils in the Qing Empire, 1832–1914*. London: Allen Lane.

Blyden, Edward W. 1887. *Christianity, Islam and the Negro Race*. London: W. B. Whittingham.

Boyd, Herb, Ron Daniels, Maulana Karenga, and Haki R. Madhubuti, eds. 2012. *By Any Means Necessary: Malcolm X: Real, Not Reinvented: Critical Conversations on Manning Marable's Biography of Malcolm X*. Chicago: Third World Press.

Carew, Jan R. 1994. *Ghosts in Our Blood: With Malcolm X in Africa, England, and the Caribbean*. New York: Lawrence Hill Books.

Carson, Clayborne. 1991. *Malcolm X: The FBI File*. Edited by David Gallen. New York: Carroll and Graf.

Cleage, Albert, and George Breitman. 1968. *Myths about Malcolm X: Two Views*. New York: Merit Publishers.

Curtis, Edward E. 2002. "Why Malcolm X Never Developed an Islamic Approach to Civil Rights." *Religion* 32, no. 3: 227–42.

DeCaro, Louis A., Jr. 1996. *On the Side of My People: A Religious Life of Malcolm X*. New York: New York University Press.

Diouf, Sylviane A. 1998. *Servants of Allah: African Muslims Enslaved in the Americas*. New York: New York University Press.

Ellis, Catherine, and Stephen Drury Smith, eds. 2010. *Say It Loud: Great Speeches on Civil Rights and African American Identity*. New York: New Press.

Essien-Udom, Essien Udosen. 1962. *Black Nationalism: A Search for an Identity in America*. Chicago: University of Chicago Press.

Evanzz, Karl. 1992. *The Judas Factor: The Plot to Kill Malcolm X*. New York: Thunder's Mouth Press.

———. 1999. *The Messenger: The Rise and Fall of Elijah Muhammad*. New York: Pantheon Books.

Gillespie, Alex. 2010. "Autobiography and Identity: Malcolm X as Author and Hero." In *The Cambridge Companion to Malcolm X*, edited by Robert E. Terrill, 26–38. Cambridge: Cambridge University Press.

Gladwell, Malcolm. 2007. "The Limits of Profiles." In *Telling True Stories: A Nonfiction Writers' Guide from the Nieman Foundation at Harvard University*, edited by Mark Kramer and Wendy Call, 73–74. New York: A Plume Book.

Gomez, Michael A. 1998. *Exchanging Our Country Marks: The Transformation of African Identities in the Colonial and Antebellum South*. Chapel Hill: University of North Carolina Press.

Hartnell, Anna. 2008. "Between Exodus and Egypt: Malcolm X, Islam, and the 'Natural' Religion of the Oppressed." *European Journal of American Culture* 27, no. 3: 207–25.

Hucks, Tracey E. 2012. *Yoruba Traditions and African American Religious Nationalism*. Albuquerque: University of New Mexico Press.

Jenkins, Robert L. 2002. "Malcolm at the White Colleges." In *The Malcolm X Encyclopedia*, edited by Robert L. Jenkins and Mfanya Donald Tryman, 352–53. Westport, CT: Greenwood Press.

LaMothe, Ryan Williams. 2011. "Malcolm X's Conversions: The Interplay of Political and Religious Subjectivities." *Pastoral Psychology* 60: 523–36.

Lincoln, C. Eric. 1994. *The Black Muslims in America*. 3rd ed. Grand Rapids, MI: Wm B. Eerdmans; Trenton, NJ: Africa World Press.

Lomax, Louis E. 1968. *To Kill a Black Man: The Shocking Parallel in the Lives of Malcolm X and Martin Luther King Jr*. Los Angeles: Holloway House Publishing.

Lowance, Mason I., Jr. 1991. "The Slave Narrative in American Literature." In *African American Writers*, edited by Valerie Smith, Lea Baechler, and A. Walton Litz, 309–25. New York: Collier Books.

Malcolm X. 1968. *The Speeches of Malcolm X at Harvard*. Edited by Archie Epps. New York: Morrow.

———. 1969. *Malcolm X Talks to Young People: Speeches in the U.S., Britain & Africa*. Edited by Steve Clark. New York: Pathfinder Press.

———. 1989. *Malcolm X: The Last Speeches*. Edited by Bruce Perry. New York: Pathfinder.

———. 1990. *Malcolm X Speaks: Selected Speeches and Statements*. Edited by George Breitman. New York: Grove Weidenfeld.

———. 1992a. *By Any Means Necessary*. New York: Pathfinder.

———. 1992b. *February 1965: The Final Speeches*. Edited by Steve Clark. New York: Pathfinder,

———. 1999. *The Autobiography of Malcolm X*. With the assistance of Alex Haley. New York: Ballantine Books.

Marable, Manning. 2011. *Malcolm X: A Life of Reinvention*. New York: Viking.

Morrow, John Andrew. 2012. "Malcolm X and Mohammad Mehdi: The Shi'a Connection?" *Journal of Shi'a Islamic Studies* 5, no. 1: 5–24.

Muhammad, Elijah. 1965. *Message to the Blackman in America*. Chicago: Muhammad Mosque of Islam No. 2.

Pinn, Anthony B. 2013. *Introducing African American Religion*. New York: Routledge.

Reed, Teresa L. 2003. *The Holy Profane: Religion in Black Popular Music*. Lexington: University Press of Kentucky.

Strickland, William. 1994. *Malcolm X: Make It Plain*. New York: Viking.

Terrill, Robert E., ed. 2010. *The Cambridge Companion to Malcolm X*. Cambridge: Cambridge University Press.

Thompson, Leonard. 1985. *The Political Mythology of Apartheid*. New Haven, CT: Yale University Press.

Tryman, Mfanya Donald. 2002. "The Chickens Coming Home to Roost." In *The Malcolm X Encyclopedia*, edited by Robert L. Jenkins and Mfanya Donald Tryman, 148–49.

Westport, CT: Greenwood Press.

Ward, Hiley H. 1969. *Prophet of the Black Nation*. Philadelphia: Pilgrim Press.

Wilmore, Gayraud S. 1983. *Black Religion and Black Radicalism: An Interpretation of the Religious History of Afro-American People*. Maryknoll, NY: Orbis Books.

Malcolm X and the Struggle for Socialism in the United States

Curtis Stokes

After some four hundred years in the English colonies and the United States, black socioeconomic well-being relative to that of non-Hispanic whites continues to be a very serious problem. A brief review of two critical indicators for well-being in America's largely pay-for-service economic system accentuates the point.[1] In a 2003 study Arthur B. Kennickell, Federal Reserve Board, reports that blacks hold 2.5 percent of the nation's total net worth or wealth, compared to 93.1 percent held by non-Hispanic whites.[2] And annualized black joblessness from 1972 to 2011, as reported in 2012 by the U.S. Bureau of Labor Statistics, went below 10 percent only seven times out of thirty-nine years and never reached what economists call "full employment" (i.e., an unemployment rate at nearly 5 percent or less); on the other hand the annualized non-Hispanic white unemployment rate in the same period never reached 10 percent and attained or came very close to attaining full employment twenty-four times (U.S. Bureau of Labor Statistics 2012).

Given their numerical minority status, which appears to have permanence, and generally left of center ideological positions, U.S. blacks seem destined to remain at the margins of American society, at least within the existing capitalist economic system. It is within this context that we will briefly look backward to the black socialist tradition from the 1890s to the 1920s, focusing on three Caribbean-born radicals, Hubert Harrison, Cyril Briggs, and Claude McKay, before examining the implications of the embryonic yet suggestively rich anticapitalist and prosocialist ideas of Malcolm X during the final fifty weeks of his life. Malcolm was of course not a socialist, neither during his years in the Nation of Islam (NOI) nor in the last year of his life. For example, during the discussion session after a 1963 speech at the University of California an attendee asked if he believed in socialism. Malcolm responded by saying what was then appropriate, "I have no knowledge of socialism" (Malcolm X 1989, 59). He always thought of himself first and foremost as a Muslim, nationalist, and revolutionary, even if that self-identification would be somewhat altered in his last year.

Like any searching intellect, especially one that had been effectively caged under the conservative black nationalism of Elijah Muhammad's NOI, Malcolm's commitment to addressing the plight of U.S. blacks and other colored populations never wavered during his period of transformation. Once freed from what he would later call Muhammad's "racist philosophy," Malcolm began constructing an appropriate organizational form, traveled to the Middle East and Africa, which had an extraordinary impact on him (now employing the language of the oppressed against the oppressors alongside that of black versus white), and interacting, teaching, and learning from an ethnically and racially diverse group of radicals, including those associated with the Trotskyist Socialist Workers Party (SWP), a predominantly white U.S. political formation. All of this contributed toward elevating his learning curve on what needed to be done to radically change the socioeconomic and political standing of African peoples, both inside and outside of the United States, as well as identifying with the oppressed around the world.

Searching for Malcolm in the New Negro Era

Though not widely known, socialism, just like liberalism, is very much a part of American political culture. Journalist and political essayist John Nichols writes, "Socialist ideas . . . have shaped and strengthened America across the past two centuries. That does not mean that America is a socialist country. . . . But it does mean that, to know America, to understand and appreciate the whole of this country's past, its present and perhaps its future, we must recognize the socialist threads that have been woven into our national tapestry" (2011, xii).[3] Included in the American socialist tradition was the important role played by exiled 1848 German revolutionaries in the election and reelection of Abraham Lincoln, as well as the fact that Lincoln and Karl Marx exchanged letters in 1864. Marx, writing on behalf of the International Working Men's Association (November 1864), said, "We congratulate the American people upon your re-election by a large majority. If resistance to the slave power was the reserved watchword of your first election, the triumphant war cry of your re-election is Death to Slavery." U.S. Ambassador to England Charles Francis Adams, the son of John Quincy Adams and grandson of John Adams, sent a note (January 28, 1865) to Marx, then residing in London, thanking him and the International for their encouragement and support (Anderson 2010; Marx 2000, 1).

Just as importantly, socialist and communist parties were instrumental in the passage of social welfare and labor policies throughout the last two centuries (e.g., the eight-hour work day, collective bargaining agreements, and other New Deal programs). Doing so against all odds, including widespread political repression, socialist organizations provided much support in defending the bulk of the laboring population (Miller 1996; Kazin 2011). But critically neither socialist nor communist parties gave sufficient attention to the race question, whether on internal relations between black and white members inside the party or in the larger society. The example of Eugene V. Debs is illustrative of the problem. Debs, leader of the left-wing of the Socialist Party of America (SPA) and its five-time presidential candidate from 1900 to 1920, while generally an opponent of racial discrimination against blacks and rightly acknowledging that "the history of the Negro in the United States is a history of crime without parallel," focused almost exclusively on class analysis. According to Debs, "I have said and say again that . . . there is no Negro question outside of the labor question—the working class struggle." And he went on to say, "The class struggle is colorless. . . . [and consequently] we have nothing special to offer the Negro" (Debs 1903, 2, 3).[4] Though this Debsian understanding of race was less true with the communist parties (born in 1919 against the backdrop of World War I, factionalism within the SPA, and the 1917 October Revolution in Russia), race and especially the national question still had to await the arrival of a handful of black radicals, operating either inside or on the periphery of those organizations, to make the case in earnest against racial injustice and for black self-determination both at home and abroad.

From the 1890s to the 1920s an assortment of black radicals, among them nationalists, socialists, and communists, were really pressing the national and anticolonial questions, including Marcus Garvey, W. E. B. Du Bois, Hubert Harrison, Cyril Briggs, and Claude McKay during a period sometimes called the New Negro era or movement. The roots of 1960s black radicalism, including that of Malcolm X, can be traced to this foundational period in black political thought; radical internationalism, the right of nations and peoples to self-determination, armed self-defense strategies, importance of black-run and black-funded political organizations, and critiquing if not rejecting capitalism while simultaneously expressing an openness to socialism were manifestations of this important African American moment. And because of their intellectual and political stature within both the black nationalist and socialist movements, Hubert Harrison, Cyril Briggs, and Claude McKay were arguably most representative of the range of early twentieth-century black radicalism. Hubert Harrison was born in St. Croix (Danish West Indies) in 1883 but made his way to the United States by 1900, where he eventually emerged as perhaps the leading class-conscious and race-conscious black radical activist and intellectual of his time, and, according to his biographer, established the first black political organization (Liberty League) and newspaper (*The Voice*) during the New Negro era. He was also an active member at different moments in the SPA, Industrial Workers of the World, and Universal Negro Improvement Association (Perry 2001).[5]

On the racial front, Harrison's pen was quick to criticize Booker T. Washington and W. E. B. Du Bois for their failings regarding the worsening socioeconomic conditions facing the black population. While traveling in Europe in 1910 Washington was reported to have said black life in the United States was improving, and just a few years later Du Bois in 1919 wrote an editorial, "Close Ranks," for the NAACP's *The Crisis*, of which he was editor, saying to black America, "Let us, while this war lasts, forget our special grievances and close our ranks shoulder to shoulder with our white fellow citizens and the allied nations that are fighting for democracy." Harrison's response: "Mr. Booker T. Washington declares to the world that all is well with the Negro. His special mouthpiece *The New York Age* said in its Thanksgiving number that the Negro had more to be thankful for than any other group of Americans. . . . I will make no appeal to the philosophy of history or to anything that may even faintly savor of erudition, because Mr. Washington and his satellites say that is bad. But I will appeal to hard facts" (Lewis 1995, 697; Perry 2001, 164–66).[6] Harrison's response to Du Bois's controversial editorial appeared in *The Voice* titled "The Descent of Dr. Du Bois"; it says, "Du Bois, of all Negroes, knows best that our 'special grievances' . . . consist of lynching, segregation and disenfranchisement." And he wondered whether Du Bois wrote the editorial in an effort to obtain employment in the intelligence division of the U.S. Army, something that had dogged Du Bois for many years (Perry 2001, 170–72, 173–74).[7]

How did Harrison understand the relationship between race-consciousness and class-consciousness? He seemed to wrestle with this topic a bit, as can be seen in two of his most important essays, "Socialism and the Negro" (1912) and "Two Negro Radicalisms" (1919); the first was written during his brief sojourn in the SPA and the other as he transitioned, however briefly, toward Marcus Garvey's Universal Negro Improvement Association. Race and class themes permeate both essays, with race underpinning all that's written, even as his hostility toward capitalism is a constant. In "Socialism and the Negro" he reminds his readers that the "crucial test of socialism" is that it must "champion" the cause of blacks "since the Negro is the most ruthlessly exploited working class group in America." According to Harrison, "Southernism" or "Socialism" was the choice facing the SPA; the party in his view chose the former and thus he left the party. In "Two Negro Radicalisms" Harrison again reminded the white radical left that blacks embrace the class-consciousness model but turn to socialism (i.e., class-consciousness) only because of the race question in the United States and elsewhere, not because of socialism itself. He writes, "Some of these newly-awakened Negroes will take to socialism and bolshevism. Here again the reason is racial. Since they suffer racially from the world as at present organized by the white race, some of their ablest hold that it is 'good play' to encourage and give aid to every subversive movement within the white world which makes for its destruction 'as it is.'" Harrison believed that economic systems come and go but race "must of necessity survive any and all changes in the economic order" (Perry 2001, 71–76, 102–5). In the midst of the horrors of Jim Crow and living not too far removed from the era of racial slavery, Harrison is confronting many of the same challenges that Malcolm X will face in the immediate post–World War II era; notably neither Democrats nor Republicans, and many on the white radical left as well, were then prepared to come to terms with the festering racial realities both in the United States and elsewhere among the colored and oppressed populations around the globe. Yet it is important to remember that Harrison was exploring all viable socioeconomic and political options available, including the socialist or class-consciousness project, which is exactly the approach Malcolm X pursued in his last year.

Cyril Valentine Briggs was born in 1888 on the Caribbean island of Nevis and made his way to the United States in 1905. He was a talented journalist, essayist, revolutionary black nationalist, and eventually committed communist activist (joined the party sometime between 1919 and 1921). Pivotal to understanding Briggs, however, was his creation of two political instruments, *The Crusader* (monthly magazine) and the African Blood Brotherhood (ABB) (preaching armed self-defense), with each existing to vindicate and lead the fight for African people wherever they reside. Briggs, like Harrison, was also a radical internationalist, especially when it concerned Africa; neither sought to "civilize" Africa or physically return American blacks to the African continent (though Briggs was partly open to the latter idea so long as it wasn't imposed on Africa). Their aim was to make the case for the right of Africans to self-determination and especially to learn from Africans.[8] *The Crusader* (September 1918–early 1922) was a magazine founded, funded, and owned by blacks; it described itself as "a magazine unbought and unbuyable [and] . . . dedicated to a renaissance of Negro power and culture throughout the world." On the other hand, the ABB was a self-acknowledged small, secret, paramilitary, regionally and West Indian–based, and armed self-defense organization. A recruiting announcement in *The Crusader* said, "Those only need apply who are willing to go the limit" (code-language meaning willing to fight and die for the cause) (1:2 and 2:29).[9]

How should we understand the most important elements in the legacy of Cyril Briggs? There are at least three that should immediately be put on the table. In an era of open and raw antiblack mob violence, evident in the "Red Summer" of 1919 (approximately fifty blacks killed, with some burned alive) and the Tulsa Race Riots in 1921 (Greenwood, a middle-class black neighborhood, was burned to the ground by white mobs backed by the Oklahoma state government), the ABB, though wrongly blamed by white media and government for stirring up troubles in Tulsa, helped to establish the principle that blacks must stand their ground when under attack. This principle would be carried forward by, among others, Robert F. Williams, Malcolm X, and the Black Panther Party. Secondly, Briggs and other pioneer black communists took their nationalistic ideas with them when joining communist parties and thus pressed the fledgling communist movement at the close of World War I to aggressively place the idea of the right of black nations and peoples to self-determination alongside the already generalized struggle for a socialist America (Williams 1998).[10] And thirdly, Briggs, like Harrison to some extent, through his journalistic pieces in *The Crusader* explored the possibility of bridging black nationalism and socialism. In a particularly direct manner, he raises the topic in "The Salvation of the Negro" (1921). Briggs said for the sake of humanity, which includes all races, he prefers what he called "the socialist co-operative commonwealth." But, again like Harrison in his "Two Negro Radicalisms," Briggs maintains that race ultimately will trump economic categories in a racially bifurcated world, especially so in the United States, and therefore blacks and other colored people would have little protection. So, Briggs concludes, "the surest and quickest way . . . in our opinion to achieve the salvation of the Negro is to combine the two most likely and feasible propositions, [namely] salvation for all Negroes through the establishment of a strong, stable, independent Negro state . . . in Africa or elsewhere; and salvation for all Negroes (as well as other oppressed peoples) through the establishment of a universal socialist co-operative commonwealth" (Briggs 1987, 4:8).[11] This statement certainly reads like an attempted marriage of Karl Marx and Marcus Garvey, melded together in ways that probably neither would find acceptable. Yet Briggs's exploration of the relationship between nationalism and socialism was an important contribution to an ongoing conversation.

Claude McKay was a Jamaican-born American poet, novelist, and revolutionary activist in the ABB; born in 1889, he arrived in the United States in 1912 and, like Harrison and Briggs, made his way to Harlem, then the cultural and political capital of the global Black world. Unlike Harrison and Briggs, he did not formally join any socialist or communist parties, but he did travel within the extant socialist political and intellectual orbit during the period under consideration. For our purposes McKay is noteworthy for two key developments, his acceptance of an invitation to participate in the Fourth Congress of the Communist International in Moscow in 1922 and his conversation, while at the congress, with Leon Trotsky; next to Vladimir I. Lenin, Trotsky was the principal organizer of Russia's October Revolution in 1917. And importantly, Trotsky's American followers, after much prodding by him, would have a mutually valued relationship with Malcolm X during the final fifty weeks of his life.

In 1920 and at the request of John Reed, a white American revolutionary journalist with close ties to the Soviet Republic, McKay received the invitation from the congress's organizers, though not being a communist party member he was not an official delegate. He was one of two blacks at the congress. Surinam-born Otto Huiswood, reportedly the first black member of the Communist Party of America, was the other black at the congress and, in his case, a delegate at the congress. McKay and Huiswood were key players on what was called the Negro Commission, charged with helping to draft the congress's "Theses on the Negro Question." Huiswood, speaking first, said, "The Negro question is another part of the racial and colonial question, and it has, until now, not received any special attention." He was followed by McKay, who said, "When I heard that the Negro question was to be placed on the agenda of this Congress, I felt . . . I would stand in eternal disgrace if I did not say something about the brothers and sisters of my race. I would particularly disgrace the Negroes of the United States since I published a poem in 1919 that has become known, which is always shoved into the limelight because of my poetical temperament as a leading spokesperson for Negro radicalism in the United States." In addition to its detailed inclusion of blacks, for the first time, as a central component in the worldwide movement to overturn capitalism and construct a socialist society, language in the 1922 "Theses on the Negro Question" points toward Lenin's 1920 "Draft Theses on the National and Colonial Questions" specifically identifying Ireland and American blacks as constituting "nations" requiring support from the Communist International.[12] This is a clear indication, at least from Lenin's perspective, that perhaps in certain situations nationalism and socialism can be bridged, an idea Trotsky further develops in forced exile during the 1930s and especially in three conversations with Trinidadian-born Pan-African scholar and Marxist C. L. R. James in Mexico City in April 1939.

McKay's account of his 1922 meeting with Trotsky appears in his first autobiography, *A Long Way from Home* (1937); we are told the meeting went exceptionally well. Trotsky inquired about the condition of U.S. blacks, as well as Africans, and was particularly interested in their "grievances and social aspirations." After listening to McKay's response, Trotsky, according to McKay, "expressed his own opinion about Negroes, which was more intelligent than that of any of the other Russian leaders . . . he was not quick to make deductions about the causes of white prejudice against black. Indeed he made no conclusion at all, and, happily, expressed no mawkish sentimentality about black-white brotherhood." He and Trotsky agreed to correspond later on issues affecting the global black population. Trotsky's 1923 letter "To Comrade McKay" reflected on the status of black-white labor relations saying, "In North America the matter is further complicated by the abominable obtuseness and caste presumptions of the privileged upper strata of the working class itself, who refuse to recognize fellow workers and fighting comrades in the Negroes." And always cautious on these matters of race due to lack of information and language challenges, Trotsky concluded, "What forms of organization are most suitable for the movement among American Negroes, it is difficult for me to say, as I am insufficiently informed regarding the concrete conditions and possibilities" (McKay 1937, 207–9). As his facility with the language improves and with continuing contact with black radicals, Trotsky will get a better handle on the status of blacks and the black-white labor question in the United States. But this encounter with McKay appears to have been beneficial to both parties and would contribute toward developing a distinctively Trotskyist approach to the race question.

Wrestling with Nationalism and Socialism for Fifty Weeks

Though the prospect had simmered for perhaps the last two of the preceding twelve years of his leadership within Elijah Muhammad's NOI, especially since his December 4, 1963, suspension for the "chickens coming home to roost" comment made immediately after the assassination of President John F. Kennedy, Malcolm publicly disassociated himself from the NOI on March 8, 1964. Of course there were many reasons for Malcolm's "split" from the NOI, but most importantly he felt the NOI was for too long moralizing and sitting on the sidelines while African peoples, at home and abroad, were dying in the streets while fighting against colonialism and racial injustice. He was now committed to rolling up his sleeves and working on behalf of blacks for momentary needs such as getting a "good education, housing and jobs," but at the same time would also say to blacks that attaining those items would not address the "main" problem facing them. As Malcolm put it, "I felt that wherever black people committed themselves, in the Little Rocks and the Birminghams and other places, militantly disciplined Muslims should also be there—for all the world to see, and respect, and discuss" (Malcolm X 1965a, 333–34). Malcolm now had a measure of freedom to think, say, and engage in the kind of work that befits a revolutionary black nationalist, which means looking beyond merely satisfying our momentary needs, however important. And he equally understood that the public and private life of a leader, including his, can and should be criticized (Malcolm X 1989, 87).

From March 8, 1964, until February 21, 1965, Malcolm had barely fifty weeks to construct a political thought that would help facilitate the emancipation of African peoples and the oppressed generally, and he would spend some twenty-six of those fifty weeks traveling to the Middle East and Africa (April 13–May 21, 1964, and July 9–November 1964), plus making a second substantial trip to Europe in February 1965. Reflecting on the continuing challenges he faced, Malcolm told Jan Carew, Guyana-born Marxist and poet, in London less than two weeks before his death, "Chances are that they will get me the way they got [Patrice] Lumumba." Despite ongoing harassment by Western governments and assassination plots during his final months, Malcolm considered these trips extremely important to his own spiritual, intellectual, and political growth, and also serving to deepen his radical internationalism by linking Africa and black America to his human rights project as well as aiding in the creation of the Organization of Afro-American Unity (OAAU), modeled on the Organization of African Unity (Carew 1994, 36).[13]

Travel, he often said, "broadens your scope," and following his conversations with African heads of state, he observed, "There was much information exchanged that definitely broadened my understanding. . . . For since coming back from over there, I have had no desire whatsoever to get bogged down in picayune arguments with any bird-brained or small-minded people" (Malcolm X 1965c, 15, and Malcolm X 1989, 155–56). Of course Malcolm had germinal ideas about the kind of organization needed for a black cultural revolution, privileging of human rights over civil rights, what kind of spirituality might result in a new human being, and an evolving sense of what constitutes black nationalism; but it was his extensive conversations and observations while abroad that really opened up his eyes about the prospects for worldwide revolution against the capitalist economic system, with the latter including people of diverse racial and ethnic backgrounds.

On black nationalism Malcolm simply brought the NOI's understanding of black nationalism to his March 12, 1964, press conference. His press release drew a distinction between two understandings of black nationalism: the "long-range" answer to the question about race in America maintains "the best solution is complete separation, with our people going back home . . . to our African homeland," while the "short-range" answer embraced the traditional 1960s call for "black control of the black community" (its politics, economics, and culture). After his two trips abroad to Mecca and visiting many African countries, Malcolm had a change of heart, at least with the usage and meaning of "black nationalism." Speaking to a group of young socialists on January 18, 1965, Malcolm now said of the term "black nationalism," "I used to define black nationalism as the idea that the black man should control the economy of his community, the politics of his community, and so forth." After having conversations with white Africans in North Africa who were revolutionaries or progressives, Malcolm said, "I had to do a lot of thinking and reappraising of my definition of black nationalism. . . . And if you notice, I haven't been using the expression for several months." The evidence strongly suggests, however, that Malcolm remained a black nationalist despite his wrestling with the term and its meaning during the last few months of his life; key here is that Malcolm's organization (OAAU) and its program were saturated with black nationalist ideas, saying, among other things, a "[black] cultural revolution will be the journey to our rediscovery of ourselves. . . . Armed with the knowledge of the past, we can with confidence chart a course for the future" (Malcolm X 1990, 121; Malcolm X 1965b, 11, 17; Malcolm X 1965b, 91).

As with black nationalism, Malcolm now reflected on the place of capitalism and socialism in his quest for an appropriate political thought. In search of a socioeconomic and political framework that would accommodate freedom and equality, Malcolm expressed hostility toward capitalism, and considering what he thought he saw in some African countries, he seemed now to have a favorable opinion about countries he referred to as socialist. In both cases, capitalism and socialism, Malcolm had not done much, if any, research; his views were more instinctive and based upon experience, observations, and conversations with various radicals, political leaders, and heads of state. When considering his speeches, prosocialist views appear especially in talks to predominantly white audiences; yet when placed within the context of his overall political development, with increasing emphasis upon a race/class dynamic in revolution making and internationalizing the black struggle against racial injustice and colonialism, Malcolm's message comes across as completely genuine. A few days after his first trip to Africa, Malcolm said, "While I was traveling I noticed that most of the countries that had recently emerged into independence . . . have turned away from the so-called capitalistic system in the direction of socialism." Was this idle talk? I think not. Malcolm went on to say he would now "begin a little investigation where that particular philosophy [i.e., socialism] happens to be." He was clearly fascinated by the socialist model. During the discussion period following his talk, Malcolm was asked about the "system" he preferred. Malcolm's reply, "All of the countries that are emerging today from under the shackles of colonialism are turning toward socialism. I don't think it's an accident. Most of the countries that were colonial powers were capitalist countries and the last bulwark of capitalism today is America." Several months later (December 20, 1964), Malcolm poses and answers his own question directed at Americans, "What are the people who have gotten their freedom adopting to provide themselves with better housing, better education and better clothing . . . none of them are adopting the capitalistic system." A capitalist, for Malcolm, is a "bloodsucker," "vulturistic," and exploits the oppressed. Clearly capitalism is not the answer, but what is? Malcolm leaves the door open to many possibilities, as he says, "I don't know. But I'm flexible" (Malcolm X 1990, 65, 69, 121).

It is worth noting here that during his last year Malcolm had a mutually beneficial relationship with the Trotskyist SWP, a predominantly white political formation. Many of his important speeches and interviews were published by *The Militant* (newspaper of the SWP) and subsequently the publishing houses of the SWP, including Pioneer Publishers and Pathfinder Books; several of Malcolm's books with Pathfinder were also copyrighted with Betty Shabazz, Malcolm's wife.[14] On

January 7, 1965, while speaking at the SWP's Militant Labor Forum (MLF) in New York City, Malcolm said, "It is an honor to me to come back to the Militant Labor Forum. . . . It's my third time here." He continued, "*The Militant* newspaper is one of the best in New York City . . . one of the best anywhere you go today. . . . I saw it even in Paris about a month ago. They were reading it over there, and I saw it in some parts of Africa where I was during the summer." And on an earlier occasion (May 29, 1964), Malcolm was not invited to the MLF, but approached the SWP about being on a "Symposium on Blood Brothers" sponsored by the MLF, with Malcolm saying once his request was accepted by the Trotskyist organization, "I couldn't resist the opportunity to come" and be part of the panel. All of this clearly shows that Malcolm had a friendly relationship with the SWP and really enjoyed the level of conversation he found at the MLF (Malcolm X 1965c, 15, 18, 19).

Another component to the capitalism/socialism observations by Malcolm was his interest in both the Chinese (1946–49) and Cuban (1953–59) Revolutions, especially the latter. And these interests suggest some resonance for the relationship between nationalism and socialism in his political thought, as Malcolm clearly had no interest in capitalism. But recall Malcolm's view that he's "flexible" regarding the necessary system to address the problems at hand. Jan Carew, interviewing Malcolm just days before his assassination, asked Malcolm "where he stood on questions of socialism and Marxism," with Malcolm hesitatingly responding, "If a mixture of nationalism and Marxism makes the Cubans fight the way they do . . . then there must be something to it." But, Malcolm continued, "We've got to learn to creep before we walk, and walk before we run." In other words, the door is simultaneously open to some form of nationalism and not closed to socialism, but more work needs to be done before embracing any system; he knew what he did not want but wasn't completely certain about what he actually wanted, at least not yet (Carew 1994, 36–37).

Conclusion

During the final fifty weeks of his life Malcolm was in search of a political thought, grounded in the African tradition, that would result in the emancipation of the oppressed. Among the components of his emerging thought were (1) identifying the fight as one primarily focused on attaining human rights (not civil rights) and importantly internationalizing and anchoring that fight in an African context; (2)

building an organization that would be at the center of affirming and defending African peoples; and (3) in the tradition of the so-called New Negro era, offering suggestively rich impressions of "socialism," admittedly anchored in an African tradition, while not denying the language of black versus white but also increasingly valuing that of the oppressed versus oppressors. All of this provides an opening toward a systemic alternative to the capitalist economic system. When commenting on the Booker T. Washington / W. E. B. Du Bois debate, Ralph Bunche aptly wrote in 1939 that, whatever their differences, "both confined their thinking within the periphery of race." Bunche continues, "when a Negro is unemployed, it is not just because he is a Negro but, more seriously, because of the defective operation of the economy under which we live—an economy that finds it impossible to provide an adequate number of jobs and economic security for the population" (Bunche 1995, 73, 76). It is this race/class dynamic that blacks, especially in a pay-for-service economy understood within an international framework, must continue to come to terms with if they are to overcome marginalization. Malcolm's quest for a truly emancipatory political thought contributes to that conversation, and as Robert L. Allen said, "Malcolm X died, but not his ideas" (1970, 40).

NOTES

1. Jaynes and Williams 1989, 33–53, and McKenney 1978. These documents provide a broad historical overview of how far U.S. blacks have come and more importantly how far they still have to go to close the racial gap in life chances between themselves and the non-Hispanic white population.

2. Kennickell 2003. See also "Wealth: Unrelenting Disparities," in Mishel 2012, 375–413, for a more detailed picture of how wealth is unequally distributed across races in the United States. Though not focused on racial disparities, the Organization for Economic Cooperation and Development, a consortium of largely rich nations, posted a report on its website ranking its thirty-four members in 2011 on a broad range of socioeconomic indicators; note that the United States ranked near the bottom on some of the most critical indicators: life expectancy (27th worst), infant mortality (31st worst), poverty (31st worst), and income inequality (31st worst): OECD 2011.

3. Like liberalism, nationalism, and even democracy, there are many meanings of what constitutes "socialism." For Karl Marx and Frederick Engels, the words "socialism" and "communism" were generally used interchangeably, especially after 1850. Socialism/communism is, according to Marx and Engels, a society brought about by

a revolution involving the active and direct participation of the working class; this postrevolutionary society is without bourgeois private property, classes and class antagonism, and a political state, and as said in Marx and Engels's *Manifesto of the Communist Party*, "We shall have an association in which the free development of each is the condition for the free development of all": Tucker 1978, 491. Considering Marx and Engels's principles above, no such society exists today or has ever existed. Still, other uses of the term "socialism," not by Marx or Engels, center on the existence of an expansive, social welfare–friendly government with perhaps a mixed economy of some kind; this use of the term "socialism" ties it to "social democracy," "African socialism," "Stalinism," "democratic socialism," etc. The assumption made in this essay is that the individuals or groups, including Malcolm X, employing the term "socialism" are themselves struggling to determine what makes sense to them.

4. The SPA, at least its left-wing, embraced Marx and Engels's understanding of the meaning of socialism yet was absolutely committed to the use of the electoral arena and strongly opposed any violent overthrowing of the capitalist economic system. The SPA was viewed overall as a softer alternative to the communist parties, born in 1919.

5. Unlike Malcolm X, as we shall see, Harrison's trajectory went from socialism toward black nationalism; though he eventually moved toward Garveyism for a while, Harrison didn't formally abandon the class-conscious model. Note that supposedly the New Negro, unlike the so-called Old Negro, was uncompromising, militant, and willing to fight and die for black rights; of course this distinction was overblown, as there were "new" and "old" Negroes in both the late nineteenth century and the first two decades of the twentieth century. Also, "radicalism" among blacks in the New Negro era crossed many boundaries, running from those calling for deep reforms but not overthrowing the entire political/economic systems to others calling for the outright overthrow of the capitalist economic system; even Booker T. Washington might be considered on some measures a black "radical" given this kind of political looseness in the definition of radicalism, especially when contrasting the private versus public side of his legacy. See Du Bois's attempt at distinguishing between the "old" and "new" Negro in "Of the Faith of the Fathers" (1903), in Du Bois 1989, 165–66.

6. The "hard facts," according to Harrison, were increasing residential segregation, disenfranchisement of blacks, and efforts to repeal the 14th and 15th Amendments to the U.S. Constitution.

7. Du Bois never received the military commission he sought, but there remains controversy among Du Bois scholars over the close proximity of the "Close Ranks" editorial and his efforts to obtain employment as a captain in the U.S. Army's Military

Intelligence Branch. See also "The Problem of Leadership" (1920) in Harrison 1997, 54–75.

8. Robert A. Hill provides a detailed and excellent biographical essay on Cyril Briggs; see his "Introduction: Racial and Radical: Cyril V. Briggs, *The Crusader* Magazine, and the African Blood Brotherhood, 1918–1922," in Briggs 1987, lxvi. This collection includes six volumes in three.

9. Though the circulation of *The Crusader* was small (circulation of some four thousand compared to several hundred thousand for Marcus Garvey's *Negro World*), it had a dedicated group of readers. And note that Robert A. Hill indicates the ABB had a membership of about seven thousand, but years later Cyril Briggs, in a letter to historian Theodore Draper, said, "at its peak it [ABB] had less than 3,000 members" (see "Letter to Theodore Draper in New York from Cyril Briggs in Los Angeles, March 17, 1958": http://www.marxists.org/history/usa/groups/abb/1958/0317-briggs-todraper.pdf; see also "The Pioneer Black Communists: Cyril Briggs and the African Blood Brotherhood," in Solomon 1998, 3–21. And according to Cedric Robinson (2000), the early membership of the ABB was almost entirely Caribbean-born and male—of ten identified by Robinson, seven were Caribbean-born while Grace Campbell was the lone woman, though she did have Caribbean ties. This is not a surprise, as Caribbean-born blacks were disproportionately represented among leading New Negro radicals, partly attributable to their skill-sets and the role that "class" as opposed to race played in Caribbean countries compared to the United States. An excellent accounting of New Negro Movement Caribbean radicals is provided by Winston James, "Caribbean Migration: Scale, Determinants, and Destinations, 1880–1932" and "Dimensions and Main Currents of Caribbean Radicalism in America: Hubert Harrison, the African Blood Brotherhood, and the UNIA," in James 1998, 7–49 and 122–84.

10. Williams's ideas about rifle clubs and armed self-defense will have resonance for Malcolm X. On the question of "self-determination," Cyril Briggs had been pushing the self-determination card since his days as a columnist at the black *New York Amsterdam News*. Of course the right of nations to self-determination is not in itself a radical idea, as it belongs to the panoply of ideas introduced during the European Enlightenment. President Woodrow Wilson himself spoke on the topics of self-determination and democracy in his "War Message to Congress" (April 2, 1917) and famous "Fourteen Points" speech (January 8, 1918). In the April 2 document he said, "We are . . . for the rights of nations great and small and the privilege of men everywhere to choose their way of life and of obedience. The world must be made safe

for democracy"; and in the January 8 speech he singled out those whom he thought should have independence or autonomy, including "Belgium," "French territory," "peoples of Austria-Hungary," "Romania, Serbia, and Montenegro," "Poland," and a few others. Not one word about the continent of Africa, with all but two states completely colonized, and of course nothing about U.S. blacks. Woodrow Wilson (April 2, 1917): http://teachingamericanhistory.org/library/document/war-message-to-congress/ and Woodrow Wilson (January 8, 1918): http://avalon.law.yale.edu/20th_century/wilson14. asp. Against this backdrop, Cyril Briggs wrote a scathing attack on President Wilson in the *New York Amsterdam News* (January 1918), where he was a columnist, wondering when America would address the plight of ten million U.S. blacks: "With what moral authority or justice can President Wilson demand that eight million Belgians be freed when for his entire first term and to the present moment of his second term he has not lifted a finger for justice and liberty for over TEN MILLION colored people, a nation within a nation, a nationality oppressed and Jim Crowed, yet as worthy as any other people of a square deal or failing that, a separate political existence": passage cited in Draper 1960, 323. His superiors at the *New York Amsterdam News* were not amused, which led to Briggs's dismissal, consequently deepening his radicalization and drift toward the communist movement.

11. In another outstanding work examining Briggs's dynamic race-class perspective, Minkah Makalani writes, "ABB radicals championed socialism not simply as an alternative to capitalism but as the basis of pan-African liberation, which they believed would only come with liberation struggles elsewhere" (2011, 60).

12. See Riddell 2012, 800, 807, and 947–51. See Lenin's "Draft Theses on the National and Colonial Question" (1920) where he writes, "All communist parties should render direct aid to the revolutionary movements among the dependent and underprivileged nations (for example, Ireland, American Negroes, etc.) and in the colonies": http://www.marxists.org/archive/lenin/works/1920/jun/05.htm. Lenin of course is listing blacks along with the Irish as constituting a "nation." Note that the quote from McKay mentions one of his famous and controversial poems, "If We Must Die," in Wilson 2000, 36; the poem includes the words, "If we must die, O let us nobly die . . . pressed to the wall, dying, but fighting back."

13. On Malcolm's trips abroad, see chaps. 3, 5–6, in Sherwood 2011, and Marable 2011. Sales (1994) provides a detailed assessment of the origin, development, and meaning of the OAAU and its broader relationship to Malcolm's political thought. Marable's *Malcolm X* is a Pulitzer Prize–winning book that has simultaneously drawn much praise and criticism. The book offers an excellent window into Malcolm's travels

abroad in his last year, especially to the Middle East and Africa. Some Marable critics say he engages in gossip about the private lives of Malcolm and Betty Shabazz, his wife (e.g., Marable suggests, without solid evidence, that they both had extramarital affairs and that Malcolm had a homosexual relationship with a white man, as well as supposedly moving ideologically closer to Martin Luther King Jr., given, among other claims, his increasingly race-neutral views). Whether one likes the book or not, Marable's wonderfully rich *Malcolm X* is now the standard against which all other biographies and conversations about Malcolm will and should be measured.

14. In the preface to Malcolm X 1992, 9, we read, "*The Militant* newspaper [is] the main publisher of Malcolm's speeches from late 1963 through February 1965."

WORKS CITED

Allen, Robert L. 1970. *Black Awakening in Capitalist America: An Analytic History*. Garden City, NY: Anchor Books.

Anderson, Kevin B. 2010. *Marx at the Margins: On Nationalism, Ethnicity, and Non-Western Societies*. Chicago: The University of Chicago Press.

Briggs, Cyril V. 1987. *The Crusader*. Edited and with an Introduction by Robert A. Hill. New York: Garland.

Bunche, Ralph J. 1995. *Selected Speeches and Writings*. Edited with an Introduction by Charles P. Henry. Ann Arbor: University of Michigan Press.

Carew, Jan R. 1994. *Ghosts in Our Blood: With Malcolm X in Africa, England, and the Caribbean*. New York: Lawrence Hill Books.

Debs, Eugene V. 1903. "The Negro and the Class Struggle" *The International Socialist Review* 4, no. 5: 257–60. www.marxists.org/history/usa/parties/spusa/1903/1100-debs-negroclassstrug.pdf.

Draper, Theodore. 1960. *American Communism and Soviet Russia*. New York: Viking Press.

Du Bois, W. E. B. 1989. *The Souls of Black Folk*. New York: Penguin Books.

Harrison, Hubert. 1997. *When Africa Awakes*. Baltimore: Black Classic Press.

James, Winston. 1998. *Holding Aloft the Banner of Ethiopia: Caribbean Radicalism in Early Twentieth-Century America*. New York: Verso.

Jaynes, Gerald David, and Robin M. Williams Jr., eds. 1989. *A Common Destiny: Blacks and American Society*. Washington, DC: National Academy Press.

Kazin, Michael. 2011. *American Dreamers: How the Left Changed a Nation*. New York: Alfred A. Knopf.

Kennickell, Arthur B. 2003. "A Rolling Tide: Changes in the Distribution of Wealth

in the U.S., 1989–2001." September. http://www.federalreserve.gov/pub/
fed2003/200324/200324pap.pdf.

Lewis, David Levering, ed. 1995. *W.E.B. Du Bois: A Reader*. New York: Henry Holt.

Makalani, Minkah. 2011. *In the Cause of Freedom: Radical Black Internationalism from
Harlem to London, 1917–1939*. Chapel Hill: University of North Carolina Press.

Malcolm X. 1965a. *The Autobiography of Malcolm X*. With the assistance of Alex Haley.
New York: Grove Press.

———. 1965b. *Malcolm X Talks to Young People: Speeches in the U.S., Britain and Africa*.
Edited by Steve Clark. New York: Pathfinder.

———. 1965c. *Two Speeches by Malcolm X*. New York: Pioneer Publishers.

———. 1989. *The Last Speeches*. Edited by Bruce Perry. New York: Pathfinder.

———. 1990. *Malcolm X Speaks: Selected Speeches and Statements*. Edited by George
Breitman. New York: Grove Press.

———. 1992. *February 1965: The Final Speeches*. New York: Pathfinder Press.

Marable, Manning. 2011. *Malcolm X: A Life of Reinvention*. New York: Viking.

Marx, Karl. 2000. "Address of the International Working Men's Association to Abraham
Lincoln, President of the United States of America. https://marxists.org/archive/marx/
iwma/documents/1864/lincoln-letter.htm.

McKay, Claude. 1937. *A Long Way from Home*. New York: Lee Furman.

McKenney, Nampeo. 1978. *The Social and Economic Status of the Black Population in the
United States: An Historical View, 1790–1978*. Washington, DC: Bureau of the Census.

Miller, Sally M., ed. 1996. *Race, Ethnicity, and Gender in Early Twentieth-Century American
Socialism*. New York: Garland.

Mishel, Lawrence, Josh Bivens, Elise Gould, and Heidi Shierholz. 2012. *The State of Working
America*. 12th ed. Ithaca: Cornell University Press.

Nichols, John. 2011. *The "S" Word: A Short History of an American Tradition . . . Socialism*.
New York: Verso.

OECD (Organization for Economic Cooperation). 2011. *Society at a Glance 2011: OECD
Social Indicators*. OECD Publishing. http://dx.doi.org/10.1787/soc_glance-2011-en.

Perry, Jeffrey B., ed. 2001. *A Hubert Harrison Reader*. Middletown, CT: Wesleyan
University Press.

Riddell, John, ed. 2012. *Toward the United Front: Proceedings of the Fourth Congress of the
Communist International, 1922*. Chicago: Haymarket Books.

Robinson, Cedric. 2000. *Black Marxism: The Making of the Black Radical Tradition*. 2nd
ed. Chapel Hill: University of North Carolina Press.

Sales, William W., Jr. 1994. *From Civil Rights to Black Liberation: Malcolm X and the*

Organization of Afro-American Unity. Boston: South End Press.

Sherwood, Marika. 2011. *Malcolm X: Visits Abroad.* Los Angeles: Tsehai Publishers.

Solomon, Mark. 1998. *The Cry Was Unity: Communists and African Americans, 1917–1936.* Jackson: University Press of Mississippi.

Tucker, Robert C., ed. 1978. *The Marx-Engels Reader.* 2nd ed. New York: W. W. Norton.

U.S. Bureau of Labor Statistics. 2012. August. http://www.bls.gov/cps/cpsrace2012.pdf.

Williams, Robert F. 1998. *Negroes with Guns.* Detroit: Wayne State University Press.

Wilson, Sondra Kathryn, ed. 2000. *The Messenger Reader: Stories, Poetry, and Essays from the Messenger Magazine.* Modern Library. New York.

Malcolm X, Black Cultural Revolution, and the Shrine of the Black Madonna in Detroit

Errol A. Henderson

Malcolm X's views have been characterized as "revolutionary nationalist," which is often contrasted with "cultural nationalist"; but this is conceptually confusing and, in light of Malcolm's black nationalist ideology, a distinction without a difference (Henderson 1997). Malcolm X's black nationalism led him to advocate "political revolution" as well as "cultural revolution"—the latter thesis is among the most undeveloped aspects of Malcolm's revolutionary ideology. Malcolm's call for black cultural revolution was consistent with his recognition that the black liberation struggle in the United States was part of a larger liberation struggle going on throughout the world.

Malcolm's thesis had a special relevance for activists in Detroit, Michigan, from the Revolutionary Action Movement (RAM), to the Freedom Now Party (FNP), the Republic of New Afrika (RNA), and the League of Revolutionary Black Workers (LRBW). But it was Albert Cleage who, through the Shrine of the Black Madonna, applied Malcolm's revolutionary precepts to the major political, economic, and cultural institution in the black community: the black church. In this essay, I examine the impact of Malcolm's thesis on black cultural revolution on the Shrine of the Black Madonna and its relevance to Detroit activists, more broadly, in the 1960s.

Malcolm X and Black Cultural Revolution

As noted above, Malcolm X's revolutionary black nationalism led him to advocate black cultural revolution. In the 1964 statement of the "Basic Aims and Objectives" of the Organization of Afro-American Unity, he stated that "we must launch a cultural revolution to unbrainwash an entire people" (Malcolm X 1970, 427). He insisted that, "armed with the knowledge of the past, we can with confidence charter a course for our future." He emphasized that "culture is an indispensable weapon in the freedom struggle" and "we must take hold of it and forge the future with the past." During the last two years of his life and up to the week before his assassination he noted that there was a "worldwide revolution going on" (Malcolm X 1970, 427). This revolution was to proceed in two stages. The first was a political revolution against Western imperialism, which was evident in the anticolonial struggles throughout Africa and Asia. The second was a cultural revolution in black America motivated by the human rights struggle of African Americans.

The human rights struggle would be manifest through either "the ballot or the bullet," in Malcolm's famous phrase, depending, in part, on the degree and extent of white racist resistance to the human rights claims of blacks. The first stage would facilitate and motivate the second stage, which would involve a cultural reawakening among black Americans, which would galvanize them to develop independent institutions to transform their societies—politically, economically, and culturally—and to establish multiracial democracy in the United States.

The centerpiece of Malcolm's formulation and program was black nationalism. Malcolm viewed black nationalism as a broad, dynamic, and evolving ideology having political, economic, and social dimensions rooted in the conception that African Americans comprised a nation that had the right of national self-determination, which meant that it had the right and responsibility to determine the political entity that would govern it. Black nationalism emerged from the national consciousness of a transnational enslaved society, whose members comprised diverse African peoples captured and transported to the United States. This diaspora synthesized an amalgam of its African cultures into an African American culture, which endured through slavery and both provided and reflected the commonalities that are the foundation of black national consciousness (Stuckey 1987). This incipient national consciousness was reinforced by the commonality of black racial oppression in terms of white exploitation of black labor through racial slavery for the black majority in the south and racist discrimination for the black minority in the north.

In addition, the galvanizing impact of the concerted effort of blacks to fight to overthrow slavery during the Civil War, the reconstitution of black family-based kin-groups after enslavement, and the institutionalization of prominent black cultural practices ensured the enduring significance of racial identification for black Americans. These factors combined to provide a sense of national identity among many African Americans and a framework for black culture (Franklin 1992). Black nationalism, which emerged from this original diasporan sense of national identity, reflected, inter alia, "a spirit of Pan-African unity and an emotional sense of solidarity with the political and economic struggles of African peoples throughout the world" (Moses 1996, 20).

Consistent with his view of the dynamic quality of black nationalism, Malcolm's incipient thesis of black cultural revolution suggests a process of systemically transforming U.S. society through the projection and institutionalization of an affirming African American culture in order to fundamentally transform the major life-giving and life-sustaining institutions of the society in order to create multiracial democracy—a clear corollary of such a revolution would be the wholesale rejection of white supremacy. This revolution could be violent, nonviolent, or a combination of both. It is this multiple quality of cultural revolution that is implicit in Malcolm's articulation of the historical and contemporary relevance of violent revolution in the United States in his "Message to the Grass Roots" (November 1963), in his argument on the prospect that the United States "is the first country on this earth that can have a bloodless revolution" in his "Black Revolution" (April 1964), and in his focus on the prospects for both outcomes in his "Ballot or the Bullet" thesis (April 1964).

Malcolm argued that revolutions in Africa and Asia were not only checking Western power in the periphery, they were providing a model of resistance to blacks in the diaspora, especially in the United States. He noted that

> As the African nations become independent and mold a new image—a positive image, a militant image . . . It has given pride to the Black man right here in the United States. So that when the Black revolution begins to roll on the African continent it affects the Black man in the United States and affects the relationship between the Black man and the white man in the United States. (Malcolm X 1989, 128)

The effect of African liberation struggles brought together the disparate strands of the global African community under a common banner of struggle, and it rejuvenated a sense of black self-determination, black pride, and black unity. Malcolm observed that "the same desire for freedom that moved the Black man on the African continent began to burn in the heart and the mind and the soul of the Black man here" (Malcolm X 1989, 168). He argued that "as the Black man in Africa got independent, it put him in a position to be master of making his own image. Up until 1959, when you and I thought of an African, we thought of someone naked, coming with the tom-toms, with bones in his nose" (Malcolm X 1989, 170). Malcolm went on to contend,

> This was the only image you had in your mind of an African. And from '59 on when they begin to come into the UN and you'd see them on the television you'd get shocked. Here was an African who could speak better English than you. He made more sense than you. He had more freedom than you. Why places where you couldn't go, all he had to do was throw on his robes and walk right past you.... It had to shake you up. And it was only when you'd become shook up that you began to really wake up.... So as the African nations gained their independence and the image of the African continent began to change, the things agreed as the image of Africa switched from negative to positive. Subconsciously! The Black man throughout the Western Hemisphere, in his subconscious mind, began to identify with that emerging positive African image.... And when he saw the Black man on the African continent taking a stand, it made him become filled with the desire also to take a stand . . . when we began to read about Jomo Kenyatta and the Mau Mau and others, then you find Black people in this country began to think along the same line. (Malcolm X 1989, 170–71)

So for Malcolm X, the "worldwide revolution," in turn, generated a cultural reawakening among black Americans. The breadth of this revolution influenced Malcolm X's view that political, economic, and social factors were often intimately tied together. They were tied in his theoretical arguments, as well; therefore, his black nationalism embraced Pan-Africanism, the spirit of Bandung, black liberation theology, and domestic colonialism.

He also noted that the status of the people throughout Africa rose no higher than that of the women in the society, which suggested the importance of challenging issues of gender in Malcolm's analysis. In addition, he argued that revolution in the United States should reflect the interests of the field Negro, which was Malcolm's characterization of the mass class strata of blacks, and reflected Malcolm's observation of the class differentiation in black America, which generated divergent interests in black communities across a variety of issues. All told, Malcolm's conception of black revolution focused on liberation from racist, sexist, and class domination.

Although Malcolm never proposed a specific theory of black cultural revolution, he thought that the manner that it would be constructed would require an engagement with the "peculiar" history and circumstances of black America that tied the political, economic, and social forces together in novel ways. He analogized the construction of such a theory to the improvisation of the jazz artist. He saw black music as one of the rare areas of black psychological autonomy that could create purely and richly African American values, aesthetics, and institutions to reflect them. No less would be required for the construction of social theory grounded in the history of black America and responding to and informing the demands of black life in the United States while providing a template for praxis to realize a better future. Where W. E. B. Du Bois evoked the "sorrow songs," Malcolm evoked the "soul" that he found at the root of the black experience and ethos. The key was to capture it, improvise, and mold it for black liberation.

But theory construction is not something one simply improvises. It comes from rigorous and disciplined study of the historical conditions and contemporary reality facing peoples. Such study would probably have led Malcolm to develop a less sanguine view of many of the African leaders whom Malcolm lauded that descended into despotism (e.g., Kwame Nkrumah, Jomo Kenyatta, and Sékou Touré). It might have dissuaded him from maintaining a position that revolutionary struggles in relatively underdeveloped Third World nations were exportable to black America, while encouraging a more systematic analysis of black social development in the United States.

In fact, one shortcoming of Malcolm's thesis was its notion that black Americans needed to follow the lead of Africans who had already embarked on anticolonial revolutionary change. Malcolm's "reverse civilizationism" correctly rejected the civilizationist theses of the pre–Du Boisian nationalists, but it failed to fully appreciate the novel, dynamic, and transformative aspects of African American culture and black political development in the United States. Such an appreciation of African American culture would demonstrate that the challenge for black Americans was not the replication of extant African culture forms, but a focus on the transformative elements of black culture in the United States—largely African American urban culture, which was more relevant to, and practicable in, U.S. society, which was/ is dramatically different from Third World contexts that Malcolm and many later theorists would draw on for their models of revolutionary change. One wonders, if Malcolm had lived to see the Watts Revolt, whether he might've reconsidered the view that black Americans lagged behind Africans in their vigor toward revolutionary social change and would've sought to channel the energy of revolt into a more lasting and impactful socioeconomic and political praxis.

In the event, Malcolm X did not have sufficient time to develop a theory of black cultural revolution before five members of the Nation of Islam (NOI) assassinated him in front of his wife, children, and supporters in the Audubon Ballroom in Harlem. Malcolm's promotion of both black nationalism and black cultural revolution would have the greatest impact on the black liberation movement following his death. This would be apparent on Detroiters of various political perspectives, and among those who attempted to push Malcolm's thesis to fruition were Albert Cleage and members of the Shrine of the Black Madonna.

The Shrine of the Black Madonna (Pan-African Orthodox Church)

By the mid-1960s, Rev. Albert Cleage of Central Congregational Church was a veteran of the black liberation struggle. He had organized with Harold Cruse, James and Grace Lee Boggs, Milton and Richard Henry (Gaidi and Imari of the RNA), William Worthy, and Conrad Lynn in the FNP; and with prominent preachers such as C. L. Franklin (Aretha Franklin's father and pastor of Detroit's New Bethel Baptist Church), U.S. Congressmen Charles Diggs and John Conyers, as well as State Senator Coleman Young, for whom Cleage's organization of the "Black Slate" would play a prominent role in his election as Detroit's first black mayor.

Cleage had been a confidant of Malcolm X who referenced him in his "Message to the Grass Roots" speech he delivered in Detroit in 1963; and he shared a podium at the historic Great March for Freedom in Detroit with Martin Luther King, who delivered an earlier version of his "I Have A Dream" speech to a Detroit crowd that some estimate as larger than the gathering that would hear the historic version in Washington, D.C. Cleage's theology had consistently been oriented to black liberation, and he was one of the few preachers of the Black Power era who wedded his theology—and not simply the rhetoric of the church or its pastor—to black liberation. This is an important distinction to make because the liberation theology of pastors such as King called congregants to dedicate themselves to their God-inspired and God-sanctioned duty of becoming involved in social justice—and not only social welfare—issues pertaining to black Americans. Cleage went beyond this and required that his followers participate in struggles for social justice for the "least of these" in the United States and abroad.

However, after his death, King's mature message—as influential as it was—could not necessarily maintain the impact it wielded while he was alive because it was tied so closely to his personal style, his personal narrative, his personal advocacy, and the sway of an ongoing civil rights movement. Thus, after King's death, "the faithful" could be deferential to his "image" and even his "message" without devoting much if any effort to emulating, much less institutionalizing, King's "practice" among themselves and within their individual churches. They could walk away from King's program of sociopolitical and spiritual activism using a variety of rationalizations after King's death. In contrast, Cleage not only transformed the message of the black church, he transformed its theology; however, unlike Malcolm, he remained within the Christian tradition. Expanding on the insights of historic black religious leaders such as Henry McNeal Turner and Bishop McGuire, he not only argued that God was black and that Jesus was a black man, he argued that Jesus was a "revolutionary black Messiah."

Further, Cleage argued that the black Church must promote a gospel of liberation rather than a gospel of salvation. A gospel of liberation insists that black liberation is the barometer of what is morally good and righteous: "that which supports the Struggle is good. That which advances the struggle of Black people is moral" (Cleage 1972, 188). Therefore, "the Black church must find its new direction in the acceptance of a new theology which holds that nothing is more sacred than the liberation of Black people" (Cleage 1972, 188). Further, he was convinced that "the theological basis for the gospel of liberation can be found in the life and teachings of Jesus. Not in his death, but in his life and in his willingness to die for the Black Nation" (Cleage 1972, 188). Eschewing the Pauline Gospels as an adulteration of Jesus's original revolutionary message to the black nation of Israel, Cleage argued that the "New Testament reflects the primitive pagan distortions that the Apostle Paul foisted upon the early church as a self-appointed apostle to the white gentile world"; but he was emphatic that "Jesus was a revolutionary Black religious leader fighting for the liberation of Israel" (1972, 3).

Cleage was not interested in simply painting Christianity black. He insisted that "you can take anything and paint it Black, but that does not make it Black if it is still serving white interests and if it still comes out of the white experience" (Cleage 1972, 14). For Cleage "a thing is not Black because it is painted Black. If it is not building a Black institution, it is not Black" (Cleage 1972, 14). This maxim was no less applicable to religion; thus, he was emphatic that "Black people cannot worship a white God and a white Jesus and fight white people for Black liberation" (Cleage 1972, 15). The fact that they did was a reflection of their acceptance of what Cleage called the white man's *declaration of black inferiority*, which was embedded and reinforced in the major political, economic, and social institutions of the United States (Cleage 1972, xxv). In his view, the *"declaration of Black inferiority* is the foundation on which American history has been built" and since slavery it has been "the framework within which the Black man was forced to build his existence" (Cleage 1972, 154).

Since "Black people are deliberately excluded from participation in the American Dream," they are outside the system as they should be; therefore, "when [blacks] demand that American institutions be restructured to include [them], or that they be destroyed as the instruments of [their] oppression, [blacks] are challenging the American way of life and ought to expect violence and conflict until the question of [their] position in American life is resolved" (Cleage 1972, 154). Cleage insists that "the Black man cannot naively assume that the white man is going to give up his privileged position without conflict. The Black man must therefore mobilize the total Black community in an attack upon repressive white institutional power" (Cleage 1972, 154).

In the clearest statement of the objective of his revolutionary framework, Cleage admonishes: "we must escape from powerlessness through the building of Black counterinstitutions and attacking the white institutional power establishment upon every front" (Cleage 1972, 154). Unlike Cruse (1967), he did not focus on attacking the cultural apparatus as the weakest sector of American capitalist free enterprise; unlike the LRBW, he did not focus on attacking at the point of production of the capitalist system; unlike most revolutionary theorists of the Black Power era, Cleage focused on attacking the multiple fronts of white racist institutional power. Here he was self-consciously following Malcolm's maxim of fighting on "all fronts"—as Paul Robeson had argued earlier—and he applied it in a way that Malcolm and many other Black Power activists had not.

The spearhead of his attack was not the black intelligentsia, the black proletariat, the lumpenproletariat, black artists, or an Afrocentric elite that had committed class suicide; it was the key political, economic, social—and cultural—institution in the black community: the black church. Convinced that "a people cannot seriously engage in a Liberation Struggle until they have developed a revolutionary theology" (Cleage 1972, 15), he recognized that the centerpiece of the transformation of black society envisioned by Black Power advocates was the transformation of the black church.

Thus, Cleage and his congregants transformed Central Congregational Church in Detroit into the Shrine of the Black Madonna. This transformation was epitomized, symbolically, in the large painting of the Black Madonna and child in the church sanctuary, but more importantly in the paradigm and program of Black Christian nationalism, which was its driving force. Cleage's black Christian nationalism began "with the basic premise that the Black church is essential to the Liberation Struggle, because it is controlled by Black people and is capable of being restructured to serve the Black Revolution" (1972, 173). Further, Cleage—who rechristened himself "Jaramogi Abebe Agyeman"—assumed that "a Black Revolution is impossible unless Black people are able to build an entire system of counter-institutions, created and designed to serve the interests of Black people as all American institutions now serve the white-supremacy interests of white people" (Cleage 1972, 173). This was Cleage's extension of the prominent practice among black nationalists of the 1960s to build parallel institutions to provide services and resources to black people and in so doing raise the contradiction between what was being provided by government institutions and social service agencies to white communities and what was being provided to blacks.

For Cleage, these counterinstitutions were available for co-optation by government and private interests of the white establishment; therefore, it was important to insure that the counterinstitutions not only serve the material, mental, and even martial interests of blacks, but also provide an independent base of political, economic, and social organization for black communities. These institutions should not be created in an ad hoc manner or simply emerge in response to transient though important issues that arise in the course of the interaction of blacks with white supremacist institutions and individuals. Cleage had learned from his earlier involvement with the FNP that it was more advantageous for the political party to be grounded in a powerful black counterinstitution rather than have the party itself serve as the basic counterinstitution from which black political organization would proceed. He insisted that in order "to build a system of counterinstitutions we must first build one basic Black institution which has the acceptance of the masses of Black people, facilities and economic stability not directly dependent on the hostile white world and the capacity to spin off all the other institutions needed for the establishment of a Black Nation within a nation" (Cleage 1972, 173–74). The obvious choice for Cleage was the black church—a revolutionary black church.

Nevertheless, Cleage realized that during the height of the Black Power era "these basic concepts are a source of general confusion to many young Black revolutionaries who have rejected religion in general and the Christian religion in particular—because it is a white man's religion, is counterrevolutionary, and serves

to perpetuate the Black man's enslavement by teaching otherworldly escapism"
(Cleage 1972, 174). Cleage asserted that

> we have now reclaimed our covenant as God's Chosen People and our revolutionary
> Black Messiah, Jesus. Slave Christianity which we learned from our white masters
> is counterrevolutionary and has served to perpetuate our enslavement. The revolu-
> tionary teachings of the Black Messiah commit us to revolution and Nation building.
> . . . We must free the Black church from slave Christianity and call it back to the
> original teachings of Jesus, and we must liberate the Black church as an institution
> and restructure it so that it can become the center of the Black Liberation Struggle.
> Young Black revolutionaries who cannot put aside their ideological hang-ups (largely
> inherited from white people) and be about this very serious business must stand
> accused of frivolity and of playing games with liberation. (Cleage 1972, 175)

For Cleage, any other starting point to the black liberation that he foresaw was
either unrealistic (e.g., separate black statehood in the United States or abroad),
untenable (interracial proletarian-led Marxist revolution), utopic (integrationism),
or liable to be easily undermined by white supremacist forces aligned against it (ad
hoc nationalist formations). He was insistent that

> we are trying to build Black institutions and our only possible point of beginning is
> the Black church. As wrong as it is, as biased as it is, as weak as it is, as corrupt as it
> is, as counterrevolutionary as it is, as Uncle Tom as it is, it is the only starting point
> we have. We have churches on every corner housed in buildings of every size, shape,
> and description. We have nominal control over it, but because of our confusion and
> psychological sickness it does not serve our interests. We have billions of dollars tied
> up in church buildings. If we are seriously interested in Black liberation we cannot
> realistically afford just to turn and walk away and leave this huge capital investment in
> the hands of the enemy. We must devise a way to co-opt it, restructure it, and make it
> the heart and center of the Black Revolution. The Black church must be programmed
> for Black liberation. (Cleage 1972, 200)

He added that

> upon this restructured institutional base we can build anything else we need. We
> can spin off economic, educational, political, and cultural institutions as rapidly as

we can train the necessary specialists. The Black church restructured as a power base can guarantee the success of any organized undertaking designed to serve the interests of Black people. . . . The Black church must program for power. . . . Only the Black church has the potential capacity to mobilize the total Black community. (Cleage 1972, 200–201)

He asserts that

the first task of the Black Church is to liberate the Black man's mind. . . . The Black church must become a teaching church. . . . It must help Black people begin to think realistically about everyday problems. This is the process by which we will move from a gospel of salvation to a gospel of liberation. We must define liberation, define struggle, analyze tactics, and develop methods for the struggle. We must look at history to find out what works and what does not work. The Black church must define liberation in terms of reality. Then we must put together the organization and structure to make it effective. (Cleage 1972, 189)

Cleage's religious project was self-consciously grounded in the social relations of the United States, which, for him, approximated a domestic balance of power system, which blacks were compelled to acknowledge, operate in, and manipulate successfully. In this framework, he argued,

Black institutions must be prepared to seek power, which means that they must inevitably face confrontation and conflict with the white power structure, because no one gives up power easily, quietly, or happily. The only way that power is transferred is through confrontation and conflict. The church is no exception. (Cleage 1972, 181)

Whether intended or not, Cleage was rejecting the supposition of many Black Power advocates who were attempting to derive lessons for black American struggles from Third World national liberation strategies such as the "war of the flea" approach or "foco" theory that emphasize the leverage of militarily weaker guerrilla bands on stronger conventional forces. Instead, Cleage's logic of struggle sought to employ the same approach that white nations had used to achieve their hegemonic positions—balance of power theory—to bring about their downfall. Importantly, "power for Black people," according to Cleage, "will not come from the barrel of a gun but from liberated minds willing to accept the theology of here and now expressed in the Black Christian Nationalist Creed" (Cleage 1972, 188).

Similarly, Cleage's contextualization of the black community in terms of institutional underdevelopment was not beholden to the domestic colonialism thesis, nor to neo-Marxist arguments suggesting the eradication of colonialism through the employment of guerrilla-based armed struggles that were also more applicable to Third World contexts. Cleage's thesis on the development of counterinstitutions was more germane to black American contexts. In fact, although he rarely used the term, Cleage's plan of action was oriented more to the logic of Malcolm X's thesis of black cultural revolution in the United States than many of his contemporaries and predecessors.

For example, he articulated the necessity of the psychological transformation of blacks to appreciate the depth of their oppression and miseducation in a manner that appreciates Malcolm X's arguments on cultural revolution. Not only was he a chief sponsor of the Detroit Black Arts Movement, but as early as 1962 he hosted a forum in his church that discussed the relationship between jazz and black nationalism featuring Abbey Lincoln and Max Roach following the release of their influential "Freedom Now Suite." Cleage endorsed the cultural revolution plank in the FNP draft platform and promoted the June 1966 Black Arts Convention in Detroit—an important forum of the incipient Black Arts Movement. Importantly, Cleage did not share other black nationalist or Marxist revolutionists' dismissal of the role of the black church in these developments, but centered them on the black church. Cleage anticipated such differences; in fact, he eschewed the notion of pursuing unity for unity's sake or even in the face of "valid reasons for uniting" such as a commonality of oppression based in black racial identity or the fear of genocide because, he argued, most rationales for black unity did not suggest how unity will "make a Black Nation come into being" (Cleage 1972, 190).

Instead, he maintained that "we must deliberately reject the values and thought patterns of the white Western world. We must consciously create a new Black mentality and value system which recognizes the equal worth of every Black brother and sister" (Cleage 1972, 190). Like Jesus, who "preached to multitudes" but "did not count on the great crowds, but on the small cadres with whom he worked," Cleage maintained that "the Black Nation will be built around small well-trained cadres" who "organize and train black people everywhere" (Cleage 1972, 222–23). These cadres would be organized through "rigid discipline during training, highly centralized controls, and carefully standardized organization structures." He fashioned the

Shrine of the Black Madonna "to use the methods of the Essene order to train cadres capable of going out and organizing Shrines, Information Centers, and cultural centers in the Black urban ghettos and rural areas of America and throughout the world" (Cleage 1972, 222). Individuals would receive a twelve-month catechism into membership in the shrine with advanced leadership training recommended. Cleage noted that other than the NOI "every other Black group tries to program with Black people the way they are (which is obviously an impossibility) or to readjust prejudices and misconceptions (which is equally impossible)" (Cleage 1972, 212–13).

An important aspect of this training focused on the development of program specialists who could institutionalize the Nguzo Saba across specific program areas, which is emblematic of the centrality of culture to the revolution that Cleage envisioned. Unlike theorists such as James Boggs and Huey Newton, he did not imagine that a revolutionary culture would emerge from a political revolution itself, but neither did he separate the struggle for cultural self-determination from that of political (or economic, for that matter) self-determination (Cleage 1972, 222–23). In 1968 he argued that "culture grows out of struggle"; but he saw this as "a power struggle" not a sartorial exercise in appropriating African dress. He admonished his contemporaries that "we have made an artificial separation between cultural revolution and the power struggle" (Dillard 2007, 254).

Cleage saw that too many of his contemporaries "are more excited about culture than they are excited about the struggle for power, because it is easier to put on African clothes than it is to struggle and sacrifice" (Dillard 2007, 254). This cultural revolution would require models of social change rooted in Afro-American processes and not expropriated from Asian, African, or Third World contexts that did not apply to black America.

In March 1968 Cleage argued that "the Negro church has prospered poorly in the North because it has been unable to relate the gospel of Jesus Christ meaningfully to the everyday problems of an underprivileged people in urban industrial communities" (Cleage 1972, 251). He was intent on changing this situation through the promotion of black Christian nationalism. Importantly, he would not only appeal to church members in the former Central Congregational Church, which included a fair measure of the "blue bloods" of Detroit's black community—including the Cleages, themselves; but he also intended to appeal to the field Negroes of Detroit. He made the Shrine of the Black Madonna a resource as well as a refuge to many of Detroit's organizing young proletarians, student organizers, and community activists—many of them representative of the lower classes whom Cleage was convinced maintained a "critical perspective and cultural authenticity" that "had been abandoned by their middle class peers"—to which Cleage wanted the black church in general, and his church in particular, to be relevant (Dillard 2007, 252–53). To this end, in large part, Cleage succeeded.

For example, the remarkable painting of the Black Madonna and child was created by Glanton Dowdell and General Baker, both members of RAM. Dowdell had honed his artistic talent serving a murder sentence in a Michigan prison from 1949 before being paroled in 1962. He had helped to organize the 1966 Black Arts Conference in Detroit that held sessions in Cleage's church. General Baker was a member of UHURU—a RAM-affiliated organization in Detroit—and by 1968, Baker would help found the Dodge Revolutionary Union Movement (DRUM), which became the core of the LRBW. Another founding member of DRUM was Marian Kramer, a prominent Detroit activist who had worked with Student Nonviolent Coordinating Committee in the south and was associated with Detroit's Black Panther Party—as several LRBW members were—as well as the influential West Central Organization. Kramer had organized tenants' unions, worked with the Westside Mothers, which was a welfare rights group, and organized against urban renewal and police brutality.

Many of the members of DRUM had been associated with the *Inner City Voice*, which was a radical community-oriented newspaper. When *ICV* staffer and activist John Watson assumed the editorship of Wayne State University's student newspaper, *The South End*—the third largest daily in the state of Michigan—he appended two black panthers on the masthead as well as the slogan "One conscious worker is worth more than a 100 students." Some of the most influential young black activists in Detroit, including Luke Tripp, Mike Hamlin, Diane Bernhard, Edna Watson, John Williams, Kenneth Cockrel, Gwen Kemp, Cassandra Smith, and Chuck and Gracie Wooten, were associated with these groups; and although not all of these individuals were associated with the Shrine of the Black Madonna, their organizations and many others were associated with the church, Cleage, or both.

Conclusion

In conclusion, in this essay I examined the impact of Malcolm X's thesis on black cultural revolution on the Shrine of the Black Madonna in the 1960s. I argued that Malcolm X's thesis of black cultural revolution is among the most undeveloped aspects of Malcolm's revolutionary ideology. It reflected his recognition that the black liberation struggle in the United States was part of a larger liberation struggle going on throughout the world. Malcolm's thesis had a special relevance for activists in Detroit, Michigan, and especially Albert Cleage, who through the Shrine of the Black Madonna applied Malcolm's revolutionary precepts to the major political, economic, and cultural institution in the black community: the black church.

A half century later, Cleage's focus on the black church and the development of counterinstitutions has been among the most influential theses and programs that embodies Malcolm's thesis of black cultural revolution in the United States.

WORKS CITED

Cleage, Albert B. 1972. *Black Christian Nationalism: New Directions for the Black Church.* New York: Morrow.

Cruse, Harold. 1967. *The Crisis of the Negro Intellectual.* New York: William Morrow.

Dillard, Angela D. 2007. *Faith in the City: Preaching Radical Social Change in Detroit.* Ann Arbor: University of Michigan Press.

Franklin, V. P. 1992. *Black Self-Determination: A Cultural History of African-American Resistance.* Brooklyn, NY: Lawrence Hill Books.

Henderson, Errol A. 1997. "The Lumpenproletariat as Vanguard? The Black Panther Party, Social Transformation, and Pearson's Analysis of Huey Newton." *Journal of Black Studies* 28, no. 2: 171–99.

Malcolm X. 1965. *The Autobiography of Malcolm X.* With the assistance of Alex Haley. New York: Grove Press.

———. 1970. "The Organization of Afro-American Unity: 'For Human Rights'" [statement of Basic Aims and Objectives of the Organization of Afro-American Unity, 1964]. In *Black Nationalism in America,* edited by John Bracey, August Meier, and Elliot Rudwick, 421–27. New York: Macmillan.

———. 1989. *Malcolm X: The Last Speeches.* Edited by Bruce Perry. New York: Pathfinder Press.

Moses, Wilson Jeremiah, ed. 1996. *Classical Black Nationalism: From the American Revolution to Marcus Garvey.* New York: New York University Press.

Stuckey, Sterling. 1987. *Slave Culture: Nationalist Theory and the Foundations of Black America.* New York: Oxford University Press.

Malcolm X and
the Cuban Revolution

Ollie Johnson

Malcolm X advocated major changes within the United States and around the world to improve the situation of Black people. In truth, Malcolm defended revolutionary changes (Malcolm X 1973; Karim 1992; Lincoln 1994; Marable 2011) including those in Latin America and the Caribbean. Significantly, Malcolm embraced the Cuban Revolution as an example of the type of serious change necessary to free Cubans from American imperialism and as an example of the type of liberating change sweeping the world. He specifically linked these international changes to the type of national change required in the United States for African Americans to be free. He repeatedly and consistently argued that African Americans must internationalize their struggle and demand not simply civil rights, but human rights.

This chapter examines why and how Malcolm X rhetorically and politically engaged the Cuban Revolution. In doing so, the chapter will emphasize the importance of uncertainty and transition in the last two years of Malcolm's life as he developed, deepened, and complicated his revolutionary logic and practices. During these last years, Malcolm left the Nation of Islam (NOI), his institutional and spiritual home for the previous ten years, spent extended time travelling abroad, and created two new organizations, Muslim Mosque, Inc. (MMI) and the Organization of Afro-American

Unity (OAAU). These last years for Malcolm represented a period in which he actively sought revolutionary collaborations around the world.

One such collaboration was with the young Afro-Cuban Carlos Moore, whom he met in the last months of his life. They shared a brief but intense interaction in November 1964. Moore had agreed to build the OAAU in Paris and Europe at the same time that he told Malcolm about his disillusionment with the Cuban Revolution. Moore admired Malcolm in 1959 and 1960 in New York, but when Moore returned to revolutionary Cuba in 1961, he could not believe the racism permeating the revolution. Moore raised his concerns about racism in revolutionary Cuba with Malcolm who at the time was much more interested in gaining international support to eradicate racism in the United States.

Malcolm X on Revolution

Manning Marable's recent biography, *Malcolm X: A Life of Reinvention*, calls attention to the dramatic life of one of America's most important twentieth-century leaders. While Marable's work covers the entirety of Malcolm's life, it obfuscates the revolutionary nature of Malcolm's philosophy and practice. While the epilogue chapter of the Marable biography of Malcolm entitled "Reflections on a Revolutionary Vision" recognizes Malcolm X as a revolutionary (Marable 2011, 479–87), at the same time, the chapter is completely inconsistent and unsatisfactory regarding how we should understand Malcolm's revolutionary commitment.

Marable seems uncomfortable with the reasonable interpretation that Malcolm X was a revolutionary who believed that (1) the United States was an evil racist, capitalist, and imperialist country guilty of oppressing and exploiting not only African Americans, but people all over the globe, (2) a revolution was necessary in the United States to overcome this state of affairs, and (3) violence was generally necessary for a revolution (Malcolm X 1992; 1970). Three examples illustrate Marable's problematic presentation of revolutionary Malcolm. Marable states "What Malcolm sought was a fundamental restructuring of wealth and power in the United States—not a violent social revolution, but radical and meaningful change nevertheless" (2011, 483). This sentence illustrates Marable's tendency to combine clear and accurate statements with perplexing clauses. Malcolm was indeed committed to radical and meaningful change. If Malcolm was committed to a fundamental restructuring in the United States, why would he have ruled out violent social revolution? In fact, he did not rule out violent social revolution. Malcolm supported and defended the need for revolutionary change in the United States. For Malcolm, revolution, by definition, involved violence and bloodshed (Malcolm X 1992; 1970).

Secondly, Marable notes "He [Malcolm X] had also come to reject violence for its own sake, but he never abandoned the nationalists' ideal for 'self-determination,' the right of oppressed nations or minorities to decide for themselves their own political futures" (2011, 485–86). Marable seems to accept the American government and mainstream media stereotype of Malcolm as a supporter of violence for the sake of violence. Malcolm believed in armed self-defense and violence when necessary in the midst of revolutionary struggle. He did not support nonviolence as a political philosophy. This explains his strong criticism of Martin Luther King Jr. and other civil rights advocates of nonviolence. Malcolm believed that it was outrageous that Black men, women, and children would allow themselves to be beaten, brutalized, and in some instances killed without defending themselves (Malcolm X 1992; 1970).

Third, Marable speculates "that Malcolm would certainly have condemned the terrorist attacks on September 11, 2001, as representing the negation of Islam's core tenets. . . . Malcolm's personal journey of self-discovery, the quest for God, led him toward peace and away from violence" (2011, 487). It is difficult to predict the behavior of leaders or to analyze how they would have responded to major events after their death. Nonetheless, scholars find it practically irresistible to not engage such hypothetical scenarios. Invoking hypothetical leadership behavior can help us compare the options or choices facing leaders. The tragedy of 9/11 was one of the most dramatic and traumatic events in American postwar history. Islamic suicide bombers hijacked four airplanes on the East Coast and attacked the World Trade Center in New York City and the Pentagon in Virginia. Another plane apparently en route to attacking a target in Washington, D.C., crashed in Pennsylvania when passengers resisted. Three thousand people were killed (Churchill 2003; Parenti 2002). While it is certainly possible that Malcolm would have condemned the 9/11 attacks, it is also possible that he would have developed an alternative response to the tragedy. For guidance, we can look to how he responded to the assassination of President John F. Kennedy in 1963 and how other radicals responded to 9/11.

On November 22, 1963, President John F. Kennedy was assassinated. The American people were shocked and in mourning. Despite being under strict orders from the Honorable Elijah Muhammad not to comment on the assassination, Malcolm described it as a situation "of the chickens coming home to roost" (Malcolm X 1973, 301). This comment, though considered unwelcome by Elijah Muhammad and much of the American public, was consistent with the speeches and analysis offered by Malcolm X and the NOI. Malcolm X regularly argued that the wicked deeds and immoral behavior of the U.S. government against African Americans and people of color around the world would have negative consequences. The murders of Medgar Evers in Mississippi and Patrice Lumumba in the Congo were examples of violence supported and sponsored by the American federal government that would bring destructive acts back on the White power structure. As a result of his comments, Malcolm X was silenced by Muhammad for ninety days. This act led to Malcolm's eventual departure from the Nation in March 1964. Following his exit from the NOI until his death in February 1965, Malcolm continued to criticize U.S. domestic and foreign policy in the strongest terms (Malcolm X 1973).

To understand how Malcolm would have responded to 9/11, it is useful to examine American policy since the 1960s. From Malcolm's death until the present day, the U.S. government has a consistent record of acts of oppression and exploitation similar to those that Malcolm condemned so strongly. These acts resulted from many interlinked structural and institutional causes such as American capitalism, imperialism, colonialism, racism, sexism, and militarism, among other factors (Churchill 2003; Parenti 2002; 2006; Hutchinson 1996). The American War in Vietnam continued for ten years after Malcolm's death. Millions of Vietnamese were killed, tortured, maimed, poisoned, and devastated as a consequence of U.S. military intervention. Thousands of American soldiers were killed in combat. The outrageousness of the war led even Martin Luther King Jr. to declare the U.S. government "the greatest purveyor of violence" on the earth in 1967 and 1968. By this time, King considered himself a nonviolent revolutionary and condemned the American government and society in terms in some respects similar to Malcolm (Ledwidge 2012, 150–60).

Malcolm's last speech before his death at the Ford Auditorium in Detroit gives no indication at all that his revolutionary impetus had become tempered as Marable suggests. In that speech, tagged "After the Bombing," in his usual fiery manner, Malcolm touched upon all the elements of U.S. imperialism especially its connection to the plight of African Americans in the United States. Malcolm's rhetoric remained radical in its indictment of racism and class oppression at the hands of Western governments.

> Tonight one of the things that has to be stressed is that which has not only the United States very much worried but which also has France, Great Britain, and most of the

powers, who formerly were known as colonial powers, worried also, and that primarily is the African revolution. They are more concerned with the revolution that's taking place on the African continent than they are with the revolution in Asia and in Latin America. And this is because there are so many people of African ancestry within the domestic confines or jurisdiction of these various governments. (Malcolm X 1992)

Indeed, contrary to Marable's contention that Malcolm was tempering his revolutionary zeal, it was during the last years of his life as he experienced the revolutionary Third World of the period, especially after he had met Fidel Castro in Harlem in 1960, that in fact Malcolm became drawn to the example of Cuba's ongoing revolutionary course.

"The Cuban Revolution—that's a revolution," he told an audience predominantly of African Americans in November 1963, "They overturned the system. Revolution is in Asia, revolution is in Africa, and the white man is screaming because he sees revolution in Latin America. How do you think he'll react to you when you learn what a real revolution is?" (Barnes 2009, 184–86)

Malcolm X on the Cuban Revolution

In January 1959, the Cuban Revolution triumphed over the government of military strongman Fulgencio Batista. Fidel Castro and other revolutionary leaders entered the capital of Havana and began establishing themselves in power. It soon became clear that these revolutionaries were committed to thorough political, economic, and social changes. Although the U.S. government had a history of military intervention in Cuba, of support for brutal Cuban dictatorships, and a permanent military base in Guantanamo, the revolutionary government wanted to establish normal relations with the United States. This would not be possible because the United States would not accept the reforms that the Cuban government began instituting (Pérez-Stable 1999; Franklin 1997).

Revolutionary government initiatives included agrarian reform, reducing the influence of foreign companies, outlawing racial discrimination, instituting a national literacy campaign, and establishing a new political order. These political acts were popular with many citizens inside Cuba. Conservative and wealthy Cubans began to disagree with the direction of the revolution. The U.S. government became increasingly hostile. In a dramatic example of opposition, the U.S. government, through the CIA, organized and financed a group of over one thousand Cuban exiles to invade Cuba on April 17, 1961, at the Bay of Pigs. The Castro government defeated the military intervention in three days (Franklin 1997, 34–46). Malcolm X saw the Cuban Revolution as part of an international trend of countries in Africa, Asia, the Caribbean, and Latin America fighting against the old oppressive systems of colonialism and imperialism. These countries wanted independence, sovereignty, equality, and respect. These were the same things that Malcolm wanted for African Americans (Mealy 1993).

Because of the early rhetoric and policies of the Cuban Revolution, Malcolm X was supportive. He had an opportunity to affirm his support when he met with Castro and other Cuban revolutionaries in New York. On September 18, 1960, Castro and a delegation arrived in New York to attend the United Nations General Assembly. However, the Eisenhower administration was already disgruntled about the revolutionary government's policies. The U.S. administration restricted the Cuban officials to the island of Manhattan and did not treat them with the respect they felt appropriate. The Cuban delegation ran into an additional problem with the Shelburne Hotel in midtown Manhattan. Because the Shelburne made exorbitant financial demands, the Cuban delegation decided to move to the Black-owned Hotel Theresa in Harlem on September 19 (Mealy 1993).

The decision to stay at the Hotel Theresa created a great deal of excitement in Harlem. Castro was able to denounce the rude treatment his delegation received and at the same time achieve a victory for personal diplomacy. In addition to speaking at the United Nations, Castro was able to meet various international leaders such as President Gamal Abdel Nasser and Prime Minister Jawaharlal Nehru at the Hotel Theresa. More important for African Americans, Castro encountered Malcolm X, other community leaders, the Harlem community, and supporters of the Cuban Revolution.

On the evening of September 19, 1960, Malcolm X met Castro in his suite in the Hotel Theresa. According to Ralph D. Matthews, one of the few journalists present, the meeting was positive. The two leaders covered many topics and generally agreed in their understanding of the national and international political situation. Castro and the Cuban delegates were treated like celebrities and received great support from the people of Harlem and New York (Mealy 1993, 41–44).

Later, in December 1964, Malcolm invited Cuban leader Ernesto "Che" Guevara to come to the Audubon Ballroom to speak to a meeting of the OAAU but due to security factors, Che couldn't make the meeting. In reading Che's apology note to the Audubon audience, Malcolm would indicate that despite the U.S. government's branding Che an "enemy," Che was in fact a revolutionary of the type that African Americans should embrace (Barnes 2009).

Carlos Moore on Malcolm X, Fidel Castro, and the Cuban Revolution

Like Malcolm X, Carlos Moore, a recent Afro-Cuban immigrant to the United States, was able to meet Castro and the Cuban delegation during their New York visit. Carlos Moore was born in Cuba in 1942. He grew up Black, poor, and the child of Jamaican immigrants to Cuba in Central Lugareño, a small rural town. He maintains that his low status was one of the reasons that he was excited about the opportunity to move to the United States and join his father who had recently remarried. Arriving in the United States at fifteen years of age, Moore felt he had moved up in the world as he attended Boys High School in Brooklyn and adjusted to American life. Living the bohemian life, he hung out at cafes, clubs, and events in Greenwich Village. Simultaneously, he developed strong ties to African Americans. He met Black community leaders such as Lewis Michaux and spent a lot of time reading at the National Memorial African Bookstore in Harlem (Moore 2008).

A talented student, Carlos Moore became politicized and radicalized while in the United States. Moore interacted with the NOI. Their street corner orators asked him why he conked his hair and dated White women. Moore heard Malcolm X and other Black leaders speak and was impressed with their Black nationalist message. However, Moore did not consider himself very religious and was unmoved by the Nation's religious and theological doctrine. Along with Patrice Lumumba, Malcolm X was one of the most outstanding leaders in Moore's incipient Pan-African worldview (Moore 2008, 73–138).

While in the United States, Moore soon found himself being asked about the Cuban Revolution. He initially didn't know much and wasn't very interested. But given the vibrant political atmosphere in New York and unprecedented political developments within the United States and around the world, Moore became better informed and soon emerged a strong defender and supporter of the Cuban Revolution. As a Cuban born and raised in Cuba and fluent in Spanish and English, Moore shortly gained visibility as a public speaker at rallies and protests in New York. Before Castro arrived in New York, Moore had begun working with the Fair

Play for Cuba Committee and the July 26 Movement. After Castro arrived in Harlem, Moore was actively on the scene (Moore 2008, 139–48).

> Night after night I addressed the hundreds who gathered to listen, shouting until I was hoarse. Those were euphoric moments. I stirred crowds into a frenzy that defied the biting cold. Since there was no doubt in my mind that Castro had reversed the situation in favor of blacks in Cuba, I fervently extolled the Revolution's success in eliminating racism. . . . I had become quite popular in Harlem's black nationalist circles, so I was all the more credible when praising the Revolution's racial achievements. (Moore 2008, 144)

It was because of his work supporting the Cuban Revolution in New York that Moore was able to meet Castro and other members of the Cuban delegation. Moore was only seventeen years old. He was humbled and exhilarated. He remembered: "My love for Fidel Castro was genuine, profound. The Revolution he ushered into Cuba was changing the face of our country. In a flicker of a second, I'd decided on my next big step in life: I would return to my country" (Moore 2008, 146). The only questions Moore had about the delegation related to its lack of racial diversity. Moore spoke with the only prominent Afro-Cuban in the delegation, military leader Juan Almeida, and learned that he was a late addition. Almeida had a special visibility in majority-Black Harlem. Moore wondered whether Almeida was only added because the delegation was staying in Harlem (Moore 2008, 145–47).

In June 1961, Moore returned to Cuba. He was sent by the July 26 Movement to work for the revolution. He was ready to give his life defending the revolution. In January 1961, Moore had already been devastated by the assassination of Patrice Lumumba, his most admired symbol of African revolutionary leadership. Shortly after arriving in Cuba, Moore experienced what he believed to be racism. Despite being fluent in English and having studied French, Moore did not receive an appointment in the foreign ministry. Moreover, he noticed that almost all the top revolutionary leaders were White. Most important, Moore lived the extreme frustration of witnessing revolutionary action against racial discrimination and segregation combined with the banning of official and public discussion about ongoing, informal racist practices and attitudes (Moore 2008, 163–72).

Moore spent two and a half years in Cuba. He had beautiful experiences as well as near fatal ones. One of the highlights of Moore's return to Cuba was meeting, working with, and translating for foreign Black leaders. Moore met and developed relationships with Brazilian Abdias do Nascimento, founder of the Black Experimental Theater, Haitian intellectual Marc Balin, and American Robert Williams, former leader of the Monroe, North Carolina, NAACP who had supported armed self-defense against White terrorist groups like the Ku Klux Klan. Williams was in exile in Cuba. The FBI included Williams on its most wanted list for allegedly kidnapping a White couple when in fact he had saved them. Moore worked with Williams on *Radio Free Dixie*, the radio program created by Williams in Cuba and beamed to the United States to encourage Americans to organize and resist racial segregation and racist violence (Moore 2008, 163–76).

Overall, Moore's return to Cuba was traumatic. He learned much from Marc Balin and Afro-Cuban intellectual Walterio Carbonell about race, politics, and history. Moore believed that Cuban racism was widespread despite the recent revolutionary measures against explicit segregation and discrimination. Moore believed that it was his revolutionary duty to denounce ongoing racism. His antiracism efforts only had the effect of getting him in trouble. Despite the advice of his brother Frank, Juan Almeida, and many others, to stop bringing up the question of race in the context of the revolution, he continued. He was warned and advised repeatedly to stop talking about racial discrimination.

Because of his observation that racism had not been effectively abolished in Cuba and his willingness to share his views with the revolutionary authorities, Moore was threatened with death, imprisoned, and placed in a labor camp. Those unpleasant experiences got his attention. Moore was given a job in the foreign ministry and, apparently, was prepared to stop criticizing the racism of the revolution. Unfortunately, he soon ran into one of the White revolutionaries (who had a leadership position in the ministry) whom Moore had earlier accused of being racist (Moore 2008).

As a result, thinking that he would be returned to a labor camp or killed, Moore fled Cuba in December 1963 fearing for his life. After months in Egypt, Moore eventually arrived in France in 1964 and stayed there for thirteen years. He wrote articles in France and eventually published the important book *Castro, the Blacks, and Africa* (1989) in the United States. With these works, Moore became the most prominent and controversial Afro-Cuban critic of the Cuban Revolution. He would be hounded by Cuban intelligence agents around the world and criticized as counterrevolutionary by former friends and allies (Moore 2008).

Malcolm X, Travel Abroad, and Crisis at Home

As a result of his comments on President Kennedy's assassination and his growing struggle with the Nation, Malcolm X left the NOI in March 1964. The last year of Malcolm's life was filled with conflict with the Nation, incomplete attempts at organization building, and international travel. This would also be the time that Malcolm's engagement with race and revolution became complicated, especially as his OAAU increasingly collaborated with the Socialist Workers Party and the Militant Labor Forum in New York.

Malcolm's break with the NOI was fraught with contention, confusion, stress, and strain. Malcolm denounced Elijah Muhammad for impregnating several of his young secretaries and for being hypocritical. The NOI leadership responded that Malcolm wanted to take over the Nation and, failing that, destroy the good name and work of the Honorable Elijah Muhammad. This conflict continued on multiple levels, including physical intimidation and violence. Malcolm and his aides had to be careful to try to avoid physical confrontations and attacks by NOI members loyal to Elijah Muhammad (Marable 2011, 297–449; Sales 1994).

In New York, Malcolm X and his supporters created the MMI on March 12, 1964, and the OAAU on June 28, 1964. These organizations provided Malcolm with a new religious and political base of operations as he tried to become more politically active than the structures of the Nation had allowed him to be. During the final ten months of his life, Malcolm travelled to or through various countries and met with many political leaders, including heads of state. Malcolm visited many countries in Africa, the Middle East, and Europe. Many of the leaders were freedom fighters and independence leaders themselves. Malcolm always explained the situation of African Americans and also tried to learn about the experiences of his hosts and advocated for mutual support. Malcolm's strong interest in revolutionary and Pan-African solidarity was apparent in his correspondence with friends in the United States and his speeches during and following his international trips (Sales 1994; Sherwood 2011).

After his split with the NOI, Malcolm X was even more committed to fighting for Black liberation by any means necessary. He wanted to work with anybody willing to work with him. This new Black united front approach to political struggle was compromised, however, by Malcolm's ongoing criticism of mainstream Black political leaders and his strong positive view on revolution. In April 1964, he outlined his perspective on revolution.

This is a real revolution. Revolution is always based on land. Revolution is never based on begging somebody for an integrated cup of coffee. Revolutions are never fought by turning the other cheek. Revolutions are never based upon love-your-enemy and pray-for-those-who-spitefully-use-you. And revolutions are never waged singing "We Shall Overcome." Revolutions are based upon bloodshed. Revolutions are never compromising. Revolutions are never based upon negotiations.

Revolutions are never based upon any kind of tokenism whatsoever. Revolutions are never even based upon that which is begging a corrupt society or a corrupt system to accept us into it. Revolutions overturn systems. And there is no system on this earth which has proven itself more corrupt, more criminal, than this system that in 1964 still colonizes 22 million African-Americans, still enslaves 22 million Afro-Americans.

There is no system more corrupt than a system that represents itself as the example of freedom, the example of democracy, and can go all over the earth telling other people how to straighten out their house, when you have citizens of this country who have to use bullets if they want to cast a ballot. (Malcolm X 1992, 50)

Later in this speech, Malcolm presented the possibility that the United States might be able to avoid a bloody and violent revolution. However, he concluded, "America is not morally equipped to do so" (Malcolm X 1990, 57).

Malcolm continued to defend revolutionary governments that overthrew corrupt systems, colonialism, and imperialism to gain control of their own land, resources, and institutions. This is part of the excitement that Malcolm felt while visiting African and Middle Eastern countries that had recently gained their independence from England and France. Throughout his international travels, Malcolm worked to internationalize the African American struggle. He drew parallels between the African fight for independence and the African American fight for freedom. He recruited allies and supporters to create OAAU chapters in Africa and Europe (Sherwood 2011).

Malcolm X traveled to Paris in November 1964. The person selected to provide his security was Carlos Moore, who was then living there in exile. Although completely disillusioned with the Cuban Revolution and with minimal personal resources, Moore remained committed to the Black Liberation Movement. During the few days that Malcolm X spent in Paris, Moore was at his side. Moore translated for Malcolm, organized a small security group, and arranged meetings with Malcolm's old friends from the United States as well as new contacts. Though Moore slept very little during Malcolm's visit, he was reinvigorated by his contact with Malcolm. The highlight of Malcolm's trip was his speech at the Salle de la Mutualité sponsored by the important cultural organization and journal *Présence Africaine* (Moore 2012; Moore 2008, 277–79; Sherwood 2011, 139–45).

While in Paris, Malcolm X asked Moore to become involved with and build the OAAU in Paris and throughout Europe. Moore accepted this responsibility although he knew this acceptance would make him even more vulnerable. His criticism of the Cuban Revolution had already gained the hostile attention of the Cuban government. Malcolm was in a very difficult situation as he was under attack by the NOI and the U.S. government. In Paris, Moore shared with Malcolm his personal experiences in Cuba and his critique of the Cuban Revolution. Moore stated that Malcolm listened closely and really didn't agree or disagree with his analysis (Moore 2012; Moore 2008, 277–79). In his public speeches and interviews, Malcolm X referred to the Cuban Revolution in a positive light. While traveling internationally, Malcolm met with Cuban diplomats, attended their events, and accepted their support (Sherwood 2011).

During their brief time together in Paris, Malcolm conveyed to Moore that he admired and had a lot of respect for Robert Williams. Moore shared how he had worked with Williams in Cuba. Although Malcolm had pleasant moments with friends in Paris, he was more serious when he was alone with Moore. Malcolm had a distinct sense of urgency in giving directives to Moore. When Moore probed, Malcolm made it clear that he did not have long to live. Malcolm believed that he was going to be killed. When Moore tried to discuss this talk of mortality, Malcolm emphasized that he was deadly serious. Therefore, it was imperative that Moore build the OAAU and organize a group to support the forces loyal to Patrice Lumumba in the ongoing conflict in the Congo (Moore 2012).

Why would Malcolm X continue to support the Cuban Revolution publicly and ask a critic of the revolution to help build the OAAU? Malcolm saw the Cuban Revolution as one of the most significant political events of the twentieth century. Egalitarian and anti-imperialist, the revolution improved education, healthcare, and social standing for Cuba's poor. Castro became world famous for challenging U.S. foreign policy in Latin America and around the world. Evidently, for Malcolm X, Moore's criticism of the Cuban Revolution did not invalidate the revolution's achievements. At the same time, Moore's support of Malcolm's Pan-African leadership and willingness to strengthen the OAAU confirmed Moore's commitment to the struggle. For Moore, the price of Cuban Revolution was too high. All potential organized, independent dissent was outlawed. This antidemocratic feature was one of the most unacceptable, especially since the now banned Black social clubs had been central aspects of Afro-Cuban cultural and political life for decades. However, in crisis and transition, Malcolm was not ready to reject the support of those revolutionaries who supported him.

When Malcolm left Paris, Moore had a new focus. He went about the process of evaluating and recruiting people for the OAAU and Congo mission. This was a delicate process because Moore was still relatively new to Paris, had few resources of his own, and was rejected by some leftists because of his criticism of the Cuban Revolution. At the same time, Moore did have the support of key individuals who had resources and contacts. Ellen Wright, the late writer Richard Wright's wife, and Mary Jane Barnet, a Canadian expatriate, believed in Moore and introduced him to people in their social, cultural, and political networks. This assistance enabled Moore to do a good job of preparing Paris for Malcolm's planned return in February 1965 to formally launch the OAAU in Paris (Moore 2012).

On February 9, 1965, Malcolm X flew to Paris to speak publicly and meet with his supporters. Moore and the other Paris-based activists were excited. To the surprise of Malcolm and his followers, after his plane landed in Paris, he was not allowed to leave the airport. After a brief exchange with French authorities at the airport, Malcolm was put on a plane and forced to return to London. Once Malcolm was back in London, Moore was able to reach him by phone and encouraged Malcolm to give his message right then, which Malcolm was able to do. This phone connection helped Moore salvage the Paris meeting. Moore and Malcolm were confused and unsure about why Malcolm had been prevented from entering Paris (Moore 2012).

What roles had the French and American governments played? What role had the American Embassy in Paris played? Malcolm demanded answers, but none were forthcoming. There was much speculation with one reason being that the French had been informed that the CIA would assassinate him while there, and thus, in order to avoid this, the French would deny Malcolm entry (Moore 2012; Sherwood 2011, 187–90). Malcolm X was assassinated in New York City less than two weeks later.

Conclusion

The United States was and is an authoritarian and imperialist country. Malcolm X recognized this reality more clearly than most African American political leaders. The United States has hundreds of military bases around the world, including one in Cuba. The American military base in Guantanamo was established over one hundred years ago as a direct result of U.S. intervention and occupation. Cuba wants the U.S. government to leave the base but has been unable to force them to leave. This is an example of American imperialism. It is unimaginable that Cuba or any foreign country could maintain a military base in the United States against the desire of the U.S. government.

Malcolm X was deeply critical of the U.S. political system and its government's treatment of Blacks. As a result, his reflex position was to be sympathetic to challenges (domestic and international) to American power and influence. In the post–World War II period, the Cuban Revolution represented the most important international challenge to American power in the Western hemisphere. Malcolm X and other Black leaders and activists saw Fidel Castro and other Cuban revolution-aries as inspirations for and possibilities of revolutionary social change.

The fact that Malcolm X, a supporter of the Cuban Revolution, was willing to work with Carlos Moore, an Afro-Cuban critic of the revolution, suggests that both Malcolm and Moore, in their own ways, backed radical social change, the struggle against racism, and Black political autonomy. Their connection was an effort to organize a transnational force for Black liberation. Because Malcolm was denied access to France in 1965, he was never able to meet again with Moore to implement their political vision. The demise of the OAAU was followed by the rise of new Black groups, such as the Black Panther Party, committed to fighting racism, imperialism, colonialism, and capitalism. Moore's experience demonstrated that one-party socialism did not necessarily provide a definitive solution to these problems.

WORKS CITED

Barnes, Jack. 2009. *Malcolm X, Black Liberation, and the Road to Workers Power*. New York: Pathfinder Press.

Churchill, Ward. 2003. *On the Justice of Roosting Chickens: Reflections on the Consequences of U.S. Imperial Arrogance and Criminality*. Oakland, CA: AK Press.

Franklin, Jane. 1997. *Cuba and the United States: A Chronological History*. Melbourne: Ocean Press.

Hutchinson, Earl Ofari. 1996. *Betrayed: A History of Presidential Failure to Protect Black Lives*. Boulder, CO: Westview Press.

Karim, Benjamin. 1992. *Remembering Malcolm*. With Peter Skutches and David Gallen. New York: Carroll & Graf.

Ledwidge, Mark. 2012. *Race and US Foreign Policy: The African-American Foreign Affairs Network*. New York: Routledge.

Lincoln, C. Eric. 1994. *The Black Muslims in America*. 3rd ed. Grand Rapids, MI: Wm B. Eerdmans; Trenton, NJ: Africa World Press.

Malcolm X. 1970. *By Any Means Necessary: Speeches, Interviews and a Letter by Malcolm X*. Edited by George Breitman. New York: Pathfinder Press.

———. 1973. *The Autobiography of Malcolm X*. With the assistance of Alex Haley. New York: Ballantine Books.

———. 1990. *Malcolm X Speaks: Selected Speeches and Statements*. Edited by George Breitman. New York: Grove Press.

———. 1992. *The Autobiography of Malcolm X*. With the assistance of Alex Haley. New York: Ballantine Books.

Marable, Manning. 2011. *Malcolm X: A Life of Reinvention*. New York: Viking.

Mealy, Rosemari, ed. 1993. *Fidel and Malcolm X: Memories of a Meeting*. Melbourne: Ocean Press.

Moore, Carlos. 1989. *Castro, the Blacks, and Africa*. Los Angeles: CAAS/UCLA.

———. 2008. *Pichón: Race and Revolution in Castro's Cuba: A Memoir*. Chicago: Lawrence Hill Books.

———. 2012. Interview by Ollie Johnson. Salvador, Bahia, Brazil. July 12.

Parenti, Michael. 2002. *The Terrorism Trap: September 11 and Beyond*. San Francisco: City Lights Books.

———. 2006. *The Culture Struggle*. New York: Seven Stories Press.

Pérez-Stable, Marifeli. 1999. *The Cuban Revolution: Origins, Course, and Legacy*. 2nd ed. New York: Oxford University Press.

Reitan, Ruth. 1999. *The Rise and Decline of an Alliance: Cuba and African American Leaders in the 1960s*. East Lansing: Michigan State University Press.

Sales, William W., Jr. 1994. *From Civil Rights to Black Liberation: Malcolm X and the Organization of Afro-American Unity*. Boston: South End Press.

Sherwood, Marika. 2011. *Malcolm X: Visits Abroad*. Los Angeles: Tsehai Publishers.

Malcolm Omowale X (Re) Turns to Africa

Pan-Africanism and the Black Studies Agenda in a Global Era

Rita Kiki Edozie

> When I was in Ibadan, Nigeria, at the University of Ibadan, the students there gave me a new name, which I go for—Omowale; they say it means in Yoruba—the child has returned.
>
> —Malcolm X, University of Ghana, May 13, 1964

Known by many names—X, Malik, Shabazz, and as the quotation above indicates, Omowale—the man who was born as Malcolm Little used names to construct and signify a self-identity throughout his conscious life and political practice. In previous chapters, we have already seen how X signified an unknown heritage from Africa. Malik and Shabazz signified a preferred religious affiliation toward Islam away from Christianity, a religion that Malcolm associated with U.S. racism and the subversion of his African identity. With both names (X and Malik Shabazz), Malcolm underscored the intersectionality of the African unknown and Islamic naming identity as markers of positive affirmation of his African identity; the former pointed to the kidnapping of his ancestors from Africa while the latter referred to his ancestors' West African heritage in Islam.

As with the larger volume, *Malcolm X's Michigan Worldview: An Exemplar for Contemporary Black Studies*, our main objective for the current chapter is to conclude the exploration, interrogation, and deliberation of the influence and impact that Malcolm X's lived experiences have on local, national, and global Black world communities in relation to the Black Studies discipline. However, our focus here will differently achieve this objective in relation to the continent of Africa and its study. In *The Geography of Malcolm X* (2006), James Tyner reveals how a study of Malcolm X helps the Black Studies scholar examine African American discourses about Africa, which not only deepens our understanding of the relationship between the two brethren but opens a window onto black America as it transformed itself during the mid-twentieth century. Tyner expresses concerns with a Black Studies scholarship that has downplayed the international forces that informed black America and caused a divorce of our understanding of the black freedom struggle from the broader, worldwide context. A study of Malcolm X in Africa rectifies such a trend in 2014 that forgets the Pan-Africanist precepts of African American thought that are so critical to our history and circumstance.

In responding to Tyner's call, in this chapter, we consider biographical aspects of Malcolm's early childhood as the son of a Garveyite who spent formative years in Lansing, Michigan, to see how this experience shaped and formulated Malcolm's own racial and ethnic identity formation in Pan-Africanist ideology and its attendant "trans-Africa" style of politics. Furthermore, we ask what insights Malcolm's Pan-Africanist identity and politics have for the evolution of the Black Studies discipline. What has been the significance of Malcolm's contribution to Pan-Africanism—to the African diaspora, to Africa, and to the notion that the National Council for Black Studies refers to as the African worldview paradigm of Black Studies? What local and community conditions in Michigan fostered Malcolm's formulation and advocacy of Pan-Africanism?

To guide these considerations, the chapter presents this discussion of Malcolm and Africa in the context of an argument about how the biography of Malcolm X helps us to examine African Americans' discourses about Africa. These discourses not only deepen our understanding of the relationship between African Americans in the United States and Africans on the continent, but open a window onto black America's Black Power globality and internationalism as it transformed itself during the mid-twentieth century (Tyner 2006). To see Malcolm X as a Black Studies exemplar for the concept of Pan-Africanism is to interrogate the discipline's agility in connecting the black freedom struggle in America to the broader, worldwide context, particularly to the African continent.

Comparatively to Martin Luther King, whose brand of civil rights agitation was liberal, Americanist, and social democratic, Malcolm's brand of nationalism was radical, transnationally diasporic, and globally Pan-Africanist. Martin advocated inclusion for the Negro and used the term profusely; Malcolm rejected the "Negro" identity label as racist and instead underscored alternative identities embedded in African heritage, Islam, and class factors. In doing so, he would formulate an ideology of Black nationalist separatism, autonomous and self-determined community development for Blacks, and especially underscored for the purposes of the current chapter, such nationalism would be transnationally political, cultural, and economically intersectional in solidarity with Africans on the continent. Significantly, the chapter will identify and discuss four such interrelated influences that shaped Malcolm's Pan-Africanism: Garveyism, the Nation of Islam (NOI), U.S. racism, and the context of African liberation in the 1950s and 1960s.

Regarding the first factor, Malcolm would learn from his parents, Earl and Louise Little, the philosophy of Garveyism as first foundations of his early Pan-Africanist formulation. Marcus Garvey's internationalism would be expressed best when he declared, "I know no national boundary where the Negro is concerned. The whole world is my province until Africa is free" (Garvey 2004, 10). To what extent could Malcolm's Garveyite roots have facilitated his own shaping of a Black U.S. identity, particularly for those African descendants in the United States who strategically identify as "African." Malcolm would say, "Twenty-two million African-Americans— that's what we are—Africans who are in America" (Malcolm X 1990, 36).

With respect to the second and third factors, the ontological precepts embedded in Black American Islam and U.S. systematic racial formation and Western colonialism, as well as the Black nationalist response, would also direct Malcolm to his African roots even if unknown as symbolized by his chosen surname "X." With the fourth influencing factor, we show how it was that Malcolm was a product of his time in the heyday of the 1950s and 1960s when civil rights occurred simultaneously with African liberation. Between 1960 and 1965, at least half of Africa's current fifty-five nation-states struggled successfully for their own liberation from colonialism. Malcolm would state,

> 1954 to 64 was the era of an emerging Africa, an independent Africa. And the impact of those independent African nations upon the civil rights struggle in the United States was tremendous. Number one, one of the first things the African revolution produced was rapid growth in a movement called the Black Muslim movement . . .

the militancy that existed in African nationalism on the African continent was one of the main motivating factors in the rapid growth of the group known as the Black Muslim movement [to] which I belonged. (qtd. in Malcolm X 1991, 40)

Through these four contextual experiences, we can see the context that shapes Malcolm's antiracist, Pan-Africanist leadership. Malcolm's Midwest-Michigan experiences and encounters with U.S. racial formation, particularly given his Garveyist father and Grenadian Black Caribbean mother, compared to King's southern experience fostered a different brand of revolutionary leadership in Malcolm. This is a leadership that privileges a rejection of the Negro identity and an expansion of Blackness to include an African ethnic identity. Formed this way, Malcolm's identity and politics of this sort further developed his Pan-Africanism.

Malcolm's Pan-African identity discourses and political practices—his Africa discourses, his trips to Africa, his establishment of and encounters with the Organization of Afro-American Unity (OAAU)—all provide a way to examine the importance of Africa for Malcolm's lived experiences and thereby a way to examine Africa as a core paradigm of the Black Studies discipline. Through his engagement with Africa, Malcolm has helped the discipline to intellectually unravel conceptual issues regarding race and ethnic identity, ethnic identity as a cultural identity on its own terms, race, ethnicity, and global political-economy and inequality, and African World solidarity movements for social justice worldwide.

Subsequent sections of the chapter will provide detail on the Malcolm Pan-Africanism impact thesis by beginning with a reevaluation of the Black Studies theories of Pan-Africanism in relation to Malcolm's vanguard shaping of the movement. We employ the biographical aspects of Malcolm's Garveyite and Grenadian childhood experiences in Lansing and Detroit, Michigan, illuminating how early twentieth-century African American communities in struggle shaped Malcolm's Pan-Africanist identity. In relation to this, next, we examine Malcolm's discourses that reject the label "Negro" and rekindle the African unknown. In a follow-up section, we elaborate Malcolm's evolutionary thinking on Africa by retracing some of his key trips to African countries: Ghana, Nigeria, and Egypt as well as Kenya, Guinea, and Tanzania. We then connect these visits to his Pan-Africanist political agitation in support of Patrice Lumumba and the Congo against imperialism.

Thereafter, we examine the OAAU, a political organization that we argue was founded as a product of Malcolm's direct engagement with Africans and modeled after the Organization of African Unity (OAU). The OAAU was established as an institution that best exhibits Malcolm's Pan-African political practice and through it Malcolm's distinctive impact on U.S. domestic Black nationalism. Concluding sections reanalyze Malcolm's impact on Africa, Africa's impact on Malcolm, and Malcolm's impact on Black Studies Pan-Africanism.

Garveyism and Black Nationalism across Borders
. . . Equals Pan-Africanism

We know that both Malcolm X and Marcus Mosley Garvey were two of the greatest Pan-Africanists known in African world history. What we need to know more about is how Malcolm was influenced by Garvey. An ideology cultivated by Marcus Garvey that climaxed in the 1920s and 1930s, Garveyism intended persons of African ancestry in the diaspora to "redeem" the nations of Africa and for European colonial powers to leave the continent. As a child, Malcolm would often attend Universal Negro Improvement Association (UNIA) meetings with his Garveyite father, Earl Little, where he would be first exposed to Garvey's separatist genre of Black nationalism presented in the argument that the African American community ought to utilize the tools and resources that it had to develop without dependence on the white man (self-determined economic development). In some of his speeches, Malcolm would often express Garveyite ideas: "Every time you see another nation on the African continent become independent, you know that Marcus Garvey is alive . . . had it not been for him, you would find no independent nations in the Caribbean today. . . . All of the freedom movements taking place right here in America today, were initiated by the work and teachings of Marcus Garvey." [1] This extract illustrates ways that Malcolm embodied his Garveyist discourses on the African diaspora identity. Through Garveyism, Malcolm foregrounded Africa in his political thought and practice and continued a long tradition of redeeming the discursive and material spaces of Africa through Pan-Africanism (Tyner 2006).

Despite the multiple iterations of Pan-Africanism (diasporic, continental, culturalist, statist, nonstatist), given that Malcolm's father was a Garveyite, follower of the Jamaican-born U.S. immigrant who established the largest Pan-Africanist movement that the world has seen—the UNIA—it is a Garveyite definition of Pan-Africanism that provides an important beginning point to understand Malcolm's own contribution to this important phenomenon. Yet Pan-Africanism predates Garvey, who similarly draws his own ideas from its long history of acting as a rallying slogan, a springboard, and an ideological vehicle for cultivating the common efforts of African diaspora and African descendant peoples to advance their political efforts globally.

Garveyism formulated an ideology of Pan-Africanism as a means to unify all Black/African descended people worldwide irrespective of their ethnic or national locations. Garvey's brand of Pan-Africanism promoted the solution to the problem of black inequality in the New World as one that required a powerful black nation in Africa, and he proposed that the formation of a strong African state could serve as home to members of the African diaspora. Garvey called his movement Black Zionism patterning his UNIA after the Jewish Legion from which he even received patronage from Jewish financiers (Tyner 2006).

Of course, Pan-Africanism has been defined universally by the varied and plural voices, perspectives, and locations of the movement's Black world agents. Black Studies presents Pan-Africanism as a brand of Black nationalism, a worldview as well as a political movement that seeks to unify and uplift both continental Africans and those of the African diaspora, as part of a "global African community." It represents a political and cultural phenomenon that regards Africa, Africans, and African descendants in the African diaspora as a single sociocultural unit. On the continent, Pan-Africanism seeks to regenerate and unify Africa and promote a feeling of oneness among the people of the African world (Esedebe 1994, 102).

Black Studies sociologist St. Clair Drake defined Pan-Africanism as a political concept developed by a group of American Negroes and West Indians between 1900 and 1945. He asserted that Pan-Africanism represented the idea that Africans and peoples of African descent in the New World should develop racial solidarity for the purpose of abolishing discrimination, enforced segregation, and political and economic exploitation (Drake 1993). Black Studies political scientist Ron Walters charted the broad scope of Pan-African relationships accordingly: among African states, among African states and African-origin states in the diaspora, among African states and African-origin peoples and communities in the diaspora, among African-origin states in the diaspora and African-origin communities in the diaspora, and among African-origin communities in the diaspora (Walters and Smith 1999). Racialistic, continental, nonstate, state, institutional, top-down, bottom-up, revolutionary, gradualist, instantist, cultural, political, transatlantic, and even trans-sub-Saharan (Okpewho, Boyce Davies, and Mazrui, 1999, 104) are additional qualifiers of Pan-Africanism.

Marcus Garvey's brand of Pan-Africanism was diasporic, originating in the Caribbean (Jamaica) in 1912, forging roots in the United States in 1914, and making strong connections with the continent of Africa with his Back-to-Africa movement. P. Olisanwuche Esedebe (1994) contends that Garvey introduced the masses to the ideas of an African nationality and an African personality. In her book *Race against Empire* (1997) Penny Von Eschen reveals ways that Garvey made African Americans conscious of their African origins and created for the first time a feeling of international solidarity between Africans and peoples of African descent. Malcolm received Garveyist Pan-African ideas as a result of Garvey's diasporic Pan-African activities across the United States.

Garveyism shaped young Malcolm by way of his family members and activist Garveyite communities among African American societies. We know that as a child, Malcolm was raised by an immigrant mother from Grenada who had first settled in Montreal and who subsequently met her husband, Malcolm's father, at a Marcus Garvey UNIA meeting in Canada. We know also that as a widow, Louise raised her children in a strict West Indian tradition. Malcolm's father, Earl Little, had been a Baptist minister and a builder who couldn't get regular work in Lansing because of his Garveyite ideas. We learn from Adi and Sherwood (2003, 123) that Garvey had visited the family many times. The circumstances that led to Earl's death—proclaimed to have been murdered by a Ku Klux Klan gang in Lansing—occurred as a result of his Garveyite preaching. We also know that Malcolm remembered his father Earl passing out pictures of Marcus Garvey at UNIA meetings in Lansing, Michigan, that attracted blacks brave enough to listen to taboo discussions of racial pride and Black Power. These early events and experiences served to shape Malcolm's development of his own Pan-African identity.

Shawna Maglangbayan (1972) classifies Malcolm in relation to Garvey who is described as a Black nationalist separatist leader struggling for the autonomous political and socioeconomic evolution of the Black world. Garveyite leaders seek ways and means to destroy the system of Black bondage. Malcolm's family experiences should also be seen in light of the struggles that Blacks have endured globally particularly as they culminated in the struggles occurring in U.S. African American communities in the 1940s, 1950s, and 1960s. In this regard, Malcolm's leadership legacy must be understood in line with the likes of Marcus Garvey, as well as with other radical Black leaders, including Patrice Lumumba, Jean-Jacques Dessalines of Haiti, and others whom she describes as Black men imbued with a racial and national consciousness against White supremacy.

Scholars who privilege Malcolm's cultural nationalism link his early childhood experiences to his joining the NOI, although such scholars also acknowledge that there were intersections between the Nation and Garveyism in this relationship as Malcolm was partially following in his late father's Garveyite footsteps here as well (Joseph 2009). For example, Malcolm's early identity formation can be seen to be directly linked to the vibrant struggles and movements occurring in Detroit and Harlem where the NOI had been organized after the heyday of the Garvey-inspired nationalism of the post–World War I New Negro (Joseph 2009). The NOI advocated personal dignity, economic self-determination, and organizational discipline in service of an unorthodox interpretation of the Islamic faith (Joseph 2009).

Both Garvey's and the NOI's distinct approaches coincided with each other in ways that would have a profound effect on Malcolm's evolution into a radical activist. While Marcus Garvey advocated the recovery of suppressed historical truths about ancient African kingdoms in order to uplift blacks in America, Elijah Muhammad, the key personality behind the NOI for over forty years, characterized whites as devils who were evil in their conscious oppression of Black peoples. As such, through these early experiences, Malcolm's unique personal and political biography allowed him to serve as a bridge between two generations of black activists: first came the veterans of the Robeson generation, who were followed by the new militants who came of age in the wake of Ghanaian independence, the Cuban Revolution, and the southern sit-in movement (Joseph 2009).

Malcolm's Race and Ethnicity Discourses

Malcolm's exemplar underscores ways that ethnicity is racialized for Blacks in America, particularly in relation to questions of heritage in Africa and the continent's associative cultural identity for Americans of African descent. Malcolm would say, "One of the things that made the Black Muslim movement grow was its emphasis upon things African. This was the secret to the growth of the Black Muslim movement. African blood, African origin, African culture, African ties. And you'd be surprised—we discovered that deep within the subconscious of the black man in this country, he is still more African than he is American" (Malcolm X 1990, 171–72).

Malcolm's early upbringing fostered his later acknowledgment of Africa in his political thought. Africa always represented a silent backdrop for Black nationalism, and Malcolm would continue in a long tradition, including Garveyism, of redeeming the discursive and material spaces of Africa through Pan-Africanism (Tyner 2006). In forging his Pan-Africanist ideology, Malcolm's racial experiences, growing up in a system of White supremacy, extended to the larger framework of ethnicity in connection to the African heritage question. Black nationalism of both the separatist and Marxist genres would lead Malcolm to advance a cultural nationalism that would culminate in Pan-Africanism.

Various factors—enslavement, denigration and contempt for Africa and all it stood for, exploration, and white definitions of Africans and their wrongly presumed nonrole in world history—created severe problems of identity for African Americans in the early twentieth century (Magubane 1987). Richard Wright argued that the Negro in America in reality constituted a separate nation, shunned and stripped, and held captive within an American nation, devoid of political, social, and economic property rights. After three and a half centuries in residence, Wright proclaimed that African Americans of the era did not feel at home (Magubane 1987). In the United States, African Americans were not accepted because of color, and this loss of identity fostered a brand of nationalism that, while it searched for Africa, was a nationalism that was also ambivalent about the continent (Wright 1995).

The fact of African descent would become the only really socially relevant historical reality about African American identity (considered Negro at the time), as it was history and the peculiar evaluations of American society that served to link African descendant peoples in the United States with the fate of Africa and its peoples (Drake 1993). Despite this fact, association with Africa was problematic because of Eurocentrism and racism. Toni Morrison formulated the term "Africanism" to capture the United States' negative discursive construction of African Americans as having originated from inferior and primitive Africans. Africanism would refer to the denotative and connotative blackness that African peoples came to signify, as well as the entire range of views, assumptions, readings, and misreadings that accompanied Eurocentric learning about these people (Morrison 1993).

Malcolm's lived experiences foreshadowed this genre of Africa exploration that Morrison describes as Africanism. He understood that negative representations of African Americans were intimately associated with negative images of the African homeland. Yet uniquely, unlike others who had explored the phenomenon before him, to redeem the identity of African Americans to counter the Africanism that flourished in American society, Malcolm turned to the place of Africa. Malcolm formulated an ideology of Pan-Africanism that would be used to challenge both racism within the diaspora and colonialism in the African homeland. At a speech at the London School of Economics on February 11, 1965, Malcolm would articulate the relationship between race, ethnic identity, and African heritage.

So because we felt that our color had trapped us, had imprisoned us, had brought us down, we ended up hating the Black skin . . . the Black blood. . . . This is the problem the Black man in the West has had. The African hasn't realized that this was the problem. And it was only as long as the African himself was held in bondage by the colonial powers, was kept from projecting any positive image of himself on our continent, something that we could look at proudly and then identify with—it was only as long as the African himself was kept down that we were kept down. (Malcolm X 2014)

In various speeches—"You Can't Hate the Roots of a Tree," "We Are Africans Who Were Kidnapped and Brought to America," "We Are Proud of Our African Image," and "You Have Been Brainwashed"—Malcolm would articulate the contours of Pan-Africanist ideology. In "You Can't Hate the Roots of a Tree," Malcolm told his African American audiences that you can't have a positive attitude about yourself and at the same time have a negative attitude about Africa. Referring to the Western racialization of the African image, he told his audience, "They made us hate our African self—our hair, color of skin, noses and even the blood of Africa in us" (Malcolm X 1965). Malcolm preached that Africa was a root that we couldn't despise. Doing so would be cutting off the nose to spite the face!

In "We Are Africans Who Were Kidnapped and Brought to America" Malcolm would reject the identity label "Negro" arguing that it was a term of self-hatred. In this speech, Malcolm articulated the contemporary oft-cited term used by Pan-Africanists when he proclaimed that "We are *Africans* who happen to be in America. We were kidnapped and brought to America" (Malcolm 1989, 24). In "We Are Proud of Our African Image," Malcolm attributed historic diaspora U.S. African descendants' hatred of the African image to the reasons why there had not been much organization in America. Malcolm argued that Africa had been in the hands of people who hated the image of Black people; as a result, African Americans imbibed that hatred. Nonetheless, African independence and self-determination would reverse this trend as African Americans began to physically interact with Africans on the continent and realize the mutual positive identity and seek to affiliate with it.

In "You Have Been Brainwashed," Malcolm called for new bridges to be built between African Americans and Africans to help Africans reach Africans in the diaspora and vice versa. In a December 1964 interview, Malcolm X told his audience that if African Americans had migrated back to Africa culturally, philosophically, and psychologically, while remaining in the United States physically, the spiritual bond that would develop between Africans and African Americans through this cultural, philosophical, and psychological migration would enhance the position of African Americans in the United States. Advocating cultural and political pan-nationalism, Malcolm explained that Pan-Africanism on this occasion would foster African American and African transnational contacts that would act as institutional foundations.

Malcolm's speeches illustrate the trajectories and contours of the evolution of the ideology of communal separatist Black nationalism and its expansion toward transnational separatism/Pan-Africanism. Malcolm would see relocation to Black Africa as a long-term strategy whereas a short-term strategy was to resolve racism and discrimination against Blacks in America. Pan-Africanism provided Malcolm with a means to expand on the idea of Black nationalism that had been heretofore too limiting. In particular, it had excluded large segments of society that were oppressed and exploited by global structures and institutions of White supremacy. Malcolm began to understand that the liberation of African Americans was inseparable from the Eurocentric international system that had to be transformed.

By June 20, 1964, on Malcolm's return from the first of his two African trips of that year, he had fully formulated a Pan-Africanist-inspired perspective on the conduct of the civil rights movement. Malcolm was fascinated by the formation of Africa's OAU and its ideals to express unity and solidarity that he compared to the splintered and factionalized civil rights movement at home. In his Declaration of Independence speech on March 12, 1964, Malcolm informed his audience that the civil rights movement must find a common approach, a common solution to a common problem that required worldwide Black unity before black-white unity.

Malcolm in Africa

In his book *Mau Mau in Harlem? The US and the Liberation of Kenya*, historian Gerald Horne eloquently illustrates the African influence on Malcolm and vice versa. Horne vividly describes Malcolm as the bespectacled militant speaking in Harlem who deployed Kenya to propel the following peroration:

> In my opinion, not only in Mississippi and Alabama but right here in New York City, you and I can best learn how to get real freedom by studying how Jomo Kenyatta brought it to his people in Kenya. . . . In Mississippi, we need a *Mau Mau* . . . in Alabama . . . Georgia . . . in Harlem, New York City! (qtd. in Horne 2009, 3)

Malcolm visited Kenya in October 1964. He described Kenya as a place that had impressed him given the Kikuyu's potential for what he described as "explosion" (Sherwood 2011). While there, Malcolm fraternized with the founding Kenyan democratic socialist nationalists such as Odinga Oginga and Tom Mboya. He also met Pio Gama Pinto, a Kenyan journalist, who had interviewed Malcolm asking him about civil rights in the United States. Malcolm replied that American legislation couldn't solve the topic of racism as it had become an inseparable part of America's political, social, and economic system. Congressman John Lewis, at that time a Student Nonviolent Coordinating Committee leader, had met Malcolm in Kenya. The meeting caused Malcolm to indicate that Africa was doing for Lewis the same thing it was doing for him—providing a frame of reference that was both broadening and refreshing (Sherwood 2011).

For Malcolm it seemed that Africa represented a land of the future faced with exhilarating possibilities and a fate in which black Americans were destined to play a key role. Malcolm traveled extensively across the continent to Ghana, Nigeria, Guinea, Tanzania, Morocco, the Sudan, Liberia, Ethiopia, Kenya, Algeria, the Democratic Republic of the Congo, and Egypt. It would seem that in Africa, he discovered mutual bonds of trust born out of shared histories of racial oppression. In Africa, Malcolm saw domestic racism as the Achilles' heel of U.S. foreign policy and sought to exploit this circumstance in the quest for racial justice for African Americans.

In his autobiography, Malcolm would write that his first trip to Africa was for three weeks as Mr. Muhammad's emissary where he travelled to Egypt, Arabia, the Sudan, Nigeria, and Ghana (Malcolm X 1992, 273). He arrived in Cairo on May 1, 1964, and went on to Cairo's suburb, Alexandria, where he met with Gamal Abdel Nasser. Malcolm admired Egypt describing it as home to the oldest civilization in the world. He described its people as a conglomeration of Black Africans, Arabs, and the mixtures resulting from empire building, conquest, and cross-Mediterranean trade (Sherwood 2011). During that first trip Malcolm flew from Cairo to Lagos, Nigeria, and on to Ibadan, where he was scheduled to meet his main contact, Professor Essien-Udom. Malcolm had first met Essien-Udom in the United States while the Nigerian professor was writing a book on Black nationalism (Essien-Udom 1962).

Malcolm was scheduled to give a major talk at Nigeria's University of Ibadan. The talk was titled "Our Struggle in the Context of the African Liberation Movement" and was chaired by the prominent Nigerian Africanist historian Professor J. F. Ajayi, who was dean of the Faculty of Arts at the time. Marika Sherwood retrieved extracts of the speech from the files of the FBI, which appears to hold the only recording.

The files reported that Malcolm argued that he spoke for Negro Americans who had been oppressed for four hundred years and remained oppressed at the time of his speech in 1964. Malcolm accused American foreign policy and media of being propagandists who had tried to divide Africans and African Americans. He decried that African Americans had been victimized by American racism in ways that caused them to lose their identity (Sherwood 2011).

Nigerians were very responsive to Malcolm's speech and his larger visit to the country. According to Essien-Udom, the Nigerians that Malcolm met saw the vision of Pan-Africanism through Malcolm. Malcolm's message that the Afro-American community should cooperate with the world's Pan-Africanists in Africa, and that Black people throughout the Americas and Africa needed to link up their struggle to impact change, resonated among Nigerians (Essien-Udom in Clarke et al. 1969, 242). Sherwood reports that Malcolm was clearly impressed by Nigeria. He wrote that the "natural beauty and wealth of Nigeria and its people are indescribable. The people of Nigeria are strongly concerned with the problems of their African brothers in America" (Sherwood 2011). Malcolm wrote about his trip to Nigeria and reported that he had been loved by Nigerians who appreciated his identity as an American Muslim and a militant. He would write that, despite Western propaganda, Africans loved African Americans and appreciated the emerging consciousness of Afro-Americans in organizing Pan-Africanism (Malcolm 1990).

From Nigeria, Malcolm went to Accra, Ghana, where Malcolm's personal and political biography began to reflect a transnational, internationalist ideology that bridged the Robeson generation and the new militants who emerged in the wake of Ghanaian independence under the charismatic leadership of Kwame Nkrumah (Joseph 2009). In comparing Nigeria to Ghana, an advisor to Malcolm noted that Nigerians were servants of American businessmen while in Ghana political awakening comes first and religion is always secondary. Malcolm had stated that Ghana had the most powerful UN voice in the continent (Sherwood 2011).

In Ghana, Malcolm would begin to envision the inner workings of a Pan-African state. In *The Amsterdam News*, March 27, 1965, he spoke about this, stating that "Thus having just arrived here in Ghana, the progressive nation that is looked upon by an increasing number of Africans today as the 'fountainhead of pan Africanism,' the remaining days of my African tour should be more interesting, enlightening and fruitful" (Sherwood 2011, 56). Malcolm was not unlike other radical African Americans of his day who were mesmerized by Kwame Nkrumah. They viewed Ghana as the potential spark that could move Africa toward a continent-wide insurgency, one that would ultimately trigger a global revolution powerful enough to meaningfully impact American racism (Joseph 2009).

By personally inviting skilled U.S. Blacks committed to Africa's restoration to help build Ghana, Nkrumah helped to build an American African expatriate community (Gaines 2006) in the country that included Harlem radicals such as Julian Mayfield, Maya Angelou, and W. E. B. Du Bois. Of the two hundred plus members of this community, the Malcolm X Committee in Ghana was formed, and it would serve to organize Malcolm's visit. When asked about their agenda in Ghana, one expatriate, named Lucy, said that she was helping Kwame Nkrumah achieve a political order that would indirectly help people of African descent achieve social justice in America. Malcolm's visit would function in this regard.

At the University of Legon at an event sponsored by the Marxist Forum in Ghana, Malcolm gave a speech titled "Will Africa Ignite America's Racial Powder Keg?" The speech recounted the horrors of the transatlantic slave trade in order to highlight connections between Africans and Blacks claiming that Blacks were Americans in name but not in reality. The speech criticized U.S. race relations using tropes that Sherwood argues later groups such as the Black Panthers would come to echo. Malcolm characterized America as an empire and a master of imperialism. In the speech, Malcolm controversially argued that the U.S. Peace Corps should be deployed to Mississippi and Alabama instead of Africa, and he noted that while South Africa preached and practiced segregation, the United States preached integration and practiced segregation (Sherwood 2011).

In 1964, Malcolm visited other Pan-African states such as Tanzania then Tanganyika on October 9–17, 1964. He had been invited to Tanzania by Abdulrahman Muhammad Babu who had become minister of economic development. The Zanzibar-born Babu was a staunch socialist and published *African Socialism* in London in 1981. In his own memoirs, Babu reported that when Malcolm X came to Tanzania, he had taken him to meet President Julius Nyerere on the day that China exploded her first nuclear bomb. Nyerere had remarked to Malcolm his very high regard for China that as a former colonial country had been able to develop weapons at par with any colonial power.

Nyerere remarked, "This is the end of colonialism through and through." Malcolm replied, "Mr. President—this is what I've been thinking all day" (Sherwood 2011, 105). In Tanzania, Malcolm published an article in the *Tanganyika Standard* on October 13, 1964, where he reported that African Americans were beginning to see their relationship with Africans as something that could not be denied (Sherwood 2011).

Malcolm went on to visit Uganda, where he met Prime Minister Milton Obote. He visited Ethiopia and made return visits to Nigeria, Ghana, Liberia, and Guinea in October–November 1964. Malcolm's trip to Guinea would also reinforce the further formulation of a Pan-African vision having previously met Sékou Touré at a United Nations meeting in New York in 1960 through Diallo Telli, the Guinean ambassador to the United Nations. In Guinea, through Telli's connections, Malcolm was warmly welcomed as a guest of Touré in his home. Malcolm would write,

> I am speechless. All praise is due Allah. They gave me three servants, a driver and army officer. . . . It is difficult to believe that I would be so widely known and respected here on this continent. The negative image the Western press has tried to paint of me certainly hasn't succeeded. The President embraced me . . . congratulated me for my firmness in the struggle for dignity. (Sherwood 2011, 132)

In July 1964, Malcolm would return to Egypt where he had been invited to participate in the OAU's Second Summit in Cairo. As a result of the culminations of his political actions at the summit, Malcolm was afforded the prestigious title "African American Prime Minister," and his political agitation at the event squarely illustrates at this time a full Pan-Africanist political practice. At the summit, Malcolm would lobby African countries to treat the African American plight as an African problem. It was here that Malcolm asked African states to bring the United States to the United Nations on crimes against African American humanity. Proclaiming that there was an identity of purpose and interests between the Afro-Americans and Africans, Malcolm warned the African heads of state, "Don't escape from European colonialism only to become even more enslaved by deceitful, friendly American dollarism" (Malcolm X 1964). In response, the OAU Heads of States meeting passed a resolution deploring racism in the United States.

Even though he had never visited the Congo, but had met Patrice Lumumba in New York City in 1960, after his trips to Africa in 1964, Malcolm became an outspoken critic of U.S. imperialist policy toward the Congo. Malcolm would denounce the U.S. militarism in the Congo, and in late 1964, Malcolm sought to collaborate with Cuban-Argentine revolutionary Ernesto "Che" Guevara in his campaign to assist the Lumumbists in the Congo. Malcolm attempted to recruit African American veterans into an "Afro-American Brigade" that would have fought alongside the Cubans and the Congolese in 1965. Just a few days prior to his death, Malcolm was denied entry into France where he had been scheduled to meet with African American expatriates interested in direct participation in the Congo struggle (Azikiwe 2011).

Practicing Pan-African Politics through the OAU and the OAAU

Malcolm was the first Black leader of the 1960s to take Africa seriously enough to go there and speak directly about conditions in the United States (Sales 1994, 101). We know that several African American scholars and civil rights leaders visited Africa. Kevin Gaines (2006) calls them American Africans. Yet few sought to relay the plight of racism experienced by African Americans to Africans in a way that underscored the intersections and connectedness of the plight of both peoples. Neither did these other African American leaders attempt to organize institutional linkages between the African American community in the United States, the African American expatriate community in Africa, and the then emergent Pan-Africanist institution the OAU in Africa (now, the African Union), as did Malcolm. Inventively, Malcolm would utilize his African visits to foster multilateral global Pan-African relations that raised the aspirations and solidarity of and among African descendants in the United States and newly liberated Africans on the continent.

Malcolm returned to the United States after eighteen weeks abroad to begin tasks that were designed to enlarge the consciousness of Afro-Americans and to reshape their sense of identity so that they would see themselves as an extension of the African peoples and part of a global Black revolution. To facilitate his objectives, leveraging from his travels to Africa between 1964 and 1965, Malcolm founded the OAAU, which would serve as a united front to engage in legitimate activities for the international recognition of the African American freedom struggle. In announcing the establishment of this secular organization, Malcolm stated,

> I have been requested and indeed it is my pleasure to announce the existence of the OAAU, to be patterned after the letter and the spirit of the Organization of African Unity (OAU). Its purpose is "to unite Afro-Americans and their organizations around a non-religious and non-sectarian constructive program for Human Rights." (Sales 1994, 106)

That Malcolm modeled the OAAU around Africa's OAU suggests the impact that his engagement with Africa had on the formulation of his politics at home. For the

U.S. African diaspora, Malcolm's OAAU would function as an important institutional vehicle for developing a Pan-African identity and consciousness; for Africa and its nationalists, it would present an African American nonstate institutional partner to strengthen Third World nationalism and Pan-African unity. The OAAU had been founded in association with Akbar Muhammad, field secretary and founder of the Revolutionary Action Movement (RAM), and Robert Williams, as well as by collaborations with James and Grace Lee Boggs, Detroiters who had written *Revolution and Evolution in the Twentieth Century*. Malcolm also collaborated to build the OAAU in Ghana with Julian Mayfield, who had initially encouraged Malcolm to develop organizing links between African American communities in the United States and African American expats in Africa.

The OAAU was patterned upon the structure of the mass-based nationalist parties that led African countries like Ghana, Guinea, Tanzania, and Kenya to independence (Sales 1994). Its organizational tactics also reflected the revolutionary movements in Mozambique, Angola, Southern Africa, and Algeria. Establishing the OAAU reflected Malcolm's transition from his previous NOI messiah thought to a philosophy and political practice more grounded in collective equality typical of liberation movements. In asking not to be assigned a decision-making role in the OAAU, Malcolm would attempt to introduce democratic decision making in the organization in contrast to the authoritarian leadership of the Nation (Sales 1994).

As a political organization, the OAAU would facilitate efforts for U.S. African Americans to compel the United Nations to grant it observer status. In doing so, it became easier for Malcolm to address the international community as a legitimate representative of African Americans as a national liberation movement. As such, Malcolm's brand of Pan-Africanism was pioneering for the U.S. civil rights era. By naming the OAAU as such—Organization of *Afro-American* Unity—and not the organization of "Black Unity" or "African Union," Malcolm would be the first revolutionary leader (black or otherwise) to consciously recognize that blacks in the United States formed a distinct African nation (Jabara et al. 1992) that would be represented at the United Nations.

Given its formation in collaboration with a group of Detroit-Clevelanders, especially Robert Williams who headed up the RAM, the OAAU would present a platform for Malcolm to be a representative and international spokesperson for revolutionary nationalism while also being a united front engaged in activities to gain recognition for the African American freedom struggle (Sales 1994). According to the "Basic Aims and Objectives" statement of the OAAU, the organization's first objective was to attack the internalization of oppression on the part of African Americans using self-defense as a legitimate tactic.

The OAAU advocated a cultural revolution to unbrainwash its peoples (Sales 1994). As a result, education assumed a high priority in the OAAU's aims whereby the organization advocated alternative schools, cultural centers, and institutions to achieve self-determination. The OAAU sought to attack the so-called powerlessness of African Americans defined by Malcolm as political, economic, and social. That is why the organization sought to expand voter registration and rent strike campaigns in African American communities. Another objective of the OAAU was to achieve a working relationship with the civil rights movement by achieving a principled reconciliation with the established civil rights leadership. On June 30, 1964, as OAAU chairman, Malcolm sent a telegram to Dr. King. "We have been witnessing with great concern the vicious attack of the white race against our poor defenseless people in St. Augustine, Florida. . . . The day of turning the cheek to the inhuman brute beasts is long over" (Sales 1994, 125).

A final objective of the OAAU was the group's lasting attempt to gain recognition from Africa's OAU itself. In Cairo, in a memo circulated to the heads of state, Malcolm would write,

> If South Africa is guilty of violating the human rights of Africans here on the mother continent, then America is guilty of worse violation of the 22 million Africans on the American continent. And if South African racism is not a domestic issue, then American racism is not a domestic issue. In the interests of world peace and security, we recommend an immediate investigation into our problem. (Sales 1994, 123)

The OAAU was a foundational and vanguard archetype of a Pan-Africanist institution fostering a Pan-Africanist movement. It would internationalize the Black nationalist struggle, foster Pan-Africanist unity and common goals, underscore a world systems approach to the African American condition, and articulate the ideology of a socialist and revolutionary vision for the civil rights movement.

Through the OAAU and Malcolm's diplomacy in Africa, African Americans would have an important impact on Africa as Malcolm's leadership through the OAAU exposed the hypocrisy of U.S. foreign policy in Africa as neocolonialist. It presented an alternative image of African Americans and their conditions to Africans. Even Malcolm would argue this when he proclaimed that, "And today you'll find that in the UN every time the Congo question or anything on the African continent is debated, they couple it with what is going on, or what is happening to you and me in Mississippi and Alabama" (Malcolm X 1964).

Conclusion

The conceptual issues on Malcolm that we have raised in the current chapter present important implications for the continuing relevance of Black Studies to reveal ongoing historical and intellectual insights and public policies for African descendant communities around the world. For example, what should African descendants in the United States call ourselves? Black, African, or Negro? Malcolm rejected the label "Negro," a racialized term imposed on African Americans by U.S. racial formation. Identifying as Afro-American would preface the later preferred identity name, African American. Malcolm's discourses on the need to reconnect with African cultural heritage present an important Black Studies theme regarding African ethnic and cultural heritage factors.

If one sees the Black Studies discipline as a comprehensive study of the African world that identifies unity, comparison, and intersection among the lived experiences of African Americans, other African diasporas in the northern hemisphere, and Africans on the continent, then Malcolm X's iconography represents an important exemplar. As did Malcolm in his public intellectualism and political practices, several Black Studies scholars have posited the African continent as a core heuristic center and thus disciplinary reference point for the discipline also increasingly referred to by its ethnic name these days as Africana Studies.

Malcolm's Pan-Africanist politics—drawn from his own racial and ethnic identity experiences that would foster his Pan-Africanist ideology—further provide Black Studies with a way to examine a long history and conceptualization of Black internationalism with Africa whose legacies, while very much still present in Black Studies disciplinary representations, surely need to be ratcheted up substantially to foster contemporary transnational convergences between the African diaspora and the African continent.

Methodological Pan-Africanism utilizes Pan-Africanism as a theoretical framework, a methodology, and an ideological tool for engaged academic Black Studies scholarship that serves to foster practical action for African heritage and African peoples throughout the world. It is a practice and an idea that Malcolm X's own lived experience magnanimously exemplified. Malcolm made distinctive contributions to

Pan-Africanism and thereby to the way that we approach Black Studies. As a public intellectual and political leader, Malcolm helped to formulate the Pan-Africanist ideology as well as build a Pan-Africanist movement. Both contributions are core attributes of the Black Studies discipline. With Pan-Africanist ideology, Malcolm articulated the intersectionality between race and ethnicity. In insisting that African Americans are neither Negro nor merely Black, but Africans in America, hence Afro-American, Malcolm would de-racialize African American identity and connect it to its rightful historical, cultural, social, and political heritage in Africa. Malcolm would also conscientize Africans on the continent to the way that they (Africans) have also been racialized through the colonial encounter. As such, Malcolm required from both estranged peoples a basis for a renewed solidarity—on the basis of race (in order to combat racial discrimination) and on ethnic heritage (rekindling the African cultural identity as well as reengaging progressively with the African circumstance)—with each other.

The discourses that Malcolm used to criticize U.S. race relations were later adopted by groups such as the Black Panthers and the Black Power movement. Malcolm's critique of American imperialism through institutions such as the Peace Corps and his United States/South Africa comparison of racial formation and discrimination have become key paradigmatic themes for Black Studies programs. Malcolm's OAAU presented an institutional framework and model for the practice of Pan-Africanism. The organization would advance revolutionary Black nationalism in the United States and link it to a revolutionary transnationalism in Africa and other parts of the Third World. The OAAU's self-styling around African national movements and its engagement with the OAU reinforced, strengthened, and paved the way for new avenues for the growth of the Pan-Africanist movement.

With regard to community relevance, Malcolm's pioneering civil rights era Pan-Africanism set the stage for a deeper and expanded contemporary cultural Pan-Africanism of the present, such as seen in the popular holiday African Liberation Day, now celebrated in Africa as Africa Day. Significantly, too, the current African Union (AU), the OAU's successor, adopts the African Diaspora Clause (recognition that the AU will include members from African heritage peoples around the world) as part of its Constitutive Act. Haiti is an official member of the AU. As for Malcolm's disciplinary relevance, as Malcolm did, most Black Studies programs observe in their programming the central role that Africa plays in the further advancement and institutionalization of the discipline. As with the program at Michigan State University, Black Studies programs across the country have imbibed Malcolm's

Pan-African vision. Most programs include course study on Africa, the study of African languages, and study abroad programming in Africa in their curricula as well as recruiting African faculty and students to convene an academic Pan-African world collegiate environment that sustains and expands Malcolm Omowale X's unity vision.

Without overtly stating it, each of the contributed chapters of the current volume has either implicitly or explicitly made core reference in their multiple and divergent themes about Malcolm to his own leanings toward Africa. They have referred to theoretical implications of his Garveyite family influences, his signifyin discourses rooted in African cultures, the legacies of his expression as a literary agent of the Black and African aesthetics, his African-Detroit politicking and cultural nationalism, his Black feminism unraveled in Africana womanism, his Africanized "Sufi" and Sunni Islam, his Africanizing of the church, his reformulation of a positive Africanist identity, and his formulation of a right-sized Pan-African politics model for the Americas.

In this respect, it is apt for us as editors and contributors of the book to conclude that perhaps Malcolm's greatest contribution to the Black Studies discipline is to underscore the need for its continued Pan-Africanist infusion of the study and practical engagement with an African world that straddles the local, national, global African diaspora, and continental communities. In our mind, this has been the key implication for *Malcolm X's Michigan Worldview: An Exemplar for Contemporary Black Studies Discipline* whereby Malcolm X has been presented as an exemplar hailing from Michigan while impacting America, Africa, and the world!

NOTE

1. "Malcolm X Speaks on Marcus Garvey": available at https://www.youtube.com/watch?v=u-01-tW—7w.

WORKS CITED

Adi, Hakim, and Marika Sherwood. 2003. *Pan-African History: Political Figures from Africa and the Diaspora Since 1787*. London: Routledge.

Azikiwe, Abayomi. 2011. "Patrice Lumumba, Congo & African-American History." *Workers World*. February 2. http://www.workers.org/2011/world/patrice_lumumba_0210/.

Boggs, James, and Grace Lee Boggs. 1974. *Revolution and Evolution in the Twentieth Century*. New York: Monthly Review Press.

Clarke, John Henrik, A. Peter Bailey, and Earl Grant. 1969. *Malcolm X: The Man and His Times*. New York: Macmillan.

Drake, St. Clair. 1993. "Diaspora Studies and Pan-Africanism." In *Global Dimensions of the African Diaspora*, edited by Joseph Harris, 451–514. Washington, DC: Howard University Press.

Esedebe, P. Olisanwuche. 1994. *Pan-Africanism: The Idea and Movement, 1776–1991*. Washington, DC: Howard University Press.

Essien-Udom, Essien Udosen. 1962. *Black Nationalism: A Search for an Identity in America*. Chicago: University of Chicago Press.

Gaines, Kevin K. 2006. *American Africans in Ghana: Black Expatriates and the Civil Rights Era*. Chapel Hill: University of North Carolina Press.

Garvey, Marcus. 2004. *Selected Writings and Speeches of Marcus Garvey*. Dover Publications.

Horne, Gerald. 2009. *Mau Mau in Harlem? The U.S. and the Liberation of Kenya*. New York: Palgrave Macmillan.

Jabara, Robert, Kumar Rupesinghe, and Gudmundar Alfredsson. 1992. *The Word: The Liberation Analects of Malcolm X*. Windsor: Clarity.

Joseph, Peniel E. 2009. "The Black Power Movement: A State of the Field." *Journal of American History* 96, no. 3: 751–76.

Maglangbayan, Shawna. 1972. *Garvey, Lumumba, and Malcolm: Black National-Separatists*. Chicago: Third World Press.

Magubane, Bernard. 1987. *The Ties That Bind: African-American Consciousness of Africa*. Trenton, N.J: Africa World Press.

Malcolm X. 1964. "Speech to the OAU." Organization of Pan African Unity. July 17. http://www.oopau.org/2.html.

———. 1965. "After the Bombing / Speech at Ford Auditorium, February 14, 1965." malcolm-x.org. http://malcolm-x.org/speeches/spc_021465.htm.

———. 1989. *Malcolm X: The Last Speeches*. Edited by Bruce Perry. New York: Pathfinder.

———. 1990. *Malcolm X Speaks: Selected Speeches and Statements*. Edited by George Breitman. New York: Grove Press.

———. 1991. *Malcolm X Talks to Young People: Speeches in the U.S., Britain, and Africa*. Edited by Steve Clark. New York: Pathfinder.

———. 1992. *The Autobiography of Malcolm X*. With the assistance of Alex Haley. New York: Ballantine Books.

———. 2014. "London School of Economics (February 11, 1965)." *Malcolm X: The Most Complete Collection of Malcolm X Speeches, Debates and Interviews Ever Assembled*.

http://malcolmxfiles.blogspot.com/2013/07/london-school-of-economics-february-11. html.

Morrison, Toni. 1993. *Playing in the Dark: Whiteness and the Literary Imagination*. New York: Vintage Books.

Okpewho, Isidore, Carole Boyce Davies, and Ali A. Mazrui. 1999.   . Bloomington: Indiana University Press.

Sales, William W., Jr. 1994. *From Civil Rights to Black Liberation: Malcolm X and the Organization of Afro-American Unity*. Boston: South End Press.

Sherwood, Marika. 2011. *Malcolm X: Visits Abroad*. Los Angeles: Tsehai Publishers.

Tyner, James. 2006. *The Geography of Malcolm X: Black Radicalism and the Remaking of American Space*. New York: Routledge.

Von Eschen, Penny. M. 1997. *Race against Empire: Black Americans and Anticolonialism, 1937–1957*. Ithaca: Cornell University Press.

Walters, Ronald W., and Robert C. Smith. 1999. *African American Leadership*. Albany: State University of New York Press.

Wright, Richard. 1995. *Black Power: A Record of Reactions in a Land Of Pathos*. New York: HarperPerennial.

Works by Malcolm X

"After the Bombing." Speech at Ford Auditorium, February 14, 1965. Malcolm-x.
    org. http://malcolm-x.org/speeches/spc_021465.htm.
The Autobiography of Malcolm X. With the assistance of Alex Haley. New York:
    Ballantine Books, 1992.
By Any Means Necessary. New York: Pathfinder, 1992.
February 1965: The Final Speeches. Edited by Steve Clark. New York: Pathfinder,
    1992.
Malcolm X: The Last Speeches. Edited by Bruce Perry. New York: Pathfinder, 1989.
Malcolm X on Afro-American History. New York: Pathfinder Press.
Malcolm X Speaks: Selected Speeches and Statements. Edited by George Breitman.
    New York: Grove Press, 1990.
Malcolm X Talks to Young People: Speeches in the U.S., Britain, and Africa. Edited
    by Steve Clark. New York: Pathfinder, 1965.
"Message to the Grassroots," November 10, 1963. Malcolm X: A Research Site.
    http://brothermalcolm.net/mxwords/whathesaid8.html.
"The Organization of Afro-American Unity: 'For Human Rights'" [statement
    of Basic Aims of the Organization of Afro-American Unity, 1964]. In *Black*

Nationalism in America, edited by John Bracey, August Meier, and Elliot Rudwick, 421–27. New York: Macmillan, 1970.

"Race Problems and the Black Muslim Religion and its Ideas." Speech at Michigan State University, Erickson Kiva, East Lansing, MI. January 23, 1963.

Speech to the OAU. July 17, 1964. Organization of Pan-African Unity. http://www.oopau.org.

The Speeches of Malcolm X at Harvard. Edited by Archie Epps. New York: Morrow, 1968.

Two Speeches by Malcolm X. New York: Pioneer, 1965.

Contributors

Zain Abdullah is the author of *Black Mecca: The African Muslims of Harlem* (2010). He holds a doctorate in cultural anthropology and is associate professor in the Religion Department at Temple University, where he is also a faculty affiliate in the Department of Geography and Urban Studies. His work focuses on the interplay of race, religion, and ethnicity, Islamic Studies and Muslims in America, African diaspora studies, globalization and transnationalism, religion and society, film, photography, and visual studies. His articles have appeared in the *Journal of the American Academy of Religion, Anthropological Quarterly*, the *Journal of Islamic Law and Culture*, the *Journal of History and Culture*, the *Middle East Journal*, *African Arts*, and other periodicals. Dr. Abdullah has earned awards from the Smithsonian Institution's Center for Folklife and Cultural Heritage, the National Museum of African Art, the Social Science Research Council, the International Center for Migration, Ethnicity, and Citizenship, and he was presented with a New Jersey State Assembly Resolution in recognition of his service to the citizens of the state. He has been quoted in the *New York Times*, the *Philadelphia Inquirer*, the *Star Ledger, Reuters-Worldwide Religious News*, and other media outlets for his work on race, Islam and immigration, intergroup relations, and other topics. Professor Abdullah serves on the Steering Committee for the Religion and Migration Group of the American Academy of Religion. As a Ford Foundation Fellow, he is currently writing a book on Black Muslim conversion and the Nation of Islam, 1955–1975. Visit his website at zainabdullah.com.

Abdul Alkalimat was born in Chicago. He has a PhD in sociology from the University of Chicago. He is professor of African American studies and library and information science at the University of Illinois. Alkalimat has been active in Black Studies from its beginning. He is a founding board member of *Black Scholar*. He has served as a special issues editor for *Negro Digest* on the Black university. Alkalimat remains an active Black Studies professor at Fisk University, University of California at Santa Barbara, the Free University in Berlin, and currently at the University of Illinois both in Chicago and Urbana-Champaign. He is also active in the Black liberation movement going back to the Student Nonviolent Coordinating Committee, Association of African American Educators, Organization of Black American Culture, Peoples College, African Liberation Support Committee, and many local struggles. Alkalimat is a publisher of the Alkalimat Listserv. Among several publications, Alkalimat is the author of *Malcolm X for Beginners* (1992), *Paradigms in Black Studies: Intellectual History, Cultural Meaning and Political Ideology* (1990), and *Introduction to Afro-American Studies: A People's College Primer* (1989).

Herb Boyd is an award-winning author and journalist and has published twenty-four books and countless articles for national magazines and newspapers. *Brotherman: The Odyssey of Black Men in America: An Anthology* (1995), coedited with Robert Allen of the *Black Scholar* journal, won the American Book Award for nonfiction. In 1999, Boyd won three first-place awards from the New York Association of Black Journalists for his articles published in the *Amsterdam News*. Among his most popular books are *Black Panthers for Beginners* (1995); *Autobiography of a People: Three Centuries of African American History Told by Those Who Lived It* (2000); *Race and Resistance: African Americans in the 21st Century* (2002); *The Harlem Reader* (2003); *We Shall Overcome: A History of the Civil Rights Movement* (2004); and *Pound for Pound: The Life and Times of Sugar Ray Robinson* (2005).

Edward C. Davis IV is a native of the South Side of Chicago and chair of the Social Sciences Department of Malcolm X College–City Colleges of Chicago. He is the first full-time faculty member in African American studies and anthropology at Malcolm X College and creates curriculum for and directs both programs. He joined the faculty at Malcolm X College in 2010. Davis earned a master of philosophy degree in anthropology in 2009 from the University of Cambridge (St. John's College) as a Gates Cambridge Scholar. In 2006, he earned a master of arts degree from University of California, Berkeley, in African American and African diaspora studies, and in 2004 he earned his bachelor of arts degree cum laude from New York University's Gallatin School of Individualized Study with concentrations in African politics, French language, and ESL education. Additionally, he has studied as an exchange student at the Institut d'Etudes Politiques (Sciences Po-Paris).

Lenwood G. Davis is a professor of history at Winston-Salem State University in Winston-Salem, North Carolina. He is currently working in the Department of English and Foreign Languages where he teaches African American culture courses. He was raised in Beaufort, North Carolina, and has studied or taught at several institutions in the United States and Ghana. Dr. Davis has published numerous articles and is the author or coauthor of over fifteen books, including *The Infusion of African American History in United States History: A Teacher's Guide* (2000), *Malcolm X: A Selected Biography* (1984), and *I Have a Dream: The Life and Times of Martin Luther King, Jr* (1973).

Rita Kiki Edozie is professor of international relations at Michigan State University's James Madison College of Public Affairs. She is also director of African American and African Studies housed at MSU's College of Arts and Letters. She earned her PhD in political science from the New School for Social Research in New York City. Dr. Edozie is author of *People Power and Democracy: The Popular Movement against Military Despotism in Nigeria, 1989–1999* (2002), *Reconstructing the Third Wave of Democracy: Comparative African Democratic Politics* (2008), *Reframing Contemporary Africa: Politics, Economics, and Culture in a Global Era* (with Peyi Soyinka-Airewele, 2010), and *The African Union's Africa: New Pan-African Initiatives in Global Governance* (2014). Professor Edozie has contributed scholarly articles and book chapters to several edited volumes and journals.

Charles Ezra Ferrell is an alumnus of Amherst College (Amherst, Massachusetts) and the University of Michigan–Dearborn where he majored in political science, black studies, and psychology. While serving as the Chairman of the Black Student Union at Amherst, he led student anti-South African apartheid demonstrations to achieve divestiture. Ferrell—a Detroit-based community activist, exhibiting portrait artist, and jazz photographer—organized the first annual Malcolm X Day Celebration in 2012 at the Charles H. Wright Museum of African American History. He is the founder and program director of the museum's groundbreaking Liberation Film Series, which is supported by eight southeast Michigan regional Black Africana departments, including Michigan State University, University of Massachusetts–Amherst, and other partner/sponsors. In addition, he is a regional account executive for a leading business analytics and data-warehousing firm.

Errol A. Henderson is associate professor of political science at Penn State University, where he teaches international relations, the analysis of war and peace, African politics, and black political ideology. He conducts research on international relations theory, analysis of war and peace, culture and world politics, and African politics as well as African American political ideology. He is the author of more than thirty scholarly publications including two books, *Afrocentrism and World Politics: Towards a New Paradigm* (1995) and *Democracy and War: The End of an Illusion* (2002). His work has been published in various journals such as *British Journal of Political Science, International Interactions, International Politics*, and *Journal of Conflict Resolution*. Professor Henderson was born and raised in the Brewster Projects on the east side of Detroit. He was a noted student and community activist and helped lead two successful student movements at the University of Michigan. As assistant professor at Wayne State University and with the support of Dr. Betty Shabazz (the widow of Malcolm X), he helped lead an extended protest to create the Africana Studies Department.

Cameron "Khalfani" Herman is a doctoral candidate in the Department of Sociology at Michigan State University. His general research interests revolve around issues concerning youth culture, community development, and urban transformations. Herman's dissertation research focuses on the provision of youth development opportunities for young people in the urban communities of Detroit, Michigan, and Atlanta, Georgia. Herman's work is guided by an interest in increasing the life chances of marginalized youth.

Ollie Johnson is an associate professor of Africana studies at Wayne State University. Ollie Johnson received his BA in Afro-American studies and international relations and an MA in Brazilian studies from Brown University. He later earned an MA and PhD in political science from the University of California at Berkeley. His first book,

Brazilian Party Politics and the Coup of 1964, was published in 2001. He coedited *Black Political Organizations in the Post-Civil Rights Era* in 2002. Professor Johnson has conducted research on the Black Panther Party, the NAACP, and other Black political groups in the United States. He has also lectured on African American politics in Brazil, Colombia, Ecuador, and Japan. His current research focuses on Afro-Brazilian and Afro-Latin American politics.

Ibram X. Kendi began his career as an assistant professor of African American history at SUNY College at Oneonta. Advised by Ama Mazama, he earned his doctoral degree in African American studies from Temple University in 2010. A native of Queens, New York, and Manassas, Virginia, he earned his undergraduate degrees from Florida A&M University. His research and teaching interests include African American history, American social history, the racial history of higher education, history of Africana Studies, civil rights and Black Power studies, student activism, the Long Sixties, black social and political thought, and American intellectual history. He has ten forthcoming or published essays on the Black Campus Movement, Black Power, and intellectual history in books and academic journals, including the *Journal of African American History, Journal of Social History, Journal of Black Studies, Journal of African American Studies*, and *The Sixties: A Journal of History, Politics and Culture*.

Joseph McLaren is a professor of English at Hofstra University, New York. He specializes in African, Caribbean, and African American literature, and his teaching and research interests also incorporate African diaspora studies. His publications include articles on jazz musicians and various literary and cultural subjects. He is author of *Langston Hughes: Folk Dramatist in the Protest Tradition, 1921–1943* (1997); he coedited *Pan Africanism Updated* (1999) and *African Visions* (2000); and he edited two volumes of *The Collected Works of Langston Hughes: The Big Sea* (2002) and *I Wonder as I Wander* (2002). He coauthored the autobiography of legendary Philadelphia-born jazz saxophonist Jimmy Heath, which will be published by Temple University Press.

Sheila Radford-Hill, author, community developer, education leader, and social activist, currently serves as executive director of the Luther Diversity Center at Luther College, Decorah, Iowa. Radford-Hill is the author of *Further to Fly: Black Women and the Politics of Empowerment* (2000), a critique of feminist theory and its impact on black women's political culture. She has written numerous articles for professional journals and independent publications and is the coauthor of several advocacy studies and reports. As an educator, Radford-Hill has twenty years of teaching, administration, curriculum-development, and program-development experience. She has lectured at DePaul University and Roosevelt University and served as a visiting professor in the African and African American Studies Department at the University of Illinois at Chicago. She is formerly a division administrator at the Illinois State Board of Education. Radford-Hill holds a bachelor's degree from DePaul University, a master's degree from the University of Pennsylvania, and a doctoral degree in humanities from the School of the Arts and Sciences at Columbia Commonwealth University. A specialist in education and social policy, she did postgraduate study in urban development at the University of Illinois in Chicago.

Ahmad A. Rahman is an associate professor of history and the director of African and African American studies at the University of Michigan–Dearborn. He is an activist/scholar. He has worked for progressive political causes since the late 1960s in Chicago and in Detroit in the early 1970s. He first discovered the writings of Kwame Nkrumah as a teenager in 1968. He was introduced to them by Ruwa Maruwa Chiri, an exile from Zimbabwe who dedicated himself to teaching African Americans about African liberation movements. Rahman received his bachelor's degree "with high distinction" from Wayne State University in 1977. He received his master's degree in history from the University of Michigan–Ann Arbor in 1999 and his PhD in history from the same university in 2006. He is the author of the book *The Regime Change of Kwame Nkrumah: Epic Heroism in Africa and the Diaspora* (2007). He is also the author of the essay "Marching Blind, the Rise and Fall of the Black Panther Party in Detroit" (2009). He is currently working on the complete history of the Black Panther Party in the state of Michigan and on the *Kwame Nkrumah Reader*.

Pamela R. Smith is a visiting assistant professor and research associate in the Department of Sociology at Michigan State University. Dr. Smith is currently directing the For Females Only project, designed to empower, encourage, and inspire young women to be strong advocates for solutions and skills that afford them positive life outcomes. Dr. Smith's work emphasizes the growing issues linked to poverty in urban America for single parents, public education, social work, and the criminal justice system.

Geneva Smitherman is University Distinguished Professor Emerita of English and Co-Founder and Executive Committee Member of African American and African Studies at Michigan State University. A pioneering scholar-activist in Black Studies and a 1973 graduate of Harvard University's Afro-American Studies master's program, Smitherman is founder and director of My Brother's Keeper, an outreach mentoring program for Detroit middle school students. Smitherman's current work focuses on African American language and language planning policy in South Africa. She was the chief advocate and expert witness for the children in *King v. Ann Arbor* (the "Black English" federal court case). Her books include *Black Language and Culture: The Sounds of Soul* (1975), the classic *Talkin and Testifyin: The Language of Black America* (1977), *Black Talk: Words and Phrases from the Hood to the Amen Corner* (1994), *Talkin That Talk: Language, Culture and Education in African America* (2000), *Word from the Mother: Language and African Americans* (2006), and *Educating African American Males: Detroit's Malcolm X Academy Solution* with coauthor Clifford Watson (1996). Her most recent book is *Articulate While Black: Barack Obama, Language, and Race in the U.S.* with H. Samy Alim (2012). Smitherman has published over one hundred articles and papers on language and education and is editor or coeditor of eight books on language. She served two terms on the Language Commission of the National Council of Teachers of English (NCTE) and on the committee that produced the *Students' Right to Their Own Language*. She is a Co-Founder and current chair of the Language Policy Committee of the Conference on College Composition and Communication (CCCC). Awards include the Educational Press Association Award for Excellence in Educational Journalism, the 1999 CCCC Exemplar Award, the 2005 NCTE James R. Squire Award for her "transforming influence" and "lasting intellectual contribution" to the field of English studies, the MSU Lifetime Diversity Award, the Marcus Garvey Foundation 50th Anniversary Award, and the 2012 NCTE Advancement of People of Color Leadership Award.

Curtis Stokes is a professor in James Madison College and was founding director (2002–5) of the doctoral program in African American and African studies at Michigan State University. He was also assistant director (1995–97) of African American Studies at Columbia University. Professor Stokes's research and teaching areas are Black politics in the United States and Michigan, as well as Marxist and radical political thought. His publications include articles and five books, most recently *Race* *and Human Rights* (2009); and he currently at work on two book projects, tentatively titled *Race and the Criminal Justice System* and *Race and Politics in the Obama Era*.

Carl S. Taylor is a professor in the Department of Sociology and in African American and African Studies, MSU Extension specialist, and senior fellow in University Outreach and Engagement at Michigan State University. Dr. Taylor has extensive experience in field research aimed at the reduction of violence involving American youth. He has worked with communities, foundations, and government agencies in understanding gangs, youth culture, and violence. Some of these organizations include the Solomon R. Guggenheim Foundation, the Charles Stewart Mott Foundation, the FBI Academy, and the Children's Defense Fund. Additionally, he serves as the principal investigator for the Michigan Gang Research Project.

Index